# FIRST FILMS OF THE HOLOCAUST

PITT SERIES IN RUSSIAN AND EAST EUROPEAN STUDIES
Jonathan Harris, Editor

# First Films of the Holocaust

## SOVIET CINEMA AND THE GENOCIDE
## OF THE JEWS, 1938–1946

## Jeremy Hicks

UNIVERSITY OF PITTSBURGH PRESS

Published by the University of Pittsburgh Press, Pittsburgh, Pa., 15260
Copyright © 2012, University of Pittsburgh Press
All rights reserved
Manufactured in the United States of America
Printed on acid-free paper
10 9 8 7 6 5 4 3 2 1

Library of Congress Cataloging-in-Publication Data

Hicks, Jeremy.
  First films of the Holocaust : Soviet cinema and the genocide of the Jews, 1938–1946 /
Jeremy Hicks.
        p.   cm. — (Pitt series in Russian and East European studies)
  Includes bibliographical references and index.
  Includes filmography.
  ISBN 978-0-8229-6224-3 (pbk. : alk. paper)
  1. Holocaust, Jewish (1939–1945), in motion pictures. 2. Antisemitism in motion pictures.
3. Jews in motion pictures. 4. Motion pictures—Soviet Union—History.   I. Title.
  PN1995.9.H53H53 2012
    791.43'652924—dc23                                    2012030693

# CONTENTS

# ACKNOWLEDGMENTS

This book emerged from two sources. One primary origin lay in conversations with Howard Jacobs, whom I was lucky enough to teach; with Libby Saxton, a colleague at Queen Mary, University of London; and with Evgenii Tsymbal, a visiting scholar there. The other source was a chance discovery of documentary film footage relating to the Holocaust in the Russian documentary film archive (RGAKFD, Krasnogorsk). First and foremost, I owe a personal and intellectual debt to these people, as well as to that archive; its staff, especially Elena Kolikova; and the archive's director, Natal´ia Kalantarova.

Once formulated, this research project would not have been realized as a book without the generous and gracious funding of the Philip Leverhulme Trust, enabling me to devote myself to research in the 2009–2010 academic year. Equally important has been the support from individuals in various quarters of Queen Mary: my immediate colleagues in the Russian department, Andreas Schönle, Anna Pilkington, and Olga Makarova; Rüdiger Görner, in the wider School of Languages, Linguistics and Film; and others in the college more generally.

Other than the RGAKFD, a number of Russian archives have provided generous assistance to me in the pursuit and completion of this project. In particular, I would like to thank the staff of the RGALI, especially Dmitrii Neustroev and the director, Tat´iana Goriaeva; Gosfil´mofond, especially Valerii Bosenko and its deputy director and guiding light,

Vladimir Dmitriev, who kindly gave me lifts, as well as its current director, Nikolai Borodachev; the Museum of Cinema (Moscow), especially Emma Malaia and the director, Naum Kleiman; and the GARF and RGASPI. British film collections have been no less accommodating to me, and I would like to thank the IWM (especially Matthew Lee), the BFI, and the National Film and Television Archive. I have also benefited enormously from the University College London's School of Slavonic and East European Studies Library, the British Library, the Russian State Historical Library ("Istorichka"), the Russian State Library ("Lenin´ka"), and the British Film Institute Library.

Friends who have helped me obtain materials and aided me in other ways include Evgenii Margolit, Nikolai Izvolov, Aleksandr Deriabin, Sergei Kapterev, Crispin Brooks, Barbara Wurm, and John Haynes. Other academic colleagues who have helped by commenting constructively and productively on various parts of this work include Karel Berkhoff, David Shneer, Olga Gershenson (whom I thank for sharing her thoughts with me and for her helpful critique of the errors in an earlier version of chapter 5), Natascha Drubek-Meyer, Valérie Pozner, Il´ia Al´tman, Valerii Fomin (even though he disagreed with the project), Julian Graffy, David Gillespie, Gil Toffell, Stuart Liebman, the members of the SSEES Russian Cinema Research Group, and participants at the numerous conference panels where I have given earlier versions of parts of the book. I would also like to thank Peter Kracht and the University of Pittsburgh Press for the interest they have shown in this project and the anonymous readers, especially the second one, whose comments helped me strengthen the book considerably.

I would also like to thank Valérie Pozner, Birgit Beumers, and Dieter Steinert for permitting me to reproduce reworked versions of previously published material in chapters 3, 5, and 7.

As with all my work, I owe an unpayable debt to Inger and Nina, who have endured, inspired, and sustained me.

I would like to dedicate this book to the memory of my friend Pete Glatter, who made me think.

In the text, I follow Library of Congress transliteration standards except for a few famous Russian names, where I have used the familiar form. Thus, instead of Il´ia Erenburg, it will be Ilya Ehrenburg. The bibliography and endnotes, however, follow the Library of Congress norms throughout.

I have also employed Russian versions of Ukrainian proper names, without diacritical marks, in the main text, because they are the forms most familiar to Western readers. I include myself in this number, as the greater part of my sources are Russian or English, not Ukrainian. Thus, I shall refer to Aleksandr and not Oleksandr Dovzhenko, to Kharkov and not the Ukrainian version Kharkiv, and likewise to Kiev and Babyi Iar, not Kyiv and Babyn Iar.

Unless otherwise attributed, all translations are my own. Consequently, most of the film titles in the book are my own translations from Russian, and the reader may encounter them elsewhere in slightly different translations.

# FIRST FILMS OF THE HOLOCAUST

Map of wartime Europe showing German-Soviet border on 22 June 1941 and places named in the text. Map by Bill Nelson.

# ⟍ Introduction

**For many,** the Holocaust has become the most important historical event of the twentieth century. Indeed, it has become part of the American experience, providing Americans a point of reference firmer even than the Civil War or Pearl Harbor.[1] As an extreme of human behavior, it informs not only the understanding of history but also contemporary politics as the international community strives to comprehend, prevent, or prosecute programs of genocide, a term itself coined to describe the Nazis' attempted extermination of the Jews.

Images, especially cinematic ones, have been a crucial means for inculcating public awareness of the Holocaust. Indeed, widespread Western skepticism about Nazi crimes was decisively defeated by screening newsreels of the camps at the end of the war. More recently, several popular films, including Marvin J. Chomsky's *Holocaust* television miniseries (1978) and Steven Spielberg's *Schindler's List* (1993), further raised mass consciousness about the Holocaust. While these are reconstructions, audiences are also familiar with fragments of the original newsreel images, which have been recycled for both authorial films, such as Alain Resnais's seminal *Night and Fog* (*Nuit et brouillard* [1955]), and TV documentaries, such as the final two parts of Thames TV's 1973 *World at War* ("The Final Solution," directed by Michael Darlow), to name but two.

Yet rarely do we pause to reflect on the genesis of the newsreel images. This oversight masks an extraordinary ignorance about the first moving images to depict the Holocaust not taken by perpetrators themselves. These little-considered films were made and shown before the newsreels showing U.S. and British soldiers liberating camps in Germany in 1945, usually regarded as the "first" films of the Holocaust. The neglected images—Soviet wartime films—are cinema's initial attempts to represent the Holocaust, the subject of this study.

Above all, identifying and examining these movies will shed new light on the apparently familiar subject of humanity's first encounter with images of the Holocaust. By shifting the focus away from the familiar territory of the 1945 U.S. and British newsreels and to that of Soviet newsreels, documentaries, and features, we can better observe how the unprecedented sights of brutality were grasped within established narrative frameworks. For the Soviets, this meant adapting representations of Nazi atrocities so as to convey a "Soviet" version of the Holocaust, to "Sovietize" it, to claim the victims as their own, a process that can be compared to American filmmakers' later tendency to "Americanize" the same events. By analyzing how Soviet filmmakers shaped and distorted their discoveries, we can better understand and guard against analogous appropriations of the Holocaust by other factions.

Such an analysis not only reveals a great deal about the effects of cultural, political, and ideological biases on Holocaust film but also illuminates the process of cinematically representing the Holocaust, the ways in which narrative tropes for its representation were elaborated. This comprises the passage from eyewitness testimony and firsthand accounts, on the one hand, to the reportorial gathering information and shaping narratives, on the other.

Finally, focusing on this body of films also enables a greater understanding of less-considered dimensions of history proper—specifically, of the initial stage of the Holocaust, the Nazis' mass murder of Soviet Jews, which began in 1941, before the construction of the death camps and gas chambers. It likewise enables a rare insight into the unique culture of the wartime Soviet Union, which experienced a distinct moment of "spontaneous de-Stalinization."[2]

## The Soviet Union and the Holocaust

Investigating Soviet wartime cinema's depiction of the Holocaust may seem a deliberately paradoxical and provocative endeavor. For one thing, it is anachronistic in that the filmmakers did not perceive these works as depicting the fate solely of Jews and certainly not as documenting the "Holocaust," for that term became widespread even in the English-speaking world only beginning in the 1960s. Indeed, Soviet authorities rejected the very notion of the Holocaust and restricted the representation and discussion of the fate of Jewish victims of the Nazis' genocidal activities as being separate from that of Soviet citizens more generally and other occupied peoples.[3] In the context of the Soviet rejection of the word, it is worth considering its coinage. This word is a deeply problematic one in that it bears long-standing Christian associations and implies sacrifice, a repellent notion when used to describe the Nazis' murder of Jews. As the philosopher Giorgio Agamben has shown persuasively, the term *Holocaust* used as a label for these horrific events possesses "a semantic heredity that is from its inception anti-Semitic."[4] Other candidates, however, have their own difficulties. The main rival term, *Shoah,* a Hebrew word for "catastrophe" that dominates usage in France and elsewhere, has unwarranted suggestions of divine retribution,[5] and the metonym *Auschwitz,* which Agamben employs, itself has the unfortunate effect of distracting attention from the millions of Jews not killed in the death camps. Consequently, I will employ the inadequate term *Holocaust* because, despite its unfortunate and unwarranted associations, it enjoys wide acceptance in the English language, especially since the 2005 U.N. resolution on Holocaust remembrance.[6]

Like many historical terms, this one is further problematic in the timeframe of events it designates. Although few serious historians would dispute that the murder of 6 million of Europe's 8 million Jews constitutes the central event that Holocaust film must strive to convey, this atrocity formed the culmination of a process that can be traced back to earlier Nazi policies of expelling Jews from German public life and ultimately from the country itself. Indeed, the roots of the Holocaust may be traced further back, to the deeply entrenched anti-Semitism that has marked Europe's Christian culture for centuries. Yet this cultural context yielded a systematic policy to kill all Jews only in Nazi Germany, so that we must seek the immediate roots of the Holocaust in the Nazis' acquisition and exercise of power after 1933.[7] Consequently, I begin my study with Soviet depictions of the Nazis' prewar persecution of Jews.

The notion that Soviet Russia may have played a pivotal role in exposing the Holocaust may seem strange. After all, popular perceptions in the English-speaking world link Russia and anti-Semitism: *pogrom* is one of few Russian-language loan words in English. This association has been passed on through folk memory as important Jewish immigrant communities came to the United States in particular: Jews made up some 80 percent of the approximately 1,288,000 who left the Russian Empire between 1897 and 1915, perceiving it as a place that violently persecuted, humiliated, and discriminated against Jews.[8] As Yuri Slezkine has pointed out, czarist Russia legally discriminated against everyone apart from the czar since it conferred no universal rights on citizens, but Jews nonetheless faced particular problems. Long-standing enmities toward Jews increased as industrial modernization began to destroy their traditional economic roles and crafts in the 1880s, leading them to migrate to urban centers. Once there, they met anti-Semitic barriers such as residency restrictions and quotas limiting entry to higher education, preventing Jews from seizing the opportunities generated by the ongoing changes to society.[9] In consequence, Jews were disproportionately attracted to the revolutionary movements and played an important part in the Russian Revolution. Even though the Bolshevik Party possessed a smaller Jewish membership (4 percent) than did the other socialist parties, some of its most prominent members, such as Lev Trotskii, Iakov Sverdlov, Lev Kamenev, and Grigorii Zinov'ev, were Jews.[10] Moreover, despite hostility to the Bolsheviks from the wider Jewish population, the Whites actively fomented anti-Semitism and conducted pogroms against Jews under their control, using the prominence of Jewish Bolsheviks as a key element in their propaganda.[11] When much of the prerevolutionary intelligentsia emigrated, the revolution offered previously undreamed of opportunities for educated Jews in particular; as an additional attraction, their loyalty was assured, for they could hardly harbor secret sympathies for the anti-Semitic Whites.

While the revolution interrupted the pattern of legal discrimination against Jews, this did little to alter grassroots anti-Semitism. Indeed, the association of Jews with the Soviet state aggravated such sentiments, even though the Bolsheviks took care to monitor, repress, and publicly deprecate such views.[12] Jews within the political elite suffered as much as others did during the Great Terror of the late 1930s, but their lack of any other homeland, which distinguished them from Germans or Poles, for example, meant that the NKVD was less likely to see Jews as potential foreign spies.[13] Nevertheless, those who replaced purged Jews in the state and party apparatus tended to come from the emerging generation of

Soviet-educated ethnic Russians, and a renewed focus on Russian cultural identity gained momentum.[14]

It is sometimes thought that Stalin was throughout an anti-Semite and that the anti-Semitic policies adopted toward the end of World War II expressed his true intentions. The evidence for this is contradictory, however, and has been effectively countered by the Russian historian Genadii Kostyrchenko, who sets out a far more convincing narrative in which these policies reflected the Stalin regime's abandonment of internationalism in favor of a growing Russian nationalism and imperial chauvinism—a populist rather than personal agenda.[15]

Nevertheless, the Soviet Union was indisputably the site of the Germans' first mass killings of Jews, which followed the Nazi invasion of 22 June 1941. Russia itself, the territory of the contemporary Russian Federation, is seldom seen as a center of Nazi killing, and compared to Poland it was not. Nonetheless, more Russian Jews were murdered than Dutch or French, although the fate of Russian Jews has been far less extensively represented or discussed than has that of their Western European counterparts, a situation that began to change only with the end of the cold war.[16] Indeed, it is possible to find even recently published books, Web sites, and so on that entirely exclude any testimony relating to the first stage of the killings, the mass shootings that claimed the lives of approximately 1.5 million Soviet Jews.[17] Moreover, a common historical sleight of hand calculates the death toll of Jews in Poland according to that nation's pre–September 1939 borders, yielding a figure of 3 million, rather than to those of the postwar state. In consequence, western Ukraine, which was incorporated into the Soviet Union in September 1939 and invaded by Germany as being part of the Soviet Union in 1941 (and which is now part of the post-Soviet state of Ukraine), still has its half a million Jewish dead conventionally added to those of Poland. The Russian historian Il´ia Al´tman goes further, arguing that the Jews living in the formerly Polish, Baltic, and Romanian territories might all more plausibly be defined as Soviet dead, since the invading Nazis began killing these 3 million Soviet citizens because they were not just Jews but *Soviet* Jews. The resulting figure of Soviet Jews killed is nearer to 3 million, approximately half of all the Jews killed, rather than the conventional figure of 1.5 million.[18] While it may seem macabre to dispute the "citizenship" of the dead in this manner, such figures nevertheless help show more broadly where and why the Holocaust occurred. The Soviet Union was the site of a brutal initial stage of the genocidal killings and as such was in a privileged position to see and represent the unfolding horror in journalism, literature, photography, and film. Recently, representations of the Holocaust in these other media have attracted public attention; examples of such representations include a major retrospective of the graphic art of Zinovii Tolkachev, whose albums contain eyewitness portrayals of the liberation of Majdanek and Auschwitz;[19] a book devoted to the Soviet Jewish photographers' depictions of the Holocaust;[20] and new studies of and translations of works by the journalists Vasilii Grossman and Ilya Ehrenburg.[21] In addition, the *Black Book of Russian Jewry* itself has been published in English and other languages, including Russian. But Soviet wartime cinema's depictions of the Holocaust have until now been all but forgotten.

## Soviet Cinema

Soviet montage cinema from the 1920s was and still is internationally acclaimed (e.g., the works of Sergei Eisenstein and Dziga Vertov), but the nation's cinematic culture from the 1930s and 1940s has received far less attention; many film critics have assumed that the coming of sound obstructed contemporary international reception of these films, whose lack of artistic worth warrants their obscurity in any event. As a number of studies have shown, however, this is at best partially true. Despite the Soviet Union's increasingly oppressive internal climate of show trials and the Great Terror, a small but influential audience in large cosmopolitan cities, such as New York and London, still saw Soviet films and associated them with sophisticated technique and the morally serious use of cinema.[22] Soviet cinema's ongoing reputation enabled these works to continue to reach Western audiences right up to and, in countries not occupied by the Nazis, throughout the war, forming a chapter in film history now largely forgotten, especially in the West.

Nevertheless, despite the almost universal ignorance of its filmic depictions of the Holocaust, the Soviet Union was the only anti-Nazi power to be occupied but still free to make and distribute its own films, uniquely positioning it to make the first cinematic depictions of liberation from Nazi occupation. Indeed, the Soviets had depicted Nazi persecution of the Jews prior the war, at least until the August 1939 Nazi-Soviet nonaggression pact. With the invasion of 22 June 1941, they began first to mention Nazi atrocities and then to make films recording them. The earliest of these films dates from the initial liberation of the southern Russian city of Rostov-on-Don in November 1941, during the Soviets' first defeat of the Germans, in the Battle of Moscow. Soviet filmmakers continued to make such newsreels throughout the rest of the war, culminating in records of the death camp at Majdanek following its liberation in July 1944 and the one at Auschwitz in January 1945. Although the Soviet productions almost always deliberately understate the distinct fate of Jews by lumping together all the Nazis' victims, including Soviet Jews, non-Jewish Soviet citizens, those of other nationalities, and political prisoners, they occasionally do explicitly identify Jewish victims. This footage thus constitutes both a visual record and an initial effort, albeit one deeply flawed and sometimes reluctant, to grasp and reconstruct the events of the Holocaust and to come to terms with its ramifications. The newsreels may be seen as a cinematic equivalent of Vasilii Grossman and Ilya Ehrenburg's *Black Book of Russian Jewry,* a compilation of documents on the Nazi extermination of Soviet Jews that was banned in 1946.[23] As the first examples of an important genre of cinema, these films deserve to be rescued from oblivion, reviewed, reconcontextualized, and reconsidered.

## Cinema's First Confrontation with the Holocaust

The historiography of the Holocaust contains a large number of accounts that trace Western society's first confrontation with the tragic events therein. Many of these accounts relate to the prewar period, as does the historian Tony Kushner's indicatively titled book *The Holocaust and the Western Liberal Imagination.* Such studies ask what Western society knew, when it knew this, and what more it might have done to save Jews from the Nazis.[24] This is of course an instructive and important line of inquiry, but curiously, such studies never discuss the Soviet Union's efforts to help the Jews—or the lack thereof. This is frustrating, for Soviet actions played an important part in the events of the Holocaust. One the one hand, the Soviets occupied a pivotal role in defeating the Nazis and thus arresting their attempt to kill all Europe's Jews; on the other, however, the Soviets' earlier failure to stop the Nazis and their signing of the nonaggression pact contributed to the Nazis' advances at least as much as Western actions did. Indeed, the partition of Poland, which resulted directly from the pact, led to the first Nazi-imposed Jewish ghettos in German-controlled Poland.

This flaw in historical focus is understandable; after all, the 1930s Soviet Union was a deeply oppressive and thoroughly illiberal society that many people would have wanted to flee, since those who took refuge there, especially from Nazi Germany, remained at risk. At the same time, however, the narrative of reactions to and representations of the situation in Germany cannot be properly understood without reference to the Soviet picture. Soviet prewar film portrayals of the Nazi persecution of Jews are a great deal more candid than either British or American images, and had they not been systematically marginalized and ignored, they might have triggered a more timely response to the international political and refugee crises faced in the last years of interwar peace.

The process by which these works were obscured was briefly interrupted to a degree during the war but has since resumed through historians' claims, for example, that the British public during World War II was sheltered from images of death and atrocity in newsreels.[25] Similar sorts of claims have been made of the United States. Yet these assertions are predicated on analyses of only British or American films.[26] They ignore the fact that Soviet films depicting atrocity had already been shown to large numbers of spectators in both countries, including the Oscar-winning *Moscow Strikes Back* (1942).

Some studies do mention that the Soviets represented the camps before British and Americans did, but they discount the footage as being "pale" (Abzug), as unauthenticated and therefore lacking "impact" (Caven), or as less immediate and entirely staged (Delage).[27] These interpretations of the Soviet films appear to be based on little or no knowledge of them, however, and seem to assume that they were not widely seen in the West, consequently had little impact, and must therefore have been poor pieces of filmmaking.

Whatever the rationale, the conclusions are not sound, for the Soviets had been showing images of Nazi atrocities since 1941, both screening them at home and sending them abroad. These were significant films that elaborated a set of conventions for representing such horrific sights. Soviet filmmakers also documented the two still-remaining death camps they discovered. When the December 1944 Soviet film of the Majdanek camp reached the West, however, it was censored, notably in France. Even where it was shown, such footage was treated with an enormous degree of suspicion,[28] for it differed in important ways from the newsreels made by the British and the Americans. For example, the Soviet films of Majdanek and Auschwitz showed fewer bodies because they depicted extermination camps in which corpses had been incinerated on a mass scale. Thus the

Soviet filmmakers had to confront a central problem in representing the Holocaust: extrapolating the scale of the dead from a killing process that destroyed almost all traces of the victims—except, as both of these films tellingly show, their material effects: clothes, shoes, and so on. To this day, museums employ such artifacts to evoke the nature and scale of the catastrophe. Moreover, the Soviet films avoid an error common in Western films, that of treating concentration camps as the epicenter of the Nazi killing machine. Instead, while they do not explain the factors, especially ethnicity, determining the different fates of those who entered the camps, they suggest that the death camps' extermination function was primary in all camps.

These films also help us understand how filmmakers and photographers among the Western liberators reacted when confronting the camps, for many of their accounts may be compared with similar reactions by Soviet camera operators. The dichotomy between witnessing these scenes and fulfilling the role of the reporter is evident in the account of Roman Karmen, who recalls himself and his colleagues overcoming their emotions as they recorded images of civilians killed by the Nazis near Moscow in 1941 and 1942 but weeping as they saw the rushes. Similarly, the American photographer Margaret Bourke-White, on an assignment for *Life* magazine, recalls truly registering the sights for the first time only on seeing the eventual prints, when "the protective veil" had been lifted.[29]

The comparison with Soviet representations of Nazi atrocities also betrays a gulf in attitudes. For instance, the British journalist Edwin Tetlow recalled: "Writing my story emptied me of emotion, restoring me to a realization that I was not a participant in the horror but a professional observer with the duty of telling others what Belsen was like."[30] By contrast, Soviet media people, from their first such experiences in Russia in the winter of 1941 to the liberation of Auschwitz in January 1945, unfailingly stressed their identification with the dead as part of their professional function. Moreover, if Soviet camera operators or photographers felt disgust at their own searching for effective compositions in the scenes before them, as the British photographer George Rodger did when filming Belsen, they did not act as Rodger did, abandoning their assignments as a war correspondent, nor would they have been allowed to do so.[31] The Soviets were less sympathetic to the expression of private, unpoliticized distress or trauma.

## Impossibility of Witnessing

Humanity's first reactions when discovering the true scale of Nazi atrocities can be understood in theoretical terms as well as from the previously articulated historical perspective. Any theorization of film representations of the Holocaust confronts a fundamental problem: apart from a few reels of film and still photographs that the Nazi mobile killing squads took of their victims in Soviet territory, as well as a handful of photographs taken in the camps, no direct documentation of the killings exists. This catastrophe continues to challenge notions of memory, history, and their representation.[32] Thus, all films of the Holocaust are in some sense reconstructions, whether capturing direct witness testimony from survivors and perpetrators or filtering material into a subsequent commentary by the immediate liberators or others.[33] Visual images recording the immediate aftermath of the liberation essentially have this same quality of secondhand reconstruction, although they may also record evidence: the corpses and other traces of the dead, as well as the scene and means of murder. In each case, the moments of the Holocaust's nearly six millions killings were not recorded, and memory intervenes between the moment of seeing an atrocity, of witnessing it, and that of recounting it in testimony, whether verbal, visual, or a combination of both in film.[34]

This gap between the event and its representation has been described in the psychoanalytically inflected notions of trauma and the *Nachträglichkeit,* or belatedness, of its expression. The most significant films addressing the Holocaust, starting with Alain Resnais's *Night and Fog,* did not appear until over a decade after the events.[35] Yet this breach between the event and images of it applies very differently to the films I will discuss. More recently, the project of mapping ethical concerns onto those of film studies, undertaken notably by Libby Saxton, has shifted the focus to the manner in which films depict such events, onto the "gaps, ellipses, silences and lacunae" in the films themselves rather than in film history. What they do not show is held to grant the greatest insight into the filmmaker's ethical vision.[36]

Yet the greatest film of the Holocaust, Claude Lanzmann's *Shoah* (1985), deliberately foregrounds such ellipses, the unrecorded images that haunt the visible ones, so as to push spectators to imagine the terrible reality that persists in the memory of those interviewed and to grasp that the most important scenes are those *not* recorded. In contrast, the films I examine here attempt to cover up and repress their lacunae. Hence, one of my main tasks in this book is to locate and begin to scrutinize these blank and blanked-out spots. Such equal attention to both the manner of depiction and the substance depicted relates to the theoretical paradigm of film and ethics; nonetheless, the work required to identify the films' significant silences about the Holocaust is considerable, and the project of doing so occupies more of the book than does explicit analysis through the vocabulary of the poststructural approach to ethics.

While the filmmakers did, in three or four instances, strive to openly depict the fate of Jews as Jews, the political climate of the wartime Soviet film industry made these exceptions rare. Even when filmmakers attempted this, they tended to avoid making Jews the exclusive focus of their films, implying or suggesting more than they showed or stated. For the most part, the filmmakers went along with the dominant wartime discourse, wherein victims were designated as Soviet, as was resistance, and both were implicitly Russian.[37] Even so, several fiction films mention the fate of the Jews or Nazi attitudes toward the Jews either at initial script stages or peripherally in the final film. Finally, some films document Nazi atrocities, in particular showing the victims of shootings and their mass graves in Russia and Ukraine or the death camps in Poland. Final films in this category sometimes mention that most of these victims were Jewish, and sometimes the initial footage clearly indicates this, but more frequently they keep silent on the matter.

In each instance, through a careful search of recently published or as yet unpublished archival materials, the silences of these films can be made to tell a significant and rarely heard story of the Holocaust. The film archives contain never released, discarded newsreel footage from camps liberated by the Soviets that identifies the victims as predominantly Jewish (in Majdanek, Klooga, and Auschwitz). The various paper archives contain camera operators' itemizations of their footage (i.e., "montazhnye listy," or dope sheets), correspondence between frontline camera operators and the studios, and earlier script versions of many of the newsreel and both documentary and fiction films, as well as internal discussions of some of the final films, all of which enable us to trace the process that Soviet attempts to represent the Holocaust had to negotiate before appearing on screen. All these sources, as well as the films themselves, can likewise be made more revealing when compared with other accounts of the events they represent, be they in government statements, journalism, literature, art, memoirs, or historiographic works. When contextualized in this manner, the films' clichés become more evident and their silences more telling. They grant us an insight into the difficulties faced and paths taken when filmmakers first attempted to portray the Holocaust. To understand this process, we need to understand how the Soviet media adapted the portrayals to their own persuasional needs—how, that is, they "Sovietized" the Holocaust.

## Sovietization of the Holocaust

In recent times scholars have described the "Americanization" of the Holocaust, a term meant to indicate the Holocaust's changing role in the United States. As Doneson points out, "the Holocaust played little if any role in the lives of most Americans, Jew or Gentile," during the events themselves, but since the 1960s it has become a central symbol in the American imagination.[38] The powerful influence of American culture, especially cinema, has meant that this process has been echoed elsewhere, especially Western Europe, to a greater or lesser extent. In the Soviet Union, almost the opposite occurred. Even though 1.5–3 million Soviet citizens perished at the hands of the Nazis for being Jewish, this aspect of Nazi crimes is glossed over or subsumed into the collective memory of the even larger number, over 27 million, of Soviet war dead: 8.7 million combatants and 18.3 million civilians.[39] The Holocaust is overshadowed by a narrative of heroic Soviet resistance, and this narrative is still important for post-Soviet Russia.[40]

Nonetheless, the Sovietization and Americanization of the Holocaust have much in common: specifically, a denial of the otherness of the Eastern European Jews, who were the Nazis' primary victims. In the case of American-made films, this entails stripping the victims of linguistic difference by making their filmic representations speak English, as well as filtering out any trace of communist politics among Jews. For example, the characters of the *Holocaust* miniseries act like postwar American or Israeli Jews rather than the German Jews they portray, let alone the wartime Polish or Ukrainian Jews who were the prime victims of the Holocaust, a characterization meant to enable spectators in the United States to identify with the victims.[41] To an extent, moreover, this Americanization involves imposing a certain optimistic construction on the material and avoiding the most gruesome aspect of the realities depicted.[42] Yet despite the partial erasure of cultural difference all this involves, the characters nevertheless retain their identities as Jews.

The Sovietization of the Holocaust in Soviet wartime film similarly involved depriving victims and eyewitnesses of language: for example, despite being photographed, no Jews were recorded in synchronous sound interviews recounting why their counterparts had died. Soviet atrocity footage frequently shows victims' suffering in a graphic manner; for example, the filmmakers often photographed the faces of the dead so as enable spectator identification, something Susan Sontag has argued to be atypical of images of the dead in the Western media.[43] But the purpose of this identification was to move the spectator to act, for the dead are presented not as an alien spectacle but as people like the spectator with whom solidarity is required. The films address the spectator, demanding a response to suffering in a contribution to the war effort figured as vengeance.[44] To rouse Soviet soldiers to avenge the dead, however, filmmakers thought it necessary to downplay the victims' Jewish identities so as to avoid confirming the Nazi propaganda leaflets' claims that the common Russian soldier was being exploited to fight for the Jews. Sovietizing the Holocaust meant editing images of Jews to appeal as widely as possible to the Soviet population, whose feared and presumed anti-Semitism might otherwise cause this call for vengeance to founder.[45] As one underground communist resister in occupied Belorussia put it: "Reckoning with the mood of the population, it was not possible in agitational work to directly and openly defend the Jews as this undoubtedly could have provoked a negative attitude to our leaflets even from our own, pro-Soviet people, or people close to us. We had to touch upon this matter obliquely."[46]

While this cautious attitude strictly rationed film images of Jewish victims as such, it also enabled Soviets to record and depict the atrocities far more widely than could U.S. and British filmmakers, whose logistical circumstances initially required them to refrain from photographing such things. This stance may be called propagandistic provided we remember that Soviet film's principal raison d'être was propaganda, a term Lenin and his disciples used habitually without negative connotations.[47] Soviet cinema's willingness to use film as propaganda, as a tool of persuasion and not just entertainment, was influential in the war, and its assertion of the right to represent atrocities for the purposes of propaganda influenced similar decisions by other nations. Nevertheless, the accusation that Soviet documentary film is all about propaganda, implying that it cannot be believed, constitutes a central reason these Soviet wartime representations of Nazi atrocities have been largely if not totally ignored by the Western public in general and film historians in particular.[48] True, these works include posed shots and reconstructions without ever describing them as such, but the Nazis (and their various collaborators) did indeed commit the atrocities shown in these Soviet films, with the exception of Irina Setkina's shameful 1943 film about Katyn, *Tragedy in the Katyn Wood* (*Tragediia v Katynskom lesu*). Yet the notion that the Soviet films are nothing but distortions seems born from a cold war hangover or a simplistic tendency to think that a documentary is either a faithful report or a complete distortion.

Indeed, the very sense of a completely reliable documentary representation is problematic, for all documentary makers shape their material and elicit performances from their subjects. Documentarians are more fruitfully seen as employing a greater or lesser degree of reconstruction, as Brian Winston has argued.[49] Moreover, such filmic representations are inherently insubstantial and must be cross-referenced with other sources. Just as, according to Walter Benjamin, the meaning of a still photograph is indeterminate without a caption,[50] much of the meaning of newsreel footage depends on the verbal characterizations that accompany it, whether the dope sheets that cameramen submit along with their original footage or the voiceover commentary later added to the newsreels or subsequent documentaries for which the images are used. In this respect, the subsequent discussions in this book will supply another verbalized contextualization to guide understanding of the films, as well as adding rarely seen images to our visual inventory of the Holocaust. But the crucial difference is that the book you hold in your hands attempts to interrogate the process by which these frames were produced.

## Testimony and Authorship in Soviet Wartime Film

These images, especially the documentary footage of Nazi atrocities, are so appalling that one might expect them to exclude the concerns of aesthetics. To consider this footage critically, however, and not just use it unreflectively as illustrative material for a predetermined narrative, we must examine the images as filmic constructs and see them as interpretations, never forgetting what is at stake ethically in these attempts to represent the Holocaust. This means asking how these images were produced, by whom, and to what purpose, as well as investigating their relation to

Soviet and wider representational traditions. Such questions enable us to overcome both the naïve presumption that the footage is a complete record and the suspicion it was faked, since a reconstructed or posed shot is no longer so misleading once it has been identified as such and when the reasons for the reconstruction have been considered.

This shift in perspective enables a refocusing on "the gaps or breaks in testimony,"[51] the discrepancies between accounts. It permits us to see that beyond Soviet films' reconstructions lies an attempt both to record and to interpret significant sites of Nazi atrocity. Nevertheless, even when we overcome the crude prejudices of viewing Soviet film as solely propaganda, we must recognize that these films do mold what they record, especially because the filmmakers had to decide what to film and how to describe events in terms of the reigning Soviet message, making the dead into martyrs whose sacrifices would be recuperated by victorious socialism.

Despite their graphic images of atrocity, then, these Soviet films shield us from the reality they portray.[52] Or rather, they place one unpleasant reality in front of an even bigger one: the Jewish deaths were not, after the logic of the socialist funeral, a martyrdom, a meaningful sacrifice or down payment on future happiness.[53]

Alongside persuasion, another key motivation behind Soviet film representations of Nazi atrocities is the logic of proof: to gather evidence of the crimes committed. Yet it is precisely this rationale, construing images of crimes as guaranteeing their own authenticity, that Lanzmann's *Shoah* rejects.[54] Such films ask whether they have the right to represent these things and are, in Jay Cantor's words, "self-examining instruments [. . .] warning us against art, uncovering its own implications."[55] A key strategy for such reflexive Holocaust films is to privilege testimony, especially oral testimony, rather than "archive images." Testimony is privileged precisely for its capacity to highlight the weak points in the broad, smooth narrative of history, especially comfortingly optimistic narratives.[56] This relates to both Americanized and Sovietized constructions. In analyzing Soviet wartime films, my purpose is to extract them from their initial Sovietizing drive not just to employ them as archive images illustrating an alternative narrative of the Holocaust but also to look for any personal testimony they incorporate. This means paying particular attention to the films' silences, gaps, and ellipses as constituting attempts to bear witness to the Holocaust that were themselves silenced, erased, and ignored. The film testimony, whether expressed in the first or third person, is cut off from the moment of witnessing as it follows the acts depicted. Nevertheless, in a small number of instances, filmmakers were able to express an immediate, personal response to the Holocaust.

## Representational System versus Individual Testimony

While Soviet wartime documentaries and features quickly established an impersonal, collective idiom of conventions and clichés for depicting Nazi atrocities, including the Red funeral, calls for vengeance, and the Sovietization of the victims, these tropes sometimes fail to completely erase traces of either the Holocaust or the filmmakers' own attitudes to it. These echoes of the event become audible especially if we examine documents that chart the films' progress, from the initial accounts and reports in camera operators' letters or diaries and newspaper articles to the reworking of material into scripts and treatments; the finished film; subsequent internal studio discussions; and finally, published reviews. Each of these stages reveals attempts to fit the event to the standard Soviet narrative of the occupation and the war. Each step mitigates individual witness testimony and distinct authorship. In a number of instances, however, screenwriters and directors managed to leave discernible individual imprints on their films' depictions of and reflections on the Nazi genocide in the East. I will pay particular attention to these as instances where filmmakers to some degree succeeded in using the medium to shape a response that is not simply the standard Soviet instrumentalization of Nazi atrocities but rather a representation using carefully selected stylistic means or deploying a particular symbolic idiom. Particularly significant here is Boris Barnet's *Priceless Head* (*Bestsennaia golova* [1942]) and Mark Donskoi's *Unvanquished* (*Nepokorennye* [1945]), which both dare to identify the Nazis' specific persecution of the Jews. This group also includes Aleksandr Dovzhenko's completed wartime documentaries and unrealized film projects, even though those works marginalize the fate of Ukraine's Jews so as to foreground Nazi violence against Ukraine and Ukrainians. Despite this grave shortcoming, however, Dovzhenko's depictions of the Nazis' genocidal actions reject the normal Soviet blandishments in favor of a bitter, intensely personal vision born of his firsthand experience of the immediate aftermath of liberation, and do so in distinct and innovative ways. These three cases yield art of lasting value that continues to grant insight, albeit fragmentary, into both the Holocaust itself and the dangers and difficulties of representing it.

In addition, however, a further category of depictions of Nazi atrocity resists being recuperated by the habitual Soviet narrative: synchronously recorded eyewitness testimony, which, since the 1961 Eichmann trial and especially since Lanzmann's *Shoah,* has become the most privileged filmic form for representing the Holocaust. As Shoshana Felman has put it: "The testimonial approach was necessary for the full disclosure of the thought-defying magnitude of the offense against the victims, and was particularly suitable to the valorization of the victims' narrative perspective."[57] Soviet cinema, however, systematically marginalized the victims' voices, and with them their perspectives, so as to better articulate the standardized Soviet interpretation of Nazi atrocities.[58] A similar filtering of testimony is evident in the work of the Soviet Extraordinary State Commission on War Crimes (ChGK), created in November 1942 to collate information about Nazi atrocities for an intended postwar trial of the perpetrators. The commission produced reports for public consumption that summarized witness testimony but systematically distorted it to fit Soviet political requirements, notably by altering witnesses' identifications of victims as Jews to characterizations as "Soviet citizens." Nevertheless, the voices of witnesses to the occupation were sometimes recorded on film, and in subsequent pages I will pay particular attention to such recordings as early forays into what has become the most important form for representing the Holocaust.

In opening our ears and eyes to these earliest cinematic representations of Nazi atrocities in the East, we can discern, beyond the constructed conventions of Soviet cinema, the testimonial power of sounds and images, where key ongoing issues in the representation of genocide were being confronted in the first films of the Holocaust.

# 1 \ "Right Off the Top of the News"

## *PROFESSOR MAMLOCK* AND SOVIET ANTIFASCIST FILM

**In May 1939,** as viewers watched a screening of the Soviet film *Professor Mamlock (Professor Mamlok)* at New York's Thalia Theatre, on Ninety-fifth Street, near Broadway, someone threw a tear-gas bomb into the auditorium.[1] This film, which depicts the Nazi persecution of an initially apolitical Jewish surgeon who "converts" to communism following Hitler's 1933 takeover, had been showing uninterrupted in New York since November 1938, when its premiere accidentally coincided with Kristallnacht, the 9 November Nazi pogroms in Germany. As one of the first films from any nation to show the Nazis' systematic persecution of the Jews, it seemed, as the *New Republic* columnist Otis Ferguson put it, "right off the top of the news"; he added that it was "closer to events than the latest *March of Time*."[2] In fact, its topicality gained it unprecedented success for a Soviet film. In the greater New York area alone, it allegedly was shown in 103 cinemas, with Jews in particular flocking to see this dramatic reconstruction corroborating the numerous eyewitness accounts of Nazi anti-Semitic persecution.[3] The film may have carried a message people needed to hear, but the tear-gas thrower, a homegrown U.S. Nazi, was not the sole obstacle to the film's being seen, for the attempts to censor or outright ban *Professor Mamlock* outnumbered similar proposals concerning any other Soviet film, even the incendiary *Battleship Potemkin*.[4] At the same time, the Soviets' own self-promotion in their depiction of Nazi anti-

Semitism, as well as the subsequent ban on this film, likewise erected barriers to the film's success.

Thus, while the film ultimately attracted a large audience in the United States, at least for a subtitled film, it has since been all but forgotten beyond occasional retrospective screenings and one-line mentions in the most comprehensive histories concerning representations of Jews or the Holocaust.[5] In other countries, where censorship was even more successful in keeping the film from the public, it is even less commonly considered.

Given the enormous importance now accorded film depictions of the Holocaust in Western culture, it may seem incredible that one of the first films of the genre—the first feature film to portray the Nazi persecution of the Jews directly as a central theme and not simply allude to it—should have been and continues to be neglected. The films conventionally seen as alerting the English-speaking world to the dangers of Nazism are the far more widely seen sixteen-minute "Inside Nazi Germany" issue of the *March of Time* newsreel (January 1938), which shows signs of anti-Jewish measures but, as a British critic wrote, no "Jew-baiting atrocities."[6] Indeed, the newsreel's stance was perceived as morally and politically ambiguous toward Nazi Germany.[7] *Confessions of a Nazi Spy* (1939) was another film both more widely seen and conventionally perceived as having been important in revealing the nature of Nazi Germany to Americans. Directed by Anatole Litvak, a Jew born in Kiev, this Hollywood film takes a more explicitly anti-Nazi stance than does the ambivalent "Inside Nazi Germany," yet it never refers to the Nazis' anti-Jewish measures. *Professor Mamlock* depicts Nazi anti-Semitism much more clearly than these other two films do and condemns it more unambiguously; indeed, its whole plot turns on this facet of Nazism. The film's disappearance from memory is thus an anomaly in film history and considerations of representations of the Holocaust.[8] Yet the erasure of the film from memory is also symptomatic of attitudes both at the time and immediately after the war.

*Professor Mamlock* met a problematic reception in the English-speaking world in part because many perceived it as emphasizing the fate of Jews under the Nazis in inconvenient or unacceptable ways. This perspective emerged, for example, in a 1943 House of Commons debate about the BBC where John McGovern, a Labour Party MP, cited *Professor Mamlock* as a film that attempts to speak for the Jews and was censored as such.[9] This claim may overstate things a bit, but the assertion is indicative in that films of that time contained virtually no direct Jewish testimony from inside

Nazi Germany; any film daring to breathe the merest hint of it was heralded as authentic—or treated with suspicion and suppressed.

*Professor Mamlock* could make some claim to offer an authentically Jewish perspective, based as it was on a play by the refugee German Jewish writer Friedrich Wolf, who imaginatively reconstructed the story's events around a photograph he had seen of a Jewish doctor in Mannheim whom Nazis there had persecuted, hanging a board bearing the word *Jew* around his neck.[10] The text was first published in the Soviet Union, where a German-language edition appeared in 1934; the play premiered in Poland later that year in a Yiddish translation. (The Polish production starred the actor Alexander Granach, who had been celebrated for his role in Fritz Murnau's German expressionist classic *Nosferatu* [1922]. Granach subsequently lived for a brief period in the Soviet Union before taking up a Hollywood acting career in which he often played a Nazi in anti-Nazi films.) The following year saw the play receive an even more successful German-language premiere in Zürich.[11] Wolf's original drama does bear a communist subtext, but this became an outspoken communist message in the Soviet film adaptation, which was directed by another Jewish refugee from Nazi Germany, the Austrian filmmaker Herbert Rappoport, and his Soviet codirector Adol´f Minkin. This interplay between the film's representation of Jews and its portrayals of communists helps reveal why Soviet depictions of the Holocaust were resisted where possible, for they struck a raw nerve in both Britain and the United States. On the rare occasions where such films represented the fate of Jews as Jews, something *Professor Mamlock* does, they combined this with a communist message in a manner that dominant Western opinion found objectionable. Even when such films overcame all obstacles and proved popular, they were forgotten as soon as practically possible. Western suspicion of the Soviets thus significantly hindered this potential means of alerting democratic opinion and eliciting public responses to the events befalling European Jews.

Before looking at the film's critical reception, we must first understand how and why, in a country with a deeply ambivalent attitude to its own Jews, a groundbreaking film portraying their persecution came to be made.[12]

### *Professor Mamlock* and Soviet Antifascist Film

Said to be "the first fiction film made about the Holocaust,"[13] the Soviet adaptation of *Professor Mamlock* received its Moscow premiere on 6 September 1938, the first of three anti-Nazi films released there that year. All three make the experience of Jews central, indicating a coordinated propaganda offensive against the Nazis, a final effort to promote an anti-German alliance comprising the Soviet Union, Britain, France, and their allies. Each of these films was adapted from literary works by refugee German antifascist writers. Grigorii Roshal´ adapted Lion Feuchtwanger's novel *The Oppermann Family* (*Die Geschwister Oppermann*) to make *The Oppenheim Family* (*Sem´ia Oppengeim* [1938]),[14] and Aleksandr Macheret loosely based *The Swamp Soldiers* (*Bolotnye soldaty* [1938]) on a memoir of that name (in German, *Moorsoldaten*) by Wolfgang Langhoff.[15] Nevertheless, *Professor Mamlock* had incomparably greater impact and so deserves more attention.[16]

Soviet anti-Nazi films are a problematic category, since they almost never use the term *Nazi,* always preferring the vaguer *Fascist.* Moreover, their target is broader than "fascism" alone,[17] principally because of the diffuse concept of fascism common in the Soviet Union, where it was seen simply as a form of capitalist state.[18] Thus many of the Soviet films in this genre are set not specifically in Nazi Germany but in fictional places bearing a composite of capitalist features. A good example is Ivan Pyr´ev's *Conveyor of Death* (*Konveier smerti* [1933]), which has anticommunist thugs adorned with swastikas, but the police uniforms are as much English as German, as is the prominence of the Salvation Army, and we see both communist leaflets and graffiti written in English, French, and German. The target is capitalism as such, denoted by the film's structural metaphor, the conveyor of death, which symbolizes the fomenting of war for munitions factory profits. Such depictions were clearly incapable of rallying an alliance of anti-Nazi powers.

The Soviet attitude to the Nazis evolved during the course of the 1930s, however, and filmmakers crafted serious attempts to court liberal anti-Nazi opinion, especially in Britain and France. Emphasizing Nazi racism provided an obvious way to do this, since the Soviet Union itself was initially constituted as an internationalist and multiethnic state guaranteeing minority rights. An analysis of Nazism along these lines was attempted as early as 1934, when the internationally oriented but soon-to-be-disbanded Mezhrabpomfil´m studios produced Vladimir Nemoliaev's film *Ruddi's Career* (*Kar´era Ruddi* [1934]), in which engineering graduates are polarized between those teasing and humiliating a Jew, Josif Weltmeyer, and those sticking up for him.[19] After a period of vacillation and association with the anti-Semitic faction, whose members soon become

Nazi storm troopers, the main character, Ruddi, eventually throws in his lot with the Jew, the former classmates sympathetic to Weltmeyer, and the striking workers. Apparently, however, no other Soviet films searched for this potential common ground until 1938.

Nevertheless, the flawed analysis of fascism in terms of a general critique of capitalism, which failed to address its racist dimension adequately, colored both the Soviets' subsequent view of the Holocaust as part of a larger phenomenon and their refusal to acknowledge the situation facing Jews specifically. The historian Larry Ceplair even identifies the Marxist view that "anti-Semitism was a symptom of the greater disease that could only be defeated by the overthrow of capitalism" as complicit in the failure of Soviet-led popular-front politics to help save Europe's Jews.[20] Still, this stance enabled Soviet filmmakers to depict the plight of these Jews, as in *Professor Mamlock,* whereas no Hollywood film dared tackle the subject until 1940. While political thinking stopped the Soviets from doing more to prevent the Holocaust, economic priorities initially equally hampered the United States and other democracies in any similar endeavor. As Jay Leyda has commented, one of the advantages of being boycotted and vilified by the Germans was that, unlike the Americans, the Soviets were not worried about losing German markets.[21] Consequently, the antifascist theme reached its apogee in 1938–39, when Foreign Minister Maxim Litvinov led the Soviet Union in its final push to form an antifascist front. The Soviets then abandoned this policy following the Czechoslovakian crisis, and in the face of insuperable mutual suspicion between their nation and Poland, the Jewish Litvinov was replaced by the non-Jewish archpragmatist Viacheslav Molotov, enabling the signing of the nonaggression pact with Nazi Germany.[22] The choice to adapt internationally celebrated literary condemnations of Nazism, banned in Germany itself, was clearly taken with an eye toward Western liberal sensibilities, as was the emphasis on anti-Semitism.[23]

A key component of *Professor Mamlock*'s attempt to influence Western opinion was its setting in contemporary Germany, not an undefined country. The film's codirector, Adol´f Minkin, claimed that this distinguished *Professor Mamlock* from earlier Soviet antifascist films: "Previously in antifascist films the action usually took place in 'a certain' country, and the time of the action was vaguely defined as 'in our time.' Working on *Professor Mamlock*, we used concrete material; we knew the place, time, and setting of the action."[24] Thus, *Professor Mamlock*'s appeal depended centrally on its ability to portray Germany convincingly. Soviet critics agreed that it did so, unlike earlier films made by Mezhrabpomfil´m studios (even though the organization specialized in such depictions); they presumably had films such as *Ruddi's Career* in mind.[25] Those films often incorporated newsreel footage—usually generic shots of Berlin traffic—alongside the acted scenes so as to convey a strong sense of place that would compensate for the fact that no Soviet film crew would be allowed to shoot on location in Nazi Germany.

Grigorii Roshal´, the director of *The Oppenheim Family,* commented on the difficulties that Mosfil´m employees faced in making sets and props for a Soviet film set in Western Europe.[26] *Professor Mamlock*'s Lenfil´m crew, however, enjoyed the advice of Herbert Rappoport, who had recent firsthand knowledge of Germany. The results were widely seen as successful. As a fellow Lenfil´m director, Il´ia Trauberg, wrote in *Komsomol'skaia pravda,* "a familiarity with the material, understanding of the atmosphere and the specific qualities of place and action make this movie free from all clichés and symbolism."[27]

Certainly Rappoport eschews many of the established clichés of Soviet films based in capitalist Europe, such as the newsreels, instead staging scenes showing, among other things, Nazis marching through the streets or burning books to create a more seamless and ultimately successful texture. But Rappoport's film was not oriented solely toward verisimilitude, as might be expected of someone who had served his creative apprenticeship, from 1928 to 1932, mostly as an assistant to the expressionist director Georg Wilhelm Pabst, working on such internationally acclaimed works as *The Threepenny Opera* (*Die Dreigroschenoper* [1931]).[28] Rappoport's use of a filmic idiom associated with German expressionism helped make the film appear more authentically German to Soviet and international audiences and lent greater persuasive power to its systematic attack on the neutral position its initially apolitical professor espouses. Especially important in this regard is the systematic use of white, a color that appears in the interiors of the clinic but also in the surgical gowns that the professor and his colleagues often wear. The gowns symbolize Mamlock's conception of the purity of the scientific world, which he expresses by saying that for him, there are only "patients and doctors, doctors and patients." This white world's metaphoric neutrality is besmirched by storm troopers, however, first when they wear their gray uniforms in the operating theater and then when they defile the professor by scrawling the word

*Jew* on his white surgical gown rather than on a board around his neck, as happens in the original play (Semen Mezhinskii, the actor playing Mamlock, claimed credit for this innovation, which was so successful that the playwright's son, Konrad Wolf, used it in his otherwise much more faithful film adaptation of 1961).[29] The expressionistic oppositions of white and gray underline how the pure world of scientific and political independence is torn apart and violated, a message implicitly addressed to the bourgeois liberal intellectual.

Rappoport also deploys another favorite motif of German expressionist directors, namely, stairs.[30] In a classic text on German expressionist film, Lotte Eisner highlighted the use of stairs to "symbolize [actors'] moods, to express their exaltation in visual terms," and "during the dialogues[,] to emphasize psychological or social inferiority or superiority."[31] Rappoport continues this tradition, as well as expressionism's broader "emphasis on textures and materials, decor and props," as a way of underpinning and reinforcing plot.[32] Thus, the film uses stairs as a motif for the fall or rise of society's and characters' hopes; on the night of the Reichstag fire, for example, storm troopers push suspects down long flights of stairs and, in one case, off them. Moreover, one of the film's most famous images (fig. 1.1) occurs when Mamlock returns to the clinic to perform an operation on a high-ranking Nazi while wearing his smock defaced with the word *Jude*; the sequence shows Mamlock ascending the stairs, flanked on all sides by storm troopers. The mise-en-scène of ascending stairs comments on the plot, symbolizing Mamlock's hopes for a return to his job and normality yet also, through the presence of storm troopers, suggesting the ultimately illusory nature of this hope. The latter message is confirmed when the professor attempts suicide on the same stairs.

By inviting Rappoport to the Soviet Union to launch his solo career as a filmmaker, the man then heading the nation's film industry, Boris Shumiatskii, was importing someone who had been involved in films with demonstrated international appeal.[33] Yet this depiction of life in a foreign country—adapted from a foreign play, codirected by a foreigner, and intended in large part for foreign audiences—was at the same time adapted to Soviet norms.

### Adapting *Professor Mamlock* to the Soviet Message

This tension between domestic and foreign priorities defines *Mamlock*. While Wolf's original play has Soviet-influenced plot features, such as the

FIGURE I.I. Mamlock's return to the clinic. From *Professor Mamlock*.

scientist or intellectual who is forced by events to realize the justice of the communist cause, as happens in an earlier film by Grigorii Roshal´, *Salamander* (*Salamandra* [1928]), the process of adapting it for Soviet cinema required further altering it to suit Soviet ideological and aesthetic norms. Wolf himself was involved in making these changes, for he was in the Soviet Union during production.[34] The most salient change was that the play's largely domestic setting was enveloped in the broader context of the communist struggle against the Nazis. For example, Rolf, Mamlock's communist son, is transformed from a peripheral character into the main protagonist, thus fulfilling Soviet film's need to stress the role of the Communist Party but at the same time highlighting the wider political context of contemporary Germany and of the "United Popular Front" against fascism, which Minkin described as a key intention behind the film.[35] This depiction of the ongoing communist underground and the suggestion that sincere or working-class storm troopers could be converted or turned back to communism reflect articles of Bolshevik faith and as such figure in almost all prewar portrayals of Nazi Germany. When war with Germany came, Soviet propaganda had to work hard to wipe away such nuanced images of Germans so as to foster a visceral hatred of the invaders without exception.

The transplanted and Sovietized plot of communist resistance evokes Trauberg and Grigorii Kozintsev's *Maxim* (1934), a film about the prerevolutionary communist underground that constitutes a landmark in Soviet cinema. Unsurprisingly, Trauberg's review of *Professor Mamlock* implicitly compares that film with his own work, suggesting that the party theme is not its strong point. Rather, the film's greatest merit is the portrayal of the central character, Professor Hans Mamlock himself, by Semen Mezhinskii, as Trauberg recognizes: "Without hesitation, the part of Mamlock can be counted among the greatest achievements of the Soviet cinema. A calm style of acting, full of inner tension, charisma and strength, that was how *Professor Mamlock* was depicted on screen, in Mezhinskii's performance. The part of Mamlock is the film's great success and merit."[36] Other critics agreed.[37] Nevertheless, the greater ideological importance of the party theme meant there was a reluctant note to the credit that reviewers accorded Mezhinskii, a stage actor playing his first film role.[38] Thus N. Kovarskii, writing in *Iskusstvo kino,* conceded that the theme of party solidarity was weaker than that of Mamlock as a character but countered that it broke new ground in showing the communist underground in a fascist state.[39]

Yet the character of Mamlock, too, had been adapted to Soviet norms. Instead of successfully committing suicide, as in the play, the professor survives to become an admirer of his son Rolf and Georgi Dmitrov, the Bulgarian leader of the Communist International who, when arrested by the Nazis and tried for the Reichstag fire, used the occasion to denounce his prosecutors. Mamlock effectively becomes a communist convert and as such dies heroically at the end of the film delivering a defiant speech to unappreciative storm troopers and a more sympathetic camera. As Kovarskii has argued, Mamlock's suicide represents the death of his old attitudes, suggesting a resurrection as a new, resisting, and political Mamlock.[40]

These politically expedient additions complement parallel cuts that dropped material in the play: Mamlock's initial expressions of support for Hindenburg; his outspoken defense of freedom of speech and democracy; and an interesting Jewish secondary character, Simon, a frequent blood donor, whose physical strength causes the Nazi Dr. Inge to question whether he can really be a "full-blooded" Jew. Mamlock's somewhat out-of-character response is to assert that Jews do physical labor in the Soviet

Union and that environmental factors, not racial characteristics, shape a human being's physique.[41] When the film's chief Nazi, Dr. Hellpach, intervenes to stress his racial theories, asserting that heroism is an Aryan trait, Mamlock counters by citing heroic Jewish figures, such as David, the Maccabees, and Samson, all of whom served as inspirations for modern Zionism as it fostered a new Jewish identity of resistance and strength and also for Soviet Yiddish culture as it fostered its own cult of Jewish heroism.[42] Later Simon obliquely refers to Zionism after Dr. Hellpach shouts "Jews get out!" and suggests they go "to Poland, Russia, Palestine." In response, Simon says: "The God of Abraham, Isaac and Jacob blesses you, his divine instrument."[43]

These changes in the representations of Jews make them conform to Soviet norms, whereby any discussion of or even reference to Zionism was virtually taboo, at least in the highly controlled environment of Russian-language film (as more demanding forms with narrower influence, the press and the stage, especially Yiddish-language venues, were less tightly controlled). Similarly, and in contrast to Yiddish cultural productions, Russian-language films downplayed the notion of Jews as resisters. Mamlock's resurrection as implicitly communist stands in contrast to his humiliation as a democrat and a Jew: his humiliation may be Jewish, but his resistance is communist. Zionism as a potential ideology of specifically Jewish resistance is edited out of the film.[44] Thus, even though *Professor Mamlock* is one of the first films to show Jews facing persecution simply for being Jewish, that is, one of the first films of the early stage of the Holocaust, where the main tools were expropriation and concentration, Annette Insdorf rightly argues that it implicitly articulates the standard universalist line identified earlier: "Jewish identity must be subsumed into larger political realities."[45] Similarly, Miron Chernenko persuasively characterizes the work as a communist film that portrays anti-Semitism only to convince spectators that the communist case is just.[46] This tendency, argues Chernenko, becomes further exaggerated in *The Oppenheim Family,* where the simplifications and distortions are even cruder; for example, that film discards the book's ambiguous main character, Gustav Oppenheim, and obliterates all reference to Ruth Oppenheim's Zionism and eventual immigration to Palestine. Nevertheless, in *Professor Mamlock*, as in other Soviet films that touch on the Holocaust, Jews are not shown to be standing up for and organizing themselves as Jews. Such a depiction would have been highly unusual for Stalin-era Soviet film, which stressed the guiding role of the Communist Party in all resistance, with a handful of exceptions during the darkest days of the war. Here again, *Professor Mamlock* points to the ulterior motives and fundamental tensions at the heart of Soviet Holocaust representation.

Yet this move to influence world opinion by depicting Nazi anti-Semitism meant that these films contrasted with Soviet cinema's prior depictions of Jews. In the 1920s and early 1930s Soviet films had often featured Jews in central roles and treated the Jewish question with some variety, but as the 1930s progressed, Soviet cinema increasingly marginalized Jews, treating them as exotic or farcical.[47] For example, Vladimir Korsh-Sablin's film *The Seekers of Happiness (Iskateli schast'ia* [1936]) had dealt with the place of Jews in Soviet society, and Lev Kuleshov's *Gorizont* (1933) dealt with the problem of Russian anti-Semitism, but such representations and considerations of Jews had, with a handful of exceptions, disappeared from accounts of domestic politics by the end of the 1930s, reappearing only with relation to other countries, such as Poland and Germany.[48]

While these initial representations of the Holocaust in Soviet film were generated with at least half an eye on the export market, domestic concerns undermined any attempts to appeal to Western liberal values by denouncing fascism as having an anti-Semitic component. These concerns included the denial and fear of a growing domestic anti-Semitism; the pathological suspicion of foreigners and all things foreign, which led to the arrest of many refugees from Nazi Germany; and the need to affirm, against all the evidence, a belief in the German working-class movement.[49]

### Reception in Russia

*Professor Mamlock* enjoyed enormous popularity in the Soviet Union, opening in sixteen Moscow cinemas, where over 370,000 spectators saw it in the first eight days after its premiere, often applauding at episodes or speeches they liked.[50] The film was promoted skillfully with large advertisements and fliers in newspapers, usually showing the image of Mamlock with the word *Jude* emblazoned on his surgical gown.[51] Mezhinskii spoke at Moscow's premier theater, the Khudozhestvennyi, where the audience gave him flowers. He was followed by the directors.[52] Over three hundred prints of the film had been made for domestic consumption by 23 September.[53] Yet a sense that the film's message was destined for foreign audiences was widespread. As one viewer commented: "The film is an object-lesson for those still 'wavering' intellectuals residing in the West."[54]

Sure enough, twenty-five prints were made for export to Britain, France, and Czechoslovakia, and a special duplicate negative was made for the United States to enable further prints to be struck on location there.[55]

While the film was ultimately intended for a Western audience, however, its portrayal of Nazi anti-Semitism sometimes became a life-and-death matter for Soviet Jews. A number of those who survived the occupation recalled *Professor Mamlock* as one of the few films that revealed the dangers of Nazi anti-Semitism to them: "We knew about fascism from newspapers and films. . . . We watched the film *Professor Mamlock,* which described Hitler's attitude towards Jews."[56] In fact, the frequency with which the film is mentioned in the Holocaust survivor testimonies collected by Steven Spielberg's Shoah Foundation suggests that it may have helped Soviet Jews to survive by impressing on them the murderous nature of Nazi anti-Semitism.[57]

Nevertheless, if this was the main lesson that Soviet Jews drew from the film, they did so by dint of their ability to read between the lines, for the Soviet press helped them very little. While the film was universally acclaimed and widely shown, critics did not especially alert spectators to the film's lessons about Nazi persecution of Jews. Although reviewers generally acknowledged the portrayal of Mamlock as the most successful dimension of the film, recounted the plot, and mentioned that Mamlock is humiliated by having the word *Jew* written on him, they did not expand on the nature of Nazi anti-Semitism. Indeed, months before the film was even released, *Pravda* set the tone by emphasizing that even though Mamlock is Jewish, his fate is "that of all of Germany's anti-Fascist intelligentsia, regardless of the blood that flows in their veins."[58]

Following this lead, other reviewers tended to elide what the film revealed about Nazi racial theories. An article in the film monthly *Iskusstvo kino* was one of the few to consider the portraits of the film's Nazis in any depth: on the one hand, the Nazi intellectual Hellpach; on the other, the thug Krause. The Nazis' special hostility to Jews and reasons for it, however, while displayed in the film, received not a word.

Similarly, while the press printed a good deal of (doubtless carefully selected) audience commentary about the film, praising its message, none of these published comments mentioned the treatment of Jews as the key aspect of the film. The Soviet media downplayed or ignored this aspect of the film, which, as I will demonstrate, would be key when it was shown abroad. Mezhinskii himself, discussing the creation of his role, was alone

FIGURE I.2. Mamlock's humiliation. From a performance of the play *Professor Mamlock* starring Walter Franck and staged at the Hebbel Theater, Berlin.

in drawing attention to Mamlock's ethnicity. First, he does so in describing the film's increasing topicality, for the German occupation of Austria occurred while they were filming: "Eyewitness accounts, books and articles about Fascism, photographs of famous German scientists, writers and artists tortured and exiled from their homeland, images of pogroms and people killed by the Fascists—all of this troubled my imagination."[59]

By using the word *pogrom* and mentioning the flood of intellectuals fleeing the country, Mezhinskii clearly evokes—though, tellingly, does not directly mention—the Nazi persecution of Jews. He then discusses how the film presents the scene of the professor's humiliation differently than the play does, deliberately repeating the word *Jew*: "Initially the intention was to have the Fascists lead Mamlock through the streets of his hometown to humiliate and degrade him, with a sign on his chest saying 'Jew' [fig. 1.2]. But in the studio, just before shooting, I came up with the fortuitous idea of tearing the surgical gown and writing the word 'Jew' directly on the gown [fig. 1.3]. The result, as we know, was positive, and the inscription was more powerful."[60]

FIGURE 1.3. Mamlock's humiliation. From the film *Professor Mamlock*.

Writing in July 1938, Grigorii Roshal´ echoed the reviewers of *Professor Mamlock* who were hesitant to mention that film's depiction of Jews, in his admission that his adaptation of the *Oppenheim Family* had toned down the novel's accentuation of Jewish victimhood, instead showing "anti-Semitism as just one of the gloomy sides of Fascist barbarity."[61] The Kristallnacht pogrom of November 1938, however, briefly made the Nazi persecution of Jews impossible to ignore.[62] Thus, when a December 1938 article compared the *Oppenheim Family* with *Professor Mamlock*, it made much wider mention of the Jewish theme in *Professor Mamlock* than had the reviews appearing when it was released, over two months earlier.[63] The events of Kristallnacht were to color the film's reception in the United States still more dramatically.

## Reception in the United States

Opening in New York on 6 November, two months to the day after its Soviet premiere, *Professor Mamlock* made a sensational impact, gaining a reputation as the first film to tell Americans that the Nazis were killing

Jews.[64] In fact, while the film does not quite do this, it was perceived as so doing because its New York release coincided with front-page newspaper coverage of Kristallnacht, the moment when "ordinary people in the liberal democracies were given the chance to confront, for the first time, the immensity of the Jewish plight."[65] *Professor Mamlock* was seen as a chilling corroboration and graphic illustration of the newspaper and radio reports. As the *American Hebrew* put it, *Professor Mamlock* "impresses upon spectators the inadequacy of words in bringing home to us the full implications of this particularly barbaric item in the Nazi program. . . . It is one thing to read about these atrocities in the newspapers, or even to hear about them from eye-witnesses; it is far more impressive, however, to see them happening before your eyes to a man with whose life, character and personality you have become familiar in the intimate and familiar way made possible by a good playwright."[66]

Responses to the movie became part of wider public realization as to the plight of Jews in contemporary Germany, despite its being set in 1933, ensuring *Professor Mamlock* unprecedented popularity for a Soviet film, a genre usually seen as "too slow and heavy and foreign."[67] Even the *Daily Worker,* the slavishly pro-Soviet newspaper of the Communist Party of the United States of America, acknowledged how exceptional this was:

> Not in the history of Soviet films shown in New York has one motion picture appealed to so wide a cross-section of people. . . . A large percentage of the nightly audience of the Cameo have never before witnessed a Soviet screenplay.
>
> It would do "Professor Mamlock" an injustice to say that its message would not have been so potent at any time during the last five years. And yet it is the Nazis themselves who are underscoring the drama with savage timeliness. It is Hitler who is conducting a grisly promotion campaign across the front pages of the world's press, driving home the film's call for unity with each terrifying headline.
>
> Audiences coming from the Cameo walk the short half-block to Times Square and look up at the electric news bulletins banding the Times Building and feel no transition from the mood of the picture. "Yes," people say to each other, "this is the way things are. This is what we just saw. It's true all of it."[68]

In contrast to reviews from the Soviet Union, even brief summaries of the film in the United States mention its depiction of Nazi anti-Semitism, the element that made it so topical.[69] In this period, the *Daily Worker,* which had a substantial Jewish readership, was especially vociferous in denouncing both Nazi anti-Semitism and the homegrown U.S. variety, which also reached its peak in this period.[70] Likewise, the *Daily Worker* emphasized *Professor Mamlock's* depiction of and relevance to Jews: "We unhesitatingly recommend it to every person who is hazy about the real meaning of fascism or who is inclined to be tolerant with it as 'just a po-litical movement.' In view of what is happening in Hitler [*sic*] Germany at present, CERTAINLY NO JEW SHOULD MISS SEEING 'PROFES-SOR MAMLOCK.'"[71] The paper used reader testimonies to amplify and illustrate this message:

> We were looking for a picture along the 42nd Street movieway.
> "How about *Professor Mamlock* over at the Cameo?" I asked.
> "The Cameo? That's where they show the Russian pictures isn't it?"
> "That's right," I answered. My Jewish friend, a dentist, doesn't like politics in any form. "But this one is about Germany—about the Nazis and a Jewish doctor."
> He perked up and looked interested for a moment. "Certainly came at the right time," he said, with a fleeting glance at the newspaper under his arm. "Too bad it's a Russian picture. How can you understand it?"
> "You'll understand it. Come on."
> He came. And he understood.

By the next day, the writer reports, the friend phoned him indignant at the Illinois censors' decision to ban the film from playing in Chicago: "My God, they call it Communist and Jewish propaganda against Hitler! Don't they want people to know what's going on?"[72]

Attempts to ban the film will be discussed later in this chapter, but the Illinois censors' charge that *Professor Mamlock* was "Jewish and Com-munist propaganda against Hitler" must be considered in its own right, as a critique of the film, since it touched a particularly sensitive nerve. In both depicting Jewish persecution and espousing a communist message, the film constituted an unstable compound where too much emphasis on communism provoked sharp criticism abroad, even from the liberal New York media, whereas emphasis on the Jews was unacceptable to the So-viets, for whom the communist message was always paramount. Indeed, before long, even mentioning the persecution specifically of Jews became problematic in the Soviet media.

In his review for the *New York Times,* Frank S. Nugent praised *Professor Mamlock* as "an engrossing, sincere, admirably played and frequently highly dramatic film" dealing with "a topic which Hollywood, with its fear of jeopardizing foreign markets, has not dared to touch." He added, however, that its dramatic impact had been lessened by "the Soviet's customary insistence upon tossing a clove of propaganda into the customary brew."[73] Nugent concluded, "none of its virtues completely counterbalances that propagandistic burden":

> Quite possibly it is of the utmost importance, in Soviet policy, to show that, in Germany the Jew and the Communist have suffered alike, and to reason, from this, that they are brothers under the paternalistic encouragement of Lenin and Stalin. It may be important in Soviet policy, but it is so far from being the entire truth that we cannot escape a feeling of resentment over such a narrowing of the dramatist's view, over the simplification of a problem which is not limited to politics but is deeply rooted as well in religious, racial and economic soil.
>
> By closing their eyes to all but the one phase of the tragedy, the Russian producers have wasted an opportunity which, by the unfortunate nature of things, has been denied the other film makers of the world. They have used the persecution of the Jews as a selfish political argument when it should have been a frontier-leveling appeal and challenge to the conscience of all liberty-loving people.[74]

In a subsequent article, Nugent expands this line of thought: "It has not been enough for the Soviet film-makers to dramatize the tragedy of the German Jew. . . . They had to bring in Dimitrov, Marx, Lenin and Stalin; they had to identify the persecuted Jew with the persecuted Communist; they had to argue that only through communism could the Jew hope for freedom."[75]

This criticism predictably riled the *Daily Worker* film correspondent, David Platt, who directly abused Nugent as "talking through his hat" for implying that the "Jewish question . . . is a racial and religious and not a political issue."[76] Platt's defense of the film echoes both *Professor Mamlock* itself and Soviet film representations of the persecution of Jews more broadly in insisting that any resistance must be led by communists. While his use of the term *propaganda* may be problematic, Nugent made an important point: the suffering of Jews differed from that of communists, for communists could and did renounce their views. Moreover, anti-Semitism does have religious and ethnic dimensions ignored or muted in *Professor Mamlock*. While these criticisms have been unconsciously echoed more recently by Chernenko, Nugent's objection to the suggestion that "only through communism could the Jew hope for freedom" anticipates criticisms made by Insdorf.[77] All three critics point to the essential fault line in Soviet films of the Holocaust: as was evident in the process of adaptation and the Soviet reception, ideological imperatives deliberately elevated communist resistance at the expense of representing the distinct fate of Jews. As I will show, when the Nazi invasion threatened the very existence both of the Soviet state and the Jewish people, this friction rose to a peak.

This turn of events may be termed a process of appropriation, a Sovietization of the Holocaust. The Jews' suffering is depicted and a solution proposed: Soviet communism, the only societal form that—in the Soviet view—can protect against the danger of ethnic persecution. For all the problems with the Soviet model, and despite the motives behind this claim (all this occurred, of course, before the postwar state-sponsored anti-Semitic campaign), the *Daily Worker* is broadly right to point out the novelty: "The Soviet Union is the first—and so far only—country to produce a film touching on this subject so vital to all countries."[78] As Nugent acknowledges, "the unfortunate nature of things" had prevented Hollywood in particular from making any films about the persecution of the Jews in contemporary Germany. When Hollywood later did begin to depict their plight, it crafted a no less distorting "Americanization" of the Holocaust, a mirror reflection of the Soviet position. In sum, each culture was determined to appropriate and depict Jewish suffering according to its own cultural and political priorities.[79] One key aspect of making the Holocaust comprehensible to Americans was the careful dissociation of Jews from communists; even where the Jews depicted were known to be communists, they were not shown as such in films from the United States.[80]

This identification of communists and Jews that exercised Nugent also played a crucial role in both Nazi ideology and the shift from expropriation, concentration, and expulsion of Jews to their extermination, which occurred after the invasion of the Soviet Union in June 1941.[81] Anxiety over this association, and fear of Jewish subversives, undermined prewar efforts to aid refugees and hampered understanding of the Holocaust, both during the war and in the immediate postwar period.[82] These fears led first to censoring *Professor Mamlock* and then to plans for dubbing the film "in an English-speaking sound track which would eliminate entirely any reference to Communism . . . 'to save the Jews from being linked to the Reds.'"[83]

Rather than revoice *Professor Mamlock,* however, the studios made films exploring the anti-Nazi theme, movies almost certainly inspired by the success of *Professor Mamlock,* but these films jettisoned all references to communism and initially did not mention Jews directly. One *Daily Worker* reader suggested enabling wider appreciation of *Professor Mamlock* by giving it an alternative English dubbing but conceded that the censors would ban the result.[84]

### Beyond New York: Censorship in the United States

Writing shortly after the film's premiere, David Platt of the *Daily Worker* had already predicted that *Professor Mamlock* would be censored.[85] On this occasion he was right, for the film ran into censorship problems in Chicago as soon as 11 November 1938, when it was condemned as "purely Jewish and Communist propaganda against Germany."[86]

In January Ohio too banned the film, with the Ohio state censors condemning *Professor Mamlock* as "harmful" and calculated to "stir up hatred and ill will and gain nothing."[87] Providence, Rhode Island, followed suit in February; the *Providence Journal* reported, "The amusement inspector held that the Soviet film tended to incite racial hatred and contained Communist propaganda."[88] The Rhode Island Supreme Court upheld this decision in July.[89] In all, attempts to ban the film were undertaken in five states, most of which were overturned by legal rulings or because of public pressure.[90]

While the bans often arose through the influence of a local German (Chicago) or Italian (Providence) community, anti-Semitism also played a role in this period of racially classified immigration quotas, and hostility to the film's communist message constituted a dominant cause. Nevertheless, *Professor Mamlock* ultimately triumphed, receiving a certificate of approval, subject to two minor cuts, from the Motion Pictures Producers and Distributors of America's Production Code Administration (the "Hays Office") on 20 February 1939. It was the first Soviet film to receive such a certificate.[91]

In an ironic twist, the Soviets themselves then censored the film, withdrawing it from daily showings at their nation's world's fair pavilion in New York in September 1939 and replacing it with Mikhail Romm's *Lenin in 1918* (1938).[92] Three days after the Nazis invaded the Soviet Union, however, it was showing again in New York,[93] but by this point Hollywood had begun to make its own anti-Nazi films, the first of which was *Confessions of a Nazi Spy*. Although there is no direct connection between the two films, *Professor Mamlock's* example emboldened those who, like the lead in *Confessions,* Edward G. Robinson, wished to make domestic anti-Nazi films modeled on the Soviet work.[94]

### Reception in Britain

*Professor Mamlock* was to meet stiffer resistance in Britain. On the eve of the film's New York premiere, the *Daily Worker* had proclaimed: "Let us say right off that 'Professor Mamlock' will be banned on sight wherever fascism has a deadly foot-hold. The Cliveden Set will probably try to suppress it in England."[95] Once again, the *Daily Worker* came close to the truth. Indeed, every effort had been made to ban even Wolf's original play.[96] The Film Society of London nevertheless screened the film in that city on 26 March 1939, since it could privately show its members films that had not yet received a certificate from the censor.[97] In a print produced and subtitled in the United States, the film immediately generated a great deal of interest in the press.[98]

   As had their counterparts in the United States, most reviews concentrated on the way the film depicted the persecution of Jews, which the popular national daily the *News Chronicle* described with particular force in an editorial following the film society's screening: "From Russia comes a remarkable film dramatisation of the tragedy of the Jews in Nazi Germany. It is called 'Professor Mamlock,' and with grim power it tells the story of a Jewish doctor who is first reviled and persecuted because of his race and then called upon to operate on a leading Nazi because of his skill. This film has already been shown in America without interference from the censors and in this country it should be given all possible facilities."[99] Many of the reviews likewise recommended the film be screened more widely. For example, the director Basil Wright, writing in the *Spectator,* declared: "One would like to recommend it most earnestly as a film for the biggest super-cinemas in London and the provinces. It would certainly be a box-office furore."[100] He was echoed, among others, by Arthur Vesselo in *Sight and Sound*: "If ever there was a Film Society film which deserved to be more widely shown, that film is unquestionably Minkin and Rappoport's *Professor Mamlock*."[101]

After this screening and the enthusiasm it aroused, the film was sent to the British Board of Film Censors (BBFC), even though the board had already announced its intention to ban the work.[102] The *Glasgow Herald* quoted the BBFC's comment on issuing the rejection: "We consider this film is quite unsuitable for public exhibition in this country."[103] The BBFC did not make its reasons explicit, but many assumed that the government had ordered the ban in an effort to appease Nazi Germany and thus avoid or delay a war (or British involvement in one). Anxieties over immigration to Palestine, then ruled by a British mandate, may also have played a role.

During April and May 1939, the film society received a number of letters from refugee-oriented charities in Hull and Liverpool, as well as the Oxford University Refugee Committee, requesting copies of the film for fundraising screenings.[104] In each case, Phyllis Morris, the society's secretary, responded by explaining that the BBFC ban applied universally: "The film has been banned for public exhibition by the Censor, and a charity performance is classed as a public exhibition." Here the consequences of the censor's decision were tangible and brutal: the refugee organizations were prevented from using the film to raise funds that could pay for refugee exit visas, for the financial bonds required from a U.K. resident, or for goods and services to help refugees already in Britain.[105] The ban cost the lives of would-be refugees who might otherwise have escaped. There can scarcely have been a darker chapter in the long history of film censorship in Britain.

London's prime venue for foreign-language films, the Academy Cinema, on Oxford Street, then applied to the local authority, the London County Council (LCC), for a license to show the film, which the theater received on 26 July 1939 partly because it submitted the film along with Anatole Litvak's *Confessions of a Nazi Spy*.[106] While the cuts it demanded were "few and very small,"[107] the council expressed a palpable tentativeness:

> Mr Reginald Stamp, chairman of the Entertainments Committee of the L.C.C., told the "Daily Herald" that the committee's action must not be considered as a precedent.
>
> "There is a tendency to introduce propaganda and attacks on persons

which are undesirable," he said. "Both films have been cut to remove this type of passage.

"But future films which contain this propaganda run the risk of being refused certificates."[108]

In addition to petitioning the LCC, the distributors applied to other councils in the London area. Surrey and Essex passed it, East Ham hesitated, and Middlesex refused the film a license.[109] London's *Daily Worker* ridiculed this further example of appeasement in censorship: "Reasons for Middlesex refusal are not given. Is it because it's a Soviet film, or is its anti-Nazi character regarded as offensive to a 'friendly' power?"[110] The newspaper expanded on the reasons for the ban the following day and encouraged its readers outside London to "insist that local authorities give it a licence" in their districts.[111]

Local authorities, however, apparently received few requests to screen the film. Apart from anything else, it would have been difficult to get hold of a print, since the Soviet Union had ceased promoting the film abroad after the Molotov-Ribbentrop nonaggression pact. The circumstances of the pact, widely seen by the British as an act of treachery ensuring war, colored the film's reception when it was finally premiered at the Academy Cinema days before the outbreak of war, on 30 August.[112]

Thus the *Spectator* and the *New Statesman and Nation,* which had both acclaimed the film on its Film Society screening in March, found different reviewers to condemn it in August. *New Statesman and Nation*'s Anthony West was the most hostile: "Perhaps because the attack on persecution and brutality comes from such a tainted source it loses most of its force."[113]

Taking a different tack, the *Observer*'s C. A. Lejeune commented on the irony of the timing, for the release of *Professor Mamlock* coincided with negotiations for the pact and its subsequent signing; he recommended escapist drama instead.[114] This preference for a cinema of entertainment and distraction over one of social critique reflected a deeply entrenched mood in Britain and played an influential role in the decisions of the BBFC, which mirrored dominant opinion in the British cinema industry. The realization that war was inevitable focused minds, however, creating a greater appetite for seriousness in film and thus making the overwhelming mood more appreciative of *Professor Mamlock*'s critique of the Nazis and depiction of the threats and crimes harrowing Europe's Jews, even if it came from a source now viewed with suspicion. As a trade publication,

*Kinematograph Weekly* was quick to pick up on the new mood, arguing that the irony of its Soviet source "in no way obstructs the picture's message" and that "the fine acting and intelligent direction, together with eloquent subtitles, enable it to be easily followed by all classes." The weekly judged that the film could be a "potential coup in 'foreign stock' for all types of halls on the strength of its urgent topicality."[115]

Following Britain's 3 September declaration of war on Germany, the film was resubmitted to the BBFC, which passed it on the condition that further cuts be made; the board made its decision on 14 September, the day before the cinemas reopened after their temporary closure for air-raid precautions training.[116] *Kinematograph Weekly* had called it correctly: the film's topicality caught the public's appetite for exposés of Nazism across the political spectrum. It even received a huge plug in Lord Beaverbrook's top-selling *Daily Express*.[117] The film was still showing uninterrupted at the Academy a month later when a letter to the *Times* asked for the ban to be lifted and for the film to be widely distributed.[118]

While the nonaggression pact may have significantly influenced the film's fate in Britain, the nation's own embarrassment over the now failed and discredited policy of appeasing Hitler played an even more important role. In contesting proposals to tighten wartime censorship under the "Emergency Powers Act," a prominent Labour MP, Herbert Morrison, now condemned the BBFC's ban as illustrating the dangers of censorship:

> As an instance of how this matter of judgment goes wrong and how we have to be careful in delegating this power, I would mention the film "Professor Mamlock." The film censors made a clean prohibition. They probably did it on advice. There was an appeal to a local authority, who passed it subject to certain cuts. When the war came, the Board of Film Censors, who had prohibited the whole film, proposed, I understand, to pass the whole film and to restore the cuts which the local authority had wisely made. The original judgment of the Board of Film Censors, and I suspect of somebody behind them, was all wrong. It was given in the days when it was thought that you must not do anything offensive to Herr Hitler or to the German Government. This matter impressed itself upon my mind as showing that the delegation of film censorship and its general administration to a body of censors appointed by the Minister would be wrong.[119]

Morrison's statement gave the film further impetus, and while *Professor Mamlock* eventually ended its run at the Academy at the end of 1939 after three and a half months, it had already moved beyond London, with successful screenings throughout the country and extensive film press coverage.[120]

Yet while appeasement had hampered the film's distribution in Britain, it completely sabotaged it in Continental Europe, with the Nazi-Soviet nonaggression pact temporarily wiping the film from the face of the earth.[121]

## A Silent Interlude

Trauberg saw the strength of *Professor Mamlock* as its capacity to depict the Nazi takeover in a way that enabled spectators to add further examples of Nazi atrocity and update the picture:

> Today, when the bestial appearance of Fascism has been laid bare, when its deceitful demagoguery has ceased to conceal, at last, its true essence of the predatory aggressor, the destroyer of human culture, the film *Professor Mamlock* may seem at first glance somewhat muted, and slightly dated in its material. The film shows the days of German Fascism's ascent to power. But the great power of art is that the spectator can supplement the action unfolding on the screen, using the latest newspaper reports from the fronts in Spain or China.[122]

Especially with respect to its reception in the United States, *Professor Mamlock* certainly enabled spectators to read the film in the light of more recent events. Yet it was at the same time a historical film, depicting a stage in Nazism already over five years out of date when it was released. While Nazi brutality and anti-Semitism remained, they had also evolved and intensified during this period. Thus Minkin demanded *Professor Mamlock* serve as an initial salvo that should be followed by further films about contemporary Germany:

> *Professor Mamlock* . . . shows Germany in the first year of Fascist rule.
>
> To show present-day Germany creaking ever more with contradictions, and exhausted by feverish preparations for new wars of conquest—that's our next task.
>
> This is an enormous opportunity for ambitious works of art, using all their creative power to target the Fascist suffocators of culture and progress.
>
> The international Fascist bandits driving humanity into a new bloody war, the growing wrath of the people against them, the struggle of

Communist Parties for freedom, peace and culture—what a grandiose and exciting theme for filmmakers!

It is the pressing duty of our cinema organizations in the coming months to begin a series of antifascist films.[123]

While the *Oppenheim Family* and *Swamp Soldiers* followed, and the latter can be seen as portraying contemporary Nazi Germany, Minkin's wish was not fulfilled. The theme petered out, although other anti-Nazi films were being planned; as late as 11 August, for example, the Politbureau approved a signed request from Viacheslav Molotov to authorize an adaptation of Feuchtwanger's *Exile* (*Exil* [1939]), which depicts a family of German Jewish immigrants in Paris after Hitler's takeover in Germany and joins *The Oppermann Family* and *Success* (1930) to form the author's so-called waiting-room trilogy.[124] This request even meant authorizing a payment of FF 35,000 to Feuchtwanger to write the screenplay.[125] Whether or not the screenplay was written or the payment issued, the film was not made after Molotov signed a rather different document: the nonaggression pact with Nazi Germany.

The nonaggression pact immediately made Soviet antifascist films impossible and *Professor Mamlock* an embarrassment; the Soviets withdrew the film from domestic circulation soon after the pact, on 1 October 1939, "until special instructions."[126] They withdrew copies showing abroad even sooner wherever the distributor operated on a terminable lease.[127] Except in Britain, where the copy of *Professor Mamlock* had been bought outright, no Soviet anti-Nazi films were made or shown until the Nazi invasion of the Soviet Union, on 22 June 1941.

Soviet cinema did of course portray Jews during the period when the Nazi-Soviet pact was in effect, but not as victims of the Nazis or in ways designed to make audiences sympathize with them. In May 1940, for example, Sergei Eisenstein submitted a proposal to make a film of the infamous anti-Semitic Beilis trial, relating the case of a Jew accused of ritually murdering a Christian in Kiev in 1913, but this was rejected as "uninteresting at present."[128] That same year, however, Aleksandr Dovzhenko and Iuliia Solntseva made the documentary *Bukovina Is Ukrainian Land* (*Bukovina—Zemlia ukrainskaia* [1940]), which portrays rich Jews from Chernovtsy, the principal city in the recently annexed Bukovina, as oblivious to the region's impoverished Ukrainians and spending their wealth to build lavish synagogues, a theme with easily discernible anti-Semitic undercurrents.

For the Soviets, the Nazi invasion of June 1941 instantaneously transformed questions about representing the Nazi persecution of Jews from issues of history or foreign policy into an internal dilemma on which the survival of the population and the system depended. At the same time, the invasion triggered a redefinition of Soviet identity through the prism of the common war effort, which further marginalized Soviet Jews from their already "ambivalent" position. Jewish persecution by the Nazis was never again to be represented in Soviet film as prominently as it had been in *Professor Mamlock*.

# 2 \ "The Beasts Have Taken Aim at Us"

## SOVIET NEWSREELS SCREEN THE WAR AND THE HOLOCAUST

**The Nazi** invasion of the Soviet Union on 22 June 1941 unleashed a new stage of the Holocaust, for the Nazis' persecution of Jews was no longer limited to humiliation, expulsion, concentration, starvation, and sporadic pogroms. As part of their ideologically conceived war against, as they saw it, intertwined forces of Jewry and communism, the Nazis immediately began systematically murdering the Jews of occupied Europe, beginning with Soviet Jews.[1] Reports of these killings began to reach the Soviet authorities probably as early as 19 July 1941, and by August information about killings throughout Belorussia, as well as in the Ukrainian towns of Vinnitsa, Kamenets-Podolskii, Zhitomyr, and Berdychev, had made Stalin aware of the Nazi intention to annihilate all Soviet Jews.[2]

Many historical studies have investigated the skepticism with which Western politicians and the media received reports of the killings.[3] Such investigations tend largely to neglect the Soviet context either through ignorance; the logistical problems, especially during the cold war, of considering this dimension alongside matters concerning the Allies; the assumption that the Soviets knew nothing; or political and cultural antipathy.[4] Furthermore, except for research appearing recently, the studies that do discuss the Soviet media have unanimously asserted that no such depictions were ever produced.[5] In contrast to their Western democratic allies, however, Stalin and the Soviet government seem to have immediately believed their sources, who were often trusted NKVD agents, and they reacted quickly: in August 1941, the month when the reports first reached Stalin, the Soviet press began to publish references to Nazis killing Jews. The radio and cinema followed soon afterward, though more circumspectly, with excerpts from the 24 August 1941 "Meeting of Representatives of the Jewish People" being broadcast on the radio and appearing as the third item in a *Soiuzkinozhurnal* newsreel (no. 84, 30 August 1941). The latter constitutes the first filmic reference to the Nazis' genocidal acts toward Jews. In the first excerpt, the famous actor and director of the Moscow Yiddish Theater (GOSET), Solomon Mikhoels, addressed Jews throughout the world. Mikhoels's speech, as published in the press, referred to the Nazis' intention to destroy the whole Jewish people.[6] The newsreel, however, setting a pattern that would continue throughout the war, omitted this reference to the bigger picture of systematic murder; what could appear in print could not appear in the more emotive and influential form of the newsreel. In the speech Mikhoels (fig. 2.1) also described a shift in Jewish identity from the historically received one of passive victims to that of fighter:

> We no longer have the strength and will to remain simply objects of violence, victims.
>
> We must no longer mournfully bear our wounds to the world.
>
> In the new, free Soviet country a totally different generation of people has grown up. . . .
>
> This generation does not know the meaning of fear. This generation cannot bear to feel itself a victim. Together with all citizens of our great country, our sons are engaged in battle.[7]

In his speech, Mikhoels described Soviet Jews as resisting and ascribed this to the influence of Soviet culture. But he also proclaimed a shift in Jewish identity more widely toward active resistance. This dual emphasis suggested that he was addressing his speech not only to the wider world of Jewry but also to Soviet Jews. Indeed, a tension between these two audiences characterized the wartime actions undertaken by Mikhoels and others, especially after the formation of the Jewish Antifascist Committee, in February 1942. In an early indication of this conflict, however, the newsreel release edited the speech to make it solely a call for international Jewry to stand in the front line against Nazism, thus avoiding the worrisome appeal to Soviet Jews to resist as Jews.

FIGURE 2.1. Solomon Mikhoels: The radio meeting of representatives of the Jewish people. From *Soiuzkinozhurnal* no. 84 (1941).

Without Mikhoels's references to a plan for destroying the Jews and to Jewish resistance, the newsreel's most explicit description of the Nazi program of genocide came in quotations from the more reliably Soviet source of Ilya Ehrenburg, whose speech, unlike that of Mikhoels, was addressed solely to the Jews of America: "Listen to the cries of Russian and Jewish women being tortured in Berdychev. You cannot stop your ears. You cannot close your eyes. . . . Jews. The beasts have taken aim at us. . . . Our place is in the first ranks. We will not forgive indifference."[8] Yet even Ehrenburg's speech is edited to remove much of his discussion concerning Nazi anti-Semitism and thus emphasize the common fate of Jews and Russians. Following the pattern established in prewar anti-Nazi films, the Soviet newsreel mentions the dangers threatening Jews in particular, but it tones down any reference to the exceptional status that the Nazis accorded them, making them similar to the Russians in this respect. Nevertheless, this short newsreel is notable for its use of synchronously recorded speeches, though voiced not by eyewitnesses but by Soviet Jews whose relatives were caught in the German occupation or whose hometowns were being overrun. The emotional charge of their appeal is all the more powerful for this blood bond with those threatened.

Before long, however, the Soviet cinema would face the task of conveying not only this kind of verbal report about the killings but also direct evidence of Nazi atrocities, as the Red Army halted the German advance for the first time in the late autumn and winter of 1941–1942, advancing across a wide front to liberate the town of Rostov-on-Don at the end of November, the Crimean town of Kerch in January 1942, and numerous towns and villages around Moscow from December 1941 to January 1942. The press had already published atrocity photos taken by the Nazis themselves and found when German soldiers were captured by the Soviets.[9] Rostov, however, presented the first case where World War II camera operators became direct eyewitnesses to evidence of Nazi atrocities, including the murder of Jews, and faced the task of conveying this brutality in documentary film.

### First Films of Nazi Atrocities

The Soviet newsreel film of the first liberation of Rostov (*Soiuzkinozhurnal* no. 114), on 29 November 1941, was released nearly a month later, on 23 December. For the first time, in a city of a half-million inhabitants including a significant Jewish population, Soviet newsreel cameramen came face to face with the aftermath of the Nazi violence against the occupied population.[10] Yet the Soviet cameramen did not simply record these sights; they also selected which images to film, how to film them, and which individual victims to name and highlight as emblematic of the wider suffering. It is important to analyze this process of shaping carefully, since any public discussion of staging, of Soviet newsreel as anything other than a record, was entirely absent from the debates around Soviet newsreel, even though some of the compositions are evidently posed. The only discussion of such matters comes in journalists' denunciations of Nazi film falsifications as "Fascist propaganda's despicable methods of rearranging the real facts" and revelations that villagers had been forced at gunpoint to smile and welcome Nazi occupiers for the cameras.[11] Purely internal reviews of newsreel items, however, sometimes discuss these issues with regard to Soviet cinema. It is important to consider them, but not because they prove that the Soviets faked their films. On the whole, they did not invent or entirely falsify so much as select what and whom to film, as well as determine how to film what they had selected. They also often demanded certain responses or actions from the people they filmed, just as the Nazis had, and established patterns and clichés of representation.

Moreover, while Rostov was the first big city to be recaptured, camera operators had already been witnessing the aftermath of smaller-scale Nazi atrocities, but it was months before they decided to film them. The journey to that point had involved a process of interpreting these sights as part of a narrative of the war, of interpreting and shaping inchoate grief and suffering as part of a meaningful message.

As they prepared for events looming on the horizon, filmmakers and others had often discussed how newsreel should cover the coming war, but they had to completely rethink their decisions once it started, for the static recording of predictable parades was swept away by the need to film the chaos of combat with mobile, handheld cameras.[12] Understandably, filming enemy atrocities did not figure in prewar plans, for this would have required, among other things, anticipating invasion, occupation, and defeat at a time when most expected a quick and easy victory on the aggressor's soil.[13] A handful of cameramen, including Roman Karmen and Boris Makaseev, had filmed air raids and their effects in Republican Spain, creating widely seen newsreel footage; they in turn had built on the example of Boris Tseitlin and Vladimir Eshurin, who had earlier filmed Italian bombings of civilians in Abyssinia. Yet no one dared imagine this experience would be relevant to recording the sufferings of the Soviet civilian population. It was precisely these initiations, however, and the wider imaginative resources for portraying violence against civilians in Soviet films, such as Eisenstein's *Battleship Potemkin* (*Bronenosets Potemkin* [1925]), that were to prove the most relevant precedents.

The newsreel camera operators initially did not dare record the tragic vistas of retreat and columns of refugees they saw during the first months of the war, for such images contradicted their earlier expectations of a triumphant Soviet advance. In some cases, they were too distressed by images of the bereaved; in others, they were simply afraid to film scenes of devastation without having received express permission, as had been required in prewar documentaries.[14] The first film to overcome this confusion was that of the liberation of Rostov.[15]

The fact that the first significant film images of Nazi atrocities came in a film about victory was no coincidence. As the cameraman Anatolii Krylov put it, there was "an unspoken orientation to film only . . . successes and victories";[16] the initial victories therefore gave filmmakers their first opportunity to begin showing the true extent of the devastation wrought by the invading forces. The Rostov footage thus established an important narrative that dominated Soviet images of Nazi atrocities, which were both preceded and followed by images of the triumphant onward march of the Red Army. Propaganda was inextricably entwined with atrocity; indeed, the latter would not have been shown without the former.[17]

### Rostov-on-Don

*Soiuzkinozhurnal* no. 114, edited by Roman Gikov and filmed by Arkadii Levitan, Georgii Popov, and Andrei Sologubov, begins with newspaper headlines proclaiming the recapture of Rostov followed by images of the generals and the battle. As the Red Army moves forward to the outskirts of town, we see abandoned German tanks and transport vehicles and dead German soldiers. This part of the newsreel culminates with Soviet tanks advancing unopposed down the streets and soldiers raising the Soviets' Red Flag on the town's central square.

This is then followed by an intertitle, "In Rostov," and images of burned, ruined, and damaged buildings accompanied by a voiceover: "The Fascist bands lorded it over Rostov for eight days. For eight days they burned and looted the town. Raped and murdered peaceful citizens." Shots of the town accompanied by this description of the Germans' actions give way to images of corpses in the street accompanying the mention of the occupiers' crimes against the population. The commentary deliberately associates two sentences with the same grammatical subject, "Fascist bands" and with a similar structure of subject, two past-tense verbs ("burned and looted" and "raped and murdered") and object ("town" and "peaceful citizens"), further underlining the parallel between the damage that the Nazis had inflicted on the town and the suffering they had inflicted on the population (figs. 2.2 and 2.3). Soviet cinema would repeat this link between ruins and the dead in many images of Nazi atrocities in the Soviet Union, above all to show the Nazis' destruction of Soviet civilization and to tie the victims to the cities, towns, and state to which they belong. A further inflection of this theme, as I will show, is to draw attention to the Nazi destruction of Russian, and sometimes Ukrainian, culture, usually by depicting ruined churches, but never synagogues. By emphasizing damage to contemporary Soviet buildings as an analogy of the human cost, the Rostov film also shifts attention away from the ethnicity of the majority of the victims. In this case, the German forces mur-

FIGURE 2.2. Footage from the recapture of Rostov, "burned and looted the town." From *Soiuzkinozhurnal* no. 114 (1941).

dered around one hundred Jews during the first occupation of Rostov, but the presentation of the dead as victims of a generalized Nazi violence toward the town and its population serves to obscure the racial motive for the crime.[18]

While it mentions Jewish victims, the previously discussed film of the meeting of "Representatives of the Jewish People" forced viewers to read between the lines if they were to glean the knowledge that most of the murdered victims were Jews; *Soiuzkinozhurnal* no. 114, however, did not even imply, let alone state, that the dead included Jews. The press did not remedy this lacuna, since the newspapers rarely divided the dead on an ethnic basis. For example, a 1 December letter to *Pravda* from those who had lived through the German occupation repeats the story of the people killed as a reprisal after a German was killed in their house, specifying that it occurred in the district of Nakhichevan´ and that there were fifty-two victims.[19] Other sources, drawing on subsequent accounts by Red Army members, refer to apparently the same incident as leading to the deaths of thirty Jews.[20] Similarly, a 7 December report in *Pravda* referred to the

FIGURE 2.3. Rostov, "Raped and killed peaceful citizens." From *Soiuzkinozhurnal* no. 114 (1941).

Germans' murder of "whole apartments, houses and districts," especially concentrating their violence against proletarian neighborhoods, illustrating this with the example of sixty-one victims from a house on a street called the Thirty-sixth Line.[21] Authenticated eyewitness testimony confirms these victims to have been Jews, among hundreds from this district who were killed for being Jewish, their corpses left on the street.[22]

Given the large proportion of Jews among the dead (indeed, they made up the majority), and even though at least one of the camera operators was Jewish, the newsreel entirely avoided indicating that any of the victims were Jewish. Its makers selected individual cases, such as the family of Professor Rozhdestvenskii, killed because someone had fired on the Germans from the vicinity of their house, or the wife of an engineer named Gordeev, who was raped and then killed. The most memorable image, however, is that of the ostensibly thirteen-year-old boy Golovlev, killed for refusing to part with his favorite pigeon (fig. 2.4).

Because this boy subsequently became a celebrated, almost mythical figure for the Pioneer movement (the Soviet politicized version of the Boy

FIGURE 2.4. Rostov, image of boy murdered by the Nazis, Vitia Golovlev/Cherev-
ichkin. From *Soiuzkinozhurnal* no. 114 (1941).

Scouts), whose members sang a song, erected a statue, and named a street
in his memory, it is possible to establish that he was in fact Vitia Cherevichkin, and his age was not thirteen but sixteen.[23] Moreover, it appears
that while he was indeed killed for refusing give up his pigeon, this was
because pigeons were a potential means of long-distance communication
and thus attracted the Nazi authorities' suspicions. The changes all seem
designed to enhance the dead boy's symbolic value. Thus, the reason for
his murder is left vague, so as to imply that this was less a savage reprisal
with its own brutal logic than a random act of irrational sadism. Likewise, the boy's age is lowered to make him less of a potential combat-
ant or serious resister and more of an innocent child victim. More than
this, however, the image has deep roots in Soviet cinema's traditions for
representing violence, which, as described by the Russian critic Evgenii
Margolit, ties the representation of children to that of violence so that the
death of a child typically calls forth what he calls "righteous" violence that
almost sanctifies the death.[24] Certainly images of children killed by the
Nazis became standard fare in the Soviets' newsreel depictions throughout

FIGURE 2.5. Rostov, Vitia Cherevichkin Park.

the war, right up to their film of Auschwitz. Indeed, in planning the film of the Battle of Moscow, the directors intended to include images of dead children even before the footage had been taken.[25] Similarly, Vitia's name change may have been intended to enhance his mythical appeal by shifting from the associations of his real name with the lower sphere of women's footwear (*cherevichki*) to those of the fictional one with the higher realm of the head (*golova*) or possibly the dove of peace (*golub*), for which he was killed, since the same Russian word denotes both pigeons generally and doves specifically. Indeed, the fact that the pigeon is still miraculously living in his hands indicates that the image was posed; even *Pravda* states he was shot *after* releasing the pigeon and not on the street, where we see him in the film, but in the park.[26] The underlying purpose once again seems to be that of making him a symbol, with the living dove implying an essential Soviet spirit of innocence and resistance the Nazis cannot crush. The effect was certainly achieved, in that Vitia and his pigeon became widely celebrated (fig. 2.5). Indeed, his was among the first of many Soviet depictions of the Nazis' victims (Zoia Kosmodem´ianskaia is the most famous) that explicitly show the corpse's face, contradicting Susan Sontag's claim that only photographs of the remote or exotic dead or dying show the victims' faces.[27] The footage of Vitia Cherevichkin shows his face, makes a spectacle of his death, and suggests that he is as typically Soviet as the presumed viewer.

This emphasis on Vitia as similar to the viewer rather than exotically distant is crucially important, for it indicates that this and similar images from Rostov serve a further purpose: to Sovietize Nazi atrocities by distracting the spectator from the Nazis' wider-scale murder, in the same district (Nakhichevan) and on the same day, of a great deal more Jews. Vitia is chosen not because he typifies the dead but precisely because he does not. Watching the film, it is impossible to discern a Jewish identity or anti-Semitic motive for his or any of the killings. Rather, the newsreel paints a picture of Germans acting from irrational and barbarous motives. They are not said to be inspired by a political ideology of antipathy to Jews and communists or desire for imperialist expansion; instead, their violence is portrayed as random, a result of a bestial nature, both theirs and fascism's generally, that is left unexplained.

The highly tendentious selection and voiceover of the film contradicts its claim to be a document. While this is a standard one-reel (ten-minute) newsreel film, it is devoted entirely to the subject of the liberation of Rostov, whereas typical newsreels contain three or four items, and approximately half the film consists of images of the atrocities introduced by a title card: "We shall not forget! We shall not forgive! Film-Documents of the Fascist Brutes' Bloody Atrocities in Rostov-on-Don." This effectively forms a short film within a film, one that proclaims itself part of the non-genre of "film documents," a designation implying little or no shaping of the material. The generic marker is an important one, for it claims the newsreel to be documenting and implicitly not interpreting, not shaping the material into a narrative aimed at persuading spectators. The Soviets would subsequently use this genre of "film documents" to show Nazi atrocities throughout the war and afterward, at the Nuremberg Tribunal; even at this early stage, it already evoked an underlying motive for filming such things: to collate evidence of Nazi crimes. This newsreel is far from a mythically pure document, however, or an objective record of Rostov as the cameramen found it.

The orientation to collect evidence and document competes with the basic cinematographic goal of creating visually striking, memorable, and persuasive shots and sequences. Both these imperatives coexist with the need to fit the evidence into a politically preestablished picture of Soviet, and not Jewish, victimhood. The Soviet cameraman Mikhail Glider expressed this tension between the call to document dispassionately and an inevitable emotional involvement when he described the experience of filming "people's suffering": "You want the camera to see precisely what your eyes see, to share your indignation and distress—in other words, crudely, . . . to 'film with feeling.' But the lens doesn't care."[28] In fact, Soviet camera operators generally succeeded in conveying their emotional orientation toward the atrocities they were documenting. The outtakes from the Rostov film convey a sense that they were searching for the most expressive rendering of the material. In addition, the filmmakers indicate their emotional reactions to all the exposed footage by using others as proxies in the Rostov film, which does not merely show corpses but cues our reactions to them through powerful images of grieving relatives. Although later wartime depictions of atrocities included officials, such as members of the subsequently established Extraordinary State Commission on War Crimes,[29] here we see the less hierarchical dimension of Soviet wartime culture—namely, its "spontaneous de-Stalinization,"[30] that is, its appeal beyond ideology and authority to the visceral, to death, grief, and hatred in a desperate effort to rally the population. This use of others' reactions may be compared to the use of so-called frame witnesses: authority figures, such as General Eisenhower, who corroborated the authenticity of the images of the camps liberated by the U.S. Army in spring 1945.[31] Although it invokes the notion of documentary, the Rostov film includes grief-stricken relatives, not frame witnesses, to channel our responses: someone who recognizes his or her murdered children seeks not corroboration but the culprit. Grief in turn cues the intended reaction among spectators: the desire for vengeance.

This approach resulted not from any individual's interpretation but from a general set of demands on Soviet camera operators and in turn on those they filmed. Indeed, eyewitness accounts of later filming in Feodosia (Crimea) in January 1942 reveal that Soviet camera crews deliberately concentrated on filming people who were crying profusely, occasionally even shouting orders to weep when bystanders appeared numbed.[32] Sometimes the emotional reaction is expressed in images of the bereaved standing beside their loved ones (fig. 2.6); sometimes it is effected through sequences edited according to the conventions of the eyeline match, through a brief tilt following some particular reaction, or through a shift in focus from the dead to the living relative.

In the newsreel at issue, the voiceover stresses the senseless nature of

FIGURE 2.6. Rostov, relatives of the dead. From *Soiuzkinozhurnal* no. 114 (1941).

the violence, with no suggestion of a methodical, genocidal plan. Indeed, as the report on the liberation of Rostov in *Pravda* put it: "The Germans didn't care whom they killed."[33] The voiceover commentary further shapes the inarticulate, silent expressions of grief and despair among the bereaved by saying that these responses are transforming into hatred for the enemy: "Thousand of inhabitants of Rostov—women, children, and old people—died, victims of savage and random violence. The tears will dry, the battle and grief will subside, but never, never in our hearts will the hatred be extinguished, the great, sacred hatred for murderers and hangmen." Indeed, in showing Soviet spectators these sights, the film aims at precisely this transformation, molding inarticulate screams into a hatred that could strengthen the war effort, be it on the battlefield or the factory floor.

Forming a neat and highly deliberate visual rhyme, the final part of the Rostov atrocity footage repeats the images that began the sequence, those of dead Soviet citizens lying on the street. Because they have already appeared, they add nothing to the piece as a document, but the repetition makes it visually more powerful by adding structural coherence. This is a document but also a great deal more.

The images of murdered civilians are followed by images of Red Army soldiers killed by the Germans. At this point the voiceover introduces the concept of vengeance, repeats the slogan from the subtitle of this film within a film ("We shall not forget! We shall not forgive!"), and asserts that these atrocities will be avenged. We then see columns of Red Army soldiers marching onward through the town. By ending one sequence with soldiers' deaths and following that with their living comrades' onward march, the film implies a victory over death, as does the earlier image of Vitia Cherevichkin; the individual soldiers we saw earlier might be dead, but the army continues their struggle. This is a wartime version of the logic in the symbolism of the socialist martyr's funeral, which the historian Catherine Merridale has described as treating death as a down payment on ultimate victory.[34] In the context of the war, the deaths will be compensated or recuperated initially by vengeance and ultimately by a victory procured through these acts of vengeance.[35] The deaths are thus transformed from the cause of inconsolable, inchoate grief into elements in a meaningful narrative of the Soviet cause's impending triumph.

Throughout these images, the soundtrack of plunging strings, including extracts from Tchaikovsky's Sixth Symphony (the *Pathétique*), serves to orient us emotionally by establishing a consistent musical trigger for such scenes. Soviet newsreels and documentaries would repeatedly use this music or works resembling it during the war to accompany images of atrocities. As do the images of children, the emphasis on the victims' relatedness to spectators, the calls to vengeance, and the compensatory onward march of the Red Army, this music helps give form to suffering, channeling images and feelings of loss so as to suggest an ultimate sense in the suffering and a response to it. This served to establish a model for subsequent Soviet film representations of Nazi atrocities, including those against Jews, whose sufferings, when depicted, had to be situated within this same template. The filmic images had a powerful impact on the public, as is evidenced by the fact that this episode of the usually twice-weekly newsreel was still showing in Moscow over a month later. It had no less of an effect on artists working in other media, such as the Jewish graphic artist Zinovii Tolkachev, who was later to create a powerful visual testimony of the liberation of the camps; his 1942 series of illustrations entitled

*Occupiers* (*Okkupanty*), made after seeing this newsreel, was his first attempt to depict the occupation in his chosen artistic medium.[36]

The importance of the film was underlined by a *Pravda* review of it, a rare occurrence for a single-reel newsreel. The review emphasizes the film's portrayal of atrocities by using as its title "We shall not forget! We shall not forgive!" ("Ne zabudem, ne prostim!"), borrowing from the similarly labeled section of the film, and includes stills from the film showing atrocities. The review analyzes little but instead amplifies the calls to vengeance articulated by the film itself, which it calls a testament as to the Nazis' sadistic nature. I will later return to this claim, made in many wartime Soviet documentaries.

### Newsreels of Short-lived Liberations: Livny, Kerch, and Barvenkovo

*Soiuzkinozhurnal* no. 114 did not identify Jews as a specific group among the Nazis' victims, a tendency continued in almost all newsreels treating other towns liberated in this period. *Soiuzkinozhurnal* no. 9, however, constitutes an exception. This newsreel, which was released on 30 January 1942 and edited by Roman Gikov, shows the liberation of Livny, a town in the central Russian oblast (administrative district) of Orlov. It displays images of Jews showing Red Army soldiers the armbands they were forced to wear and includes close-ups of those armbands (see figs. 2.7 and 2.8). The voiceover explains: "The Fascists forced the town's Jews to wear these armbands." This short segment unambiguously identifies the Nazis' forced humiliation of Jews but not the rationale behind it or other aspects of concentrating the Jewish population, such as forcing them into ghettos.

The footage in this report was taken by Boris Vakar, M. Gol´dbrikh, Izrail´ Gol´dshtein, Evgenii Mukhin, and Grigorii Ostrovskii, and while it is easy to imagine that the two camera operators among this group with obviously Jewish surnames took these images, the lack of a corroborating document precludes certainty. As is typical for Soviet newsreel films, identifying a personal vision, a political or aesthetic authoring of these images, poses insuperable difficulties. Whereas David Shneer has attempted to define a Jewish gaze in his discussion of Soviet Jewish photographers, the question of authorship with regard to still photography remains far clearer than it does for newsreel films.[37] Even where the cameramen's personal investments as Jews suggest that they filmed the Jewish subjects, the footage was edited and a commentary added by someone else in Moscow, someone who may have had a completely different attitude. Certainly the

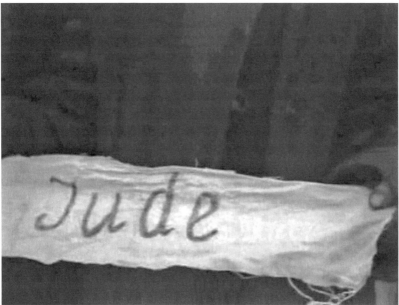

FIGURES 2.7 and 2.8. Livny, "The Nazis forced the town's Jews to wear these armbands." From *Soiuzkinozhurnal* no. 9 (1942).

voiceover to the Livny newsreel fails to seize the opportunity to explain the wider picture of Nazi treatment of Jews. Thus the collective nature of Soviet newsreel tended to dilute any sense of a personal vision and any sense of a Jewish gaze, with one or two rare exceptions, as I will show.

Despite this episode's importance, few newsreel images of formerly occupied towns and villages and the Nazi atrocities in them reveal anything about the Nazis' specific attitude to Jews. This is a particularly yawning omission in *Soiuzkinozhurnal* no. 10 (6 February 1942). This newsreel, edited by Nikolai Karmazinskii, contains footage that Mikhail Oshurkov had recorded in December 1941 in Bagerovskii Rov (also known as the Bagerov Trench), just outside the Crimean town of Kerch, which the Red Army had briefly recaptured; Oshurkov's material includes images of a mass gave uncovered to reveal the bodies of 7,000 Soviet citizens.[38] The film is the first cinematic attempt to show a Nazi mass grave, such as that at Babyi Iar, where Soviet Jews had been and were still being shot and buried by the tens of thousands. As such, it makes some attempt to evoke the process by which the town's inhabitants had been led from the town, split into small groups, and shot with submachine guns.

The film's treatment of these events contrasts with those in other media. For example, whereas the newsreel shows an otherwise anonymous man wearing a white scarf who is grieving by the bodies of his children (fig. 2.9), Evgenii Khaldei's photographs of this man, shown grieving by the corpses of his wife and daughters, were labeled to identify him as Grigorii Berman, whose surname suggests that, like most of the victims, he and his family were Jewish.[39] Similarly, Il´ia Sel´vinskii's poem about Kerch mentions Jews as numbering among the victims; the poem was published not only in the newspapers but also in a brochure devoted to the subject that named victims such as Nahum Rappaport, enabling readers to surmise that Jews were prominent among the victims (fig. 2.10).[40]

One film did contain material implying that such victims were overwhelmingly Jewish: *Soiuzkinozhurnal* no. 27 (30 March 1942), edited by Irina Setkina and filmed by Leon Mazrukho, a Jewish cameraman who would later direct postwar antifascist films on the subject of war crimes trials, such as *In the Name of the Living* (*Vo imia zhivykh* [1964]).[41] The newsreel depicts the liberation of the small town of Barvenkovo, in Ukraine's Kharkov Oblast; Barvenkovo, a town recaptured by the Red Army and held until May the following year, is covered in an item entitled "We Shall

FIGURE 2.9. Kerch, Grigorii Berman grieving at the loss of his family. From *Soiuzkinozhurnal* no. 10 (1942).

FIGURE 2.10. Kerch, image of Nahum Rappoport, murdered by Nazis. From "We Shall not Forget! We shall not Forgive!"

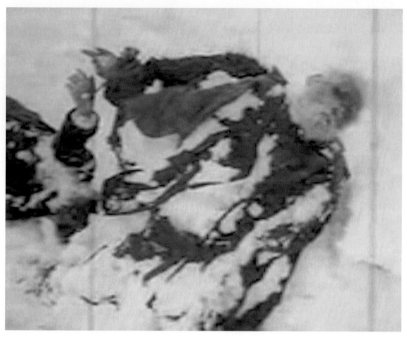

FIGURE 2.11. Barvenkovo, image of Iakov Reingold, murdered by Nazis. From *Soiuzkinozhurnal* no. 27 (1942).

Not Forget, We Shall Not Forgive—Film Documents of the Gory Evil Deeds of the Fascist Occupiers" ("Ne zabudem, ne prostim—kinodokumenty o krovavykh zlodeianii nemetsko-fashistskikh okkupantov"). As this item runs, the voiceover mentions the "elderly worker Iakov Reingol´d" and shows an image of his frozen corpse tied to that of his daughter, Tat´iana (fig. 2.11). Nevertheless, the commentary attempts to dispel any thought that he might have been killed because he was Jewish, stating: "These peaceful citizens of a little Ukrainian town became victims of Fascist barbarity. They were tortured by executioners in German uniforms. They were killed simply because they were Soviet People."

Conveying this message required some effort, for the town's Jewish inhabitants apparently had been forced to wear Star of David armbands. Footage omitted from the finished film clearly shows this, but the images of the dead were deliberately selected so as to conceal this unambiguous visual marker of their Jewish identity (cf. figs. 2.12 and 2.13).

The massacre at Bagerovskii Rov, however, lay on a completely different scale to that of the atrocities depicted in this film about Barvenkovo,

FIGURE 2.12. Barvenkovo, dead woman murdered by Nazis, armband visible. Outtake from *Soiuzkinozhurnal* no. 27 (1942). Courtesy of RGAKFD.

FIGURE 2.13. Barvenkovo, dead woman murdered by Nazis, armband not visible. From *Soiuzkinozhurnal* no. 27 (1942).

where it seems fewer than one hundred victims were found, and those shown in the Rostov film (although Rostov would suffer something similarly massive when it was occupied for a second time in the summer of 1942). Nevertheless, the newsreel of Kerch attracted less public attention than the Rostov film had, for it was not the first depiction of Nazi atrocities, and its release coincided with that of the most significant filmic treatment of Nazi atrocities: the documentary film of the Battle of Moscow compiled from newsreel footage and released in February 1942.

### Defeat of the Germans near Moscow

By far the most influential and widely disseminated images of the Nazi occupation appeared in a film about the Battle of Moscow. This film, a brilliantly rewritten and reedited version of which was widely shown in the United States and won an Oscar in 1943, was the first feature-length Soviet documentary of the war. Its depiction of the first significant defeat inflicted on the Nazis in a land battle was combined with images of the atrocities they had committed in the towns and villages of the Moscow region briefly occupied at the end of 1941. The greater scope of the feature-length documentary format enabled the film to provide expanded depictions of these atrocities and present these images in new ways that further shaped audience responses to them.

Yet these developments resulted less from individual decisions than from political interventions, including those by the Political Directorate of the Red Army, which, in the preamble to a directive issued shortly after the Rostov film came out, had criticized newsreel images of reoccupied areas: "The face of the German army of looters, its mass atrocities in the districts liberated by the Red Army, and the destruction of artifacts of Russian culture and civilization are all shown weakly, impersonally, with no documentation, and there are no shots of the moments of the recording of atrocities."[42] Even though the Rostov film does individualize victims to a degree, doing so, for example, with its images of Vitia Cherevichkin, Professor Rozhdestvenskii's family, and Gordeev's wife, it does not display any damage to specifically Russian cultural artifacts or the investigation as to what happened (footage omitted from the film, however, does include images of Soviet soldiers taking down reports from the inhabitants). Later films would illustrate the processes of drafting protocols and gathering witness testimony, particularly after the Soviet Extraordinary State Commission on War Crimes was created, in November 1942, but

FIGURE 2.14. Woman mourning daughter murdered by Nazis. From *Defeat of the Germans near Moscow*.

*Defeat of the Germans near Moscow* instead presents Red Army personnel as they treat the wounded and stand contemplating the dead.

Unlike the Rostov film, this longer work encompasses images of captured Germans that emphasize their disheveled and somewhat pitiful—or contemptible—appearance. These shots are combined with images of the bereaved, often in close-up and of greater duration, conveying and evoking emotions far more effectively than the brief newsreel could. For example, the film's editors used an eyeline match to transform one woman's grief over her defiled and murdered daughter into a gaze of vengeful hatred, concretized through the addition of the word *murderers* in the voiceover, which is addressed to the Germans (figs. 2.14, 2.15, and 2.16). The verbalization and editing work together here to overcome the "indeterminate" nature of photographic images and turn them into an unambiguous call to arms.[43] Moreover, the film's manner of showing not just individualized victims but also relatives mourning individual victims frames the gaze and underlines the sense that the dead are related to the spectator, too. The mourners are further concretized by being tied to di-

FIGURE 2.15. The voiceover appears to vocalize her cries: "No mercy!" From *Defeat of the Germans near Moscow.*

FIGURE 2.16. The voiceover apparently continues to speak for her: "Murderers!" From *Defeat of the Germans near Moscow.*

rect speech, albeit spoken not by them but by the voiceover (there is no way of ascertaining whether they uttered the words voiced in this way).

In addition, *Defeat of the Germans near Moscow* outstrips the earlier Rostov film in its number of images showing Red Army soldiers, some of them depicted in medium-range or close-up shots to endow them with far more individuality than the earlier film ever reveals. In particular, they are shown in detail reacting to Nazi atrocities. In one sequence, for example, a soldier removes his hat and bows his head in a mark of respect for the dead Soviet civilians he sees (figs. 2.17 and 2.18). The eyeline match leads into various images of German atrocities that follow, more than the soldier can plausibly see at one time. Not simply a witness, he is constructed here as the subject of vision, the soldier who, having seen what the Nazis do to his people, will fight more uncompromisingly. The sequence ends by returning to the close-up up of the soldier, who now replaces his hat and marches on, into battle, alongside his comrades. Grief and vengeance are thus deftly linked through the more explicit intimation of a brief secular and military funeral, and they are recuperated by a much more significant victory.

*Defeat of the Germans near Moscow* further differs from the Rostov film in suggesting that Nazi violence was not simply random and animalistic but born of a "hatred toward our Soviet people," a sentiment suggesting some kind of ethnic hatred, though one directed against all Soviet citizens. Yet this film goes much further than *Soiuzkinozhurnal* no. 114 in its detailed and specific portrayal of the Germans' destruction of Russian cultural artifacts, including traditional houses and churches, as well as the homes of Tolstoy and Tchaikovsky. Where the images of Rostov were anonymously civic, those of the Moscow region are explicitly Russian. The effect is to shape images of suffering so as to imply a narrative of Russian national victimhood; while the victims are identified as Soviet, the cultural destruction is described as Russian. Because the film describes the ruination and destruction of culture in a way that echoes the human suffering, the consistent identification of that culture as Russian ends up rubbing off on the way the dead are conceptualized.

Even though the Jewish populations of these recaptured towns near Moscow were small compared to Rostov's, significant numbers of the dead there were Jews. Between 150 and 200 Jews were killed in the Moscow Oblast, and some 100 to 150 were killed in the Kaluga Oblast; in the Kalinin region, the Nazi occupation cost as many as 1,250–1,500 Jewish

FIGURE 2.17. A Red Army man mourns. From *Defeat of the Germans near Moscow*.

FIGURE 2.18. The person mourned by the Red Army man. From *Defeat of the Germans near Moscow*.

lives,[44] and only the ease of evacuating to Moscow prevented a higher toll. The press contained some coverage of Nazi persecution of Jews at this time, referring, for example, to the creation of a ghetto in Kaluga and the fact that Jews there had to wear armbands.[45] Footage of Nazi atrocities in Kaluga had appeared in the seventh installment of a special newsreel series devoted to the Battle of Moscow, *For the Defense of Beloved Moscow* (*Na zashchitu rodnoi Moskvy*), dated 12 January 1942, but it incorporates no images of identifiably Jewish suffering. Indeed, this newsreel claims that the victims had been killed because they were Soviet people. In the town of Kalinin itself, 200 of the 400 people whom the Nazis killed were Jews. *Defeat of the Germans near Moscow* has a brief section on the retaking of that town, but the commentary fails to explain the reasons for half the murders committed there.[46] Similarly, Nikolai Kagan, one of the eight Young Communists shown hanged in Volokalamsk, was a Jew, but this fact is evident only from his name, which some of the newspaper accounts provide, and neither the papers nor the newsreel specifies his ethnicity.[47] Instead, the images of Nazi atrocities are given a universal, ethnically nonspecific character, although colored, as I have shown, by artifacts of specifically Russian culture.

### Synchronous Sound and Testimony

One factor that helped filmmakers shape their narratives is the decision to dispense with synchronous sound footage. In their initial plan for the film, however, which they laid out in December 1942, Il´ia Kopalin and Leonid Varlamov envisioned incorporating oral testimony from eyewitnesses as some form of synchronous sound: "The population of the liberated towns joyfully greets the fighters of the Red Army, tells them about the Fascist atrocities and the travails of the German forces around Moscow."[48] This was soon expanded, making explicit the intention to record speech from these people for use as synchronous sound: "Record on sound the tales of Soviet people who were living in the German occupied districts, tales about atrocities and marauding."[49] In the final film, however, the only Soviet citizen heard speaking is Stalin as he made his 7 November speech on Red Square. The difficulties the filmmakers had in recording this speech— they had to get Stalin to reenact it in the studio—illustrate the logistical and technical challenges that Soviet filmmakers faced throughout the war when attempting to create synchronous sound footage.[50] Nevertheless, the filmmakers clearly valued the emotive power of such footage, and since the technique, typically employed as a means of conveying oral testimony, is now held to be crucially important for contemporary representations of the Holocaust and of traumatic or indeed any historical experience whatsoever, it is worth considering why the filmmakers' initial intentions were not realized in the finished film.

One problem was simply the shortage of sound-recording equipment, which at that time was bulky and had to be carried in a separate van. Any cameraman who wanted sound footage had to order the equipment and wait rather than immediately record unfolding events, as could be done with the portable but silent Eyemo camera then in use. This means that wartime Soviet documentary cinema was, with certain significant exceptions (see chapter 4), essentially silent. Sound was added later, in the studio. Roman Karmen discussed this issue, remarking in 1942: "Our newsreels are not sound films, but silent films with sound added." He continued:

> There have been few attempts to get in the thick of events with sound apparatus. This is not done enough. Items such as the interrogation of prisoners, the account of a collective-farm woman from a village liberated from the Germans. When she told her tale of woe, I simply could not come to terms with the fact that I didn't have sound recording apparatus with me. Later we came back and tried to reproduce her account, but we weren't successful.
>
> (KATSMAN: You made a sound recording?)
>
> We didn't manage to: we should have recorded her when I heard her for the first time. If I had had a sound technician, I would have winked at him to switch on the apparatus without anyone noticing, and I would have recorded 120 meters of the collective farmer.
>
> We tried to make a sound recording of the life of an aerodrome: the loading of bombs, and all kinds of sounds and so on. I have high hopes for the portable sound devices, which should arrive from the USA.[51]

It remains unclear whether the U.S. government ever sent portable sound-recording devices as part of the lend-lease agreement to help the Soviet war effort, but synchronously recorded sound remained the exception, rather than the rule, until the end of the war.

An illustration of the problems facing Karmen can be found in the synchronously recorded sound footage taken in Volokolamsk, where he attempts to get some villagers to recount their experiences under the Nazis. Several women stand next to a group of Soviet soldiers as a voice from behind the camera says, "Tell them what happened when the Germans were here, tell the soldiers." The women then all speak at once, saying that the Germans stole warm clothing from them and threw them out of their own homes and that Germans billeted in their houses kept them away from their stoves. The effect is chaotic, and the soldiers look bored and uninterested in these women's tales of woe. Worse, the words are barely comprehensible as the villagers talk over one another, and background noises, such as that of a low-flying plane, further distract. The decision to conduct a collective rather than a one-on-one interview seems to reflect an attempt to compensate for the lack of direct political control over the message by giving interviewees a sense that they were speaking in public rather than in private. The intention is presumably to create an account of the occupation that emphasizes the common suffering of the villagers and the Soviet people, precluding any inconveniently personal accent. Unfortunately, the result, a technically deficient cacophony, prevents any kind of coherent message from emerging. Technical problems were compounded by ideological factors such as fears that the unpredictable freedom of the personal interview would yield politically unacceptable points of view, and all such footage was discarded from the finished work, which functions largely as a silent film.

As a result of all this, eyewitnesses to the occupation were not permitted to verbalize their experience on film. Note that the two cases regarding which Karmen particularly regretted being unable to record involved eyewitness accounts of the occupation, for both occupied and occupiers might have granted spectators a deeper insight into the occupation in general and the Holocaust in particular. At the same time, the witnesses might have said things that contradicted the dominant view, so the filmmakers abrogated this privilege; instead, the voiceover commentary repeats their words or summarizes their experiences indirectly.

## Silent Footage as Testimony

We do, however, still have the silent film footage shot immediately after the Soviet liberation of previously occupied territories. To what extent do these images possess testimonial power? In their influential discussion of testimony, Dori Laub and Shoshana Felman take an ambiguous stand on the status of visual images: on the one hand, they emphasize the importance of verbal testimony and its highly personal, intransmissible character; on the other, they insist on casting witnessing as a form of seeing.[52]

For Soviet camera operators, the footage of Nazi atrocities they produced on arriving at the various Nazi crime scenes constituted a form of testimony. When matched up with memoir accounts of filming those events, such footage regains its personal quality. Thus, while their later war memoirs tend not to reflect on their experiences of witnessing the aftermath of these atrocities, several cameramen did provide accounts, published in the press when their films were released, in which they reflect on the way they or their colleagues had reacted to the initial sight of these scenes. The reports repeatedly describe a tension between their emotional reactions and their purpose in filming these sights: to expose the true nature of Nazism for the outside world, for a war crimes tribunal, or for posterity. Thus Roman Karmen describes the delayed emotional reaction of his colleague Aleksandr El´bert: "When El´bert filmed the corpses of collective farmers tortured by the Germans and dumped in piles on the snow, the camera did not shake in his hands: he knew that every meter of film, every frame, would be a terrifying document denouncing the Fascist hangmen. But when these images are shown on the screen, I see the brave cameraman's eyes moisten."[53] This delayed shock reaction, in which the emotional response to horrific revelations of Nazi violence is initially repressed in order to further the war effort, is a significant and distinctive aspect of Soviet reactions to Nazi atrocities. Similarly, the codirector of *Defeat of the Germans near Moscow,* Kopalin, stressed the emotional involvement of the filmmakers as they edited the sequences portraying Nazi atrocities: "Sometimes we cried watching the screen. Our fists clenched when we saw the corpses of peasants shot outside villages, or women with babes in arms peppered with submachine gun fire."[54]

The filmmakers overcome their personal distress for the sake of the task in hand. Thus, while the images are saturated with an emotionally heightened empathy toward the victims that stresses their common identity with the persons behind the camera, often themselves from a Jewish background, as was Karmen, all such individual and ethnically specific considerations are subordinated to the need to present an image of universalized Soviet suffering. Quite apart from the various decisions about selecting scenes to shoot, these images are highly vulnerable to many forms of manipulation; for example, they might be combined with footage taken at a different time or place or with a misleading, manipulative commentary.

Given this universalizing tendency, can these images of the dead and their loved ones yield any insight into the Holocaust, which has proved to be elusive and resistant to coherent testimony? The answer to this question is a resounding yes. The dismissal or, in a sense, misappropriation of these images is not unusual. Footage of the camps shot by British and American filmmakers also rarely identifies subjects as Jewish, and similarly inaccurate captioning frequently accompanies still photographs; as Janina Struk has shown, such misleading captions have repeatedly been attached to images of the Holocaust.[55] The testimonial power of the footage in *Defeat of the Germans near Moscow* depends entirely on painstaking work to identify the subjects and contextual information about the cameramen, the directorial or institutional instructions given to them, and most important, the discarded images. Performing this kind of analysis lets us recognize this film as a document of the Holocaust containing a yawning gap at its center, with the fate of the Jews specifically unspoken or glossed over, but a document nonetheless. The film shocks us with its graphic images of violence against the innocent, which truly do intimate the brutal nature of the Nazis' policy of racial conquest in the East but conceal the reason for the Jewish deaths under the occupation so as to make the film a more effective instrument of propaganda with an equal appeal to all Soviet citizens.

### We Shall Be Avenged!

The tension between document and propaganda evident in *Defeat of the Germans near Moscow,* between the need to record crimes for ultimately legal purposes and the use of such images to motivate the Red Army, is especially acute in the 1942 film *We Shall Be Avenged! (Otomstim!).* This film, which uses the two-reel special-release newsreel format employed later for Soviet films of the liberation of Nazi death camps,[56] is subtitled "Film Documents of the Monstrously Evil Deeds, Atrocities and Violence of the German-Fascist Invaders." Indeed, it takes its title and opening line from an official document: the Soviet foreign minister Viacheslav Molotov's 6 January 1942 "note" on war crimes,[57] the second of the four notes on Nazi war crimes that Molotov published during the war and the first document published by the Allies to refer to the systematic murder of Jewish civilians.[58] The film quotes its opening paragraph: "The German invaders engage everywhere in plunder and whole scale extermination of the Soviet population, stopping at no crimes, no brutality or violence, on the territories which they have temporarily occupied or still continue to occupy."[59]

The film, however, goes nowhere nearly as far as Molotov's note does in detailing specifically anti-Jewish violence, largely because it was intended solely for domestic consumption. Nonetheless, it does attempt to justify its status as a document by compiling images of Nazi atrocities up to this point, including those in the previously discussed Rostov, Moscow, and Kerch footage; by supplying some names, including that of Iakov Reingol´d from Barvenkovo; and by estimating the numbers of those killed in various places. As with many newspaper reports, anyone relying just on this source would have had to read between the lines to establish that there were Jews among the victims, let alone that the Nazis targeted them disproportionately. Like the Soviet documentaries and newsreels discussed previously, however, this film is not only a document but also an emotive, agitational use of factual material, with the familiar soundtrack of plunging strings and appeals to spectators, especially Red Army soldiers, to seek vengeance:

> If you don't want to give the Germans, with their sinister weapons, the house where you lived, your wife and mother, all that we hold dear, know that no one will save her if you don't. No one will kill him, if you don't. . . .
> Over there, beyond the front line, they are waiting for you!
> Over there our children, women and old people are waiting for you—set them free.

Paradoxically, this film provides the kernel of the one that the Soviet prosecution presented as evidence of Nazi war crimes at the Nuremberg Tribunal, though with a completely different and much more descriptive voiceover and without music. Reedited for a new audience, the footage was made to articulate a similar narrative of Soviet suffering, but with a different intended message adapted to the court's legal and international setting.

## Reception in the West

The Soviets' efforts to record these sights were informed by a desire not only to motivate their own population but also to appeal to opinion in the West. Shortly after seeing *Defeat of the Germans near Moscow,* the Leningrad playwright Vsevolod Vishnevskii started work on a scenario for a documentary about the blockade. He saw depictions of Soviet losses as particularly important for the film's impact on the Allies: "It should be a film with very deep international resonance—a tale of Leningrad's heroism, the resilience of its citizens. A challenge to England and the USA:

that's how to fight! All your 'losses' can't even be compared with Russia's."[60] When *Defeat of the Germans near Moscow* was exported in 1942 and shown first in Britain and then in the United States, it drew praise for its combat footage, which was then unrivaled by any British- or American-made documentary, but its portrayal of Nazi atrocities provoked the most debate.

The key question for the film's critics was whether cinema has the right to depict such scenes. London's *Daily Telegraph* objected to the representation of Nazi atrocities and expressed concern that children be spared these sights.[61] The dominant view, however, was that voiced by a critic for the British left-wing weekly the *Tribune,* who argued that spectators needed to see the film so as to grasp both Nazi brutality and Soviet sacrifices:

> Because this is no fancy glory-story but a record of actual happenings, we are shown the body of a baby frozen at its mother's breast in the snow, we see our comrades hanging on the gallows outside the small towns, or heaps of men, or what once were men, who had been locked into farm buildings which were then mined. "What is the use," asked a friend, "of witnessing such things? What good can it do?" There are several answers. This is mine.
>
> We have to see such things. Imagination is not enough. It is too comfortable a way of thinking of our brothers' sufferings. In total war, such as that which the Russian masses are undergoing, to witness these horrors forces our comfort-loving minds to grasp the actual meaning of our comrades' sacrifice. Imagination, it is true, can be a torture but it can also be a soporific. "Too horrible even to think about," we say. In the war before Moscow nothing was too horrible for the Nazis to do, and it is our duty to see for ourselves by what means Russia has saved us.[62]

This defense of *Defeat of the Germans near Moscow* was reprinted in the United States by the *Daily Worker* when a substantially reedited and rewritten version of the film came out there under the title *Moscow Strikes Back* in August 1942. The *New Republic* critic Manny Farber saw the "unflinching" portrayal of such sights as making the film's depiction of the war more significant than any to be found in films produced in his own country.[63] Yet the sympathy that the film aroused for the Soviets through its depiction of Nazi atrocities presented a problem. At the 1943 Oscars ceremony, Lowell Mellett, an official with the U.S. Office of War Information, asserted that the country would not allow foreign powers to gain control of its film market.[64] Hollywood's response was swift: commissions soon went out for several films, including Lewis Milestone's *North Star* (1943), that would use American actors to depict the war in the Soviet Union and be politically and economically controlled by U.S. studios. Whereas the Soviets might be said to be Sovietizing the Holocaust, the Americans were Americanizing the war as a whole, including the eastern front. These films nevertheless tended to depict violence less explicitly than their Soviet counterparts did, particularly with respect to civilian populations. Moreover, while some famous American-made documentary films were compiled from Soviet footage, such as the "Battle of Russia" installment of Frank Capra's *Why We Fight* series, American filmmakers did not make many documentaries of the war in Russia. Indeed, they were unable to shoot any footage of their own on the eastern front, even though Anatole Litvak and Capra sought permission in March 1944 to enter the Soviet Union so as to film the Red Army (they planned to use ten camera operators and two writers in the project).[65] Such documentaries on Soviet themes as Americans did make incorporated no scenes of genocidal violence either against civilian populations generally or Jews in particular.

In this context, *Moscow Strikes Back* stands out from all other films made in the United States (as well as Britain) during the war, for these strove not to show civilian dead. Significantly, this is one of the areas where the commentary, written by the later blacklisted left-wing author Albert Maltz, departs substantially from the original film's; in addition, the remake's completely new voiceover commentary, spoken by Edward G. Robinson, gives a much stronger sense of the immense scale of the killings (although it still underestimates them) and stresses the deliberate *mass* killing of innocents: "These are not dolls but children. The vandals stripped them first. No accident. The slaughter of the innocent by official order. No isolated incidents. Policy. Not hundreds of bodies like these, not thousands, but tens of thousands. No words, no statistics can sum up the brutality of a generation reared by Nazis. Massed torture, massed murder by order of the high command."

This film follows the original one in making no attempt to identify the ethnicity of the dead; nonetheless, Maltz uses the images to stand for the mass murder of tens of thousands, a fact derived from other sources, and in so doing conveys a better sense of the Nazis' systematic killing in the East. His film betrays a hint of the Holocaust. Moreover, placing the blame on orders from the high command and the Nazi system rather than on the barbarous and bestial nature of Germans as a whole, as the Soviet source does, gives a stronger sense of the "Final Solution" taking shape as the film was being made and adapted, a time when reports of this genocidal program were beginning to filter through to the United States. Nevertheless, even though these images of Nazi mass murder reached American and British audiences three years before the 1945 images of the camps did, film historians have recognized those films, not *Moscow Strikes Back,* as the Western public's first confrontation with images of the Holocaust.[66]

Yet the film has been marginalized and forgotten for reasons unrelated to Soviets' failure to identify Jewish suffering as such; after all, Western films showing the liberation of the camps, too, seldom mention Jews.[67] Rather, this film was and remains widely unacknowledged as a revelation about the nature of Nazism because Western audiences distrusted its peculiarly Soviet combination of documentation and persuasion (i.e., propaganda). In this *Moscow Strikes Back* is not unusual. Information about Nazi atrocities, including those committed against Jews, did filter through to the British and American publics, but most commentators suggest that few believed them. As Deborah Lipstadt put it, there was a "chasm between information and belief."[68]

As early as November 1941, the U.S. press published reports of German murders of Jews in Odessa and Kiev, but these atrocity stories and reports of the camps were equated with propaganda.[69] In addition, the papers often buried the stories, which "created another barrier between public information and belief," and in any case, all stories coming out of Russia were treated with suspicion.[70] In the rare instances where Soviet Jews were mentioned, domestic anti-Semitism in the United States and Britain compounded distrust of Communist Party propaganda.[71] As a consequence, Jews were more likely to attract sympathy if they were described as being from Poland rather than the Soviet Union, and this emphasis has colored Western views of the geography of the Holocaust ever since.

Thus, Walter Laqueur argues that the images of Bergen-Belsen were shocking not because they told people something they did not know but because until then, "the statistics of murder were either disbelieved or dismissed from consciousness."[72] Nicholas Pronay, one of few Western critics to mention that Soviet footage of Nazi atrocities had been shown in the West before the films of the camps in spring 1945, suggests that in Britain, disbelief and distrust of the Soviets was compounded by visceral anti-German sentiment that led people to expect the Germans to commit atrocities, given the chance. Consequently, according to Pronay, British audiences saw footage of the camps not as a revelation but as proof of what was already known, though previously unproven.[73]

As a result, the revelation in *Moscow Strikes Back* failed to sink in with the wider public in either Britain or the United States. As Barbie Zelizer put it, until the liberation of the camps, "the atrocity story did not have a place in [American] public discourse."[74] The atrocity story did have a place in the Soviet Union, however, where these images were treated as the key representations of Nazi genocide, after which all further discoveries, including those of the death camps and the extent of Jewish suffering, were treated as illustrations supplementary to the initial shocking images of Nazi killings of Soviet citizens in Russia.

Soviet filmmakers had successfully translated incoherent screams of grief into sense; in doing this, they had created conventions for conferring meaning on the war's death and suffering. Atrocities could be represented, but they could not be ethnically differentiated; in addition, they required compensation through a number of representational templates designed to suggest an emotional, political, or military response to the deaths of the victims, such as, most commonly, shots showing bereaved relatives or Russian soldiers paying their respects and marching onward. These formed a certain visual language, an idiom with which to articulate pain and suffering. The filmmakers thus helped establish a representational system that, along with ideological factors, acted to mute attempts to represent the specifically Jewish Holocaust.

When it came to reporting Nazi atrocities against Jews, Soviet newsreel and documentary filmmakers labored under tight restrictions, and they had little scope in which to challenge the representational clichés. These restrictions were rooted in the very nature of newsreel and documentary filmmaking as well, for the Nazis' genocidal acts often occurred beyond the reach of Soviet arms and lenses. Given that synchronously recording sound for in-depth interviews with witnesses was technically challenging as well as ideologically suspect, artistic, imaginative reconstructions (i.e., fiction films) became a crucially important alternative by which filmmakers could attempt to get at the truth about events in the Nazi-occupied territories. Only with the help of the imagination could filmmakers attempt to represent the realities of the Holocaust as it unfolded. Here too, though, they were to meet insurmountable ideological barriers.

# 3 \ Imagining Occupation

## PARTISANS AND SPECTRAL JEWS

The nature of Soviet newsreel and documentary film enabled it to respond quickly to the unexpected challenges of representing the war, and such works began to play a greater and far more important role than they had done previously. The elements intrinsic to feature films, such as writing scripts, building sets, and shooting many takes of scenes, means that they take longer to make than do most documentaries; because of such time-consuming elements, together with the disruption caused by the evacuation of the major studios of Moscow, Leningrad, and Kiev to the far east, the first feature-film depiction of the German invasion (Ivan Pyr′ev's *Secretary of the Regional Party Committee*) came out only at the end of 1942. By this point, wartime documentaries and newsreels had established certain conventions for representing Nazi atrocities—close-ups of grieving relatives, funerals, calls for vengeance—as I discussed in the previous chapter. For all its advantages of immediacy, however, documentary strictly limited the role of imaginative reconstruction. While some films incorporated footage taken by cameramen who had been dropped behind enemy lines, as did Vasilii Beliaev's documentary *The People's Avengers* (*Narodnye mstiteli* [1943]), even these could do little more than show the aftermath of German rule following the recapture of previously occupied territories or reproduce the verbal recollections of witnesses, the latter an approach little employed by Soviet documentary makers. Thus newsreel and documentary were unable to depict life—or death—under the occupation. Feature films employing dramatic reconstructions with actors possess evident potential advantages in helping audiences understand what was happening under Nazi rule. Only fictionalized accounts could hope to depict the Holocaust as it unfolded and was experienced by its victims.

At the same time, feature films accord directors greater potential freedom to interpret and impose something of a personal authorial vision on the material at hand, and the Soviet scriptwriting and studio system worked to control matters so as to ensure that a broadly consistent vision of the war emerged. As was the case with documentaries, mentions and unambiguous images of the Nazis' persecution specifically of Jews were removed, usually at or before the script stage. Despite these efforts at control, however, Soviet studios did release several films that either directly depicted or at least touched on the fates befalling Jews under the Nazis; when analyzed in terms of their images and implications, these films constitute an important, albeit slim, early chapter in Holocaust film.

### Fighting Film Collections

Although Soviet studios were still making features during the war's first year, fewer such works appeared than had in previous years, and the gap was filled both by unbanning and rereleasing prewar antifascist films, including *Professor Mamlock,* and by creating acted shorts grouped under the rubric *Fighting Film Collections* (*Boevye kinosborniki*). This genre was initially conceived on 24 June 1941, two days after the invasion, when Leningrad filmmakers suggested to their bosses the idea of "novellas" (i.e., filmed short stories) on war themes grouped into anthologies or collections (*sborniki*).[1] The idea was passed on from the Lenfil´m boss to the government's minister in charge of cinema, Ivan Bol´shakov, and approved by the authorities at Mosfil´m. The first was released on 2 August 1941, and the last, number 12, was released on 12 August 1942. This short format dominated Soviet screen representations of the war throughout the first year after the German invasion. While the early issues included a few documentaries, the majority were short subjects conceived as an attempt to dramatize or reconstruct events described in the Sovinformbureau's laconic news reports. The resulting shorts illustrated events and actions with little consideration as to character, motivation, or deeper explanation. Writing of the genre in 1947, the critic Vitalii Zhdan emphasized this concentration on episode and event:

These were newsreel-style short stories [*novelly-khroniki*]; the artist was not yet in a position to distance himself from the exceptional drama of real life. He was struck by the very power of events. It was important to grasp them correctly and register them. It seemed as if the meaning itself of what was occurring, the meaning of that which people had done[,] was so important that it spoke for itself. . . .

The basis of the newsreel-style film short stories was the event and not the person. It was natural and to be expected that for the first days of the war what counted was the individual episode and not the overall picture of events.[2]

This approach was soon to appear excessively schematic and simplistic, but it offered advantages, too. Specifically, it allowed the liberation of a certain emphasis on the event that gave writers more room to leave aside the bigger picture, the "generalization" or "typicality" referred to in Soviet criticism. For Soviet cinema, this notion of the wider meaning behind phenomena provided a crucial means of unifying and standardizing the message; as a result of its hegemony, no feature film released even in 1942–1943 devoted significant attention to the situation now facing Europe's Jews. The *Fighting Film Collections,* however, constituted a sphere where the homogenizing power of the Stalinist cultural system was for a short time shaken in such a way as to permit the expression of unorthodox messages. Because of this temporary disruption, then, the first treatment of the theme of the Holocaust came in this short format, appearing in *A Priceless Head* (*Betsennaia golova* [1942]), directed by Boris Barnet and produced by the TsOKS studio in Alma-Ata.

### A Priceless Head

*A Priceless Head* relates the story of a Polish partisan, Jozef Grochowski, whose acts of sabotage lead the Nazis to put up posters offering 5,000 marks for information leading to his capture. Using a structure ambitious for this form, Barnet's film then develops two parallel plots. First, a Jew wearing a Star of David armband sees the poster from a distance; though not permitted to walk on the pavement, he treats the poster as a sign of distinction when the text is read to him it (figs. 3.1 and 3.2). Second, the mother of a sick child visits her neighbor, a physician, begging him for help, but the doctor explains that the child's problem is a lack of food, and the mother must sell something to get money for provisions. Having nothing left to sell, the mother puts on stockings, her best hat, and lipstick,

FIGURE 3.1. The Jew barred from the pavement. From *A Priceless Head.*

intending to prostitute herself. At this point the doctor enters and offers to sell his stethoscope, an offer rejected as useless. The fugitive Grochowski then bursts in, and when he understands the situation, he proposes that the woman turn him in and get the reward (he explains that he has escaped four times already and will do so again).

The woman goes out and fetches some Germans, whom she leads up the staircase in her building; instead of betraying Grochowski, however, she takes them past her door, enabling the fugitive partisan to escape through the flat of the previously introduced Jew, who appears to live in the same building. The woman is now arrested, and she descends the staircase with the doctor and her child. The Nazis then shoot the doctor for insulting them, but before he dies, he passes the child over to the Jew, and the Germans lead the woman, the Jew, and the child he holds across the snow, at which point they are rescued by Grochowski's partisans. In the denouement, the Nazis raise the price on the wanted poster to 10,000 marks and add a new poster alongside it: that of the woman, who in the link to the next film in the collection is shown broadcasting antifascist radio messages, along with Grochowski.

Unfortunately, all journalistic references to *A Priceless Head,* at all

FIGURE 3.2. The Jew sees the poster. From *A Priceless Head*.

stages of its production, pointedly ignored its Jewish dimension, which makes it almost impossible to state with certainty whether the Jewish plot-line evident in the final film was present from the beginning, in the initial screenplay, or added later. The first such reference appeared in *Vecherniaia Moskva* on 29 October 1941; this article described the plot but said nothing whatsoever about the Jewish character.[3] The article states that the hero is not just the partisan Grochowski but the whole Polish people, yet it focuses on the woman as the representative of this group. Of course, this emphasis on the Polish people as a whole may be interpreted as including the Jews among them.[4]

Other factors, however, suggest that the Jewish theme was present from the screenplay's very inception. For example, the title's ironic inversion, whereby the price on Grochowski's head and his status as an outlaw is treated as a sign of distinction, is suggested by the nameless Jewish character, and an analogous humorous turnaround can be found in other works by the screenplay's Jewish coauthor, the Moscow Arts Theater and film actor Boris Petker. For example, in the comedy *Mary Archer's Dissertation* (*Dissertatsiia Meri Archera* [1950]), a cold war agitational play, Petker displays a similar sensitivity to language's susceptibility to ironic subversion when he ridicules a cynical American congressman who mentions the plight of African Americans solely to gain votes, but the politician's hypocrisy is exposed when his daughter marries a black man and bears his child.[5] The similarities in irony and concern with racial persecution here suggest that Petker probably wrote the dialogue involving the Jew.[6]

Although the screenplay was ready in October, the evacuation of Mosfil´m and Lenfil´m studios to Alma-Ata in October 1941 evidently delayed the production of *A Priceless Head,* and reports that production had started did not appear until January 1942. At this point it was expected to be finished by the end of January,[7] yet the film was released in June. When mentioning the film's cast and crew, the various reports about the film identify Vladimir Shishkin (Grochowski) and Vera Orlova (the woman) from the outset but say nothing about Moisei Gol´dblat (the Jew) or Nikolai Cherkasov-Sergeev (the doctor). They do, however, mention two prominent actors who do not figure in the final film: Maxim Straukh and Vsevolod Pudovkin.[8]

As the production schedule for this film continued to slip (as did the schedules for many other films during this period), Ivan Bol´shakov, the minister for cinema, criticized the slow pace of filmmaking at Alma-Ata.[9] In response, the studio agreed to cut the number of scenes in each screenplay so that shorts would be completed in two to three months.[10] Finally, on 1 June, *A Priceless Head* was given a high-profile release in thirteen Moscow cinemas, but it ran for only a couple of weeks, probably a little less than normal.

While not reviewed in *Pravda, Izvestiia,* or *Literatura i iskusstvo,* the only wartime film publication, the film did receive coverage in *Vecherniaia Moskva,* which largely panned the effort: "The directorial solution is stagey [*kamernyi*], in a genre close to melodrama; the images of the main characters are not sketched out in sufficient depth. The art of the film short story is a great, complex and subtle art. The ability to reveal the full depths of the human character in it with a few simple strokes is the key to the craft of the film short story; its core."[11] This criticism was echoed and amplified the following month in an article that reflects on the film short story form more broadly:

> The tendency of some actors towards saccharine sentimental embroidering of reality and fake pathos can be explained by their insufficient knowledge of reality and an abstract, drily theoretical conception of the person.

Saccharine melodrama is characteristic not only of many shorts on the war theme. It can be found too, for example, in the recently released film short story *A Priceless Head,* directed by B. Barnet. Here too an external descriptive "layer" alternates with a supersentimental "layer." The central scene of the film—the imaginary betrayal by the mother—cannot possibly cause the spectator anxiety. Even before the mother goes to meet the German patrol, apparently so as to receive 5,000 for the head of the anti-Fascist, the spectator already knows full well that the woman could not commit this kind of base act. She says this to Wladislaw [*sic*].[12] This follows from her overall behavior. It is not surprising that the whole protracted path of the mother down and up the staircase, energetically emphasized by the music, does not create a powerful emotional effect and even seems forced: the situation and the character clash. This is why the director is forced to "lay it on thick" with fail-safe shots such as that of a mother at the bed of her dying child so as to manipulate the spectator's emotions. Despite all its superficial effects, the film remains one of those works which barely touch the spectator's feelings.[13]

The claim that we do not believe the heroine capable of betraying the partisan to save her child exposes the reviewer's Soviet reflexes rather than the film's shortcomings; as Louise McReynolds and Joan Neuberger have shown, Soviet melodrama was distinct in privileging the public over private.[14] In a normal Soviet film, the heroine would chose the common good over her child, but Barnet's merit lies in his ability to persuade us, at least briefly, that she might not. He does something similar in a number of his previous films, notably *By the Deep Blue Sea* (*U samogo sinego moria* [1936]). Otherwise, this criticism of Barnet's film as melodramatic is to some degree justified, since the dominance of the emotional is precisely the nature of Barnet's cinema as a whole.[15] Indeed, the decision to give the central role to Vera Orlova strongly suggests that Barnet intended to echo that form, for the actress had made her name in Iakov Protazanov's prerevolutionary melodramas. Likewise, the director's admirers willingly agree that his cinema is "stagey."[16] He had a tendency to reduce everything to powerful interior scenes where actors dominate rather than rely on mass scenes. Thus, these criticisms were not unusual for his films, and it was not unusual for his films to attract sharp criticism for simply typifying his own distinctive style and approach. Of the four features he made in the early 1940s, two were never released, and one was removed from distribution soon after release without being reviewed.[17]

Criticisms of the entire series that Ivan Bol´shakov published just after the war further hint at the dimensions of this film unacceptable to the authorities: "This *Film Collection* differed sharply from all the previous in its extremely primitive nature and low ideological and artistic level. The basic flaw of the film short stories it contained was that their plots were farfetched and unlifelike."[18] The notion of Barnet's plot as "made up" and "unlifelike" may be seen as implied by the idea of melodrama, since by definition melodrama diverges from reality, making criticism of the film somewhat predictable. The critics seem to have been choosing an easy target so as indirectly to censure aspects of the film that were difficult to denounce openly. The first unspoken rebuke seems to center on the domestically set melodramatic dimension of the film, which emerges from, on the one hand, the film's treatment of prostitution and its powerful sexual charge and, on the one other, the way it portrays the war, which it presents mostly off-screen.

The other implicit reproach involves the Jewish plotline and the Jewish character. As was often the case during the Stalin era, but especially in the highly ambiguous ideological atmosphere of the war, critics were unsure how to react to Jewish elements. This partly explains why few critics reviewed the film; they lacked any clearly acceptable way to discuss this dimension of it, and the few who did mention the film chose to ignore its Jewish plotline. Whereas anyone who reviewed *Professor Mamlock* had to mention that the main character is Jewish merely in recounting the plot (though Soviet critics generally avoided elaborating on this), critics reviewing *A Priceless Head* simply avoided mentioning the Jew, who is after all a secondary character. It is one thing to depict Jews' persecution at the hands of Nazis but quite another to reaffirm the significance of such portrayals by repeatedly verbalizing them in reviews. In remaining largely silent about the Jewish elements in this film, these reviews parallel newspaper and newsreel reports of atrocities that mention Jewish names of victims without pointing out that the victims were Jews and were persecuted as such. As Il´ia Al´tman suggests, readers of such reports understood not only that the Nazis were targeting Jews but also that they were not to talk about this. Viewers of *A Priceless Head* understood exactly the same thing with respect to the film's fictional tale. But precisely what did *A Priceless Head* tell spectators about the plight of the Jews under Nazi rule?

*A Priceless Head* differs from most Soviet cinema in being set in an unnamed town in Poland and thus identifying a specifically Jewish per-

FIGURE 3.3. Moisei Gol´dblat in *A Jew's Happiness*.

secution. Unlike the newsreels of the time, the film emphasized the persecution of Jews as Jews, not as Soviet citizens (see chapter 2).[19] This message
is confirmed first in visual terms through the depiction of an orthodox
religious Jew as a key character. The character wears a dark (presumably
blue) Star of David on a white background, and the man playing the part,
which the credits list simply as "The Jew," is a prominent Jewish actor,
Moisei Gol´dblat, who had played Solomon Mikhoels's fellow schemer in
a popular Yiddish comedy of 1925, *A Jew's Happiness,* also known as *Jewish Luck* (*Evreiskoe schast´e*), and had been pivotal in the development of the
Yiddish-language theater in the Jewish autonomous region of Birobid-
zhan in 1937–1938.[20] Gol´dblat was thus strongly associated with Yiddish
culture and Jewish roles (fig. 3.3).

Second, "the Jew" verbalizes his Jewishness both by stating he suffers discrimination simply for being Jewish and by showing his hostility
to the Nazis through ironic comments; for example, on hearing that the
poster describes Grochowski as having "no distinguishing features," he
muses, in admiration, that the partisan is "an ordinary man" (*obyknovennyi
chelovek*). Gol´dblat turns in a clever and, albeit brief, at times subtle performance that uses irony in a style akin to the ethnically marked manner

described by Patricia Erens, whereby a Jewish character is defined as such by his irony.[21]

But the Jew's subversion is not simply verbal. Rather, his acts of resistance are more or less plausible attempts to save lives, first that of Grochowski and then, in a less likely scenario, that of the child. Indeed, while he is not named in the credits, the doctor addresses him as "Mr. Toive," which appears to evoke the Yiddish word for benefactor, *bal-toyve*. If so, the epithet is appropriate, for his actions save lives, with the first instance being the most significant in the context of the film.

The film offers only the faintest of indications as to the forced segregation, discrimination, destitution, and starvation prevailing in the ghetto. For example, in showing the Jew as banned from walking on the pavement, a form of persecution closer to those enacted through Nazi Germany's Nuremberg Laws, it falls far short of showing the true misery of Nazi persecution in 1941 Poland. Ignorance about the plight of Polish Jews, however, is unlikely to have motivated the decision to limit things in this way. Although sometimes patchy, Soviet press coverage of the situation in Poland, even after the Nazi invasion of the Soviet Union, was nevertheless sufficient to form a representative picture of the situation.[22] If the decision to show the Jew as not isolated in a ghetto was prompted by something other than ignorance, it presumably arose from the filmmaker's desire to create an image or make a point. By making the Jew a neighbor of both the female protagonist and the doctor, living not just on the same street but in the same building, Barnet was able to evoke a sense of the whole of the Polish population, Jew and non-Jew, united in resisting Nazi rule, a conception of the film mentioned as early as October 1941, when it was still at the script stage.[23] Moreover, the fact that the Jew intervenes to save Grochowski's life on the stairs is vitally important when seen in the context of the use of the staircase as a symbol throughout Barnet's work.

Beginning with his earliest silent films, *Girl with a Hatbox* (*Devushka s korobkoi* [1927]), and *House on Trubnaia Square* (*Dom na trubnoi* [1928]), Barnet used the image of the staircase to represent a space where the private and public spheres meet (fig. 3.4). As the mother descends the staircase in *A Priceless Head,* the spectator cannot tell whether she intends to betray Grochowski or to help him escape and in the process almost certainly condemn herself to death. This heart-rending choice between private and societal motivations is unusual in Soviet wartime film, where unreflective self-sacrifice is the ideal and the norm, particularly in this genre of film

FIGURE 3.4. Steps in Barnet's *Girl with a Hatbox*.

FIGURE 3.5. The Jew and Grochowski meet on the stairs, where the Jew offers his apartment as an escape route. From *A Priceless Head*.

shorts.[24] The conflict is played out melodramatically in the setting of the staircase, but the Jew too must intervene in order to guarantee Grochowski's escape (fig 3.5). He too participates in the microcosm of Polish political life playing out on the staircase, and his intervention is vital to saving the resister. Indeed, the parallel between the Jew and the mother is further strengthened when she decides not to betray Grochowski while looking at the very same poster that the Jew contemplates earlier in the film.

But the film is more than an attempt to represent the situation in Poland under Nazi occupation through Barnet's own symbolic language for exploring private-public tensions and a melodramatic coloring; it fits its depiction of Jews into certain representational clichés in Soviet cinema as well. Most important here is the pattern evident in Soviet film since *Professor Mamlock,* where violent resistance tends to be depicted as incompatible with a marked Jewish identity. As Annette Insdorf puts it: "Judaism can inhibit resistance."[25] Thus, while the woman becomes a partisan at the end of the film, the Jewish character, as well as the child, disappears inexplicably. As I mention in chapter 2, the image of the child as a victim or potential victim of aggressors has deep roots in Soviet film culture.[26] Evgenii Margolit's suggestion that the child is associated with the part of the masses unable to resist aggressors in the conscious manner of the communist is relevant here. The Jew, ironically distant and evidently opposed to the Nazis but presumably limited in potential for resistance by his religion, is, like the child, a victim (albeit implicitly) of the Nazis.[27] Yet the film ignores the dramatic potential of any such victimhood, whether the child's or the Jew's.

Barnet's film thus displays many elements conventional in other works of Soviet cinema, but within that genre it remains a brave initial attempt at using a distinctively personal manner to depict the tragic fates inflicted on Jews during the Holocaust. Still, though it has been the subject of several retrospectives and studies, its unique depiction of anti-Semitic oppression has been recognized only by Margolit, who nevertheless sees *A Priceless Head* as an important film primarily for being a distinct and significant expression of Barnet's directorial talent and vision.[28] Margolit's primary concern, however, is to place the film in the broader context of the director's psychological concerns, system of imagery, and style, seeing it as a "reconnaissance" for Barnet's true masterpiece of the war years, *It Happened One Night (Odnazhdi noch'iu* [1945]), which it resembles in its representation of the heroine, its domestic setting, and its use of a staircase both as a symbol and as the setting for the central dramatic scene. But *A Priceless Head* is more than just a preliminary sketch; rather, it is significant in its own right for representing the Holocaust in a personal manner through Barnet's melodramatic mode and central symbol, the staircase. Indeed, in some respects it may be said to anticipate the Polish director Aleksander Ford's landmark postwar film about the Warsaw ghetto, *Border Street* (*Ulica graniczna* [1949]). First and foremost, though, it constitutes Soviet film's initial attempt to explore what the Nazis were doing to Jews. Its reception reveals that this was a difficult theme and that anyone expressing it would be criticized, although probably not directly. Barnet, whose ancestry was not Jewish but English, certainly never returned to the theme; indeed, he lost an opportunity to do so just before *A Priceless Head* came out in 1942, when he was removed from the production of a film about partisans based on an Aleksei Kapler script.[29] This film ultimately became *She Defends the Motherland*.

## Feature Films

Whereas Barnet's film touches on the situation confronting Jews in Poland, most depictions of or references to the Holocaust in Soviet wartime feature films occur in movies concerning the occupation of Soviet territories. For wartime Soviet cinema, depicting the occupation meant depicting partisan warfare, since becoming a partisan was seen as the only loyal reaction to Nazi rule. Yet just as the partisan movement lacked any coordinated directive to help the Jews, feature-film depictions of their plight were extremely sporadic and highly marginal.[30] Moreover, the emphasis on heroic resistance meant that these films were unlikely to display the Nazis' decision first to brutally murder the very old and very young among the Jewish population left behind in the occupied territories.

### "I Want to Live"

One script submitted to Kiev film studios in June 1942 did place the Jewish situation at its heart: "I Want to Live," by the Yiddish-language poet David Bergelson. "I Want to Live" tells the story of a Jewish collective farm on the right bank of the Dneipr when the Nazis seize and occupy it in the first days of the war.[31] Rather than concentrate on partisan resistance, the film develops the prototype of *Professor Mamlock* by portraying a Jewish refugee from Germany, Professor Kronblit, who refuses to give the Nazis the logbook for his experimental factory. Like Wolf's Mamlock, he initially intends to commit suicide as a protest against the Nazi occupation, but he is dissuaded from doing so by the central character, Avrom-Ber, a tailor who insists that suicide is not the proper Jewish response to oppression. Throughout centuries of persecution, he asserts, the Jewish people have defiantly affirmed, "I want to live!"[32] Although the script portrays the Jews of the occupied town as actively resisting, it accentuates their will to live in the face of Nazi attempts to annihilate them as Jews rather than any violent struggle, resistance, or vengeance. The script contains Ukrainian characters, too, but its emphasis on the Nazis' treatment of Jews as separate from that of other Soviet citizens and its evocation of Jewish cultural models of resistance rather than Soviet ones meant that it was destined never to be produced.

By contrast with this script, approved and completed Soviet films are most eloquent about the exceptional fate of Soviet Jews in their silences, in what they do not show and do not say. For many of the films I examine in the following pages, we can trace the process whereby eyewitness, journalistic, and literary materials were reworked so to as to exclude or muffle any reference to Jews or the Holocaust.

### Secretary of the Regional Party Committee

Ivan Py´rev's *Secretary of the Regional Party Committee* tells the story of Stepan Gavrilovich Kochet (Vasilii Vanin), a Communist Party regional committee secretary who energetically organizes first the sabotage of local infrastructure and then, after the Germans occupy his town, the partisan resistance. The Germans infiltrate his detachment with a spy, but Kochet ultimately identifies the culprit and tricks him into setting up an ambush in a church where the Nazis are destroyed. Acclaimed as the first Soviet feature film to depict the war directly, it came out in October 1942 to relieved, ecstatic reviews. A review from *Literatura i iskusstvo* illustrates this response: "Cinema has long been preparing for this day. Indeed, too long. The year and a half since the start of the war [has] been filled with preliminary work and sketches, from the point of view of film's present tasks. The short stories of the *Film Collections* were just a first and distant step towards the solution of the wartime theme. The audience has long been waiting for this day. . . . This, in essence, is the first feature film containing solely the characters and events of the Great Patriotic War."[33]

The film was adapted from a play by the Jewish screenwriter Iosif Prut, whose family was later trapped in occupied Rostov-on-Don. Prut had volunteered as a frontline newspaper correspondent the day after war broke out (doing so along with the veteran Soviet documentary maker Dziga Vertov); working as a journalist had allowed him to visit partisan units preparing to drop behind enemy lines. The screenplay was already complete by October 1941, and the aesthetic of the film shares much with the style of the simplistic plots used in the *Fighting Film Collection*. As one critic puts it, "The makers of the film *Secretary of the Regional Party Committee* to a great extent remain in thrall to the 'dashing' agitational plots of the *Fighting Film Collections,* tending towards superficial, full-frontal assault-style solutions, to the 'livening up' of material with the help of adventure plot and melodramatic elements."[34]

Nevertheless, while the film does not greatly differ from the original play, the two works diverge significantly in their treatments of the Holocaust. Prut's play introduces the character of Rotman (Boris Poslavskii), a more analytical but less decisive alter ego to the brutally assured Kochet, who bears the Jewish forename and patronymic Abram Solomonovich, which the film inexplicably changes to the no less Jewish Semen Abramovich. The representation of Jewish participation in the partisan movement is significant in itself, since depictions of partisans typically downplayed such participation.[35] In Prut's play, Rotman is addressed first by Kochet and then by the Nazi general in ways that explicitly identify him as Jewish and that acknowledge both the extent of Nazi violence against Jews in particular and the especially virulent anti-Semitism of individual Nazis.

In the key episode, Kochet's arrest when visiting the town undercover leads first Rotman and then Kochet himself to suspect that a traitor has infiltrated the partisan ranks. All those who knew of Kochet's trip become suspects, including Rotman and a character named Orlov, who is indeed the spy. In running through the list, Kochet rules out Rotman: "Rotman! The blood of his brothers, with which the Fascists have drenched the earth, his whole life is a cast-iron guarantee. We can count out my friend Rotman!"[36] The play has given us no sense that the Nazis are drenching the earth with Jewish blood and no sense until now that the Nazis have any particular fate in store for the Jews trapped in occupied territories. Indeed, we might ask how Kochet is supposed to know this within the play's diegetic world and whether it is not strange that he states the claim as if it was common knowledge when no one, not even Rotman, a prominent character, has mentioned it. The film includes a scene where Nazis kill civilians en masse (fig. 3.6), but nothing indicates that Jews number among

FIGURE 3.6. The killing of civilians. From *Secretary of the Regional Party Committee.*

them, let alone make up a significant proportion; rather, the victims, who are shown only in long shot, almost from the perspective of the murderers, appear to have been rounded up randomly as a reprisal for an incident in the previous scene, when someone shoots a German soldier hoisting a Nazi flag over the town.

The film version addresses this problem by cutting out these references to Rotman's Jewishness and the Nazis' murderous anti-Jewish actions. This alteration damages the film, for Rotman remains among those who knew of Kochet's trip, yet he is not mentioned among the suspects in the subsequent inquiry (fig. 3.7). This may seem a continuity error or strangely trusting assumption, yet the situation functions to portray Rotman more as a facet of Kochet himself, and he takes on more of Kochet's own strength than in the original. In erasing his Jewishness, the rewritten script also erases Rotman's distinctive difference as a character.

Rotman's Jewishness is further downplayed in the film's final scene in the church, when the Germans think they have captured the partisans. In the play, Orlov, the Nazi spy, jeers the archaic word "Judaean" (*Iudei*) at Rotman, and the Nazi general present at the incident addresses words of mocking triumphalism first to Kochet and then to Rotman, whom he

FIGURE 3.7. Identifying the traitor: Rotman, Natasha, and Kochet. From *Secretary of the Regional Party Committee.*

clearly addresses as a Jew: "And you, dog, . . . I'll crucify you!" Later, in an ironic reversal, Rotman accuses the German of being a crucifier, the traditional anti-Semitic insult.[37] The film version discards this reversal, removing these references to Rotman's Jewish ethnicity by having the German general promise to crucify not the Jewish Rotman but the Russian Kochet, a threat that comes across simply as an expression of sadism with no specifically Nazi racist or ideological hue and is less effective as a result. This would not be the last time a Soviet film accepted a relatively ineffective characterization, such as that of an idiotic and sadistic Nazi, to avoid the topic of Nazi ideology and its anti-Semitic component.

### She Defends the Motherland

It is possible to trace the process wherein filmmakers reworked material so as to remove references to the Holocaust in other depictions of the occupation and partisan struggle from 1942 and 1943; examples include Igor´ Savchenko's *Partisans of the Ukrainian Steppes* (*Partizany v stepiakh Ukrainy,* also known as *Ukraina* [1941]), released in March 1943. One film, however, did retain its source material's marginal reference to the fate befalling Soviet Jews under the Nazis: Fridrikh Ermler's *She Defends the Motherland* (*Ona zashchishchaet rodinu*), released in May 1943. This film tells the story of Praskov´ia Lukianova (Vera Maretskaia), a happily married mother and tractor driver who becomes a partisan leader consumed by vengeance after seeing her soldier-husband die of Nazi-inflicted wounds and then witnessing the Nazis murder first other wounded Red Army members and, after that, her son. Unlike the previous films about the occupation and partisans, whose scripts essentially relied on third-hand press reports, the screenplay for this film was developed from Aleksei Kapler's own experiences as a journalist accompanying a partisan detachment fighting behind enemy lines in the Novgorod district of the Leningrad Oblast during February 1942. Kapler initially recounted his experiences in a series of articles for *Pravda* and *Izvestiia,* which he later released in book form as *Behind Enemy Lines* (*V tylu vraga*).

These brief articles show Kapler researching intensively, attempting to get as much information as he can from those he interviews so as to build up a rounded picture of life in the occupied territories. His subjects include a woman who has lost everything and is consumed by hatred for the Germans, the prototype for the character of Praskov´ia, the film's heroine, but he also carefully portrays the difficult theme of collaboration with the Nazis. To illustrate this aspect of the occupation, he recounts the story of one repentant traitor who comes over to the partisans. Relating how the man came to realize the error of his ways, Kapler writes: "Time passed; he saw German atrocities, their persecution of the Russian people, and the Jews."[38] This seems to have been an indirect way of confessing to complicity in these murders, and the collaborator begs the partisans to kill him. They oblige.

The theme of collaboration is reworked in Kapler's stage version of essentially the same story that became the film, and here it is Praskov´ia's husband who, assumed dead, has in fact survived and been living in the occupied territories and working for the Germans. As with the traitor figure in the journalistic account, the husband makes a confession of sorts that in fact leaves many questions unanswered; as the other characters say, he was in the town of Kurganov, where the Germans killed everyone but him.[39] He is implicitly assumed to have collaborated in mass killings of Soviet citizens, presumably including Jews, but this assumption is not spelled out.

In the final film, the figure of the traitor is changed to that of an anon-

FIGURE 3.8. Kolkhoznik proposes to accommodate to the Nazis because they kill only Communists "and the Jews." From *She Defends the Motherland*.

ymous kolkhoznik who says: "Weren't you in their hands? You were. Did you see them kill everyone they laid their hands on? Are the Germans stupid [*tozhe razbiraetsia*]? No sir! Communists, well of course, they certainly won't spare them. And the Jews [accompanied by gesture that suggests "of course"]. But why touch us? Germans, like any other people, need farmers; that's why they won't bother us!"[40] (fig. 3.8). In response, Praskov´ia stands up and shoots the peasant in the back as he walks off, concluding, "While we live, we fight." The film clearly endorses this reaction to the collaborator's anti-Communism, implicit anti-Semitism, and pragmatic wish to accommodate to Nazi power, although it does not clearly indicate whether it is all three sentiments or any single one that provokes the summary execution. Yet the episode, which treats the crucial theme of collaboration in a quite different way from its treatment in the journalistic works and the play, is significant. The kolkhoznik's words appeal to the villagers' shared experience of Nazi rule: the Nazis kill only communists, because they used to be in control, and Jews, without explanation. That is, contrary to their portrayals in newsreels, the Germans have been highly selective in choosing their victims. Yet the film has shown nothing of the kind. Instead, it presents rather indiscriminate violence against wounded Soviet soldiers and a child (Praskov´ia's son). The traitor's words thus open a strange new off-screen space of atrocities against Jews and communists, one apparently known to all but never shown, despite the film's general willingness to depict atrocities and their transformative effect on the main character.

Although puzzling in this way, the collaborator's verbalization of the Nazis' systematic murder of Jews goes somewhat further than anything in Kapler's earlier treatments of the material. Perhaps it was added by the writers credited with the final version of the screenplay, Mikhail Bleiman and Ivan Bondin, but it was more likely the contribution of Fridrikh Ermler, a signatory to Soviet Jewry's August 1941 appeal to the Jews of the world.[41] Here once again, we see a Jewish filmmaker, like some of the newsreel cameramen, straining to convey the particular nature of the Jewish predicament. Certainly the change cannot be attributed to Kapler, whose name was removed from the final credits, for by this time he was in the Gulag, sent there after Stalin found out about the writer's affair with Stalin's daughter, Svetlana. While Kapler's screenplays, including that for *She Defends the Motherland,* did not emphasize his Jewish background, this cut no ice with Stalin, who scolded his daughter: "Couldn't you find yourself a Russian!" Svetlana concluded that Kapler's Jewish identity particularly annoyed her father.[42]

Ermler's treatment of the occupation was notable in showing how Nazi atrocities transformed a peaceful mother and wife into a weapon of war wholly consumed by the desire for vengeance. *Pravda*'s review makes this point: "Such women as the heroine of the film, Praskov´ia Luk´ianova, have often been the subject of reports from the front, their faces turned to us from posters, enjoining us to vengeance, but for the first time the film *She Defends the Motherland* brings us right up close with their life and fate, face to face with the heroine herself."[43] Such images, however, were familiar not only from news reports and posters but equally from newsreel and documentary films; indeed, the film was probably made under the influence of *The Defeat of the Germans near Moscow,* which I discuss in the previous chapter. In any event, it certainly dramatizes the transformation wrought in a relative who contemplates the death of the loved one, that is, someone who directly undergoes the experience of bereavement portrayed powerfully in that earlier film and other newsreels like it. This may be seen as an attempt to take the newsreels' and documentaries' images of the bereaved mother's call for vengeance and give that drive toward revenge a back story that would produce a deeper and more lasting impression on spectators. In a bitter twist of fate, Vera Maretskaia, the actress playing Praskov´ia, received news that her own husband had been killed at the front just before the final day of filming.[44]

This dominance of private emotion as underpinning publically oriented actions has more than a whiff of the melodrama typical of works by the film's initial director, Boris Barnet. It is thus no surprise that the generally more cautious and politically orthodox Ermler had been hostile to this dimension of Kapler's script and was already asking to be removed from the production in April 1942, arguing that he did not know the Russian countryside and felt no sympathy for the central characters.[45] Ermler's misgivings were echoed by G. Aleksandrov, head of the Soviet Central Committee's agitprop section; writing just before the film's Moscow release, Aleksandrov criticized the emphasis on grief rather than rational, political motives for Praskov´ia's conduct and leadership role among the partisans: "The main character, Praskov´ia Ivanovna, according to the filmmakers is an advanced Soviet woman, who shows herself during the whole course of the film to be a mother poleaxed by grief, having lost her son and husband. She is more likely to make audiences feel pity and sympathy for her than see her as a conscious warrior, defending the freedom and independence of her land. The director of the film did not show sufficiently convincingly why Praskov´ia became the leader of the partisan detachment."[46]

This portrayal of grief's leveling effect and its primacy over authority with respect to the war effort had clearly begun to worry the likes of Aleksandrov. Nevertheless, the film was released in Moscow on 20 May 1943 and screened widely. The film was then exported to Allied nations. The Soviets particularly sought to promote a specially dubbed English-language version in the United States; with this version, bearing the title *No Greater Love,* they hoped to penetrate the U.S. film market further than they ever had before. However, American audiences matched Russian ones in finding it difficult to empathize with the emotional journey of the central character, and the film was less successful than the dubbed documentaries that preceded it. Howard Barnes, writing in the *New York Herald Tribune,* complained about this issue:

The Russians pull no punches when they make a war picture. . . . Violence is the burden of this new screen drama from the U.S.S.R. From the *Wehrmacht's* wanton destruction of a collective farm, to the final sequence in which the villagers wrest their community back from the German invaders briefly by guerilla fighting, killing, torture and rape are the chief components of the continuity. The result is a film that is as unrelieved as it is grimly persuasive. M. Bleiman and I. Blondin have written their script almost as an imagined documentary and Frederick Ermler has staged it savagely. . . . Unquestionably it is difficult for American audiences, who have no direct knowledge of actual invasion, to appreciate the full impact of "No Greater Love." It is frequently more impassioned than artful. The photography leaves much to be desired.[47]

A different Russian film, however, would ultimately provoke the most noteworthy discussion concerning depictions of screen violence, and it contained nothing about the plight of Soviet Jews.

### The Rainbow: "Now There Are New Laws in Art"

Throughout its production, Mark Donskoi's 1944 film *The Rainbow* omitted any reference whatsoever to the horrors then facing European Jews, but its brutal depiction of the Ukrainian occupation warrants consideration for the way that it portrayed the Nazi mentality, the criticism about its representation of Nazi atrocities that it provoked on its U.S. release, and the manner in which these rebukes affected its director.

The film contains unremittingly brutal images of the occupation. In one scene, German soldiers take hostages to extract grain from the already underfed population; throughout, villagers are required to wear numbers. Other scenes show Soviet prisoners of war starving and without boots; the interrogation and torture of a pregnant partisan, Olena; her further torture and subsequent execution along with that of her infant son immediately after he is born; and the similar treatment of a boy who tries to bring her bread. Moreover, it reinflects the clichés of such depictions with a scene where all the villagers watch Olena's ordeal at the hands of the occupiers, but in secret, from the windows of their homes, vowing vengeance under their breaths.

Most important, the film paints a plausible portrait of the Nazi perpetrator, Kurt Werner, his realistic characterization in part the fruit of interviews that the director had conducted with captured Germans.[48] Instead of being the all too common sadistic caricature, the resulting image is that of a functionary, a shallow carouser who would rather spend time with his Russian mistress, Pusia, but nevertheless conscientiously carries out his duty to interrogate, torture, and kill the partisan woman, Olena Kostiuk, and her baby. Examinations of the Nazis' ideological makeup were intrinsically problematic for Soviet filmmakers, since anti-Semitism formed a central dimension of the Nazi worldview, equaled only by hostility to communism. Even celebrated filmmakers could find their works deemed unfit for release, as happened to Vsevolod Pudovkin and Iuryi Tarych's film *The Murderers Leave for the Road* (*Ubiitsy vykhodiat na dorogu* [1942]) and Grigorii Kozintsev's *Young Fritz* (*Iunyi Frits* [1943]), not only because they depicted Nazi police repression in a way that too closely resembled Soviet police oppression but also, at least in part, because they mentioned Nazi anti-Semitism. The difficulties of representing Nazis stretched even to the actors performing the roles. Hans Klering, for example, was a 1930s German communist refugee who had been arrested at the start of the war, and Donskoi had to spring him from the Gulag to play the part of Werner.[49] Thus Donskoi and Klering trod very carefully with this character, emphasizing Werner as a morally desensitized functionary rather than an ideological zealot.

All this adds up to a film that depicts Nazi genocidal violence in Ukraine without ever mentioning Jews specifically, even though many of the crew members and actors were Jewish, as was Oskar Kurganov, the man who wrote the newspaper article that formed the basis for Wanda Wasilewska's novel, also entitled *The Rainbow,* which would be used to create the film's screenplay. That article, however, about a partisan from the village of Uvarovka, in the Moscow Oblast, concentrates solely on Aleksandra Dreiman, the prototype for Olena, and does not mention the Nazis' murder, also in Uvarovka during November 1941, of approximately forty villagers, including thirteen Jews—eight women and five children. These mothers and their children were not deemed appropriate subjects for journalistic treatment.[50] Kurganov used much the same approach as had the makers of the 1941 Rostov newsreel, choosing one incident as a central, mythologized image and ignoring the massacre of the town's Jews. The image of loss was constructed so as to marginalize the story of the Holocaust, an instance, once more, of remembering to forget.

Wasilewska's transposition of the story to Ukraine made her omission of Jews still more anomalous, for that republic contained the Soviet Union's greatest Jewish population and thus was the site of that popula-

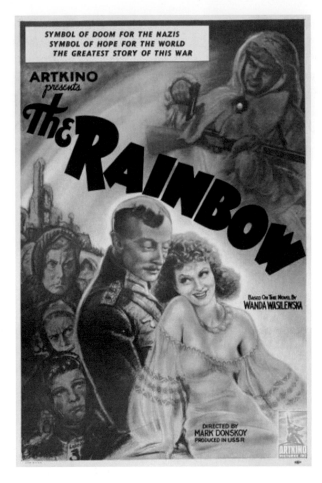

SYMBOL OF DOOM FOR THE NAZIS
SYMBOL OF HOPE FOR THE WORLD
THE GREATEST STORY OF THIS WAR

ARTKINO
presents

The RAINBOW

Based On The Novel By
WANDA WASILEWSKA

DIRECTED BY
MARK DONSKOY
PRODUCED IN USSR

FIGURE 3.9. Poster used in the United States for *The Rainbow.*

tion's highest losses during the Holocaust. In any case, when the film came to the United States in October 1944 (fig. 3.9), its depictions of violence provoked discussions that say much about American attitudes to film representations of the Holocaust. Those discussions would in turn lead Mark Donskoi to place the plight of Jews at the center of his next film, which also depicted the Nazi occupation of Ukraine.[51]

Several critics, including Bosley Crowther writing in the *New York Times,* attributed the brutality shown in the film to its factual basis: "in the light of authenticated deeds, the catalogue of horrors here recorded must be accepted as the grim impress of truth."[52] Howard Barnes, of the *New York Herald Tribune,* similarly wrote, "Very like a documentary, it makes no compromise with horror. . . . It is as savage as any film account which this reviewer has witnessed."[53] However, these same scenes of horror provoked other prominent critics to condemn the film, as the *New Republic*'s Manny Farber did when he called it "a mad-eyed simplification unsurpassed in war films." Farber particularly objected to the conclusions the film draws from this violence: "Since the Russians and their country have felt Nazi cruelty as much as anyone, it is understandable that their movie makers see the war almost wholly as an affair of killing, cruelty and revenge. But their method, in this film, of showing it as that is the narrowest possible and one that results for the audience in no understanding of the problem of the Nazis beyond the fact that vengeance must be taken on them."[54]

This view was echoed by the film reviewer for the *Nation,* James Agee, who objected that *The Rainbow* did not attempt to "understand or illuminate" the Nazis' atrocities but rather exploited the representations of them "to demolish one's moral and aesthetic judgment by splitting both and by turning the split forces of both against each other." Revealingly, Agee comments that it is "almost of a piece with war itself."[55] Of course, Soviet cinema, unlike that of Hollywood, *was* entirely consumed by the war and could not afford the luxury of objectivity. Showing consistency, Agee was later to condemn American-made anti-Japanese films as well as the American and British newsreel images of the concentration camps liberated on the western front in the spring of 1945.

While these criticisms make valid points in that the film clearly does attempt to exploit grief so as to channel it into vengeance, as the Soviet documentaries had done, they often betray a sheer inability to accept the mind-numbingly violent reality being displayed and the extent of the Wehrmacht's complicity in these crimes. Thus Farber found depictions of unprovoked Nazi violence difficult to believe, but as we now know, this was the reality of the war in the East in general and the Holocaust in particular.

This debate followed a few months after the discovery of Majdanek, the first Nazi death camp to be brought to light; those reports, too, were widely disbelieved at the time (see chapter 6). The parallel between the film's portrayal of Nazi atrocities and the reality of the camps was made by Jessica Smith, a well-briefed *New Republic* reader who responded to Farber:

SIR: Mr. Manny Farber's review of "The Rainbow" . . . is really an insult to your readers as well as to the Russian people, of whose epic sufferings and heroism it records but one terrible episode.

Alexandra Drayman was a Russian woman, who went out to live in the woods and cook for the guerillas when her native village was occupied by the Germans. She was pregnant, and only at the very last minute returned to her village to have her baby. The Nazis caught her and tortured her to make her reveal the whereabouts of the guerilla band. They drove her barefoot through the snow at night, poking her with bayonets. They threw her into a freezing shed, where her baby was born. Next morning the German commandant called her in and offered her baby's life in return for the information about her comrades. When she refused, he murdered the baby before her eyes. Then they murdered her and threw her into the river.

This story is true. So is the story of Majdanek, with its poison chambers, its death ovens, its hundreds of thousands of pairs of shoes of men, women and babies, stripped from them before they were murdered and carefully stacked and classified to be sent on order to different parts of Germany.

Wanda Wassilevska wrote a novel about what happened to Alexandra Drayman and the others in the village, a novel based on what has happened to millions of Russian people, and she also wrote the film version, which faithfully follows the novel. This picture is perhaps as close as the American people will ever come to the reality of what the Russian people have endured.[56]

This reader, then, defended the film as an accurate record of the facts. When Donskoi learned of the critical reviews, he likewise attempted to justify his film's depictions of violence by insisting that his stories had been taken from life:

I never invented subjects for the films I made during the war. . . . I scooped them by the handful from life itself.

I spoke to people who told me of what had happened to them or to their near ones in the terrible days of the enemy-invasion of our soil, and their stories were introduced as episodes and incidents in my pictures. . . . With some of the heroes of my films I could speak, others I could neither see nor speak with them, for they were dead. And of them their friends told me.

No matter how beautiful it may be, even the whitest of lies remains a lie, but no matter how appalling at times the truth may be, it will always be beautiful, for it is the truth.[57]

Writing in 1944, Donskoi recalled distributing the first copies of Wasilewska's story to frontline soldiers in autumn 1942. Their outraged reaction was one he hoped to repeat with his film, too:

> I wanted audiences who saw my film to say with the same undying hatred for the Germans: "The bastards!"
>
> People can get used to a lot of things. But it is impossible to get used to the rule of the Germans, just as it is impossible to get used to hangings, to the terrible ringing of frozen corpses, the child's head riddled with bullets. Now new rules of art have arisen. They have been born from our grief, our blood, our hatred towards the enemy, and the sacred love towards those in the enemy's power.[58]

At no point does Donskoi attempt to explore the potential tensions between the desire to document and the drive to elicit a sense of moral outrage from the spectator, the contradictory twofold purpose that informs these Soviet wartime portrayals of Nazi genocidal violence, be they documentary or features. Yet it is precisely this sensibility, this sense that the war entitles or rather obliges the filmmaker to show death and atrocity graphically in order to elicit action in response, that made Donskoi's film such uncomfortable viewing and disturbed American critics.

Despite these defenses, which appealed to the film's factual source, *The Rainbow* was based on a novel that was drawn from a journalistic source only loosely grounded in fact. More generally, the testimonial bases of the various films described in this chapter were typically thin, for though Jewish scriptwriters often attempted to convey their anxiety about the fate of their people, most relied on the press or interviews with eyewitnesses for firsthand accounts to rework as screenplays. Likewise, the studio-based films were all made in the Soviet Far East, by directors and crews with little or no direct experience of the front, occupation, or the recently liberated areas. As such, their representations were more faithful to the conventions of Soviet film than to the realities of the Nazis' genocidal violence and the Holocaust. Donskoi set his next film in Kiev, which had recently been occupied, and attempted to draw more deeply on eyewitness testimony to show the fate of the city's Jews at Babyi Iar.

While Donskoi had been making *The Rainbow* in Ashkhabad, Turkmenia, another Soviet filmmaker, Aleksandr Dovzhenko, was at the front in Kharkov and Kiev working on a two-part documentary about the liberation of Ukraine, as well as writing a screenplay aimed at producing a truly personal testament about that victory and the ultimate price that his native land and its inhabitants had paid for it: *Ukraine in Flames*. Dovzhenko's aim was similar to that of Donskoi—namely, to transgress the rules of art so as to depict the unprecedented. Dovzhenko, however, was at this point a writer-director at the height of his creative powers whose international reputation gave him considerable room to maneuver; the combination of these attributes and firsthand experience of the front would result in a body of work that portrayed the genocidal programs being conducted in the East in a more profound and moving way than had been done previously . . . yet still with little or no mention of the Nazis' primary target, the Jews.

# 4 \ Dovzhenko

## MOVING THE BOUNDARIES OF THE ACCEPTABLE

**In contrast** to most other wartime Soviet directors of documentaries or features, Aleksandr Dovzhenko went to the front and viewed the aftermath of Nazi atrocities firsthand. Between February and October 1942, he worked first as a journalist and then as an army political instructor; after that, he inspected murder sites and interviewed witnesses as a member of the Ukrainian Commission Investigating German War Crimes, to which he was appointed in April 1943. All these expriences profoundly affected his filmmaking career.[1] Other filmmakers spent time at the front as well, notably cameramen, a quarter of whom were killed in action, but they were typically required to produce short items for newsreels that were then edited by directors in Moscow who had been uninvolved in the filming process. However technically effective these depictions may have been, they quickly established and then followed conventional patterns for representing Nazi atrocities. The upshot was that regardless of their talent, ethnicity, or personal ties to the occupied territories, wartime Soviet documentary filmmakers rarely found themselves in a position to impose a personal vision on their films.[2] Yet Dovzhenko was a legendary figure in Soviet film, a director of international stature who, like Eisenstein or Vertov, had created a distinct personal style and subject matter. No other similarly significant screenwriter or director was able to depict the Nazis' occupation of and genocidal policies in the East in a way that both incorporated a distinct directorial style and drew on firsthand experience of the front and newly liberated areas.

With his beloved Ukraine entirely under Nazi control and his parents trapped in occupied Kiev, Dovzhenko had an intensely personal investment in his wartime films. In addition, the war rendered the central themes of Dovzhenko's art—death, mourning, memory, and Ukrainian identity—more urgent than ever. These motivations combined with his position and experience to produce two documentary films, the first of which, *The Battle for Our Soviet Ukraine* (*Bitva za nashu sovetskuiu Ukrainu* [1943]), ranks among the most important and powerful wartime documentaries and constitutes an important part of Dovzhenko's oeuvre, although it has not been recognized as such. Yet this engagement promised a great deal more, for Dovzhenko's journalism, literary output, public pronouncements, and private reflections produced during his research for the documentaries led to an artistically and politically ambitious screenplay, "Ukraine in Flames" ("Ukraina v ogne"); had this been produced, the result would have been the most important film of the war, an immense contribution to cinema's initial attempts to portray both the Nazis' pursuit of genocide in the East and, implicitly, the Holocaust. Unfortunately, Stalin and the Central Committee condemned "Ukraine in Flames" for its Ukrainian nationalist undertones in January 1944, after which Dovzhenko found himself ostracized and unable to publish, let alone produce, his film projects, with the exception of a weak second documentary: *Victory in Right Bank Ukraine and the Expulsion of the German Invaders from the Boundaries of Soviet Ukrainian Lands* (*Pobeda na Pravoberezhnoi Ukraine i izgnanie nemetskikh zakhvatchikov za predely ukrainskikh sovetskikh zemel'* [1945]).

Yet while Dovzhenko's wartime films and unrealized film projects surpassed all other contemporary works in frankly portraying the full horror of Nazi mass murder, savage reprisals, enslavement, and starvation, they depart from the accepted narrative of "Soviet" suffering only to emphasize more or less explicitly ethnic Ukrainian victimhood. The suffering of Jews as Jews is marginalized and passed over in silence almost as much as it was in other wartime documentaries. Nevertheless, Dovzhenko's works present images of the events now called "the Holocaust by bullets," including the Babyi Iar massacre, in Kiev, and the slaughter at Drobitskii Iar, in Kharkov, doing so in a way worth considering in the wider context of film representations of the Holocaust and its theorizations.[3] Dovzhenko's first public responses to his experience at the front, however, were literary: his wartime stories, which offer powerful images of heroism and reflect on both the traumatic moment when Soviet forces retreated from Ukraine and the subsequent Nazi occupation. Yet his wartime "notebooks" are more ambitious, for they constitute initial attempts to depict the Nazis' genocidal acts and to reflect on such attempts.[4]

## Dovzhenko's Theorizations of the Representation of Atrocity

Dovzhenko fills his notebooks with references to Nazi atrocities, but more important for my purposes, he also ruminates on the very representation of atrocity in art and journalism. In doing so, he grapples with something that has been described as one of the enduring problems of depictions of the Holocaust in art: whether it is permissible or even possible to endow such senseless suffering with the meaning implicit in art, and if so, by what means.[5]

In March 1942, shortly after arriving at the front, Dovzhenko expresses a certainty that art can and must represent the horrors of war: "Reality has become more terrible than imagination. It must be shown as it is. The human spirit is being tested to its limits, limits that the world didn't even suspect. Books and films about our experience must crackle with the horror, suffering, anger, and fortitude."[6] This immediate sense that the atrocities must be depicted in art was a powerful one, and Dovzhenko ultimately came to see that the war offered an opportunity to get away from the clichéd approach of Soviet journalists writing, "the same one-sided, saccharine nonsense that they wrote before the war about socialist construction," and in particular to do so by portraying suffering more honestly.[7] Thus, seizing the opportunity for greater artistic license than he had been permitted since the 1920s, Dovzhenko immediately began to reflect on ways of portraying atrocity and fictionalizing episodes, such as one set in a Nazi POW camp that he subsequently used in short stories and "Ukraine in Flames."

But only a month later, in April 1942, the filmmaker started to express doubts: "Today as yesterday and tomorrow, the newspapers are glutted with accounts of such cruelties, such inhuman deeds committed by the enemy, that the mind boggles and one does not even feel anger, only an ordinary reflex of disgust. It would be no different even if we were Dantes or Michelangelos. These events cannot be contained by the mind. No one reads these accounts any more. They are like cries of pain or groans of despair."[8] Here, the sheer overload of the Soviet media's highly predictable and clichéd accounts discussed in chapter 2 makes Dovzhenko become indecisive about portraying these horrific scenes and doubt that even the greatest artists could depict them meaningfully. In a fictional dialogue, moreover, Dovzhenko represents the voice of the people who do not want these terrible sights represented because they do not want to remember them:

> "What are you writing and photographing?"
>
> "We're making notes, immortalizing your suffering and charred corpses and frozen, butchered children."
>
> "They're so terrible."
>
> "They are terrible. What horrors those cursed butchers have brought! We'll write it all down and paint a picture."
>
> "Well, maybe you shouldn't. Maybe you ought to forget about it. You can't bring the dead back to life, and we can't live on memories of horror. We have to forget."
>
> "What?"
>
> "Otherwise it's better to die. We have to live with good things in mind. Write about good things for us. Teach us about the beautiful and the good. We want to be happy, if only for a little while."
>
> "That's a delusion."
>
> "Maybe. But have pity on us."[9]

Compared to his colleagues working in journalism and the newsreel genre, Dovzhenko was afforded the relative luxury of thinking through this dilemma. His doubts remained private, however, for in August 1942 Dovzhenko produced one of the most powerful of all wartime public statements on the need to represent atrocities and the horrors of war in art in general and in cinema especially. In a speech at an evening of American and British cinema held in Moscow, Dovzhenko clearly outlined why he thought that war films should pay particular attention to atrocity:

> Today and tomorrow the boundaries of the acceptable in art will have to be moved.
>
> That which in the interests of taste, and of the aesthetic demands of the age, was considered prohibited as too terrifying, too cruel—this has forced its way onto the screen. . . .
>
> Today, unprecedented base and evil deeds, sadism and insults, hatred towards man, and hatred towards humanity have forced their way on to our screens. Today we need to drag on to our screens the Fascist

mass child-killer, hangman, murderer of the wounded, the elderly, and children, the destroyer of cultural artifacts, the asphyxiator and murderer of whole peoples.

Today we need to drag on to the screens of the world, as if to the courthouse of the nations, not simply evil deeds, perversions, base acts, and not simply deceit and horror, but acts that are so vast, wide-ranging, terrible and shocking, the likes of which the world has never seen, and no one imagined in their moments of greatest pessimism.[10]

This speech seems to represent something of a resolution in Dovzhenko's thinking, where he concludes that the epoch requires artists to move the borders of the permissible in art; as he says, previously unthinkable sights have forced themselves onto the screen. His language emphasizes the impersonal. Filmmakers are, he suggests, compelled to respond to this entirely unprecedented situation and to represent its horrors.

In attempting to react to this unprecedented situation, however, Dovzhenko is nonetheless able to draw on precedents—namely, the prior resources of his own films, especially those of the 1920s, in which death and mourning in the context of an antiwar pathos played an important part. Most relevant here is *Arsenal,* his 1928 film of the Bolshevik Revolution in Ukraine, which uses lengthy images of static women as a motif of the bereavement and mourning of the dead in World War I. Diverging from most other revolutionary cinema, however, Dovzhenko's evocation of loss does not end there; indeed, even the film's depiction of the revolution itself is, in the words of Vance Kepley Jr., "counterpointed by sotto voce misgivings about the human costs of revolution."[11] Death and the process of grieving are also central themes in Dovzhenko's subsequent films *Earth* (*Zemlia* [1930]) and *Ivan* (1932), which attempt to counterbalance those aspects of life with a sense of continuity grounded in nature, cultural tradition, and the perspective of revolutionary transformation.

Thus Dovzhenko, an artist whose works already attempted to elaborate images of loss, brought a completely new dimension to the depiction of the Nazis' pursuit of genocide. As an eyewitness at the front with an immense personal investment in depicting the events then afflicting his own parents and almost all his native country, Dovzhenko confronted the devastating experience of the war quite differently than did most of his fellow film directors, whether they made documentaries or features. Instead of presenting images of death and bereavement as a means to spur Soviet soldiers to vengeance, Dovzhenko chose a different path, for as his note-books make clear, he was most struck by the bereaved women he had met, whose grief does not translate into a call to action. Whereas the previous documentaries had silenced these widows and childless mothers through a standardizing, universalizing, Sovietizing voiceover, Dovzhenko tries to hear and convey the voices of those for whom the price paid has been too much and for whom liberation will not and cannot compensate for the numbing pain of their suffering.[12] Dovzhenko is an artist not content to forget the dead, heroes or otherwise, and not willing simply to endow images of atrocity with the conventional Soviet sense of redemption conferred by martyrdom for a cause.

### The Battle for Our Soviet Ukraine

Dovzhenko's wartime documentaries have long been neglected.[13] Even the contemporary scholars who mention the director's wartime works focus mostly on the ban on "Ukraine in Flames" and his fall from grace within months of *The Battle for Our Soviet Ukraine*'s October 1943 premiere.[14] (Indeed, the ban somewhat truncated the praise for that documentary at the time.)[15] One reason for this neglect has been the assumption that the film is fundamentally a compilation because its footage was shot by over twenty-three cameramen without any directorial control. In fact, however, though Dovzhenko of course had wielded no control over the captured German footage as it was filmed, ample evidence indicates that he did control the Soviet cameramen, either directly or through a proxy, in addition to editing all the amassed footage.[16]

The title credits for *The Battle for Our Soviet Ukraine* list Dovzhenko solely as the artistic director and the author of the commentary, movingly spoken in voiceover by Leonid Khmara, himself a Ukrainian educated in Kharkov. The director's credit went to Dovzhenko's wife and long-standing creative partner, Iuliia Solntseva, along with Iakov Avdeenko, an established director from Ukrainian newsreel studios who was able to advise Dovzhenko and Solntseva on documentary film, a relatively new field for the husband-and-wife directorial team.[17] One cameraman whose footage appears in the film, Valentin Orliankin, explains that while Dovzhenko was more often at the front than in Moscow, Avdeenko too stayed at the front throughout the film's production as part of one or another group of frontline cameramen. Avdeenko's role seems to have been to ensure that people took the kind of images Dovzhenko required, especially when he was absent.[18]

The arrangement meant that Dovzhenko and Solntseva were able to give specific instructions to camera operators, demanding that they photograph atrocity and death. One of them, A. Brantman, complained to Solntseva that he could not find any entirely burned-down villages, having turned up only isolated burned-out dwellings; he reported that he had proposed setting fire to the latter for dramatic effect but was prevented from doing so by owners who intended to use the remaining structures, either rebuilding them or using them in their present state. As this demonstrates, the cameramen not only worked from instructions but also intervened in what they were filming.[19] The emphasis on images of destruction revealed here was a deliberate approach, as is similarly clear from Dovzhenko's own instructions to the frontline cameraman Vladislav Mikosha in 1942. Mikosha recalled that when he returned to Moscow after having filmed the heroic but unsuccessful defense of Sevastopol, the director told him "to show people's suffering unflinchingly," adding:

> Death, tears, suffering. There lies a tremendous life-affirming force. Show the sufferings of the soldier wounded on the field of battle. Show the hard drudgery of the soldier. Film the death of the soldier. Do not flinch: you can cry, but you must film it. . . . Everyone must see it. Tears can fill your eyes, but you must film it. . . . Everyone must see how and why he is dying. . . . Film the enemy, his bestial appearance. . . . . I'm not talking about any old German—he is the same as you or I. . . . I'm talking about the evil done by the Fascists. About the barbarity and pedantry with which they shoot our people, burn our villages and towns, cripple our land. All this is the true appearance, the true face of the Fascist beast, the enemy of humanity, the barbarian of the Twentieth century. . . . Some day our children will look to these images to learn the price of life, the price of peace and the horror and stupidity of war."[20]

Dovzhenko, moreover, was present during the battle for Kharkov, as his notebooks and other witness testimony confirm, where he could have further influenced some of the filming, giving similar instructions to cameramen.[21] Here and at other points while making the film, Dovzhenko was a witness on the scene of liberation. This made him something completely different from the newsreel editors assembling films in Moscow from other people's footage over which they had minimal control.

Consequently, as Valérie Pozner's study has shown, Dovzhenko's film stands out from other films of the liberation of Kharkov by dwelling on the town's destruction rather than its liberation and reconstruction.[22] Dovzhenko can thus be said to have exercised a considerable degree of authorship over the film, not just selecting and editing the footage and writing the accompanying voiceover, as has previously been assumed or argued, but even in determining how cameramen selected subjects, posed them, and photographed them.[23] Relative to other wartime documentaries, however, *The Battle for Our Soviet Ukraine* is most marked in its use of synchronously recorded sound.[24]

The film included ten synchronously recorded sound sequences, whereas the norm for a Soviet wartime feature-length documentary was to employ only one. These recordings range from a recital of a poem in Ukrainian, to soldiers in a trench singing a Ukrainian folksong, to a motivational speech by an officer before the battle. Half of them, however, are recordings of eyewitnesses as they react to or recount German atrocities. These include the first sequence, that of wailing women in Kupiansk lamenting over the disinterred bodies of their loved ones, and direct-to-camera addresses by the Kharkov University professor of medicine Lev Nikolaev, who was imprisoned and beaten by the Germans, as well as by Doctor Shingeladze and Sergeant of the Guards Pavel Korovkin, who both tell how four hundred wounded Soviet soldiers were killed when Germans set fire to the hospital where they were convalescing.

Yet perhaps the most striking of these scenes shows women recounting the murders of their loved ones. The power in this segment emerges from both the content of the women's tales and the anguished and emotional way they recount them, with not just the camera but also the microphone capturing long takes of the women's struggles with their own tears. It emerges, too, from the way this sequence relates to the episodes around it, the film as a whole, and the wider contexts of Soviet wartime cinema, Dovzhenko's own films, and the place of testimony in contemporary documentaries about war and the Holocaust (fig. 4.1).

The first woman recounts a tale of finding her husband (or possibly son) three days after he was killed, frozen in the fields. She sobs as she tells this story, but though she mentions taking him to the cemetery, she draws no conclusions from her account and issues no call to vengeance. The second woman tells how her son was shot in the eye and his chest cut

FIGURE 4.1. Blind woman's testimony. From *Battle for Our Soviet Ukraine*.

open. She ends her story by asking why the Germans humiliated her son's corpse. This almost unanswerable question is followed by one that closes the next testimony: "I think the child suffered. My darling son, why did the enemy make you suffer? What had you done to deserve it? What did you die for?" The final woman's story, of being blinded by the Germans, similarly ends with a question, one that the woman herself succinctly answers by blaming the Germans for her injuries. While the sequence ends with this explanation for the suffering, apparently corresponding to representations of the German violence as irrational and indiscriminate, the answer is inadequate, and the single, simplistic response is outweighed by the three questions. This imbalance becomes even greater when we consider that the questions "Why did you die?" and "Why did you suffer?" are not questions habitually asked of the dead or left substantially unanswered in Soviet wartime films. Normally, any such questions are asked to conjure an immediate response, with an emphasis on explaining, recuperating, and Sovietizing death. In this sequence, no voiceover intervenes to contextualize or explain the bigger picture, and while the triumphant procession of the film narrative as a whole largely offsets the haunting

FIGURE 4.2. Blind woman. From *Battle for Our Soviet Ukraine*.

questions of the bereaved women, Dovzhenko grants the spectator a significant freedom to reflect on such questions; as a consequence, they remain disturbing even after the film ends.

Dovzhenko's decision to end this sequence with the testimony of a woman blinded by the Germans is significant, since the capacity to bear witness is usually based on sight. In this case, the woman recounts the moment when she lost her sight, and the camera shows her in close-up, drawing attention to the scars on her face and her unseeing eyes (fig 4.2). Whereas the other women mourn dead sons, the final witness is herself a victim, and the evidence and indexical trace of Nazi violence appear not just in her words and tears but in her face itself. But even here, her scarred face would tell us nothing without her verbal testimony. The speech, not the image, plays the decisive role.

The figure of a mourning woman played an important role in Soviet wartime propaganda as a whole, but it was usually a silent image, the words those of a voiceover commentary ventriloquizing calls for vengeance, as occurs in *Defeat of the Germans near Moscow*. But Dovzhenko's mourning women are more than a visual motif; they speak, creating a sense that these are the authentic voices of the grieving, whose suffering is given the space to express itself rather than being summarized, ventriloquized, and instrumentalized.[25]

This sequence is followed by the apparently compensatory sight of renewed harvesting and the Red Army's advance, but that in turn ends with entrenched soldiers giving a melancholic rendition of the Ukrainian folksong "Galia the Barmaid" ("Shinkarochka Galia") as an expression of the 1943 harvest (*zhniva* in Ukrainian), the likes of which, according to the voiceover, will never be repeated. This harvest comes to symbolize not just the process of forgetting injuries suffered but also rebirth. The effect is a powerful restatement of death as part of a cycle ultimately of renewal, a theme famously articulated in Dovzhenko's own silent classic, *Earth*.

This approach to the use of sound was a revelation for Dovzhenko's fellow filmmakers. At a discussion in the "House of Cinema," for example, Vsevolod Pudovkin and Sergei Gerasimov were quick to rate the film as far superior to anything previously produced about the war, particularly in its use of sound. As Gerasimov put it: "We must definitely reproduce the sounds of the war; people's voices, husky and tired, the certain haziness of the sound and its fragmentary quality—all this comes close to the truth. This is genuine. This immersion in authentic material conveys the sensation that the film is real. This is broadly the approach to form I want to promote in future."[26]

Dovzhenko found encouragement at this discussion and championed his film as a model for documentary cinema: "Newsreel has barely used any sound footage. It has not recorded the exceptional people of the epoch, or their voices, so that in many years' time we would be able to hear our generals, the defenders of Stalingrad and so on. We need to leave ourselves in the future thousands of portraits, film portraits that will be even better than if we have portraits painted by artists."[27] Though he did not voice it in public discussion, this desire to synchronously record the human voice was evidently stimulated by Dovzhenko's desire to emphasize Ukrainian identity as well. While the film's voiceover is in Russian, interspersed with occasional Ukrainian words, such as the one for Germany (*Nemetchina*), the majority of its synchronous sound footage is in Ukrainian, even though populations in Kharkov and across eastern Ukraine predominantly speak Russian. In particular, most of the witnesses speak Ukrainian, and the underlying purpose is clearly to stress the Ukrainianness of the suffering.

Moreover, as Gerasimov notes, the film's final effect depends largely on its makers' bonds with Ukraine: "The success of this film lies in the fact that it is made by people with blood ties to Ukraine. If it had been made by someone from outside, a neutral, it would not have turned out like this. What is needed is self-belief, awareness and unmediated participation in the war[;] then the idea will be realized correctly."[28] Gerasimov even expressed the wish for a more Ukrainian-sounding voiceover performed by Dovzhenko himself: "My only regret is that the voiceover is spoken by Khmara. It would have been better if Dovzhenko himself had spoken it. The accent itself and intonation have been somewhat lost. I heard him on the radio, and have heard him in life several times. The way word and intonation combine in his speech is very effective. You need a Ukrainian accent here, whereas the fact that the speech is somewhat refined and polished in Khmara's pronunciation spoils and reduces the effect, undermines it."[29]

Dovzhenko used synchronously recorded sound to emphasize Ukrainian rather than Soviet suffering, and this goal certainly had a point. Even ignoring the approximately 900,000 Jews killed in Ukraine, it is likely that Ukraine's war dead outnumbered those of any other nationality, with probably 5–8 million Ukranians losing their lives.[30] Indeed, during the war Dovzhenko repeatedly expressed doubts that the Ukrainian nation would survive: "Hitler will undoubtedly be defeated, it's true, but he has destroyed Ukraine."[31] As Kate Brown has shown, however, the Holocaust and the war led to an ethnic homogenization of Ukraine, transforming it into an "unambiguously Ukrainian nation-space."[32]

The French historian Annette Wieviorka argues that individual testimony appeals to the heart and not to the mind. It elicits compassion, pity, and indignation, which risk undermining coherent historical narrative.[33] By using synch sound testimonies, Dovzhenko highlighted individual feelings, especially loss, but also ethnicized it as Ukrainian, privileging national over the overarching "Soviet" narrative of suffering,[34] a focus that Soviet authorities ultimately found unacceptable. In addition, this emphasis on Ukrainian suffering also meant that Dovzhenko's film remained completely silent as to the separate, still bleaker fate of Ukraine's Jews.

One of the film's most powerful sequences shows Drobitskii Iar, the ravine outside Kharkov where, as the film's voiceover says, "the Fascists shot 14,000 citizens of the town." As the viewer confronts an image of the entire common grave, opened to reveal lines of partially decomposed corpses,

FIGURE 4.3. The mass grave at Drobitskii Iar (Kharkov). From *Battle for Our Soviet Ukraine*.

the narrator commands attention: "Look at us, you who are living; do not turn from our terrifying pits. We cannot be forgotten or silenced. We are many. We are an enormous multitude in Ukraine! Do not forget us! Make Germany pay for our suffering!" (fig 4.3). Instead of attributing words to the bereaved, as most Soviet films do, or interviewing some of them, as he does elsewhere, Dovzhenko here makes victims themselves speak in the name of the dead, who cannot be silenced or forgotten. But while he makes the dead articulate the familiar call to vengeance, Dovzhenko also stresses the need to contemplate them. Indeed, he arranged and photographed a number of skulls, not only those found in the ruins of the hospital where the Germans had killed wounded soldiers by burning them alive, but most notably that of a dead woman apparently disinterred from Drobitskii Iar, posing her so as to make her look directly at the spectator (fig. 4.4). We are being told to look at the dead, but at the same time, they are looking back at us, addressing us, reminding us of our responsibilities as ethical agents—as Saxton has put it, "implicating us inescapably in the production of meaning" and entreating us not to contemplate passively but to act.[35] The response demanded of the spectator is ultimately active,

FIGURE 4.4. A woman's skull, from Drobitskii Iar, appears to gaze into the camera. From *Battle for Our Soviet Ukraine*.

namely, a contribution to the war effort conceived as "vengeance," which is thus entirely consistent with the aim of most Soviet newsreel depictions of atrocities. Dovzhenko's film is extraordinary only in the means it uses to effect this call. The impossible dead witness, central to the question of testimony in memory of the Holocaust, is made to speak.

Yet this image of a dead woman also indicates a problem in both Dovzhenko's film and Soviet wartime documentaries more broadly. We know little or nothing of the woman whose corpse addresses us. She speaks in Dovzhenko's words, voiced by a professional announcer. Had she been able to do so, she might well have told a different story, and her intonation would certainly have been different. Instead, she is made to articulate a narrative of Ukrainian suffering. In a further gesture unusual for Soviet documentaries, Dovzhenko again underlines the Ukrainian identity of the dead by estimating the number of Ukrainian victims who lie in such "pits" (*iamy*) across the region; though he states an accurate figure, however, the statistic avoids and misrepresents the fact that the majority (over 10,000) of the people massacred at Drobitskii Iar were killed for being Jewish, not Ukrainian, and that these pits, which can be found all

FIGURE 4.5. Professor Efros mentioned as being persecuted for being a Ukrainian intellectual as film shows images of ruined Kharkov University buildings. From *Battle for Our Soviet Ukraine*.

over Ukraine, were filled overwhelmingly with Jews who fell victim to the Einsatzgruppen. Thus, by combining a skillfully composed voiceover with shocking images of the mass grave of Kharkov Jewry, Dovzhenko grants audiences a powerful sense of the immense scale of mass killings in the East. At the same time, however, he audaciously shifts the victims' identity away from the misleading one of "peaceful Soviet citizens" to imply that they are ethnic Ukrainians even though they are overwhelmingly Jews.

Further demonstrating this to be a consistent tendency in the film, an image of the ruined building that had housed the University of Kharkov building appears as the voiceover reports that Doctor Efros, a professor of mathematical sciences, was killed here, and then implies that he was killed in an effort to destroy Ukrainian learning and cultural life (fig. 4.5). In fact, recent sources on the Holocaust in Ukraine identify this man, Aleksandr Mikhailovich Efros, a professor of physical and mathematical sciences, as a Jew who was killed for being Jewish, a victim not of the persecution of Ukrainian culture but of the Holocaust.[36]

It is tempting to see Dovzhenko's silence on the separate fate of Ukraine's Jews as particularly important in the light of the unproven accusation that the filmmaker participated in persecutions of Jews when fighting for Symon Petliura in the Russian (and Ukrainian) Civil War,[37] as well as his reported anti-Semitic outbursts in the 1930s. Possibly more significant, although not necessarily reliable, is a denunciation made to the NKVD in March 1943, where he is quoted as referring to Jews as "sabotaging" and eternally hating Ukrainian culture.[38] Counterbalancing such accusations, Dovzhenko's wartime journalism denounces Nazi anti-Semitism as early as the day after the invasion, an unlikely gesture for a committed anti-Semite since such denunciations were not required of authors, and his posthumously published wartime notebooks mention that the Germans killed Jews first, something that could never be stated outright anywhere in film during the war.[39] The record of his films is similarly mixed. Some of his earlier films, including *Arsenal* (1928) and *Shchors* (1939), depict Jews sympathetically or neutrally as an integral part of Ukrainian life who were threatened by the forces of Ukrainian nationalism during the civil war. *Bukovina Is Ukrainian Land* (1939), however, employs a synagogue that wealthy orthodox Jews built in Chernovtsy, the capital of Bukovina, as a symbol of the oppression of the poor, especially Ukrainians, under Austro-Hungarian and Romanian rule. Christianity is not singled out in this manner, suggesting an anti-Semitic undercurrent to this film's call to protect the rights of persecuted Bukovina Ukrainians. Then again, Dovzhenko's *Liberation* (1940), a film that celebrates the annexation of western Ukraine and western Belorussia as a consequence of the Nazi-Soviet nonaggression pact's dismemberment of Second Republic Poland, repeatedly mentions and condemns Polish persecution of not just Ukrainians but also Jews, which further illustrates this mixed record. In short, Dovzhenko remained a champion of Ukrainian culture and the rights of Ukrainians throughout the greater part of his career, and when he perceived Jews as an obstacle to these interests, he was capable of resorting to anti-Semitism, whether in private outbursts or in cinematic clichés. As Liber has argued, such outbursts carried less risk than did complaints about the greater Russian obstacle to Ukrainian cultural and political aspirations.[40]

Whether or not the wartime NKVD report of Dovzhenko's anti-Semitism is correct, Dovzhenko's silence regarding the fate of Jews in *The Battle for Our Soviet Ukraine* can be seen as part of the increasing virus of

Soviet anti-Semitism, especially in Ukraine, where Ukrainians were not solely victims of the Nazis; during the occupation, significant numbers actively facilitated and participated in murdering Jews.[41] After the liberation in 1943, Jews returning from evacuation often faced hostility from their Ukrainian neighbors, particularly but not solely if they attempted to reclaim their residences or possessions.[42] Late wartime and postwar anti-Semitism, in part emanating from the Central Committee, as well as apparently spontaneous pogroms (e.g., the one had that transpired in Kiev in 1945), frightened Jewish survivors into silence.[43] Likewise, for all the merit in his innovative use of the documentary medium to portray Nazi atrocities, Dovzhenko's film constitutes an even greater distortion than do other Soviet documentaries of the war. By portraying Nazi genocide in Ukraine as directed at POWs and Ukrainian citizens, without so much as mentioning the specific fate of Jews, it helps silence Jewish attempts to convey the story of the Holocaust by proposing to enlist the murder of Jews in the cause of a Ukrainian nationalism antipathetic to their interests.

Dovzhenko strove to present a more rounded picture of the occupation in his screenplay "Ukraine in Flames," which he had been writing at this same time. This entailed the portrayal of Nazis and Ukrainian collaborators, which in turn required the depiction of Nazi anti-Semitism.

### "Ukraine in Flames"

On completing *The Battle for Our Soviet Ukraine,* Dovzhenko was nervous about its reception. As he wrote in his notebooks:

> We completed *The Battle for Our Soviet Ukraine* today. I don't know what the government will say about it. Maybe the film will be banned or I will be forced to mar it by cutting the difficult and unheroic scenes. But I am convinced of one thing: the film is absolutely correct. In what does its truth inhere? In the grandiose woe of retreat and in the incomplete joy of advance.
>
> Only newsreel reporter X can put on his brave act and try to fool the world by concealing the tragic truth: the destruction of Ukraine by the Germans and sometimes even by ourselves, owing to difficult circumstances.[44]

Nevertheless, even though it emphasizes "the price of victory," as Dovzhenko put later put it, *The Battle for Our Soviet Ukraine* won universally positive reviews on its theatrical release in October 1943. This encouraged the director to pursue his interpretation of the war in "Ukraine in Flames," for which the documentary would be something of a preliminary sketch.[45]

A reviewer for the popular weekly *Ogonek,* however, felt the need to stress that Ukraine was the cradle of Russian civilization and to compare *The Battle for Our Soviet Ukraine* to the famous medieval epic from the Kievan Rus era, *The Lay of Igor's Campaign* (*Slovo o polku Igoreve*).[46] More than any other, this review hinted at anxieties and tensions related to Dovzhenko's renewed emphasis on the particular nature of Ukraine's suffering.

The central event in "Ukraine in Flames" is the Soviets' loss of the republic in the summer and early autumn of 1941 and the subsequent Nazi occupation. The action follows the main characters, the Zaporozhets family, symbolically named to evoke the spirit of Ukrainian national pride associated with the Ukrainian Cossacks of the same name. The family consists of a father and mother, five adult sons, and a daughter. The sons leave for the front and the mother is killed, strafed by an enemy plane, after which the focus turns to the father, Lavrin, and the daughter, Olesia, who endure all the horrors of the occupation, from a concentration camp to slave labor in Germany. Although he intends ultimately to serve the partisans as a double agent, Lavrin becomes stigmatized as a collaborator when he agrees to work for the Germans. As he had with *The Battle for Our Soviet Ukraine,* Dovzhenko intended to emphasize the price paid for the occupation especially by Ukrainians. Indeed, the price is greatly amplified in this particular case, for Ukrainians are said to have suffered more than any other nation in the war—which is true only if Europe's Jews are not counted a nation.[47] This suggestion alone was enough to make his film suspect to the Communist Party, but Dovzhenko went a great deal further into life under the occupation, not only touching on taboos such as the hypocrisy and incompetence of the Soviet rulers as they retreated, abandoning Ukraine in the face of the 1941 German advance, but also portraying the Nazis' contempt for what they see as the Soviets' vain attempt to appeal to class rather than nation.[48] Dovzhenko also reopened older wounds, such as that of collectivization and the Ukrainian famine of 1932–1933, hinting that these were factors motivating collaborators' anticommunism. Indeed, the basic attitude toward the occupied in "Ukraine in Flames" is a sense of sympathy, understanding, and even guilt arising from the fact that Soviet state had abandoned them to this fate.[49] Needless to say, Stalin took a different view, blaming those who had been occupied.

Despite all this, the scenario was initially praised by Nikita Khrushchev, Dovzhenko's protector and then the head of the Ukrainian Communist Party. Only when Stalin himself read it were alarm bells sounded, and Khrushchev immediately ditched the Ukrainian director.

Although this screenplay is normally explored only in the light of its ban, it presents a picture of Nazi mass killings in Ukraine, including killings of Jews, through a portrayal of Nazi ideology and Ukrainian collaboration of a depth unprecedented at the time. This was difficult terrain, as Kozintsev and Pudovkin had found out a year earlier when their films depicting Nazis were banned (see chapter 3). Indeed, the comparison between Dovzhenko's film and those of Pudovkin and Kozintsev can be instructive, for unlike those earlier works, which portray only stereotypic fictional Nazis, Dovzhenko's screenplay incorporates a portrait of the historical Reichskommissar of Ukraine, Erich Koch, as he gives a speech in Kiev: "Death to the Slavs, death to Bolshevism, death to the democratic indiscipline of clamoring minorities, death to the Jews!"[50] In the screenplay, Koch's immediate audience consists of German officers, but the address is broadcast throughout Nazi-occupied Europe, and in it he goes on to promise land in Ukraine for anyone wanting it. This aspiration is made concrete in the fictional characters of Ernst von Kraus, a colonel in German intelligence and a veteran of Germany's 1918 occupation of Ukraine, and his son, Ludwig, a lieutenant. Dovzhenko uses these characters to explore a tension between the traditions of the Prussian officer class and the Nazis; military successes and the conquest of Ukraine resolve this potential conflict, however, and Ernst's objection to Ludwig's mass killings are easily overcome. Yet even here Dovzhenko presents Ukrainians as the primary victims; in the previously quoted passage, for example, killing Jews is presented as secondary to killing Slavs. In fact, however, the Nazis prioritized killing Jews and Bolsheviks over Slavs, who were for the most part to be starved or worked to death, and in some cases even assimilated, but not systematically annihilated.[51]

The screenplay does contain one episode in which an elderly Ukrainian makes comments suggesting the Nazis' persecution of Jews to be common knowledge: "They'll beat up the Jews in the towns, and then they'll start on us."[52] Nevertheless, this remains some distance from acknowledging that hundreds of thousands of Jews are being killed in cold blood, implying as it does something more like sporadic violence. Moreover, while this seems to make it clear that the Nazis prioritize anti-Jewish violence over that against ethnic Ukrainians, the statement expresses not so much explicit solidarity or sympathy for the Jews as an implicit fear that the Nazis will not content themselves with "beating" the Jews but will next attack Ukrainians.

Furthermore, "Ukraine in Flames" depicts ingrained anti-Semitism as an important component in the outlook of a Ukrainian collaborator, Zabroda. A former kulak who has returned from Siberia to settle scores during the occupation, Zabroda insultingly calls Lavrin Zaporozhets an "old friend of the Jews" (*zhidovskii bat´ko*), presumably because as the former chairman of the collective farm, the latter man favors the Communist Party, and Zabroda, like the Nazis, associates communism and Jews.[53] The two trade insults, with Zabroda condemning Zaporozhets for the crimes of communism and Zaporozhets condemning the crimes of Nazism, including pogroms: "They spat in each others' eyes: Siberia and sufferings, famine and death. They spat in each other's faces: Hitler, German pogroms and fires, hangings, slavery and the violent hatred of the whole world for Hitler."[54] Much as Ermler does in *She Defends the Motherland,* analyzed in chapter 3, Dovzhenko repeatedly refers to the persecution of Jews here but never shows it. We see Nazis calling for anti-Jewish violence, a Ukrainian collaborator attracted by it, and other Ukrainians aware of but not condoning it, but in each case, it is only one item on a list of Nazi crimes. Throughout the screenplay it remains peripheral to the plot, which contains no Jewish characters; indeed, no Jews are so much as mentioned by name, and while some scenes depict the hanging or imprisonment of Ukrainians, and the screenplay offers an important exploration of the issues of memory and forgetting with regard to the experiences of women *Ostarbeiters* (slave laborers), none of the film's scenes attempt to reconstruct the genocidal killings of Jews. Had "Ukraine in Flames" been made into a film, the result would have powerfully conveyed the genocidal nature marking the Nazi occupation of Ukraine, but Dovzhenko's prime concern was the Ukrainian nation, whose very existence he saw as threatened. Consequently, a finished film would have at best mentioned the Jews in passing, just as earlier Soviet depictions of the occupation had done.[55]

In part, the decision to ban "Ukraine in Flames" shocked Dovzhenko because his powerful and indeed overwhelming compulsion to make a significant film about the war sprang from ethical as much as aesthetic imperatives. He recognized, however, that others might see things differently: "No one needs my story; evidently only panegyrics are needed."[56] Nevertheless, this did not stop Dovzhenko from attempting to complete a sequel documentary about the liberation of the rest of Ukraine and trying to rewrite "Ukraine in Flames" in a more acceptable form.

### Victory in Right Bank Ukraine and the Expulsion of the German Invader from the Boundaries of Soviet Ukrainian Lands

After the devastating setback of "Ukraine in Flames," Dovzhenko still attempted to complete what he considered the second part of his documentary on the liberation of Ukraine, perhaps in part because Ivan Bol´shakov had authorized production of that film on 28 December 1943, before the worst of Dovzhenko's humiliation and ostracization.[57] Archival materials relating to the film reveal that he planned to make something similar to *The Battle for Our Soviet Ukraine,* with the later work functioning as a sequel.[58] The synchronously recorded sound sequences he planned, however, either were never made or turned out to be of inadequate quality; as a result, the final film has few such sequences, most of them speeches by Khrushchev or Marshall Zhukov, and was greatly inferior to the previous work.

The sequences Dovzhenko planned to shoot included one of a blind boy sitting on the banks of the Dneiper playing a *kobzar* (an eight-stringed balalaika) and singing songs with lyrics by Ukraine's national poet, Taras Shevchenko; the final sequence was to show the Ukrainian-speaking traditional peoples of the Carpathians, the Gutsuls, playing their *trombity* (long bugle-like instruments similar to Swiss alpenhorns). The director's instructions state: "The sounds of the *trombity* must resonate like a call to arms."[59] Clearly Dovzhenko intended synchronous sound to play as large a part in this film as it had in the previous one, and the effect would have been equally powerful.

In addition, however, it appears that Dovzhenko and Solntseva were planning episodes that would have made *Victory in Right Bank Ukraine* a significant attempt to understand the occupation, collaboration, and the Nazis' genocidal pursuits. In a letter dated 5 April 1944, Solntseva requested synchronously recorded sound footage of Ukrainian nationalists: "Make sound recordings of three or four Ukrainian nationalists. Their accounts. Their present position. What they fought for. What Hitler promised them and so on and so on. We are interested in Nationalists who have lived all this period—the 25 years of Soviet rule—in Germany. Or those who became such at the moment the war began. Record the most 'obscene,' 'die-hard.' Using them will make it easier to portray traitors."[60]

If "Ukraine in Flames" was anything to go by, rendering these portraits would have meant depicting the ingrained anti-Semitic thinking of such Ukrainian nationalists and would thus have granted insight into perpetrators of the Holocaust. The filmmakers further planned to include a sequence entitled "Babyi Iar"; archival sources indicate that this segment was filmed but failed to meet technical standards.[61] It is hard to be sure, but this sequence seems to comprise two takes of synchronously recorded sound footage showing a former Red Army soldier talking about his experience as one of three hundred Soviet POWs who were forced to burn the corpses of some one hundred thousand Kiev citizens in Babyi Iar (this footage can be found at the Russian State Archive of Film and Photo Documents). The victims' ethnicities remain unspecified, though other evidence demonstrates that the majority were Jewish. The man says that he was one of the twelve who escaped and concludes: "We managed to escape, and so we can tell the whole world, and our country, about the barbarous acts that the German scum carried out in our beloved Kiev."

If this is indeed the footage to which the correspondence refers, it is possible that the "technical deficiency" consisted in the fact that this man was a former prisoner of war, a category of witness treated with great suspicion by the Soviet authorities. Had these sequences been filmed (in the case of the Ukrainian nationalists) or included in the final film (in the case of the Babyi Iar footage), *Victory in Right Bank Ukraine* would have been a markedly different film that would have offered significant insight into the Holocaust in Ukraine.

Dovzhenko and Solntseva's authority was evidently not what it had been in 1943, however, before the condemnation of "Ukraine in Flames," and the two filmmakers were unable to command the resources or exert the control over the footage that they had previously enjoyed; indeed, the cameramen who were officially allocated to them were reassigned to shoot immediately topical material for newsreels rather than images for this more demanding and ambitious documentary. With time running out, a group consisting of "three camera operators, the producer and the supervisor" was sent to the front to record enough material simply to finish the film, and the ambitious plans for synchronous sound sequences were discarded.[62]

As a result, the finished film includes little footage of Nazi atrocities. To compensate, Dovzhenko's commentary announces a rather novel approach to depicting Nazi crimes, stating that the film will show only a tiny proportion of these atrocities: "We shall refrain from showing horrific sights in this film. We shall not burden the soul with the contemplation of death. We shall not talk of German atrocities, without number and without precedent, of the mother's grief, of Soviet children's gaping wounds, of the millions driven into servitude, of the one in four Ukrainian houses burnt down and of the innumerable ruins of our towns. We shall present to humanity only the most insignificant part of the evil deeds that have been recorded."[63] In keeping with this approach, while the film shows the liberation of Odessa and culminates with that of Lvov, the most important sequence depicting the suffering of Ukraine's civilian population consists in scenes showing the liberation of Kiev, where Dovzhenko's commentary emphasizes above all the fact that the city is deserted: "But why is there no one to meet them? Where are the people? Where are the joyful crowds of the population of Kiev? There is no population of Kiev." Indeed, Dovzhenko reports this sense of desertion and the absence of human life as having been his first impressions on entering the recaptured city on 7 November 1943, mentioning this reaction in his notebooks from that time: "The more I look at Kiev the more I realize what a terrible tragedy it has lived through. Most of the population is gone. Only a small group of impoverished, exhausted people [is] left. No children, no girls, no young men. Only old women and cripples. The world has not seen anything like this in centuries. Before the war Kiev had a population of one million; now there are only about fifty thousand people among the ruins."[64] The film elaborates on this sense of absence, explaining where the dead have gone:

> Here is the population of Kiev. What kind of dour reception is this in the smoke? As if in a dream. How few of them there are. No one recognized the population of Kiev on this day; in fact, they had ceased to recognize themselves, so much had the hard times changed them. Two years of Fascist captivity, like two centuries lived beyond the boundaries of the human, in a plundered city, had left a heavy stamp upon their souls.
>
> Two hundred thousand citizens of the town shot, tortured to death, hanged or poisoned in gas-vans. The others were deported or driven away, hidden in the woods, the ravines, and the graves.

FIGURE 4.6. The empty mass grave at Babyi Iar. From *Victory in Right Bank Ukraine.*

Here people were rounded up with dogs, and people hid, like animals.

In Babyi Iar alone the murderers shot more than one hundred thousand ill-fated citizens. Babes in arms were buried alive in the earth with their murdered mothers, and the earth could be seen rippling, shuddering from the movements of living people.

Here people cried, screamed, cursed, and bid final farewells.

Here small children saw sights unknown to the imagination of the great Dante, who wrote *Inferno.*[65]

The reference to Babyi Iar is accompanied by footage of the site as a group of Soviet military officials found it in November 1943, a grave emptied of its dead (fig. 4.6). It is clear how the former POW's testimony would have fitted in here, for this man was one of those forced to destroy the corpses in the ravine. Instead of explaining the absence of corpses in this way, the camera shows a series of images of the dead, some partially decomposed and still lying buried and some apparently killed recently. It shows grieving relatives, too, and accompanying the final line about small children witnessing unimaginable events, an anxious-looking child stares directly into the camera before the lens turns to ruined buildings and huge piles of rubble.

While the POW's discarded testimony would have enabled Dovzhenko to dwell further on the sense of the destruction and the absence of evidence for the mass murder at Babyi Iar, as well as the problem of finding witnesses, he does illustrate the account of the massacre with images that imply or suggest the true horrors of this site. On a first viewing, these images distract our attention from the uncanny emptiness of the place and from the limitations facing cinema when trying to depict what occurred in the most significant site of Nazi murder in the Soviet Union, whose very name came to stand for the "the Holocaust by bullets." In fact, however, these images are not of Babyi Iar, so that the problem of representing the dead of whom no trace remains returns to haunt the film, and us, its spectators.

In 1945 Dovzhenko rewrote "Ukraine in Flames" as a new screenplay, "Chronicle of Flaming Years" ("Povest′ plamennykh let"), in a further attempt to depict the Nazis' occupation of and mass slaughter in Ukraine, motivated by his compulsion to bear witness and need to grieve: "Only one thing do I need. Not to be deprived of my tears and sorrow for the fifteen million of my suffering people who are dead."[66]

Unfortunately for Dovzhenko, the growing certainty of victory led Soviet authorities increasingly to downplay its price. Although all Dovzhenko's finished documentaries and unfilmed screenplays attempted to offset the suffering of war with some sense of the victory, "tears and sorrow" were no longer a desirable message for the Soviet system, whose functionaries now felt unable to acknowledge the huge cost of the victory, for doing so would have entailed examining the terrible errors of the war's first years—hence the final decision to estimate the total Soviet war dead at a ridiculously low seven million.[67] Dovzhenko's reworked material in "Chronicle of Flaming Years" was thus doomed to suffer the same fate as had "Ukraine in Flames"; having antagonized the leadership, it was never filmed in his lifetime.

Dovzhenko's portrayal of Nazi mass murder in the East was equally controversial in the West. Dovzhenko's name ensured that his films would be of interest there, and *The Battle for Our Soviet Ukraine* was sent to Britain soon after its Moscow premiere. Dovzhenko even stated in his diary that he had made the film with at least half an eye on international audiences: "Iuliia and I made this film more for the whole world, and less for our own audiences."[68]

Nonetheless, the film's frank depiction of Nazi atrocities made it the most heavily censored Soviet wartime film to be shown. In Britain, where a version was made with a commentary by Alexander Werth, the BBC's Moscow correspondent, the film lost eleven minutes, reduced to a less grisly sixty-minute version after the BBFC demanded more than forty cuts to images of corpses (e.g., the one shown in fig. 4.4) and calls for vengeance. Bol´shakov complained to the British about the cuts of these "horrors," arguing that they stripped the film of a great part of its value.[69] Nevertheless, it still presented images of horrific acts committed by the Nazis against the civilian population, including a communal grave in Kharkov, and eyewitness testimony in interviews of atrocities.[70]

As Mikhail Kalatozov reported in December 1943, the film encountered similar difficulties in the United States, where censors demanded the removal of all corpses and "horrors."[71]

But censorship was not the only issue. By the time the film came to the United States (where, in an unintentionally ironic move, it was given the title *Ukraine in Flames*), American-made footage on the brutal fighting in the Pacific, as well as the popularity of American films on the Soviet theme, had reduced the appeal of documentaries about the eastern front. The U.S. version of *The Battle for Our Soviet Ukraine* was limited to specialist cinemas and failed to achieve the wide draw of *Moscow Strikes Back*.[72] The news incensed Dovzhenko: "America has refused to see my *Battle for Our Soviet Ukraine*. She didn't even want to look at the blood she is buying with her canned bacon. Curses on you, ladies and gentlemen of America, with all your prosperity and your gentle smiles. My father and mother and I and all the Ukrainian people curse you."[73]

Dovzhenko's film was both a more explicit and a more thought-provoking depiction of Nazi war crimes than had ever been sent to Britain or the United States. However, his film was mauled by the censors in both places, and audiences proved unresponsive to his message. The wider Anglo-American public would believe the scale of Hitler's exterminatory policies only when shown images of the concentration camps filmed by their own.

In "Chronicle of Flaming Years," however, Dovzhenko returned to the theme of the mass grave that he had explored in his documentaries about Drobitskii Iar and Babyi Iar. This time he depicted the story of Antonina, a Ukrainian woman who, having fallen into a pit during a mobile killing squad operation, was left for dead but crawled out at night and survived.[74] Once again, Dovzhenko's narrative attempts to define the Nazi-inflicted suffering of Ukraine as Ukrainian. Another filmmaker, however, arrived in Kiev nearly eight months after its liberation to make a feature film depicting the occupation.[75] After interviewing individuals who had, like Dovzhenko's fictional Antonina, survived the Einsatzgruppen Aktion at Babyi Iar, this man, Mark Donskoi, became determined to make a film that portrayed the Nazis' persecution and extermination of Ukraine's Jews as well. Shortly before Dovzhenko finished the screenplay for "Chronicle of Flaming Years," in September 1945, Donskoi had completed his film, *The Unvanquished,* at Kiev studios.

# 5 \ Mark Donskoi's Reconstruction of Babyi Iar

*THE UNVANQUISHED*

**When Aleksandr** Dovzhenko arrived in liberated Kiev in November 1943, his dramatic fall from grace had just commenced, but when Mark Donskoi got there a few months later, in the summer of 1944, he stood at the peak of his reputation as a filmmaker. His earlier film of the Ukrainian occupation, *The Rainbow,* had been released in January of that year to universal acclaim, leading to his being awarded the Stalin Prize First Class and his admission into the Soviet Communist Party; now he was committed to another film about the occupation, an adaptation of Boris Gorbatov's Stalin Prize–winning novel *The Unvanquished,* published the previous year.[1] While Donskoi saw the project as something of a sequel to his earlier work, the new film was to present a picture of the Ukrainian occupation dramatically different from that in *The Rainbow,* which had emphasized heroic, uncompromising resistance but kept silent as to the fate of Ukraine's Jews specifically.[2] Unlike many Soviet wartime films, which sought to marginalize depictions of anti-Jewish persecutions, *The Unvanquished* would depart radically from its literary source precisely to amplify and extend the depiction of such persecution. What caused this transformation?

Primarily, this shift seems to have arisen from the director's firsthand experience: as an Odessan Jew, Donskoi's native city had been occupied and its enormous prewar Jewish population annihilated, along with much

FIGURE 5.1. Mark Donskoi's war correspondent ID, valid 7 June–31 December 1944. Courtesy of Muzei kino.

of Soviet Jewry. It is hard to imagine that this did not affect the director personally. Moreover, in June 1944, Donskoi received accreditation as a war correspondent that enabled him to move freely in Kiev, liberated only months earlier, researching and conducting interviews about the occupation (fig. 5.1). He appears to have immediately visited Babyi Iar, where he interviewed witnesses and survivors, and also spent a great deal of time in private conversation with Zinovii Rodianskii, a cameraman who had filmed Nazi atrocities at the site.[3] In addition, filming for *The Unvanquished* began on 23 August,[4] just weeks after the liberation of the Majdanek death camp, and Gorbatov, who not only had written the novel but, with Donskoi, coauthored the subsequent screenplay, had visited and written about the camp for *Pravda* (see chapter 6). Perhaps this experience led him to expand his novel's material about the slaughter of Jews or to let Donskoi do so.

The debate provoked by the U.S. release of *The Rainbow* in the autumn of that year further encouraged this expansion; as the discussion in chapter 3 details, the film met harsh criticism in the United States for its depiction of Nazi atrocities and for articulating the Soviets' savage hatred toward the occupiers. Donskoi was shocked that his portrayal of the occupation had provoked such hostility.[5] In defending the film, he argued that it reflected actual events, and perhaps this line of thought led him to anchor the subsequent film even more strongly in the "real" basis of eyewitness testimony and genuine locations. Moreover, the emphasis on Soviet interethnic harmony and the Nazis' murder of Jews is possibly intended as a riposte to his American critics, whom Soviets perceived as being as particularly responsive to the Nazis' attacks on Jews, as is evidenced by Solomon Mikhoels's fundraising trip to the United States, Canada, and Britain in 1943. Once again, an attempt to reckon with a Western audience was influencing a Soviet depiction of the war.

### The Unvanquished

*The Unvanquished* tells the story of a master metalworker named Taras Iatsenko (played by the prominent Ukrainian actor Amvrosii Buchma) and his family in an unnamed Ukrainian town during the Nazi occupation (1941–1943).[6] Taras returns to work only at gunpoint, and even then he leads passive resistance to the new regime at the factory. His children include one son, Stepan (Daniil Segal), who leads the partisans; another son, Andrei, who is stigmatized for having surrendered to the Germans; and a daughter, Nastia, who joins the partisans and is hanged by the occupiers. The film ends with the town's liberation by the Red Army (including a now redeemed Andrei).[7]

While the film encompasses several aspects of the occupation, including partisan warfare and the dilemmas facing workers and peasants under Nazi rule, its most remarkable dimension emerges in a secondary plotline following a Iatsenko family friend, the Jewish doctor Aron Davidovich Fishman, played by Veniamin Zuskin; one of the Moscow Jewish Theater's most famous actors, Zuskin had also starred in Vladimir Korsh-Sablin's wildly popular Jewish-themed comedy *Seekers of Happiness* (*Iskateli shchast'ia* [1936]). Donskoi and Gorbatov gave much greater importance to Dr. Fishman than the character enjoys in the novel; though Fishman appears in the film only three times and receives little screen time, the role was nonetheless significantly expanded from the marginal part the character plays in the literary source.[8]

From the very first scene, where Dr. Fishman is shown treating Iatsenko's granddaughter, the film reveals the story of Dr. Fishman and the town's other Jews through Taras's eyes. This immediately establishes a parallel between Taras and the physician and presents a vision of interethnic harmony between Ukrainians and Jews under Soviet rule.

This opening scene ends with Aron Davidovich refusing to hide in Taras's house out of a sense of duty to his patients. We are not told why he should want to stay with Taras, for the particular danger facing Jews is not spelled out. In addition, no one explicitly refers to his ethnicity, though his name (especially his patronymic, which translates as "son of David"), his appearance, the casting of Zuskin to play him, and even his profession would almost certainly have led most Soviet viewers to surmise that Dr. Fishman is Jewish. Nevertheless, the offer to stay makes sense only if one is aware that the Nazi threat was greater for Jews than for other Soviet citizens. The film thus appears to hint at the dire situation of Jews under Nazi rule, as did the numerous newsreels that named obviously Jewish victims.

Never a subtle director, however, Donskoi was not willing to confine himself to allusions. The next time we see Aron Davidovich, he is selling his possessions at the market; evidently, the occupying regime has removed him from his position as a doctor. When Taras sees Fishman in this scene, his eyes are immediately drawn to the Star of David armband the doctor is wearing on his sleeve, and the editing emphasizes this through a close-up of Taras looking at the armband, underlining Dr. Fishman's Jewish identity more explicitly than anywhere else in the film (figs. 5.2 and 5.3). The scene ends as the two characters flee a roundup, and fearing the worst, Fishman entrusts his granddaughter to Taras. The plotting and editing here once again stress the parallels between the two men in their shared concern for their grandchildren.

The film's broader structure also invites viewers to compare the resistance of Taras's son Stepan; the apparent collaboration of Vasilek, the sweetheart of Taras's daughter Nastia and now a member of the German-controlled police; and the secret resistance of Ignat Nesoglasnyi, a kolkhoznik. The film shows Dr. Fishman to be suffering the most under the occupation and makes it clear that he does so because he is a Jew. The "director's literary scenario" also tries to develop a counterpoint to the scenes of resistance and interethnic harmony, as it does, for example, in a scene where the German commandant and one of his officers discuss how to foment tensions between Ukrainians and Russians and refer to their plan to kill the Jews first, without hiding it, before employing more subtle measures to destroy the leaders of the Russian population.[9] As a clear reference to the Nazis' particularly fierce hatred for the Jews over other Soviet citizens, the scene was cut. Donskoi nevertheless managed to portray the murder of Jews in a scene where Taras and the doctor meet for the final time, when Taras is marching in a funeral procession for a fellow metalworker whom the Nazis killed for his defiance. The mourners come across virtually all the town's Jews being led away to be shot, and seeing Dr. Fishman among them, Taras bows to him. Fishman is surprised and asks Taras whether he is really bowing to *him*. Taras replies: "To you and your sufferings." Fishman replies: "Thank you, human being" (fig. 5.4).

FIGURE 5.2. Taras encounters Aron Davidovich at the market. From *The Unvanquished*.

FIGURE 5.3. Insert of Taras looking at Aron Davidovich's armband. From *The Unvanquished*.

FIGURE 5.4. Aron Davidovich's last words, addressed to Taras, "Thank you, human being." From *The Unvanquished*.

These are his last words. During production, Donskoi was told to remove this scene, but he insisted on its importance.[10]

Taras remains rooted to the spot, watching the column of Jews being led away. The director's literary script had Taras muttering under his breath: "Goodbye Dr. Aron Davidovich. Forgive me: there was no way I could save you."[11] The film then shows the Jews in a ravine where they are shot. This episode stands out from the rest of the film, for it is the only time the Jews are shown through an impersonal narrative focus. Previously we had seen them, figured in the character of Fishman, only through the eyes of Taras when he encounters the doctor; here, for the first time, we see Jews not just in the person of the doctor but as a group, and their fate is portrayed as a matter of intrinsic interest. At their previous two meetings, we could draw a parallel between Aron Davidovich and Taras, but here only contrasts are possible: the Ukrainians are persecuted for specific acts of resistance; the Jews are all killed solely for being Jewish.

While these three episodes do not occupy the majority of screen time, for the film treats many aspects of the occupation, they constitute by far its most poignant subplot. The scene of the mass killing provides the film's emotional and visual climax, as is evident from the way the narrative seems to lose direction after it. Like many others, Donskoi faced a difficulty fundamental to attempts to depict the Holocaust in narrative form: the incompatibility of such a traumatic scene with narrative as such, an issue that has been described in a number of theorizations of memory with regard to the Holocaust, especially that of trauma theory.[12]

Nevertheless, the film does continue, and despite apparently having witnessed the destruction of the town's Jews, Taras never mentions what he has seen. This silence weighs down the scene following the massacre as Taras listens to the innocent song sung by the doctor's granddaughter; he cannot communicate his knowledge of her family's fate to her. Grief here is not instrumentalized but incommunicable. The presence of the doctor's granddaughter serves as a reminder of the theme of Jewish persecution, with Taras's family hiding the girl from the authorities. Here the film anticipates the trope of the Jewish child hidden by Gentile resisters, in essence the story of Anne Frank, whose diary and its screen and stage adaptations have long ranked among the most influential images of the Holocaust in the West.[13] Like Anne, Dr. Fishman's granddaughter is discovered, but unlike her, and in a departure from Gorbatov's novel, she is saved by Vasilek, a police officer working for the partisans.[14]

The fact that the one major character who appears to be a collaborator is in fact a partisan typifies the film's treatment of the Ukrainian population, implying a deep solidarity among all Soviet citizens and a refusal to collaborate among Ukrainians.[15] But Ukrainian police uniforms are clearly visible in the scene of the Jews' massacre, and Taras apparently stands alone in his concern for Aron Davidovich's fate; we see no one else reacting to the mass slaughter of the town's Jews. Indeed, Aron Davidovich is not just moved but also surprised by Taras's bow, which suggests the exceptional nature of this respect.

In any event, while this emphasis on the warm relations between these two people might appear to misleadingly imply interethnic harmony, the focus on the fate of the one Jewish girl who survives strikes the most problematically optimistic note. In clutching her doll, Dr. Fishman's unnamed granddaughter serves, as Margolit has argued, as an image of embryonic motherhood, functioning as an image of hope, of the future of the Jewish people (fig. 5.5).[16] Here *The Unvanquished* may be accused of falling into the same trap as Spielberg's *Schindler's List,* that of emphasizing a single individual saved as cause for optimism to counterbalance the morally dev-

FIGURE 5.5. Aron Davidovich's granddaughter with her doll. From *The Unvanquished*.

astating perspective of the unimaginably greater loss of life. Such a move looks more like the Americanization of the Holocaust than the Sovietization of it. Moreover, while this is just an episode, and the film does not return to the theme of the Jews in its last half-hour, it nevertheless ends upliftingly with the liberation of the town and a call for reconstruction. These optimistic distortions, however, arise from the economy of filmic representation, from the need to continue a story and project a future for the Jewish people and Soviet society. They do not detract substantially from the originality and power marking the representation of the massacre. This extraordinary episode warrants careful consideration not just in its mobilization of filmmaking's technical and narrative resources but also in its interaction with historical events, its approach to reconstruction.

## Babyi Iar: History, Authenticity, and Reconstruction

Gorbatov set his novel in the Donetsk region in eastern Ukraine, including recognizable locations, such as Ostraia mogila, that identify his hometown of Voroshilovgrad (now Lugansk), where he had conducted interviews after its liberation in February 1943.[17] The book represents events in that town, including the murder of its Jewish residents.[18] The massacre of the Jews in Voroshilovgrad happened much as similar events did elsewhere in occupied Soviet territory: in November and December 1941, eight thousand Jews were ordered to assemble and then were taken outside the city and shot by units of the Einsatzgruppen.[19]

Donskoi's film, however, was filmed at the Kiev film studios immediately after the liberation. Donskoi conducted interviews with witnesses to and survivors of Nazi atrocities in Kiev and filmed the massacre scene on the actual location of Babyi Iar (fig. 5.6). The importance of the massacre scene for Donskoi is evident from the fact that he expanded it from a single sentence in Gorbatov's novel: "The Jews were shot somewhere outside the town."[20] This is very much a directorial intervention added to the original source. The film does not explicitly name Babyi Iar, but as Donskoi made clear in discussions of the film, he had this historical reference in mind in shooting the scene and based it on eyewitness testimony concerning events there:

> We began making the film *The Unvanquished* in Kiev as soon as the city was liberated by the Red Army.
> We had to sidestep mined areas in choosing our location site.
> Ruins and rubble served as real life settings.
> At every step we met people who became our assistants, people who reestablished the truth and who understood the nature of the Germans all too deeply and exactly.
> When we were filming the scene showing the shooting of Jews at Babyi Iar, we received consultation on this scene from people who had miraculously lived through this butchery, people who had been shot on this very spot. They had been wounded, and in the dead of night, they had crawled out from under the mounds of dead bodies among which were their own kith and kin.
> They escaped alive, and these witnesses of the monstrous Nazi atrocities now helped us to reproduce the appalling truth for the annals of history.
> Leah Gershman is not a fictitious person. Leah Gershman was one of those who lived through experiences that no words can describe.
> These people not only helped us to recreate this ghastly scene in all its truth and fearsomeness. . . [but] also fired our emotions.[21]

Given that virtually all postwar Soviet accounts claimed the scale of Jewish suffering to have been far lower than it was, identifying the episode

FIGURE 5.6. Filming *The Unvanquished* at Babyi Iar, 1944. Courtesy of Emma Malaia.

as a depiction of Babyi Iar was a provocative move, for the name was effectively a code for the wider "Holocaust by bullets" and for the fact that those murdered were Jews killed for their ethnicity rather than for being Soviet.[22] Reenacting such massacres for the screen remains a controversial approach to depicting the Holocaust, and the Holocaust survivor Elie Wiesel has condemned the reenactment of the Babyi Iar massacre specifically:

> Certain productions dazzle with their authenticity; others shock with their vulgarity. *Night and Fog* on one side, *Holocaust* on the other. Up against Hollywood superproductions, can poetic memory hold its own? Me, I prefer it. I prefer restraint to excess, the murmur of documentary to the script edited by tear-jerk specialists. To direct the massacre of Babi Yar smells of blasphemy. To make up extras as corpses is obscene. Perhaps I am too severe, too demanding, but the Holocaust as filmed romantic adventure seems to me an outrage to the memory of the dead, and to sensitivity.[23]

While Wiesel's comments are directed against the *Holocaust* miniseries, produced in the United States, they may be applied to Donskoi's film, too, at least to some degree. While its highly Soviet seriousness of moral purpose dispels any potential charge that it is a romantic adventure, it too attempts to elicit from us the kind of emotional response associated with art by showing people pretending to die. Donskoi too "direct[s] the massacre of Babi Yar." The question is whether Donskoi's film does something worthwhile, either by telling us something about the Holocaust that was not already known or by conveying a sense of the events more profoundly or to a wider group of people than previous efforts had managed to do.

Curiously, much the same question was raised even before the film was released, in an industry screening at the Artistic Council of the Ministry of Cinematography, in Moscow. The actor Boris Babochkin, famous for his performance in the title role of Georgii and Sergei Vasiliev's wildly popular prewar film *Chapaev* (1934), objected to the portrayal of the mass killing as moving but not art: "I consider that this scene is inadmissible, because it does not contain the essential elements of art. It has the gory naturalism of *guignol,* it cannot fail to distress you, but this cannot be considered an element of art. I feel that we do not have the right to show such scenes to our public."[24]

Donskoi's film was defended by the director of 1930s Lenin films turned 1960s liberal Mikhail Romm: "I don't agree with Babochkin that we shouldn't show the scenes of the shooting. . . . If, in these last years[,] the extermination of three and a half million Jews has taken place in Europe, and we haven't uttered a word about it, didn't say anything about it in our films, and if in this film the mass extermination of Jews is shown in a single image, then I believe we must keep these images."[25] Indeed, Romm's justification for depicting the massacre ultimately proved the one most often advanced: the need both to make the public aware of the fate of the Jews and to comment on, condemn, and commemorate this event. Yet doing so in a feature film raised crucial questions—namely, whether cinema possesses the appropriate means to do this and what those means might be.

The film's representation of the massacre broadly repeats what we know from eyewitness accounts: armed soldiers and police officers accompanied by dogs drive the town's Jews to a ravine in the countryside where the victims are then shot. The episode in Donskoi's film, however, differs from the actual events in certain significant ways that serve to articulate a distinct directorial commentary on the events depicted.

Thus, for example, witness accounts reveal that the victims were made to undress before they were shot, but the film does not show this.[26] Instead it shows Aron Davidovich in his shirt sleeves and a piece of clothing

FIGURE 5.7. Scarf snagged on a tree. From *The Unvanquished*.

snagged on a bush and fluttering in the wind. Perhaps considerations of prudery or decency dictated this change, but the scene nevertheless subtly suggests the actual circumstances of the victims' deaths while restoring a certain dignity that their murderers had stripped from them (fig. 5.7).

Donskoi would return to the emblem of a black scarf snagged against a tree, using it in his 1962 film *Hello, Children (Zdravstvuite deti)*, where a Japanese child's latent traumatic memory of the nuclear bomb blast in Hiroshima returns when she sees an almost identical scarf snagged on yet another tree. In addition, the first scarf evokes a further Soviet representation of the Holocaust in a series of paintings by Zinovii Tolkachev, one of which, entitled *Taleskoten,* shows a tallit, a Jewish ritual prayer shawl, snagged on the barbed-wire fence around Majdanek. This image stands out from the rest of Tolkachev's series as the only one to identify victims as Jewish, although it does so somewhat subtly, in a way that might be opaque to many non-Jewish viewers. For some it has an optimistic dimension: "the garment is not just caught on the wire, it waves in the breeze like a flag. It is a symbol not only of the dead, but of Judaism's ability to rise triumphant over the camps."[27] Ultimately, though, it serves as a symbol of loss, and this image of the tallit has been interpreted as referring to

FIGURE 5.8. Aron Davidovich appearing to pray. From *The Unvanquished.*

God's failure to respond or intervene to save his chosen people.[28] Given Gorbatov's visit to Majdanek, which almost certainly coincided with Tolkachev's time there, Donskoi probably knew of this image. Even so, though his black snagged scarf may invoke Tolkachev's *Taleskoten,* it is far more unambiguously despairing than Tolkachev's image.

Donskoi's depiction of the massacre also appears both to evoke Judaism as a marker of the victims' identity and to imply the absence of God. Thus, the scene begins with frames of a machine gun firing from the top of the ravine, but the camera then shifts to a group of Jews who, though in the ravine, seem not to be under fire. An image of clouds passing across a dark sky then ensues, apparently an attempt to re-create the point of view of victims who are looking to the heavens and perhaps hoping that God will intervene or desperately appealing to God to do so. Aron Davidovich is one of the figures shown in close-up here. The impression of an appeal to God is strengthened as the dramatic nondiegetic music pauses (fig. 5.8).[29]

Many eyewitness accounts describe Jewish victims of the Nazis reciting Hebrew prayers prior to death, asserting the sometimes long-dormant Jewish identity for which they were being murdered, even in the face of the despairing doubt that the Holocaust cast on the existence of a divine order. As the poet Abraham Sutzkever wrote while trapped in the Vilnius ghetto: "I feel like saying a prayer—but to whom?"[30] Donskoi's film expressionistically silences the sounds of gunfire and occludes any images of violence to permit these images of implied prayer, albeit apparently silent, that render the victims' last thoughts. In doing so, Donskoi restores to the victims a measure of the dignity that they might otherwise have found in different deaths, a dignity denied them by their executioners. Indeed, Taras ends the previous scene by saying of his metalworking colleague: "They not only deprived you of an honorable life, but also of an honorable death." This comment is even more appropriate to the Jews than to Taras's colleague, and the sequence of the massacre seems to impart a solemn majesty to their last moments. Indeed, the convoy of Jews being led to their deaths interrupts the metalworker's funeral procession, as if the murder of the Jews continues and consummates the metalworker's funeral, which we never see completed. The impetus and focus of the mourning shifts from the Ukrainians to the Jews.

The aesthetic force of the sequence emerges in part from its resonance with the great themes that Donskoi repeated throughout his work as a director: death and religious beliefs and rituals pertaining to it. Yet this scene portrays death quite differently than does Donskoi's previous film, *The Rainbow,* where the main character's murder is immediately avenged by the execution of a collaborator.[31] Indeed, as I showed in chapters 2 and 3, Soviet portrayals of Nazi atrocities typically assert or suggest that such deaths will be avenged by victory, as with the tradition of the socialist martyr's funeral.[32] *The Unvanquished* stands out in this respect because the massacre of the Jews does not elicit a call to vengeance, even though the director's screenplay describes the music as doing so.[33] The sequence does not immediately give way to images of the onward march of victory or a successful partisan operation. Moreover, the Jews do not die with words of defiance, predictions of victory, or Soviet patriotism on their lips, as they do in Ehrenburg's depiction of the same events in his 1947 novel *The Storm* (*Buria*).[34] This shift of emphasis seems to have been an important one for Donskoi, as he deliberately moved away from an early version of the scene that resembled Ehrenburg's approach, in that Aron Davidovich was forcibly led to his death, struggling against his captors, and shouting defiant but inaudible words.[35] Instead, the doctor dies while seeming to intone a presumably Jewish prayer. Nonetheless, as with other Soviet films that depict the persecution of Jews, such as *Professor Mamlock* and *A Priceless Head,* insisting on the victims' Jewish identity carries a cost: they must become passive victims, for active resistance must be identified with others—in this case, the Ukrainian characters, especially Stepan, a Communist, and Nastia, a member of the Young Communist League.[36] Yet it is precisely this crucial insistence on the victims' Jewish identity that elevates the film above other Soviet wartime depictions of the Holocaust, making it a powerful response to the Babyi Iar massacre as yet unsurpassed in fiction film.

Donskoi's depiction of the mass killing also responds to and reworks another Soviet cliché, namely, images emphasizing child victims as an index of extreme Nazi cruelty. The director's screenplay has an old man with hair "as white as the moon" holding up a child to the sun in protest at what is happening. In the final version of the scene, Donskoi expressed his emotional involvement by having his own son, Alexander, play a child with dark curly hair whom the old man holds (fig. 5.9).[37] The extratextual fact of this casting takes the Soviet habit of encouraging the spectator to identify with the Nazis' victims one step further. Although it is not evident to the uninformed, it provides a haunting but encrypted declaration that the filmmaker is personally implicated in the Holocaust.

Such an identification with the victims is an extremely important dimension of the scene, since many wartime images of the Holocaust were taken either from the perpetrator's point of view, as was the extant footage of Einsatzgruppen killings, or in a highly dehumanizing manner, as was most of the footage showing the liberation of concentration camps, especially that taken by British and American camera crews in Germany (see chapter 6). In *The Unvanquished,* the fate of Europe's Jews has until this point been refracted through the perspective of the Ukrainians, as it is in the literary source, through Taras's meetings with Aron Davidovich. In this scene, however, as was previously mentioned, the camera follows the column of Jews after Taras has left with the funeral cortege. The camera's point of view is mobile and suggests an omniscient narrator's perspective, with a dominance of high-angle setups framed neither as the point of view of the Nazis, that of the Jews, nor even that of a third-person witness. Indeed, while Aron Davidovich is the only familiar character here, he is not especially prominent but rather one of several people briefly portrayed in a close-up or medium-range shot. The effect is to shift our attention from him as an individual to the Jews as a whole.

Donskoi's film further differs from accounts of the events at Babyi Iar

FIGURE 5.9. Donskoi's son, Aleksandr. From *The Unvanquished*.

in following the pause with a scene showing a line of advancing soldiers shooting the gathered Jews (fig. 5.10). Witnesses to the massacre, however, have said that most victims were made to lie face down on the ground, at which point the members of the killing units shot them in the backs of their necks; in other cases, the victims were shot from behind as they stood at the edge of the ravine.[38] The director's screenplay, too, pictures people being shot at the top of the ravine and falling in,[39] but in the image of the advancing line of soldiers firing into the crowd, Donskoi seems to have been influenced more by the Odessa steps sequence from Sergei Eisenstein's *Battleship "Potemkin"* than by concerns for strict historical accuracy. We even see the image of a small girl staggering toward the soldiers and begging for mercy only to be shot, further echoing Eisenstein (fig. 5.11). This departure from the historical record seems to have sprung from a desire to exploit the cinematic potential of the site and to create a more cinematically moving and engaging image. This is problematic territory, for contemplating such a powerful scene can yield a form of aesthetic pleasure, and any sense of pleasure in viewing such images is deeply troubling, as Wiesel's remarks suggest.[40]

FIGURE 5.10. Reconstruction of massacre of Jews at Babyi Iar. From *The Unvanquished*.

FIGURE 5.11. A wounded girl stumbles towards her executioners. From *The Unvanquished*.

Yet Donskoi, working from the basic premise of Soviet cinema, whose prime function is to educate and inform, chose to reconstruct the scene. Having made this decision, he was compelled to make the scene as effective as he could, even if this meant taking liberties with historical detail, since he could convey the awful nature of the events only if the scene could shock and move the spectator. Donskoi also accorded himself a certain creative freedom in depicting the Jews with armbands; Kiev's Jews were never forced to wear them, because they were killed only ten days after the initial occupation. In reconstructing the scene at Babyi Iar, however, itself a metonymic image for the Holocaust by bullets, Donskoi was not seeking to represent events in Kiev but creating something of a composite image of the Holocaust in all of Ukraine, incorporating details from a number of sources and elaborating on them through his imagination and talent as an artist so as to produce an image that relates the underlying story of the massacre in a way no documentary record of the atrocity could ever hope to match.

## The Fate of the Film in the Soviet Union

At the previously mentioned Artistic Council discussion of the film, Mikhail Romm stated that the film would be successful both domestically and abroad.[41] He was wrong on both counts. *The Unvanquished* was the first postliberation Kiev studio production, a further sign of the esteem in which Donskoi was then held. The location scenes appear to have been completed by the end of October 1944, leaving only the studio work to be finished and prompting newspapers to mention a potential release date of February 1945.[42] The film was actually finished in June, when it was discussed at the Artistic Council meeting, but it was not released until autumn, opening in Moscow on 15 October 1945 and in Kiev a week later, on 23 October—four months after the Artistic Council discussion and nearly a full year after the close of location work.

Unsurprisingly, the council's discussion focused on the sense that the film deviates from the original literary source. This troubled a number of those present, including Babochkin[43] and Ivan Pyr'ev, who objected in particular to the expansion of the doctor's role at the expense of other material. Pyr'ev criticized the scene showing the massacre of the town's Jews, calling it a "theft of what was in the story" because it sidelined the sufferings of other, Slavic characters.[44] In other words, Donskoi's depiction of the Jewish victims' deaths steals from the wider Soviet and Russian suffering. Writing later and publicly, however, Pyr'ev employed more measured, less transparently anti-Semitic tones, describing the film as an example of a director's too close identification with his actors, making it hard to say where the director ended and the actor began and culminating in a sort of "naturalism."[45] "Naturalism" was a frequently used code word for depictions that contradicted established political conventions. Nevertheless, after Gorbatov crucially intervened in the debate to defend Donskoi's interpretation of his novel as true to life and to insist that he had no complaints as to its adaptation, the film was passed for release.[46]

Despite these travails, the press in both Moscow and Kiev greeted *The Unvanquished* with a fanfare of publicity involving weeks of eye-catching advertisements. In Moscow it was shown in eleven of the city's biggest cinemas. In half-ruined Kiev it initially appeared in four cinemas, but within four days this number has fallen to two because the Frank Borzage film *His Butler's Sister* (1943), starring Deanna Durbin, pushed it from the prominent Pioneer cinema, and by 3 November it had disappeared from Kiev screens altogether.

Something similar happened in Moscow, where on 29 October the film suddenly vanished from those eleven Moscow screens, replaced by an older Deanna Durbin classic, Henry Koster's *Spring Parade* (1940), with no explanation. The ads for the film disappeared at the same time, but the film clearly had a certain word-of-mouth appeal, for it was shown in various cinemas in Moscow until the end of November, when it was replaced with a special-release newsreel of the famous soccer match between Chelsea FC and Dinamo Moscow.

There had clearly been a high-level decision to end publicity for the film and to withdraw it from the most prominent cinemas without actually banning it. These developments occurred just days after *Pravda* published an ambivalent review of Donskoi's film. This review, which appeared on 24 October 1945, was written by Sergei Borzenko, who had been named Hero of the Soviet Union and was a highly authoritative figure.[47] Borzenko emphasized the theme of labor as being the most successful in the film and praised Buchma's performance, but he ended his article by implicitly yet unambiguously condemning Donskoi's treatment of the Jewish theme:

> The film has some contentious moments. On the whole V. Zuskin, People's artist of the RSFSR [Russian Soviet Federative Socialist Republic], played the role of Doctor Aron Davidovich expressively, but

in his performance Aron Davidovich submits to his fate too much. The filmmakers were unsuccessful in their depiction of the scene of the mass shooting of Soviet people by the Nazis. In the film our people are shown going to their death unflinchingly and humbly, whereas from life we know that in such cases even those not strong in spirit broke up paving stones and threw them at their murderers.[48]

Not only does this review virtually ignore the character of Fishman, but it never mentions the word *Jew* and criticizes the passivity of the victims, which, as I have discussed, challenged the representational cliché of the dead as martyrs to a meaningful Soviet cause. The victims' passivity is a vital part of depicting their identity as Jews, since unlike other Soviet citizens, Jews were killed whether or not they actively resisted the Nazis. While a number of earlier reviews had praised the film, with writers for *Pravda Ukrainy* and *Komsomol'skaia pravda* among those touching on the Jewish theme, reviews in *Pravda* were widely perceived as authoritative and often expressed Stalin's own opinion.[49] Consequently, the film soon faded from view, though without having been banned. That would not happen until 20 May 1952, when it was formally removed from circulation "definitively."[50]

### Reception of the Film in the West

The film was forgotten in part because it is uneven, hiding its most powerful story within a more clichéd and diffuse one and thereby losing dramatic impact. Moreover, even before the end of the war, audiences and critics in Britain and the United States were already tired of war-related films in general and were losing their recently acquired appetite for Soviet war films in particular. British distributors thus rejected the film, and the same weary attitude was evident at the film's New York premiere as *The Taras Family* on 7 December 1946. Nevertheless, Bosley Crowther of the *New York Times* praised the film as superior to other recent films in the war genre and specifically mentioned "the machine-gunning of the Jews . . . pictured in a dramatic and horrible scene."[51]

A sense that the film dwells on past atrocities at too great a length and with too vengeful a tone dominates the *Variety* review: "The overlong cycle of Russian films treating with Nazi brutality—and in this case, coupled with fierce demands for revenge—is followed through in *The Taras Family*."[52] Nevertheless, *Variety* does discuss the film's portrayal of persecution of the Jews: "Heralded as the first Soviet film to dramatize the Nazi discriminatory policy against the Jews in German-occupied Russia, *Taras* actually focuses on a Russian family (Slavic) and Teutonic efforts to force reopening of an arms factory. Jewish question is treated in a few episodes, dramatically—the most effective in the film, one, a terrifying hunt for Jewish hideaways; the other, a brutal mass slaughter. The latter has impact despite some sloppy . . . camera work."[53]

Broadly then, audiences in the United States were typically attentive to the film's portrayal of the persecution of Jews, but their flagging interest in war films limited its reception there. In France and Italy, whose populations had been denied the Soviet view of the war during the occupation and were now receptive to it, the situation was largely reversed. The film garnered acclaim when it was shown at the 1946 Venice Film Festival,[54] after which the influential film critic Umberto Barbaro (1902–1959), writing in the Italian Communist Party daily *L'Unità,* praised *The Unvanquished* above all for its exploration of "resistance and war": "The only people who do not appreciate the themes of the Resistance and the War are either those who did not experience it or those who think they came through it unscathed: these are topics we will never tire of expanding upon or talking about as long as there exists in Europe and in Italy incomprehension of that part of our most recent history which we would want everyone to understand."[55]

Still, notwithstanding all its praise for the discussion of resistance and war, Barbaro's review says nothing whatsoever about the film's Jewish theme. French reviewers similarly avoided mentioning the victims' Jewishness, although they paid a great deal of attention to the massacre itself. The first French screenings appear to have occurred on 4 May 1949, when the film was shown in three Parisian cinemas. One review praised it for sequences such as that of the massacre and the return of Taras, as well as for its beautiful photography, but criticized it for having too many long scenes in the same location.[56] Here too none of the published responses explicitly refers to Jews, although the previously mentioned review and at least one other person characterize the massacre scene as one of the film's most effective episodes.[57] The most striking evaluation comes from a viewer named Andrée Arnaud: "Only those who suffered the occupation can understand and judge. A moving film, even its slowness was only too meaningful. Was the oppression not itself interminable? . . . Propaganda! Some will say. I would answer those people: a necessary reminder."[58] Despite this belated French and Italian appreciation for the film's portrayal of the occupation, the film made little impact in the West and was soon forgotten. An untimely Holocaust film, *The Unvanquished* was probably not shown anywhere else outside the Eastern Bloc.[59]

### And in the East . . .

Despite its lackluster reception in the West, *The Unvanquished* made its greatest impact with Eastern Europe's emergent new cinema and left its most lasting legacy in Poland, where the film was screened in May 1946 under the title *Fathers and Sons*. In particular, its use of real locations for reconstructing witnessed memory anticipated and inspired the Polish director Wanda Jakubowska, whose film *Last Stage* (*Ostatni etap* [1948]) stands among the first feature films to depict the war's anti-Jewish atrocities and thus is seen as "a special landmark in the history of the Holocaust film."[60] *Last Stage* was filmed at the Auschwitz camp by Bentsion (Boris) Monastyrskii, the director of photography whom Donskoi had used as well.[61] This kinship points to *The Unvanquished* as the hitherto unacknowledged progenitor of a genre of Eastern European feature films of the Holocaust made in the late 1940s; this group includes the Czech director Alfred Radok's *Distant Journey* (*Daleka Ćesta* [1948]) and the Polish director Aleksandr Ford's film *Border Street* (*Ulica Graniczna* [1949]).

Recent histories describe these films, some of which have only recently come to a wider public, as possessing an authenticity deriving from their makers' temporal and spatial proximity to the events reconstructed in them.[62] Mark Donskoi's film can be added to the list of rediscoveries; indeed, it is a pivotal film that clearly paved the way for Jakubowska and others.

This proximity suffers from its own blind spots, however, and some critics have argued that the moral polarities and melodramatic action of Jakubowska's film undermine the power of its "apparent authenticity, deriving from the actual location and the firsthand experience of those involved in its making."[63] Chernenko similarly criticizes the emotional excess of these films' "sentimental-naturalistic cine-lamentations."[64] While meant as criticisms, such observations apply equally to *The Unvanquished*; the production's proximity to events and the filmmakers' access to witness testimony endow the film not only with its aura of authenticity but also with its powerful emotional tenor.

Certainly some critics, including the writer Konstantin Simonov, already perceived *The Unvanquished* to be less a reconstruction of recent events than a historical film, one to be measured by the yardstick of history.[65] Yet as Romm had pointed out, the murder of Soviet Jews had hardly been represented at all on the Soviet screen; indeed, it had received precious little attention in the press and literature. In view of the film's pioneering theme, it would be harsh to demand of Donskoi's film the distance and objectivity associated with the historical voice. Made in the immediate aftermath of the events it depicts, *The Unvanquished* is squeezed between conflicting imperatives. On the one hand, it is still colored by the wartime imperative to show Nazi atrocities as part of a propagandist strategy; on the other, its representation of the Babyi Iar massacre resists the moral economy of compensation by vengeance or victory, with that representation standing somehow outside the film, looking forward in its attempt to visualize an often marginalized aspect of the Holocaust and commemorating the victims and their profaned grave. Even before the war ended, the price paid for victory was increasingly deemed an untimely subject for Soviet propaganda, and the depiction of atrocities was no longer seen as an important subject for cinema.[66] Soviet newsreel cinema had to negotiate the same shifting demands on filmmakers at the liberated death camps at Auschwitz and Majdanek.

# 6 \ Liberation of the Camps

**On 24 July 1944** the Red Army liberated the Majdanek death camp, near Lublin, Poland. Despite the catalog of appalling Nazi crimes already uncovered by the Soviets, all who saw the first captured *Vernichtungslager* were shocked by the industrial efficiency and sheer scale of the murder perpetrated there.[1] Recognizing the news value of this discovery and needing to prove their moral superiority over the Nazis, the Soviets hastily sent a group of writers turned journalists, including Konstantin Simonov and Boris Gorbatov, to report on this death camp, the first to be captured.[2] All the reporters promised to send their material at the same time, but Simonov broke his promise by wiring his material to Moscow before the others transmitted theirs.[3] His first article, published in the Red Army daily newspaper, *Krasnaia zvezda,* on 10 August, was followed by two more in the next two days.

Filmmakers were on the scene as well. In fact, Polish cameramen had entered the camp minutes after the Nazis had vacated it.[4] They were soon followed by a Soviet film crew under Roman Karmen, whom the political directorate of the Red Army had just assigned "the special task" of documenting the most important events involving four fronts (a type of military unit), including actions by the First Belorussian Front, whose operations encompassed the Lublin region; the directorate issued Karmen a letter of introduction to this effect just one day after the camp had been liberated.[5]

During the course of August 1944, both the Soviet and the Polish camera crews set about producing a film record of the camp. All the footage was dispatched to Moscow for the addition of a soundtrack, and these efforts resulted in two films: the Soviet special-release newsreel *Majdanek,* edited by Irina Setkina and approved for release in the Soviet Union on 18 December 1944, and *Majdanek Death Camp—the Cemetery of Europe (Vernichtungslager Majdanek—Cmentarzysko Europy,* henceforth referred to by its subtitle), a Polish film edited under the direction of Aleksander Ford and first screened three weeks earlier, on 27 November, in Lublin.[6] Nonetheless, though the discovery of the death camp site was unprecedented, Soviet and Polish cameramen produced footage that fitted the evidence into a preexisting template, muting and downplaying the extent of Jewish suffering to suit the priorities of Polish or Soviet ideological priorities. At the same time, these priorities themselves were shifting. As the war progressed beyond the borders of the Soviet state, Nazi crimes could no longer be presented simply as an injury to the Soviet spectator that demanded vengeance. Filmmakers negotiated this transition into more unpredictable territory with difficulty.

### Majdanek: Making Sense of the Unprecedented

There is a widely accepted sense in which the discovery of the camps marks a profound break in Western culture, most famously expressed by Theodor Adorno's aphorism "To write poetry after Auschwitz is barbaric."[7] While compelling reasons motivate the use of Auschwitz as a metonymic image for the Holocaust as a whole—the single largest number of people were murdered there–the moment of shock at the discovery of this killing factory is conventionally associated in the West with the photographic and newsreel reports of concentration camps in Germany, including Bergen-Belsen, Dachau, and Buchenwald. This is puzzling, for the concentration camps, brutal and murderous as they were, did not focus on the immediate industrialized murder of Jews deemed unable to work, a function that Majdanek and Auschwitz combined with that of the concentration camps and that constituted the sole purpose of four camps in the East: Bełżec, Sobibór, Treblinka, and Chełmno.[8]

The discovery of the death camp at Majdanek antedated that of the western concentration camps by many months, and thus the case can be made that the films of Majdanek mark, or should mark, a privileged point in this traumatic break in culture. Stuart Liebman articulates this case, arguing that although the Soviets had previously recorded and shown images of Nazi atrocities against civilians and POWs, *Cemetery of Europe* was "the first film to develop visual and narrative strategies to dramatize the unprecedented story of German brutality in a camp," doing so with "shots of barbed-wire fences, crematorium ovens and gas chambers."[9] In fact, cinematic representations of concentration camps had appeared as early as the 1938 Soviet film *The Swamp Soldiers,* where barbed-wire camp fences figure prominently.[10] Thus, while the Polish and Soviet films recording and recounting the Majdanek death camp attempted to represent a phenomenon without precedent, the devices and images they employ were at the time a mixture of the innovative and the ingrained.[11]

These filmic precedents affected both teams, including the Poles. Ford's Polish team, which comprised the cameramen Wladyslaw Forbert, Olgierd Samucewicz, and Stanislaw Wohl and the scenarist Jerzy Bossak, had to work in an environment strictly controlled by the Soviets, who had already elaborated a number of conventions for portraying Nazi atrocity. With respect to the film the Poles produced, moreover, it is difficult to establish which cameraman took which images. *Film Documents of Atrocities Committed by the German–Fascist Invaders,* the Soviet film shown at the Nuremberg Tribunal, attributes all its footage from Majdanek to the Soviet team, with the Polish cameramen receiving no credit, though this may well be an unjust lapse.[12] Whatever the truth of the matter, the Soviets clearly took a great deal of the footage, including much of that in the Polish film and no doubt vice versa. Along with the Poles, all three Soviet cameramen (Roman Karmen, a veteran of the Battle of Moscow and many other campaigns, as well as Viktor Shtatland and Avenir Sof´in, who both shot footage appearing in Dovzhenko's *Battle for Our Soviet Ukraine*) were credited for the photography on the Polish film, as they were for the film that Irina Setkina edited in Moscow. These three cameramen drew and expanded on their own and their colleagues' considerable experience of portraying Nazi genocidal violence dating back to 1941.[13]

Similarly, Setkina was perceived as a reliable editor whose work was consistent if unremarkable, a member of the newsreel studio's "old guard"[14] who would thus tend to standardize the content to a certain Soviet stylistic and ideological norm within the generic boundaries of the two-reel special-release newsreel. Indeed, she had edited a number of films depicting Nazi atrocities, from the Soviet film of Katyn (discussed later) to that of Kerch.

As a result, both films follow the established templates to a greater or lesser extent. The Sovietizing tendency was strongest in Setkina's film, but *Cemetery of Europe* can productively be understood by comparing it to the Soviet film along these lines and considering it in the context of the norms governing wartime Soviet documentary films' previous portrayals of Nazi atrocity.

In their opening scenes, both films follow the pattern shaping many Soviet atrocity depictions, tempering their ghoulish revelations by beginning with footage of victory, such as the liberation of Rostov in *Soiuzki-nozhurnal* no. 114. The two films show Lublin's inhabitants joyfully receiving the Soviet and Polish troops who liberated their city. Having presented these uplifting images, both films add that the world found out about Majdanek at this time and then set about showing the crimes the Nazis committed there. They share a key strategy to convey the camp's gristly realities, with both following the Polish-Soviet Extraordinary Commission for Investigating the Crimes Committed by the Germans in the Majdanek Extermination Camp in Lublin. Thus *Majdanek* shadows the commission's investigations to reveal in detail the camp's most shocking dimension: the systematic, industrialized manner in which people were killed with Zyklon B in the gas chambers.[15] As images of the gas chambers appear, the Russian commentary explains that the victims were told they were going to have a shower. The film also shows the extraordinary commission officials examining crematoria where, the voiceover points out, corpses were incinerated.[16] Earlier Soviet films had already used this form of "frame witness" to authenticate war crimes, but typically the witnesses included a relative whose distress at the loss of a loved one demanded more than the dispassionate investigation of crimes. The distress demanded further that the spectator react emotionally and functioned to articulate the call to vengeance and to battle.[17] For all its horror, *Majdanek* attempts to temper and otherwise mediate the spectator's response to the crimes through the template of an investigation by the authority figures on the extraordinary commission, who serve as a surrogate for the spectators themselves.

In contrast, while *Cemetery of Europe* immediately introduces the commission, even naming its members, from the outset it attempts to appeal more directly to the spectator through synchronous sound footage, intercutting the dry verbal evasions of the captured SS guards with a passionate testimony by a Polish officer, Second Lieutenant Tadeusz Budzyń, a former prisoner of the camp whose testimony to the commission unveils the true nature of the crimes that the perpetrators deny having committed. Ford's film also manipulates its spectators' emotions by first mentioning that the gas chambers were disguised as bathhouses and then showing an actual bathhouse; the voiceover then identifies the image as that of a real bathhouse, after which the film turns to an image of a disguised gas chamber. Thus this film, the first to show Nazi gas chambers, exploits the spectator's expectations in this bitterly ironic manner and, in doing so, anticipates Spielberg's use of a similar device in *Schindler's List*.

The image of the gas chambers, the Holocaust's ultimate crime scene, has been seen as key in the representation of the Holocaust, even as "haunting it," since nobody subjected to one could have survived.[18] Any footage of these gas chambers had to have been produced not by the victims of the crimes committed there but only by the perpetrators or, as with the films at issue here, the liberating forces.[19] Both the Russian and the Polish films show the gas chambers, explaining their function by combining images of them, including one of a peephole through which guards could watch their dying victims, with those of the visit by the joint extraordinary commission (fig. 6.1). Of the two films, *Cemetery of Europe* more effectively uses the image of the peephole, which Ford conveys through a brief tracking movement toward it, thus emphasizing the sadism of the Germans guards who watched the victims' deaths (and, as Saxton argues, potentially pandering to such sadism in the spectator).[20] In contrast, Setkina's film describes the Nazis as watching not the victims' deaths but the effects of the Zyklon gas, implying that their principal concern lay in verifying the smooth operation of the killing system. The Soviet film's dispassionate language here and the accompanying montage serve to ensure that the spectator's perspective mirrors that of the commission. Unlike the Polish film and many earlier Soviet films, Setkina's film shows us the site for a legal reason: to establish the Nazis' guilt and their lack of compassion rather than their active sadism. The Soviet film thus acts as a guarantee of authenticity, one dependent on a "logic of proof" Claude Lanzmann attempts to counter in his film *Shoah*, which relies almost solely on survivors' testimony.[21] In showing the unprecedented sight of the gas chambers, then, Setkina's *Majdanek* evokes the same legal rationale of collating evidence of atrocities that had motivated Soviet cameraman since 1941, a rationale that contrasts with the intense emotional pitch of Ford's film.

The reality of the death camp presents a problem for this approach,

FIGURE 6.1. A gas chamber peephole. From *Majdanek*.

since the crematoria were meant to destroy the remains of the victims, leaving few corpses to incriminate the perpetrators. The sole sequence that truly conveys the unprecedented scale and industrial nature of the killings is one that shows what the Russian commentary calls "material evidence" of this scale, namely, the mounds of the victims' personal effects, such as children's toys, glasses, passports, and especially shoes. As Liebman has pointed out in his analysis of Ford's film (although Setkina's film uses the same shot), the low-angle shots of the mountains of shoes are made particularly telling by the way in which the camera tilts to reveal their seemingly unending quantity.[22] The result is a powerful metonym for the almost unimaginable destruction of the camp, which has left footwear as the only remaining trace of the tens of thousands of victims (fig. 6.2).

Yet using images of footwear in this way cannot be plausibly seen as Ford's invention, since similar images appear in Soviet journalistic accounts of Majdanek, starting with Simonov's. Indeed, photographs of footwear taken by the Red Army photographer Oleg Knorring (fig. 6.3) were published in *Krasnaia zvezda* alongside the first of Simonov's articles, and those were followed by photographs from Iakov Riumkin that were

FIGURE 6.2. Victims' shoes. From *Majdanek*.

published in *Pravda* on 11 August 1944 alongside the first of Boris Gorbatov's two articles on the liberation of the camp.[23] Simonov describes these piles as "perhaps the most gruesome evidence of all of what went on" there:

> How many pairs of footwear there are here it would be hard to say. There may be a million, there may be more. They spill out of the hut through doors and windows. At one spot, the weight of them has thrust out part of the wall, which has fallen outwards together with piles of shoes.
>
> Every form of footwear is to be found here, torn Russian military top-boots, Polish soldiers' boots, men's shoes, women's slippers and, what is grimmest of all, thousands upon thousands of pairs of children's footwear, bootees, shoes, sandals, ten year old children's, eight year old's, six-year old's, and even babies' shoes.
>
> It is hard to imagine anything more gruesome than this sight, the silent witness to the destruction of thousands of men, women, and children. If one climbs over the mountains of shoes to the rear part of the shed one realises the meaning and significance of this monstrous storehouse. Here are stacked in separate piles tens of thousands of shoes,

FIGURE 6.3. Victims' shoes at Majdanek. Photo by Oleg Knorring.

heels, vamps and leather clippings. Here were cut out and sorted parts of shoes that as a whole were unfit for wear—soles, heels, vamps—all sorted separately. Like everything else in the death factory, this storehouse was organized on strictly utilitarian lines. Nothing belonging to the slaughtered victims was to be wasted, neither clothes nor shoes, nor bones nor ashes.[24]

Thus, while the cameramen probably selected the image of footwear only after journalists and photographers had already employed it as a "silent witness," a trace of the camp's otherwise completely silent and invisible victims, the segments nevertheless reflect the moment when the Majdanek films grasp the impossibility of representing those victims. Not only do they have no graves, but they have truly left no identifiable bodily remains. Only their effects survive.

Commenting on photographs of the Majdanek camp published in the *London Illustrated News* in October 1944, Zelizer says: "Unlike the images of later camps, few pictures of dead corpses were as yet published."[25] Yet this was the point. The Soviets did not refrain from showing images of corpses; rather, Majdanek had been organized so as not just to murder Jews but to obliterate them. This was the very nature of the death camps, as Primo Levi argued, since the true witnesses were the victims who "die[d] or disappear[ed] without leaving a trace in anyone's memory."[26] Yet the Majdanek films do show some corpses to illustrate the other primary means of murder that the Nazis used in the camp: a bullet in the back of the neck, a technique they had used throughout the first stage of the Holocaust, when the Einsatzgruppen were killing Jews throughout the Soviet Union. The films' images of mass grave exhumations resemble ones that Soviet newsreels had been showing since 1942. In so doing, Soviet filmmakers had become adept at ensuring that their images of the dead conveyed the required message. Thus, both films list the nationalities of people killed in Majdanek, illustrating this through the images of various different passports and ID cards, and enumerate the countries of origin of those transported to their deaths in the camp, as well as naming some famous victims. But neither film mentions Jews. Neither intimates the disproportionately high number of Jewish victims of the camp; the Soviet film cites the figure of 1,380,000 victims without breaking it down into ethnic groups. This figure has been since revised downward. According to the most recent research, the camp's victims number between 80,000 and 250,000 people. Opinions differ, but in publishing the most widely accepted figures, the United States Holocaust Memorial Museum and the Majdanek Museum assert that most of the victims were Jews.[27]

Faced with the reality of a Nazi death camp oriented above all toward the extermination of Jews, the Soviet film in particular attempted to shape the evidence collected to a predetermined narrative wherein the Nazis killed people of all nationalities from all over occupied Europe. An examination of the fourteen reels omitted from both Setkina's and Ford's films reveals that when interrogated, the captured SS men were frank as to the identities of their victims. One guard stresses, as if in mitigation, that those gassed in the camp were mostly Jews and never Soviet prisoners of war. Later, when the Soviet interrogator reads a list of nationalities similar to the one that appears in the Setkina film, an SS guard named Ternes intervenes to include Jews: "Juden waren's." The Soviet interrogator works hard to foist his predetermined narrative on the German and insists, in a mixture of Russian and German, "Ne tol´ko Juden" ("Not only Jews").[28]

As I have shown in my discussion of films and uncompleted projects by Pudovkin, Iutkevich, and Dovzhenko, as well as in Donskoi's abandonment of initial plans for *The Unvanquished,* portraying Nazis could be tricky, in part because it was hard to mask their anti-Semitic focus. Indeed, almost all the discarded synch sound testimonies confirm that the overwhelming majority of victims were Jewish. At a hearing of the extraordinary commission, a Frenchman named Corentin Le Dû stands up and says that he arrived at the camp with 350 French captives, some Poles, and "many, many" Jews.[29] When asked again, he stresses that there were many Jews, a few Poles, and many Russians. He then continues to describe how all these Jews disappeared immediately, the same day they had arrived. When asked, he states that they were gassed. As Liebman points out, the "Dutchman" Benem who appears in the film is also Jewish, but both films deliberately conceal this fact.[30]

In both films, this refusal to identify the victims as Jewish arose from the ongoing Soviet approach to representing the Holocaust, and though they both confront and attempt to convey the unprecedented, they deliberately bend the material away from the plight of the Jews under Nazism.[31]

Because they were intended for different audiences, however, the Soviet and Polish films treat witness testimony differently. Ford's film uses a great deal of synchronously recorded sound footage, including accounts from four non-Polish inmates and testimony from the Polish witness to the extraordinary commission, a man named Budzyń, and it ends with a Polish Catholic funeral ceremony and the singing of the Polish patriotic hymn "Rotę," which the audience perceives as having been synchronously recorded but was actually performed by a Red Army choir in Moscow.[32] By including these specifically Polish elements, Ford follows a Soviet tendency to suggest that the victims are part of the same group as the spectator. Thus, despite its subtitle, which suggests an attempt to treat the camps as a symbol of oppression across all Europe, the Polish film deliberately downplays the victims' Jewish identities in an effort to appeal to Poles, who were its primary intended audience.[33]

Although Setkina's film retains the final scene of the Catholic mass for the victims, its lack of any synchronous sound and explanatory detail in either the voiceover commentary or the intertitles detaches the images from their specific focus on Polish victims, transforming the mass into a more generalized image of mourning. Unless the material was intended strictly for Polish consumption, the Soviets resisted any narrative that privileged Polish suffering, just as they resisted narratives privileging specifically Jewish victimhood, and this was not a message they wished to convey either to their own population or internationally. Thus the Polish hymn is largely denuded of its ethnic specificity, just as the various eyewitnesses are ventriloquized by the voiceover commentary. Whereas Ford's film was intended to appeal primarily to Poles, the Soviet film was designed to appeal to a wider, international audience.

## The Presentation of Victims as "Like Us"

Ford's strategy of representing concentration camp victims as similar to the intended spectator, of effectively suggesting that "this could have been you or your loved ones," is nonetheless colored by the approach to representing victims of Nazi genocidal violence that the Soviets had used since the end of 1941. Whereas Sontag has argued that photography shows faces of the dead only when the victims are exotic, Soviet films of Nazi atrocities deliberately erase any sense of difference, of otherness, in order to appeal to a sense of solidarity and provoke an active response.[34] Sontag's account nevertheless does aptly apply to British and American representations of the camps, which display the victims as not entirely human and certainly "not like us." Robert Abzug makes a similar point:

> These soldiers found themselves capable of confronting the awful tasks of sorting the living from the dead, breathing the fetid air, and walking amidst untold human misery only by partially shutting off their senses and emotions. They also distanced themselves from the scene around them by making a basic distinction between themselves and the dead or liberated. If the liberator defined the helpless victims of Nazis as not quite human, then he could defend himself against thinking that this might have been his own fate. Such a strategy, a part of the liberator experience at every camp, was illustrated in Al Newman's Nordhausen report that appeared in *Newsweek*. He captioned one part of the story "These Were Men" and later characterized the liberated prisoners as "creatures—you could not by any stretch of the imagination call them human beings." It was Newman's way of describing in the most graphic way possible the destruction that had been wrought in the lives of the Nazis' victims. At the same time, by making these individuals something other than human, he could push from his mind the realization that anyone could be brutalized into such a state, that one's normal existence and even life was so fragile.[35]

While there were exceptions (e.g., Morris Parloff, a Jewish American who identified with the victims powerfully),[36] soldiers, reporters, and politicians from the United States tended to perceive concentration camp survivors as being "like a foreign race": "They could just as well have been from Mars, or from Hell. The identities and characters of these Jewish survivors rarely were personalized through interviews or individualized through biographical sketches; rather, they were presented as a mass, and often as a mess, a petrified, degrading, and smelly one, not only by newspaper reporters but by some of the most powerful general officers in the Allied high command. This depersonalization made it more difficult for the survivors' trauma to generate compelling identification."[37]

In contrast, Ford uses synchronous sound to humanize and give voice to the prisoners, so that they come across as human beings inviting identification with their suffering rather than distanced pity for it. Like Dovzhenko, Ford was striving to particularize and "nationalize" the suffering that occurred in the land of his birth. In doing so, he created a far more personal and artistically distinct film than the universalizing Soviet version was. Emblematic of this contrasting approach was Ford's decision to end his film with a religious funeral ceremony.[38]

### Making Sense of Death: War Crimes, Mourning, Vengeance

Again, the notion of film as evidence and the emphasis on the war crimes commission was important for Setkina's *Majdanek,* but this film bears a subtitle that invokes a different logic: *Film Documents of the Monstrously Evil Deeds of the Germans in the Extermination Camp of Majdanek, in the Town of Lublin (Kinodokumenty o chudovishchnykh zlodeianiiakh nemtsev v lagere unichtozheniia na Maidaneke v gorode Liublin).* The emotive phrase "monstrously evil deeds" and attribution of it to the Germans as a whole evoke the Soviet media's earlier wartime strategy of ascribing the crimes less to human beings than to some kind of monsters and seeing this generalized lack of humanity as a facet of the Germans as a whole.[39]

*Majdanek's* final words, however, return to the legal rationale, with the voiceover stating that Hitler, Himmler, and the SS are to blame for these atrocities. The voiceover commentary ends there, succeeded by a silent sequence that an intertitle labels "Liberated Lublin declared mourning for the victims of Majdanek." This introduces the discourse not of justice but of mourning, of the Roman Catholic funeral. We then see a funeral service being held in Lublin.

The incorporation of this third, specifically Christian, response to Nazi violence through a discourse of mourning seems drawn from Ford's film, in which it makes perfect sense as an appeal to specifically Polish sensibilities, yet it has something of a destabilizing influence here, for the funeral service in *Majdanek* is not a Bolshevik rite but a Catholic one, and it does not end with a political slogan. Rather, it serves as a kind of coda. Death is here integrated not into the economy of defiance, vengeance, or the law but rather the (unverbalized) Christian religious discourse of heaven and resurrection—all of which is woefully inadequate for making sense of the Holocaust, especially given that its primary victims were Jewish. Nevertheless, this response to death is more open-ended than are the discourses of vengeance or justice that had hitherto dominated Soviet portrayals of Nazi genocidal atrocities; it at least recognizes the loss and rupture of death.

Given the unprecedented scale and industrial efficiency of the death camp, and with the new problems of representing not just Soviet dead but Polish and other European victims as well, the majority of whom were Jewish, the Soviets' tried and tested templates became less effective. When it was no longer a matter of survival, the logic of vengeance or of the protection of loved ones that had been deployed to stimulate last-ditch defense no longer made sense. Likewise, the sheer numbers of the dead seemed to so undermine the idea of martyrdom, of meaningful sacrifice redeemed in an ultimate victory, as to make it absurd. As the established narrative about Nazi atrocities lost relevance, uncertainty reigned. Indeed, journalists, filmmakers, and others representing the liberation of Majdanek were more unsure than ever as to what was permitted and what was not. For example, Boris Gorbatov omitted any reference to Jews in his original report on the camp, but he found himself overruled by Aleksandr Shcherbakov, the secretary of the Central Committee and head of the Soviet Information Bureau, which had been set up to control the wartime media—and a man alleged to have been that committee's most anti-Semitic member. Shcherbakov, however, inserted a reference to Jews before allowing the report to be published in *Pravda*.[40] Similarly, when the joint Polish-Soviet commission on Madjanek published its declaration on 16 September, leading articles in *Pravda* and *Izvestiia* referred to the camp's Jewish dead. As Berkhoff has demonstrated, no consistent policy had yet been established: "despite a transparent effort to deemphasize the Jews murdered in Poland, they were not always omitted."[41]

FIGURE 6.4. A Jewish victim's clothing. From *Klooga Death Camp*.

FIGURE 6.5. An outtake of a Jewish victim's clothing. From *Klooga Death Camp*. Courtesy of RGAKFD.

This ambiguity was once again evident when Soviet camera crews discovered the gruesome aftermath of the Klooga concentration camp, near Talinn, in Estonia, in September 1944. While the extraordinary commission reports published in the newspapers did not identify the victims' ethnicities, the one-reel special-release newsreel of the camp, photographed by the Leningrad cameramen Efim Uchitel´ and O. Ivanov, mentions Jews as well as Russians and Estonians among the three thousand victims whom the Nazis killed as the Red Army approached. It does not mention that they constituted approximately half of those killed, but the final footage is nevertheless unusual among Soviet films of the camps in showing an image of a victim's uniform with the Star of David prominently displayed (fig. 6.4).[42] When showing the clothing that victims were made to remove and leave lying on the ground, moreover, the discarded footage repeatedly shows the numbers and symbols revealing these items to have belonged to Jewish prisoners (fig. 6.5). Likewise, the cameramen's own dope sheets list the names of the few survivors, such as Motel´ Naumovich Ass and Abram Moisevich Vannik; while these documents do not identify them as such, their names indicate that they were Jews (the finished film, however, does not include these names).[43] The fact that these people's names were recorded and that the cameramen took many images that unambiguously identify the victims as Jewish is a testament to the fluid situation and lack of clear guidelines warning filmmakers from referring to the Nazis' murder of Jews.

### Distribution and Reception of *Majdanek*

Despite all they had already been told of Nazi atrocities, Soviet citizens were shocked by the August 1944 newspaper reports on Majdanek coming from Konstantin Simonov, Boris Gorbatov, and Evgenii Kriger. The BBC correspondent Alexander Werth described the effect:

> As they advanced, the Russians had been learning more and more of German atrocities and the enormous number of killings. But, somehow, all this killing was spread over relatively wide areas, and though it added up to far, far more than Majdanek, it did not have the vast monumental, "industrial" quality of that unbelievable Death Factory two miles from Lublin. . . . Everybody had heard of Babyi Yar and thousands of other German atrocities; but this was something even more staggering. . . . The effect of Majdanek was enormous, not least in the Red Army. Thousands of Russian soldiers were made to visit it.[44]

Simonov's three articles about Majdanek were then translated and circulated throughout the world, often combined with unattributed photographs of the camp by Iakov Riumkin and others.[45] Despite their sensational content, however, or perhaps because of it, the world treated these print and photographic revelations with skepticism. Similarly, when Werth filed a report for the BBC later that month, it was rejected as Soviet propaganda.[46] It took the British and American discovery of concentration camps to convince the West that Majdanek was not a hoax. But the Nazis knew better, and the coverage led Hitler to curse his men for not having covered up all the damning traces.[47] Within months of these reports, the Germans began to dismantle and destroy the crematoria of the Auschwitz camp and other evidence of their crimes.[48]

As the films show, however, the Nazis had attempted to cover up their crimes at Majdanek, the earliest of which dated back to the start of 1942. Thus, the second, final reel of Setkina's film concentrates on overcoming the Nazis' attempts to conceal the crimes by burning their victims' bodies in crematoria and on bonfires. The camera shows us a number of details of the crematoria, some with charred human remains still in them. It also shows charred bones left over from bonfires. These revelations are at each point corroborated by footage of extraordinary commission officials investigating the crimes committed at the camp, visiting the gas chamber, inspecting the crematoria, and questioning perpetrators. In this way, the film joins print journalists in the effort to defeat the Nazis' attempt to obscure what had happened. This goal of verification is supplemented by the use of eyewitness accounts from both survivors and the guards, with their words rendered in direct speech in the voiceover commentary.

Despite its shocking and chilling revelations, *Majdanek* received lackluster distribution in the Soviet Union, with one-week screenings, running 4–12 January 1945, in two of Moscow's newsreel cinemas, Novosti dnia and Vostokkino.[49] The ambivalence of the Soviet response is evident in the fact that the press listed the film but did not advertise it. Even more crucially, neither of the key Soviet publications, *Pravda* and *Izvestiia,* reviewed it; indeed, it seems not to have been reviewed at all, which again suggests reviewers' fears of dealing with the sensitive subject, a circumspection entirely understandable in the light of the inconsistent media coverage of Nazi persecution of the Jews.[50]

But again, Soviet citizens were not the principal intended audience. The primary purpose in making the Soviet version of the material from

Majdanek lay in showing international audiences what the Nazis had done and to persuade a skeptical world of the realities of the death camp, as is indicated in the decision to send Roman Karmen to the site, for he was the Soviet documentary filmmaker consistently entrusted with projects destined for external consumption. Realizing that purpose could also serve to bolster the Soviet Union's moral authority over the Nazis, which had been seriously undermined in April 1943 when the Nazis had revealed that the Soviets had murdered Polish officers and others in Katyn during 1940, a claim corroborated by the Polish government in exile. Indeed, Ford's film refers to the murder of Poles at Lublin castle as "another Hitlerite Katyn."[51] To counter the Nazis' (well-founded) allegations, the Soviets released a shamelessly falsified film in March 1944 entitled *Tragedy in the Katyn Forest* (*Tragediia v Katynskom lesu*), also edited by Irina Setkina, which deceitfully blamed the Nazis for the NKVD's crime.[52] Yet despite the fact that one is a falsification and the other is essentially truthful, *Tragedy in the Katyn Forest* and *Majdanek* bear formal and structural similarities to each other. They both define themselves as belonging to the genre of "film documents," they both show the work of investigative commissions and foreign journalists, and they both end with a Christian funeral for the dead. Unfortunately, the Katyn film's bare-faced deceit helped undermine Western confidence in Soviet film revelations of actual Nazi atrocities and has been an important factor preventing the world from taking these wartime films seriously.

Thus, when Setkina's *Majdanek* reached France in April 1945, it was initially banned because of, as the censor put it, "the emotions it would not fail to arouse in the families of the deported, many of whom are still without news of their loved ones. Can be passed once the situation of French deportees is clarified."[53] Yet it may have helped publicize Nazi atrocities more indirectly. The French film historian Sylvie Lindeperg stresses the fact that the British and Americans had yet to decide to photograph and publicize their findings as they liberated the camps in the West.[54] The Soviet film thus antedated decisions to record such sights and probably helped convince the British and the Americans to photograph what they found at the camps.

The temporary French ban provoked howls of protest and was lifted later that month when the film was acclaimed by the likes of the left-wing critic Georges Sadoul as an important contribution to the documentation of Nazi atrocities, a subject that critics on the Left saw as being too often glossed over in the postliberation climate.[55] Shortly afterward, at the end of April, a shortened version of *Majdanek* was shown in the United States (this version ran only fourteen minutes, though it included additional footage of SS guards being hanged).[56] By this time, however, in part because they had become aware that the Soviets were already showing such things,[57] American and British cameramen had filmed the liberation of camps in Germany and shown these images to their domestic audiences.[58]

Unlike the Soviet film, this footage was seen as coming from a reliable source and therefore as being undeniable. Even though none of these later films documented the death camps, as *Majdanek* does, they forced audiences in the Western world to recognize the depths and scale of Nazi brutality.

Yet all these sites of atrocity were dwarfed by Auschwitz.

## Auschwitz

Although Auschwitz was the most murderous of all Nazi camps, Boris Polevoi's *Pravda* article was the only significant Soviet media coverage of its liberation on 27 January 1945. In general, journalists and authorities in the Soviet Union paid far less attention to the liberation of Auschwitz, a site now synonymous with the Nazis' murder of Jews, than they had to the smaller camp at Majdanek, a difference that probably reflects their increasing uncertainty concerning the appropriate way to present such matters. As late as 18 January, in fact, the units that would end up liberating it had not been informed of the camp's existence or given orders to capture it.[59] Nevertheless, in May 1945 the Soviets released *Auschwitz,* a two-reel special-edition newsreel that even mentioned Jews, albeit only in a list of victims. This deeply flawed film of the camp's liberation and its aftermath nevertheless left a significant trace, its footage recurring frequently in visual representations of the Holocaust, from *Night and Fog* to *The World at War* and beyond. Its value as a document and act of testimony can be enhanced immensely by analyzing the film in the light of the technical, personal, and political decisions that influenced its making.

No film crew accompanied the troops that liberated Auschwitz, but the cameraman Kenian Kutub-Zade claimed to have arrived there the following day, 28 January.[60] On 7 February the Central Documentary Film Studios, in Moscow, received a telegram from Mikhail Oshurkov, who led the film group attached to the Red Army's First Ukrainian Front and had filmed mass graves at Kerch in 1942; the telegram read: "We are filming the Auschwitz camp."[61] The first five hundred meters of film was sent the following day, on 8 February, eleven days after the camp's liberation.[62] Given that the cameramen would have needed to research the situation before beginning to shoot this footage, they probably had arrived on the scene as quickly as had their counterparts and print journalists in Majdanek, at most a week after the camp had been liberated. Some of this first footage, which presents a general picture, including an aerial view of the camp, appears in the final film, for it shows snow on the ground, and the snow had melted by the time the later footage was taken.[63]

On 15 February Oshurkov then requested that a further cameraman with a portable lighting source be sent by plane to film the work of the Soviet Extraordinary State Commission on War Crimes.[64] Frontline camera operators, who principally filmed images of battles, did not carry lighting apparatus, since they filmed in natural light. To record the extraordinary commission activities, including its members' visit to the gas chambers, the film group needed lights. Evidently, then, the film quickly evolved beyond a run-of-the-mill newsreel. Its production now required not only lighting but also more film stock, which Oshurkov repeatedly requested, complaining about its lack and receiving it only in early March.[65] He also requested synchronous sound recording equipment but was told that it was in use by film crews with the Second Ukrainian Front.[66] Thus the Auschwitz film contains no synchronously recorded interviews with survivors. The fact that authorities did not immediately redeploy sound-recording equipment, which was in short supply, suggests that filming Auschwitz was not a priority for the decision makers of Central Documentary Film Studios, just as the camp's liberation was not a priority for the Red Army.

On 19 March Oshurkov sent a further 2,500 meters of material to Moscow, saying it should be combined with the earlier footage. He also advised the laboratory to develop the film with care, stressing that it had been taken in difficult circumstances.[67] These instructions were followed, but authorities in Moscow did not send Oshurkov an assessment of the Auschwitz material until 3 April: "editor Braslavskii stop evaluation of Auschwitz material by cameramen Kutub-Zade and Vorontsov stop cameramen sent footage of great importance stop work carried out on good professional level stop episodes chosen and filmed with clear correct orientation stop cameramen avoid the dangers of naturalism in footage of atrocities and at the same time convincingly portrayed picture of death camp stop especially mention excellently compiled dope-sheet stop material accepted for special release stop will also use footage of Auschwitz sent earlier recommending cameramen for award."[68] But what did the authorities have in mind when they spoke approvingly of the "selection and filming of episodes with [a] clear [and] correct orientation" and the "avoid[ance of] the dangers of naturalism in footage of atrocities"?

## "Correct Orientation": Analysis of the Film

The cameramen who documented Auschwitz faced the complex task of not just filming in accordance with strictures in place during January, February, and March 1945 but also anticipating the demands that would inform decisions in April, when the material would be assessed, and May, when the film would be released. But attitudes to the depiction of Nazi atrocities shifted unpredictably in Moscow, making this task particularly difficult. Nevertheless, the cameramen could be pretty sure that unacceptable expressions of "naturalism" would include any undue concentration on images that identified the dead as Jews. Thus, while many close-ups show triangular symbols on inmates' chests, none display the Jewish inmates' Star of David, formed of two equilateral triangles. Indeed, in a series of images showing inmates' badges, the one person who raises his arm across his chest to reveal his tattoo instead of his badge is Berthold Epstein, who was probably Jewish.

There is an element of indecision, however. As with the film of Majdanek, *Auschwitz* communicates the central problem of representing the camp's absent victims in large part by showing images of the piles of effects plundered from them. The cameramen take images of shoes, suitcases, and clothes, but none of these images indicates that most of the victims were Jewish, even though an unpublished extraordinary commission report of 4 March mentions that "a considerable quantity of outer clothes" bore sewn-on "mass-produced signs in the form of six-pointed stars with the word 'Jude' inside the star."[69] Still, though they avoided showing close-ups of clothes bearing the Magen David symbol, the Soviet newsreel cameramen did film a pile of tallits, the Jewish ritual prayer shawls, lying in the open air with a breeze fluttering the edge of one or two (fig. 6.6). The huge pile of these shawls unambiguously established the enormous number of Jews killed at Auschwitz, a fact that is not otherwise evident from the footage. This image was not included in the final cut of the film, nor does the voiceover identify the majority of those killed at the

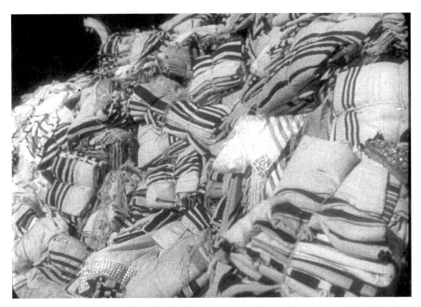

FIGURE 6.6. An outtake of a pile of tallits. From *Auschwitz.* Courtesy of RGAKFD.

camps as Jews. Yet the fact that this powerful image was filmed at all indicates the lack of certainty that reigned in the depiction of Jewish victims: the cameramen would not have squandered film stock on such an image if they had been certain that the editors would not include it in the final film.

Like the earlier films of Majdanek, *Auschwitz* attempts to confront the unprecedented problems of representing a death camp using the means that Soviet filmmakers had employed since the first year of the war, and the results are equally ambiguous. Thus, the Soviets selected and shaped what they saw so that their images conformed to their concepts about the best way to represent Nazi atrocities.[70] In *Auschwitz,* this is evident from the prominence of child victims and survivors—for example, the image of soldiers picking up tiny vests as the voiceover states that children's clothes were destined for Germany and the focus on the autopsy of a pregnant young woman and her fetus (fig. 6.7). Probably the film's most memorable image is that of a crowd of children, 180 twins whom Josef Mengele spared from the gas chambers for use in medical experiments, who pull back their left sleeves in unison to reveal their tattooed numbers (fig. 6.8).[71] Here the commentary points out that all the other children who arrived at the camp were exterminated. While it does not mention that these twins are all Jewish, this sequence nevertheless constitutes an attempt to convey

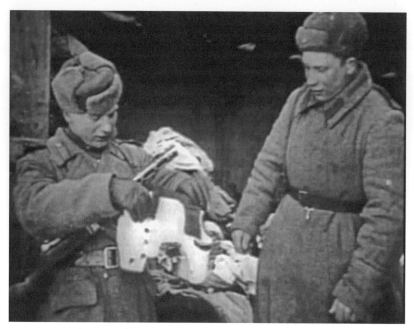

FIGURE 6.7. Red Army soldiers with children's clothes. From *Auschwitz*.

the central problem of representing Auschwitz survivors: their fate was exceptional, since children under ten were generally gassed.

According to both the film and the Soviet war crimes commission report, the Red Army found 2,819 survivors at the camp when it was liberated,[72] and children, who had constituted a large proportion of the camp's victims, made up only a small minority of those survivors. The prominence that the film gives them is thus best understood in the context of previous Soviet representations of atrocities, a tradition stretching back to the film of Rostov. The murder (and torture) of children symbolizes a moral extreme, and the Soviets used such images to sanction their war effort as righteous. For the Nazis, however, the murder of children was the ultimate act in pursuit of genocide. The Soviet film, like those before it, fails to grasp this dimension of the symbol it employs. Moreover, whereas previous depictions of the deaths of children were calculated to stimulate an emotional response in the spectator, particularly a drive toward vengeance on the battlefield, this was no longer an appropriate strategy now that the war was over, as it was by the time the film was released. When showing the war crimes commission's medical examination of children,

FIGURE 6.8. Rescued Jewish twins. From *Auschwitz*.

the film deliberately tones down the emotional pitch with which an earlier draft of the voiceover evoked their previous existence, cutting the following words: "Once they lived their youthful lives. The children played and enjoyed their parents' love. Cheerful, happy, rosy-cheeked, they blossomed on the Earth. And then . . ."[73]

Moreover, *Auschwitz* does not show the faces of the dead, as many earlier films had done, in part because the dead are no longer Soviet but rather foreign. This appears to have been a deliberate decision taken by the editor, since the initial footage taken by A. Pavlov, one of the first cameramen on the scene, included close-ups of Russians and Belorussians. Presumably he looked for such victims so as to articulate a narrative of Soviet suffering, or a Soviet perspective on it, as did the initial Sovinformbureau report, which quoted a Russian eyewitness,[74] but this was discarded in favor of a different narrative.

Similarly, there is little attempt to emphasize that these children are like the spectator, and the testimony lacks any personal dimension. The contrast is evident when we compare the film to the series of charcoal drawings produced by another individual present at the newly liberated camp, the Soviet graphic artist Zinovii Tolkachev. He later recalled viewing hair shorn from the dead and seeing a ribbon identical to one worn by his own daughter; when viewing the shoes, he saw a pair identical to ones she wore.[75] Moreover, his series of drawings showing the camp, *Auschwitz,* personalized the images of the shoes by showing a woman identified as Liza holding a shoe, the last trace of her daughter.[76] Tolkachev's art uses many elements of imaginative reconstruction, as it does in a scene of the gas chambers, forcing viewers to identify with the victims whose individual fates and personal suffering are etched in their faces and demand an emotional response. Similarly, the most successful journalistic accounts of the death camps, such as Vasilii Grossman's article "The Hell of Treblinka" ("Treblinskii ad" [1945]), also attempted to imagine the final thoughts of the condemned as they arrived at a camp.[77]

This is precisely what the Auschwitz film generally fails to do, although its makers did sometimes reconstruct scenes and events that the cameraman did not witness. Discarded footage shows an absurd sequence of inmates crowding against a gate and striving to get out. Soviet troops arrive and open the gates to set them free, at which point the prisoners embrace their liberators before leaping around and rejoicing. This grotesquely faked shot is then repeated from a different angle under the gates bearing the legend "Arbeit macht frei." In the 1980s the cameraman Aleksandr Vorontsov told the filmmakers Bengt and Irmgard von zur Mühlen that the sequence was not included in the final film because it was too far from the truth; for the most part, the liberated inmates could hardly stand, let alone jump for joy.[78]

But some reconstructions did make it into the final film. Given that Oshurkov had to order lighting apparatus to film the interior shots, the footage showing the barracks must have been filmed in late February or early March. According to the von zur Mühlens, the barracks occupants shown in this footage were Polish women sent to the camp after the Warsaw uprising in September 1944; they had been asked to return to the camp to illustrate the conditions there (fig. 6.9).[79] The difficulty described by Levi—namely, that the only possible witnesses were survivors, whose fates made them atypical of the overwhelming majority of those sent to the camps—is here taken to an extreme, with healthy non-Jewish survivors performing the conditions suffered by doomed prisoners and doing so weeks after the camp's liberation.

FIGURE 6.9. Reconstructed scene with Polish women. From *Auschwitz*.

This strategy was dictated in part by the film crew's failure to obtain apparatus to synchronously record verbal testimony from eyewitnesses. Had the crew possessed this equipment, the final film could have incorporated survivors' descriptions of the conditions, thus avoiding any need to reconstruct them. Nonetheless, an earlier draft of the voiceover script, written no later than 20 May (i.e., a week before the final film was approved), bears a faint trace of an intention to listen to survivors' voices. The script attempted to evoke the sense that these women could bear witness through its use of second-person address to spectators, inviting them to ask survivors to recount their experiences during the sequence filmed in the barracks where the Polish women are named and shown: "People were living here already in the next world, cut off from everything, surrounded by horror and torture, in expectation of the inevitable. Ask Elena Jablunska, Stanislawa Kszeczkowska, Olimpia Prusikowska, ask Franczeska Murawska, what she endured at her seventy-five years—why did the Fascist murderers need their lives?"[80] The final version merely lists names: "People lived here cut off from everything, surrounded by horror and torture. Elena Iablunskaia, seventy-three. Stanislava Kshechkol′skaia, fifty-four. Olimpia Prusinov′skaia, sixty-five. Why did the Fascist murderers need their lives?" The invitation, addressed to spectators, to ask these women, which deploys the rhetorical power we saw in Dovzhenko's wartime documentaries, became in the final film simply a list of names and ages. Moreover, their names, rendered in the Polish form in the first version, have become Russified and distorted, downplaying their ethnic difference from Russian-speaking viewers.

Another instance where the theme of absent testimony, of the impossibility of finding "complete witnesses," is addressed poignantly occurs in the earlier version of the voiceover accompanying the images of the twins being led away from the camp, before the film shows images of the crematoria and gas chambers, where the narrator contrasts "living" and "silent" witnesses: "The last victims and the living witnesses of Nazi atrocities have left the camp. Is it deserted? No, there still remain the silent witnesses." The final version removes any reference to witnesses: "The camp. Has emptied. But there remain the indelible traces of Nazi atrocities. They provide evidence."[81] This scene introduces the widely discussed images of the gas chambers, which stand at the center of questions about the possibility of representing the Holocaust, and the first draft of the voiceover accompanying it both addresses the scarcity of testimony about events there and explicitly proposes the images of the crematoria and the gas chambers as "silent witnesses" to the Nazis' crimes. The original voiceover script thus hints at the inadequacy of inanimate buildings as witnesses to Nazi crimes, a technique deployed in Soviet newsreel since 1941, whereas the final film glosses over the issue.

The shift in the voiceover may have stemmed from the fact that while the film was completed after the war had ended, it was largely made before the 8 May 1945 capitulation.[82] The final version of the voiceover anticipates the Nuremberg Tribunal and the decision there to focus on documents rather than witnesses so as to avoid any emotional excess that might be prejudicial to justice and the creation of a legal precedent.[83] Similarly anticipating the Nuremberg Tribunal, the film's subtitle refers to "film documents of the monstrous crimes of the German government in Auschwitz" (*Kinodokumenty o chudovishchnykh prestupleniiakh germanskogo pravitel′stva v Osventsime*). Thus, whereas the Majdanek film refers to "evil deeds" (*zlodeistva*), the Auschwitz film calls similar events "crimes" (*prestupleniia*). The difference here is that between a moral conceptualization of actions as evil and a legal definition of crimes, suggesting that they must be answered by a postwar legal process rather than in battle. *Auschwitz* does this more consistently than *Majdanek*.

In an analogous shift away from emotive and moral terminology, the final film discarded many earlier descriptions of the camp as hell or a form of death, just as it discarded the evocatively descriptive list of the various kinds of women's hair discovered: "women's hair. The hair of blondes, brunettes, the auburn-haired, the ashen-haired, the golden-haired, once soft, fragrant, living. Here it is packed into bales."[84] Similarly, the final cut resists personalizing the thirst for justice, which borders on retribution in the earlier version, in its final image of Soviet doctors inspecting the sick, that of a Hungarian boy identified as Wenkel, who was shot in the head for sharing his bread with a starving neighbor. The voiceover addresses him in the second person and explains why the SS trooper shot him in the head: "Not to kill him, but as a warning. A skull injury, paralysis of the arm and leg. How is your hand? Walk up and down the room. Don't worry, we'll make you better! So you can walk all over the world, to the ends of the Earth to find your torturers. We'll find them all."[85] This gives way to a series of photographs of the Nazis who ran the camp, and the accompanying words ("Take a good look at them. Remember them.") seem to be addressed not just to the spectator but also to the maimed boy and to imply that we should help find these people to assist his presumed quest for a personal settling of scores.

The final version of the film ends with an intertitle quoting the call from Stalin, Roosevelt, and Churchill for an international tribunal to judge war criminals. This note, that of a call for justice as a response to Nazi atrocities, ultimately prevails over all others, including that of mourning, which the film also invokes, but in a far less religious manner and with less emphasis on the culturally Polish character of the ceremony than either Majdanek film used.

## The Reception of the Auschwitz Film

As I have discussed, the production of *Auschwitz* was a protracted process, and even though its footage had been praised by the studio at the beginning of April, the film did not come out until the end of May. It seems likely that authorities delayed releasing the film until the war had ended and the war crimes commission had published its report on the camp, which came out on 8 May. The film was then passed for internal distribu-

FIGURE 6.10. *Auschwitz* advertisement from *Vecherniaia Moskva,* 30 May 1945.

tion on 28 May and shown in Moscow in a low-key run in three cinemas for three weeks beginning 31 May (fig. 6.10).

Whereas the Majdanek film had failed to receive a single review, one journalist, A. Krol´, dared to review *Auschwitz* for the Russian-language Kiev newspaper *Pravda Ukrainy.* Krol´ stressed the film's importance: "Everyone must see this film: not even the most powerful description can take the place of that which the camera has registered dispassionately."[86] While it is hard to be certain, this is probably the same A. N. Krol´ whose name appears on a list compiled by G. F. Aleksandrov, the Central Committee member in charge of propaganda; this document lists largely Jewish journalists whose "poor quality" articles had appeared in the Soviet press during June 1945.[87] However, while the fact of its publication is significant, the review itself largely just summarizes what the film shows and says nothing of Jewish victims, instead seeing the film as arguing that people were killed in the camp for their resistance to the Nazis: "guilty solely of loving their country and refusing to become Fascist slaves."

Despite the tentative domestic reception, Oshurkov, who was at this point back in Moscow, sent a telegram dated 15 June 1945 to his replacement as political commander of the First Ukrainian Front: "Film of Auschwitz received very well and released on screens of the USSR stop taking measures to send copies to your address."[88] Primarily, though, as was the Soviet Majdanek film, *Auschwitz* was always intended for foreign consumption. But the end of the war and emerging cold war tensions meant there was little appetite for such films. For example, although a copy of the film appears to have been sent to France soon after its release, the French were not keen to show it, apparently waiting some months to do so.[89] Nevertheless, in October 1945 the magazine *Paris-cinéma* referred to *Auschwitz* as even more realistic than the other two Soviet atrocity films, *Majdanek* and *The Kharkov Trial*.[90]

The film was most widely exhibited, however, in the Soviet occupied zone of Germany, where the Soviets screened specially edited versions of these films to show the Germans the crimes committed by the Nazis. From 1 June to 1 October 1945, Soviet production facilities struck sixty-nine German-language prints of *Auschwitz* and thirty-seven of *Majdanek*.[91]

A further objective in making this footage was to compile evidence not only to inform and influence domestic and international opinion but also to provide damning material for the planned international tribunal investigating Nazi war criminals. With the war over and preparations for the tribunal underway, Soviet film of Nazi crimes was positioned to meet the legal purposes for which it had supposedly always been intended. Footage from both *Majdanek* and *Auschwitz* was included as a crucial part of the film the Soviets submitted in their indictment at Nuremberg.

# 7 \ "The Dead Never Lie"

## SOVIET FILM, THE NUREMBERG TRIBUNAL, AND THE HOLOCAUST

**From the** moment they first began filming Nazi atrocities, in autumn 1941, the Soviets had invoked a legal rationale for doing so. As Roman Karmen said, "every meter of film, every frame, would be a terrifying document denouncing the Fascist hangmen."[1] The footage was to be shown at a future trial of the Nazis, demonstrating their crimes, especially those against the Soviets, to the whole world. This aspiration to legal redress was widespread in the Soviet Union, which, having suffered more losses than any other state involved in the war, became an important force calling for retributive justice against the Nazis. This call began with Molotov's four "notes" on war crimes, the first issued in November 1941; all four refer to notions of law contravened by Nazi atrocities. Other documents, too, invoked juridical notions, including the Supreme Soviet's 19 April 1943 decree declaring that Axis personnel and their accomplices found guilty of committing crimes against the Soviet Union would be publicly executed or sentenced to lengthy prison terms,[2] and the November 1943 Moscow Declaration. All these pronouncements proved crucial in paving the way to an international trial.[3]

Nonetheless, though Soviet newsreel makers and other journalists sincerely strove to record evidence of Nazi crimes as just that—crimes—it may seem strange that the idea of judging Nazis in a court originated in the pronouncements of Soviet leaders, since the Soviet Union itself was notorious for its extrajudicial detentions, deportations, and murders, as well as torture, forced confessions, show trials, and a general contempt for the rule of law.[4] As I have shown, however, the legalistic imperative had throughout the war coexisted uneasily with the desire to show images of Nazi atrocities so as to spur Soviet citizens to greater efforts toward victory. Ultimately, the calls for some sort of legal process were part of a wartime propaganda strategy aimed partly at bolstering the Soviets' image with their British and U.S. allies but above all at reestablishing the Soviet government's moral superiority among its own citizens, whom the war had shown to be so alienated that they were often attracted to the Nazis.

Soviet officials, then, understood the proposed judicial procedure primarily in terms of propaganda, along the lines of the 1930s Moscow show trials, but other factions warmed to the notion of an international tribunal during the course of the war, and as the proposed process took shape, it gained backing, particularly in the United States. While the proposed format included the didactic, not to say theatrical, elements of a show trial, the proceedings were given a legally robust basis guaranteeing their judicial integrity, despite Soviet involvement.[5] The consequence was the Nuremberg International Military Tribunal of Major Nazi War Criminals, a groundbreaking attempt to demonstrate the benefit of due process for international conflict. The tribunal was equally important for creating a framework that shaped the early understanding of the Holocaust, in particular by establishing the figure of six million Jewish dead "with the authority of a non-Jewish international agency."[6]

The trial incorporated novel means to achieve its aims, one of them being film admitted as evidence of the Nazis' crimes. Historians have paid significant attention to the two films that the U.S. team compiled and showed at the proceedings, *Nazi Concentration Camps* and *The Nazi Plan,* both directed by George Stevens, but they have tended to ignore the Soviet films, the most significant of which was *Film Documents of Atrocities Committed by the German-Fascist Invaders* (*Kinodukumenty o zverstvakh nemetsko-fashistskikh zakhvatchikov*; hereinafter referred to as *Film Documents of Atrocities*).[7] Given the suspicion that all information of Soviet provenance received, this disparity probably arose, at least in part, from an unease regarding the film's trustworthiness. Indeed, *Film Documents of Atrocities* was essentially a reedited compilation of footage that had been used for motivational or propagandistic ends in wartime Soviet newsreels and documentaries. The voiceover was more descriptive, but the polemical purpose behind the original material contradicted the title's claim that this was simply a document.

Whatever its polemical origins, the Soviet film was submitted as evidence relevant to the tribunal's most groundbreaking legal dimension: the indictment for "crimes against humanity," which has been described as "the first successful international prosecution for genocide."[8] Moreover, *Film Documents of Atrocities* in some respects outshines the other primary film shown as evidence at the trial, *Nazi Concentration Camps.* Though it suffers from significant shortcomings (e.g., it underplays Jewish victimhood, a fault shared with *Nazi Concentration Camps*), the Soviet film gives us far greater insight into the Holocaust than does the U.S. film, and if analyzed and contextualized carefully, it can correct some of the imbalances in representations of the Nazis' genocidal project that the trial is said to have initiated or perpetuated. As such, it constitutes an unjustly neglected early film of the Holocaust.

### *Film Documents of Atrocities* as a Framework for Understanding the Holocaust

While the trial as a whole is now widely accepted as having created significant and worthwhile legal precedents and marking a milestone in our understanding of the Holocaust, several historians, including Donald Bloxham, have argued that it misleadingly represented the Nazis' attempt to exterminate the Jews.[9] The significance of the Nuremberg Tribunal has grown dramatically over recent decades, a consequence both of the Holocaust's enormous importance in contemporary Western thinking and of the role that the tribunal's prosecution for crimes against humanity has played in setting a precedent for various subsequent such endeavors, such as the U.N. Security Council Resolution of 25 May 1993, which established the statute of the international criminal tribunal for the former Yugoslavia.[10] But it was not always thus, and scholars have debated the trial's legacy in American popular memory from the 1946 judgment itself until 1960. For example, the issue stands at the center of a colorful dispute between the historians Lawrence Baron and Peter Novick. While reluctantly conceding that the tribunal did not focus on the Holocaust, Baron has maintained that its ruling on crimes against humanity and war crimes was important in mentioning the Nazis' genocidal acts targeting Jews. Novick, however, has argued that the issue of genocide was peripheral to the proceedings and received little press coverage in the United States, so that it had little impact on public perceptions of the trial there.[11] Novick's position may be the better supported; for example, an influential 1977 history of the tribunal by Bradley F. Smith barely mentions the Holocaust and characterizes the tribunal's chief merit as its having "sharply limited the utility of such concepts as . . . 'crimes against humanity' in any future victors' trial."[12]

Indeed, the tribunal did not adequately emphasize the Jewish dimensions of the Nazi atrocities or the disproportionality of the consequent Jewish suffering. In addition, it contributed to three other distortions: first, it did not distinguish between concentration camps and death, or extermination, camps; second, it overemphasized the camps while marginalizing the Einsatzgruppen killings; and third, it failed to individuate or dramatize the victims sufficiently. Each of these three shortcomings is reflected in and perpetuated by *Nazi Concentration Camps.* In contrast, while *Film Documents of Atrocities* similarly fails to identify the staggeringly many victims it shows as Jewish, mentioning them as a group just once, it is superior to the U.S. film on all three counts: it shows images of the *extermination* camps of Auschwitz and Majdanek; it does not emphasize camps to the exclusion of Nazi mass shootings; and it far more successfully creates emotionally effective images of the victims, helping spectators to identify with them.

With respect to the first distortion, Bloxham argues that in eliding the difference between concentration camps and extermination camps, the tribunal hindered the emergence of "the proportional—let alone the conceptual—importance of the Holocaust," for "crimes against the Jews were subsumed within the general Nazi policies of repression and persecution."[13] This elision dominates *Nazi Concentration Camps,* which focuses exclusively on the concentration camps that U.S. and British troops liberated in Germany. As Lawrence Douglas argues, *Nazi Concentration Camps* "understands the crimes to be the consequence of aggressive militarism rather than genocide."[14] It consequently never mentions Auschwitz or the other death camps, Majdanek, Treblinka, Sobibór, Chełmno, and Bełżec, which do not even appear on the first draft of the map shown at the beginning of the film.[15] Indeed, the trial as a whole paid little attention to Auschwitz, let alone Treblinka, Sobibór, Chełmno, or Bełżec.[16] In contrast, *Film Documents of Atrocities* culminates with images of Majdanek and then Auschwitz, including the now familiar details of the gas chambers, the Zyklon B canisters, the crematoria, and the piles of effects. The commentary gives the now discredited initial Soviet figures for the dead in the two camps: 1,380,000 for Majdanek (current figures suggest between 80,000 and 250,000 died) and 4 million for Auschwitz (current figures suggest 1.1 million died; see chapter 6).[17]

This focus on the concentration camps relates to the second distortion as well, for although most of the Jews whom the Nazis murdered were killed in death camps, which the tribunal tended to conflate with concentration camps, the initial phase of the Final Solution began with the invasion of the Soviet Union and the mobile killing squads, or Einsatzgruppen, which were barely understood at the tribunal—the prosecution produced only one witness, Otto Ohlendorf, in relation to them.[18] An understanding of the variety of groups involved in the Einsatzgruppen killings would have helped tribunal officials to more firmly grasp the breadth of German military complicity in the atrocities; their absence from the proceedings allowed prosecutors to present the Wehrmacht and other non-SS organizations as largely guiltless, a narrative the British and U.S. governments in particular wanted to emphasize so as to enable the formation of a stable postwar West Germany.[19]

These two distortions in *Nazi Concentration Camps* arose in part from the fact that the British and U.S. troops had not liberated any of the death camps in the East, let alone seen firsthand evidence of the Einsatzgruppen killings, a situation that placed Soviet filmmakers in a far better position to tell how the Nazis killed Jews before they set up the death camps. *Film Documents of Atrocities* reflects this fact, for it avoids focusing on camps as the sole locus of Nazi murder and instead depicts the aftermath of a whole series of Nazi crimes in Russia, moving westward through Ukraine, Latvia, Estonia, and Belorussia before ultimately depicting the death camps at Auschwitz and Majdanek.

Finally, the Soviet film ameliorates the third distortion, too. Ostensibly in pursuit of objectivity, the trial's organizers chose to focus on documents rather than witnesses, a decision that privileged establishing legal precedent over capturing the public imagination.[20] Bloxham has argued that the trial consequently failed to dramatize the fates of the victims: "it neglected to ensure that the victims were given the stage. In consequence, few non-German and no Jewish names, faces, or stories were engraved on the collective consciousness."[21] The tribunal thus focused on the Nazi defendants, who have dominated films of the trial ever since. Certainly, *Nazi Concentration Camps* offered no individuated images of victims. As

Delage has pointed out, the Soviet film does name many of the victims, particularly in the initial footage from Russia, but he sees this as part of a "brutal" representational strategy, excessively harrowing in its graphic depiction of the bereaved relatives' distress.[22]

But such criticism overlooks the attempt in *Film Documents of Atrocities* to do what *Nazi Concentration Camps* does not. Because it includes images drawn from films that were intended to appeal to spectators' emotions, the Soviet film frequently emphasizes individual victims and presents them as connected with the viewer; it individuates the victims to elicit greater sympathy, sometimes by showing faces or giving names and sometimes by adding biographical detail, as it does when relating the tale of the boy identified as Vitia Golovlev, in Rostov, who it mentions was killed for refusing to hand over his dove (see chapter 2). While the commentary does not press the point, as the original newsreel's narrator does, the implication of the sequence remains: this could have been *our* child. Likewise, the first half of *Film Documents of Atrocities,* which is set entirely within the Soviet Union's pre-1939 borders, is dominated by the images of mothers, fathers, sons, or brothers grieving at the discovery of a dead loved one, scenes familiar from Soviet newsreels. As had the narration in those works, the commentary often spells out their relationships to the victims, and the camera pays particular attention to powerful expressions of grief, rendering the emotions in close-up and presenting the dead as related to the spectator. These frame witnesses constitute the rhetorical strategy most widely deployed by the Soviet film. Whereas the U.S. film shows U.S. and German military personnel and civilian officials witnessing the camps and evidence of Nazi atrocities there, the Soviet film initially shows Soviet citizens confronting the aftermath of the other atrocities, only afterward turning to the Red Army soldiers and members of the Soviet Extraordinary Commission on War Crimes witnessing the aftermath of such things.

Whereas the U.S. filmmakers sought above all to collect evidence,[23] the Soviet filmmakers intended to rouse their people to resist the Nazis, and the images in *Film Documents of Atrocities* exude this emotional involvement, despite being reinflected with a new commentary for their new, strictly judicial purpose. Moreover, despite the sworn affidavit that precedes *Film Documents of Atrocities* and attests its historicity, the Soviet films that provided the source material articulated this emotive call to action through a significant degree of reconstruction and conscious manipulation: the dead were chosen, identified carefully, and often posed or rearranged. The living were sometimes told how to react to loss or to the camera.

Although the narrative loses emotional intensity as the film moves into Poland and Germany, where images of grieving relatives are less prominent, it retains this strategy even in the Auschwitz footage, where it names a number of the surviving inmates, all of them Polish women. Child survivors appear here as well, and the commentary states that the Nazis killed children and induced pregnant women to give birth prematurely as the films shows a Red Army doctor performing an autopsy on a dead premature baby. This emphasis on the incarceration and murder of children not only serves as a trope in Soviet film but also restates the genocidal nature of the Nazi regime, whereas *Nazi Concentration Camps* focuses on that regime's aggressive militarism and repression of political opponents.

Nevertheless, *Film Documents of Atrocities* shows all other victims only by extension with Soviet victims. By starting with the Soviet Union, the narrative makes Soviet victimhood the paradigm and shows Nazi violence as effectively beginning in the Soviet Union and continuing from there. Indeed, the narrative emphasizes Russian victimhood above all. After watching the film, the Soviet playwright and journalist Vsevolod Vishnevskii spelled out the film's intended lesson: "The moving scenes when the mothers find their murdered children. How humanly terrifying and understandable is the scene when the mother carefully brushes off the dust, the straw from the collar and head of her son. Why did they kill you—those rosenbergs [*sic*] sitting over there? Because you are Russian."[24] This message was reinforced, as it had been in films such as *Defeat of the Germans near Moscow,* by one of the other films the Soviets submitted at Nuremberg: *The Destruction of Works of Art and Artifacts of National Culture, Wrought by the Nazis on the Territory of the USSR* (*Razrusheniia proizvedenii iskusstva i pamiatnikov natsional'noi kul'tury, proizvedennye nemtsami na territorii SSSR*), which concentrates on damage to architecturally important Russian buildings, especially churches and monasteries, as well as the destruction of places of historical interest linked to Russian writers and composers. No images of the synagogues that the Nazis ruined or defiled interrupt this catalog of damage to the Russian cultural heritage.

With its commentary, *Film Documents of Atrocities* is a deeply flawed account of the Holocaust or even Nazi genocidal practices in the East more broadly. As a silent film, however, despite the imprint of its original propagandist intent and Soviet geographical bias, this footage still has more potential to illuminate the Holocaust than does *Nazi Concentration Camps*. Indeed, one could use the footage in *Film Documents of Atrocities* to create a plausible film detailing a number of the major stages of the Holocaust from the beginning of its systematically murderous phase on 22 June 1941. Doing so would require nothing more than adding an entirely different voiceover detailing, among other things, the ethnicity of the victims, much as has been done for the Soviet footage of the liberation of Majdanek and Auschwitz.[25]

Although *Film Documents of Atrocities* represents Auschwitz, it says virtually nothing about the fact that mostly Jews were killed there. Like *Nazi Concentration Camps,* the Soviet film mentions Jews only once, in a list indicating the nationalities of concentration (or death) camp victims. It also goes out of its way to mention the deaths of Soviet prisoners of war, interrupting its otherwise strictly chronological order to show footage of a camp near Landsdorf, Silesia, where Soviet POWs were starved to death; this is inserted between images of atrocities in Lublin castle and at Majdanek, just outside Lublin. This, as well as the identification of many victims in the camps as Soviet POWs, participates in a sustained effort to ensure that the spectator sees the Soviets, and not the Jews (or any other group), as having suffered most at the hands of the Nazis.

From the Soviet perspective, the over 3 million Soviet POWs who were killed by the Nazis mattered more than the approximately 1.5 million Soviet Jews they murdered.[26] Certainly, as Berkhoff and others have argued, the Nazis' elimination of Soviet POWs may be considered genocidal.[27] Moreover, it overlaps with the Holocaust proper, for as Pavel Polian points out, "the Holocaust, as a system for the destruction of the Jewish race, began both conceptually and chronologically with the systematic murder of Jewish prisoners of war."[28] Nevertheless, even though the Soviets emphasized the notion of genocide, albeit not yet employing this newly coined term, they deliberately understated the particular nature of Jewish suffering, as they had already begun to do with increasing but not yet complete consistency toward the end of the war.

This emphasis on Soviet POWs is evident from the very first sequence of *Film Documents of Atrocities,* which utilizes footage from Rostov taken in November 1941, when the town was recaptured after an eight-day Nazi occupation. The Einsatzgruppen had murdered up to a hundred Jews during this occupation,[29] but the original newsreel fails to identify a Jewish identity for any of the victims shown. The same is true of the images of Babyi Iar, near Kiev; of Drobitskii Iar, near Kharkov; and of Kerch, Taganrog, and other places where the majority of victims were Jews. The sole exception occurs in an image from Klooga that briefly shows a dead prisoner's Star of David insignia, but the commentary does not point this out. In thus marginalizing the fate of Jews, however, the Soviets differed little from the other participants in the tribunal. For example, in his introductory speech on war crimes and crimes against humanity in Western Europe, which lasted several hours, the French prosecutor, François de Menthon, mentioned Jews only once, when he said that they had been discriminated against;[30] moreover, the chief U.S. prosecutor, Robert Jackson, thought that the trial as a whole would not be successful if it was seen as too "Jewish."[31]

The decision to begin the film with images from Russia may be justified by its organizational principle; apart from the previously noted significant exception, incidents are ordered chronologically, paralleling the order in which the Red Army liberated the named towns and discovered the atrocities. The commentary refers to dates when the atrocities occurred or, in many cases, when they started occurring. The presentation thus foregrounds Russia and Russian suffering by presenting it first in the narrative, associating it with the initial sight of horror. Everything that follows seems to confirm what we already know about the Nazis from their deeds in Russia.

Indeed, whereas the footage in *Nazi Concentration Camps* has been described as unprecedented,[32] much of *Film Documents of Atrocities* would have been familiar to anyone who had viewed Soviet wartime newsreels and compilation documentaries, for it comprises footage that had been appearing in such works since 1941. Previously, however, such distressing footage had usually been offset by uplifting images of the Red Army marching onward. With the war won, *Film Documents of Atrocities* was left with presenting an unalleviated succession of gruesome images of the dead, though it accompanies the footage with a less emotive, less agitational, and more descriptive voiceover.[33]

The issue of the voiceover commentary points to a further, inherent difficulty in the use of such footage. Such films' attempts to reconstruct what occurred will always be inadequate, all the more so in cases where the Nazis destroyed the evidence, leaving no corpses to disinter. While the Soviet film intimates the scale of the killings by showing the victims' effects, nothing remained of the dead but "graves in the air," to use Paul

Celan's celebrated image.[34] Attempts at using documentary film to provide faces and individual stories flounder before the unrepresentability of the gas chambers.

Eyewitness testimony, of course, provides one approach to overcoming this problem. The Soviet film, however, contrasts with the U.S. film in its complete absence of synchronously recorded interviews.[35] This lack did not arise from technical limitations, since the archives of Soviet wartime film include several synchronously recorded interviews with eyewitnesses, but all such synch sound footage was deliberately and systematically excluded from *Film Documents of Atrocities*. Instead, the visible dead dominate. Where we see the living, their words are at best summarized in indirect speech. This bias against witness testimony characterizes Soviet wartime documentary as a whole, as well as prewar films of show trials, such as Il´ia Kopalin's film *The Verdict of the Court Is the Verdict of the People* (*Prigovor suda—prigovor naroda* [1938]) and Roman Karmen's documentary film of the Nuremberg Tribunal itself, *The Judgment of the Nations* (*Sud narodov* [1946]; subsequently released in English as *Nuremberg Trials* [1947]). Nonetheless, the Soviets' first wartime attempt to film trials included a great deal of synchronous sound footage, granting the witnesses and the bereaved a voice.

### *Justice Is Coming*: Precursors and Precedents

Beginning with the first war crimes trial, at Krasnodar, in the northern Caucasus, the Soviet leadership in particular saw such prosecutions "as an instrument of propaganda—as a means to publicize German atrocities committed on Soviet territory to bolster the country's moral authority internationally."[36] This was especially important in the wake of the Nazis' revelations about the Katyn massacre in April 1943. The Soviets thus used the public trial of Nazi collaborators in Krasnodar, held during July 1943, as an opportunity to film legal proceedings involving Nazi crimes, the first such film to be made. The result was a twenty-minute special-edition newsreel, *The People's Verdict* (*Prigovor naroda*), directed by Irina Setkina, which attracted little public attention even in the Soviet Union when it was released in September 1943, less than two months after the trial had ended.[37] The fact that the Nazis were tried here in absentia, with only Soviet collaborators present in the dock, limited international interest, for the proceedings could be discounted as another Soviet show trial, like those of the late 1930s.[38] After all, the defendants were tried under the infamous article 58 of the Soviet penal code, "anti-Soviet activities," which as Alexander Solzhenitsyn commented, covered pretty much anything.[39] Such an impression was not dispelled by the film's title, which recycled that of a 1938 film about the show trials.

The Krasnodar trial film, the first in this genre, nevertheless placed synchronously recorded witness testimony at its center, allocating very little space to the prosecutor's speech. It also included interviews with individuals in the crowd of people who had come to watch the executions of the collaborators, asking them to elaborate on their knowledge of these crimes. While no one says anything that contradicts the message required by the Soviet authorities, presumably because political exigencies dictated that the filmmakers omit such footage, the emphasis here rests on the common Soviet people as the key agent in passing judgment on the accused; as the film's title states, this was "the people's verdict." The film presents the state as merely the instrument of retribution, not its agent.

Krasnodar was followed by a long series of Soviet-run trials, the first being the most significant. That trial, held in Kharkov during December 1943, constituted the first instance in which captured German Nazis were prosecuted in person for their crimes, including the killing of Soviet Jews. This received even greater coverage in the Soviet press and on Moscow radio than had its predecessor.[40] Again a film was made of these proceedings, but this time it was a more ambitious feature-length documentary entitled *Justice Is Coming* (*Sud idet,* released in English as *The Kharkov Trials*); Il´ia Kopalin, who had codirected *The Defeat of the Germans near Moscow,* directed this documentary, which was distributed widely in Moscow beginning 18 January 1944.

This documentary was then sent to the United States and Britain, where a July 1944 London *Times* review dubbed *The Kharkov Trials* "perhaps the most important film the war has yet produced."[41] The attention it attracted there, and later in France, may well have influenced the decision to film in the courtroom at Nuremberg.

Again, the Soviet Union held more trials like the one in Kharkov, producing films of these legal proceedings, and some conventions emerged. As does *The People's Verdict, The Kharkov Trials* presents a condensed version of prosecution speeches, witness statements, and cross-examination, but the latter film includes far more images of the Nazis' victims than does the former. In doing so, it served as a model for Karmen's film of the Nuremberg Tribunal, *The Judgment of the Nations.* Unlike the Kharkov and

Krasnodar films, however, Karmen's film contains no witness testimony and very little synchronous sound footage of cross-examination. Instead of letting viewers hear their voices, the filmmaker interspersed images of the victims of Nazi atrocities within sequences showing the trial, doing so to shocking effect.

### The Judgment of the Nations

The Nuremberg Tribunal bore purposes beyond the solely legal, for it was also intended to be a spectacle that would publicly demonstrate Nazi guilt. As such, the proceedings were defined by tension between representation and justice, or pageant and process.[42] Indeed, this conflict has marked not just the Nuremberg Tribunal but all subsequent war crimes trials.[43] As pageant, the trial certainly generated enormous media interest; the over three hundred European and American press and radio correspondents covering the trial were joined by over one hundred cameramen, filmmakers, and photographers.[44]

The Soviets sent Roman Karmen to cover the proceedings (fig. 7.1). Karmen, who drew on his experience in filming the war, faced the not inconsiderable task of producing a feature-length film that would summarize the generally tedious year-long proceedings from the Soviet perspective but in a dramatically engaging way, one that could appeal to the wider forum of world opinion. Events outside the courtroom, however, transformed the political landscape, complicating his task still further. On 5 March 1946 Winston Churchill gave a speech at Westminster College, in Fulton, Missouri, where he coined the term "the iron curtain," effectively beginning the cold war.[45] Journalists in the Soviet Union and elsewhere lost interest in the trial, seeing it as an inconvenient expression of a wartime alliance that had already fragmented.

Karmen felt this ambivalent situation keenly. Writing from Nuremberg that summer, he mentioned the "very cold attitude of the Studio" and "voices about the film being unnecessary."[46] In fact, he was given mixed signals: Ivan Bol´shakov, the minister for cinema, encouraged him, while Karmen's own studio bosses told him that his pieces for newsreels covering the trial, such as *At the Trial of the Major Nazi War Criminals in Nuremberg* (*Na protsesse glavnykh voennykh prestupnikov v Niuremberge* [1946]), were not well received.

Moreover, the atmosphere within the Soviet Union was becoming increasingly repressive, with suspicion particularly directed at those who

FIGURE 7.1. Roman Karmen's Nuremburg ID card. Courtesy of Muzei kino.

had links to the West and Jews, making Karmen doubly an object of suspicion. Indeed, he had good reason to fear that he was being scrutinized closely, for the Soviets' delegation to Nuremberg included Chekists (security officers) such as Captain P. I. Grishaev, subsequently in charge of persecuting the Jewish Antifascist Committee.[47] Such constant scrutiny by the secret police added to the pressure that the filmmakers and other members of the delegation felt simply in doing their work. For example, the Soviet prosecutors had been directed both to evaluate each document submitted in evidence so as to determine whether disclosing it would undermine the interests of the Soviet Union and to prevent the prosecutors' committee from using any documents found to be damaging.[48] Reactions to defendants' "anti-Soviet" statements were monitored so closely that G. N. Aleksandrov (an investigator on the Soviet team) asked that denunciations on such matters stop, for, he said, they were "creating a nervous atmosphere and hindering work."[49] Instead, the Politbureau appointed Andrei Vyshinskii, of the Moscow show trials fame, to head a newly created Nuremberg-based commission assigned to control the Soviet contribution, after which the NKVD sent Stalin almost daily telegrams describing the course of events.[50]

Despite these pressures, Karmen immersed himself in the work creatively, waiting patiently to catch revealing poses from the defendants with his hand-held Eyemo camera.[51] He duly delivered his completed film a little over a month after the verdict, and *The Judgment of the Nations* was released in the Soviet Union on 23 November 1946.[52]

In seeking to render the protracted and often dull proceedings in an engaging way, Karmen placed the accused at the center of the film.[53] He did not, however, attempt to emulate the Soviet caricaturists, such as Boris Efimov and the triumvirate who signed their pictures "the Kukryniksy," who portrayed the Nazi leaders as grotesque and repulsive animals whose appearance was entirely consonant with their heinous crimes (fig. 7.2). While actors in Soviet and other feature films had used this approach before (and would again), such an obviously manipulative technique would have been inappropriate for a documentary and difficult to adapt to that genre in any case.

Other accounts of the trial, such as the one by the *New Yorker* correspondent Rebecca West, emphasized the defendants' banality, anticipating Hannah Arendt's famous "banality of evil" thesis expressed with regard to the Adolf Eichmann trial in Jerusalem in 1961.[54] This view was shared by the Soviet prosecutor M. Raginskii, who commented on the discrepancy between the insignificant appearance of the accused and "the colossal evil they had inflicted on humanity."[55]

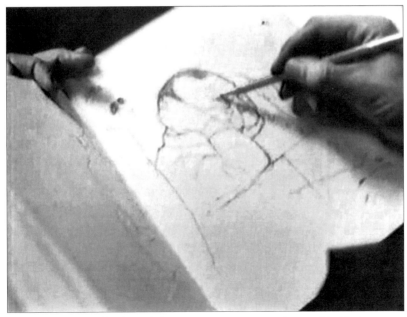

FIGURE 7.2. Kukryniksy (artists) drawing Göring. From *Judgment of the Nations*.

Karmen's method for revealing an underlying depravity was to look for nervous ticks:

> Karmen understood that the main thing was to show the criminals themselves on screen, to convey a truthful, accurate picture of those whose names were pronounced with curses by millions of people. At the same time, as an artist who had devoted his craft to the struggle against Fascism, Karmen, photographing these people who had committed the most terrifying crimes in the world, could not remain impassive. It was precisely this strength of feeling that suggested to him, as a cameraman, the manner in which his film should be constructed and filled it with the passionate polemical tone of political journalism.
>
> Over the course of many years of observing human behavior while he was making his films, Karmen had become used to noticing his subjects' facial expressions, the involuntary or habitual gestures that a person makes without realizing it. From these little details a living portrait can be formed. It is possible to capture these funny gestures with the camera lens and the portrait will be humorous, or you can also create a savage caricature. A different kind of approach was required for the "characters" in the Nuremberg Tribunal. . . .
>
> Göring, now slim and crumpled, began to cover his face with his hand, and then he wiped his neck.
>
> "It's as if he can feel the noose," thought Karmen. "The noose. . . . " Göring's nervous reflex called to mind a multitude of thoughts. Or rather pushed his thinking in a certain direction. Armed with his camera, like a hunter after his prey, he began to lie in wait for the enemy. Now Karmen did not take his eyes off the bench where the criminals sat, so as not to miss this expressive gesture. "Surely," thought Karmen, "Göring will wipe his neck again[;] Hess, the lying, squirming hypocrite, will lift his hand up to his face again."
>
> The filmmaker was willing to wait for days. His calculations proved correct. Soon the affectation and poses deserted the accused.[56]

When these defendants' various nervous mannerisms were combined with images of the crimes committed on their watch and their statements justifying such actions, they came to seem like expressions of repressed guilt. Thus Karmen uses Hess's gesture of raising his hand to his head to symbolize not just Hess's apparent memory loss in particular but also that of all the Nazis who pretended to have forgotten about their crimes (fig. 7.3). The image introduces a long train of images of the Nazis in their pomp. Es-

FIGURE 7.3. "We will remind you, Hess." From *Judgment of the Nations.*

sentially, Karmen used the Soviet avant-garde's Kuleshov effect, whereby meaning not inherent in the separate shots is created through their combination. In this case, the effect was created by the virtuoso editor Elizaveta Svilova, herself the wife of a living legend of the avant-garde, Dziga Vertov. Svilova's unparalleled editing skills gave *The Judgment of the Nations* its final form, and the credits duly listed her as coeditor.

Curiously, the film's fascination with the moments when the Nazis were confronted with their crimes dominates firsthand accounts of its screening, in both contemporary journalistic pieces and subsequent memoirs.[57] Indeed, Karmen had aspired to capture such moments at least since 1941, when he recorded the shock of an SS man as he was made to look at the bodies of his victims.[58] Commenting on the same anticipated confrontation of Nazi perpetrators with their crimes, Ilya Ehrenburg wrote: "Fascism brings death. It does not want to look at itself. Germany fears the mirror: it farcically covers it up. . . . But we shall drive it to the mirror, we shall force the German Fascists to look at themselves."[59] Karmen's Nuremberg film thus uses montage to create a scenario wherein all the Nazis are unnerved and disturbed by images showing the consequences of their actions. While the film's organization and presentation is important, however, and its depiction of Nazis is dramatically engaging, those aspects remain less important than its analysis of Nazism and the Holocaust. This analysis depends not just on the images chosen but also, and even more heavily, on the way in which the voiceover commentary describes them.

### The Evolution of Karmen's Film and Its Commentary

The voiceover commentary constitutes an element absolutely central to Karmen's account of Nazism and the Holocaust. The final draft of this commentary was written by Boris Gorbatov:

> Boris Gorbatov became involved in the work on the film. As someone who had traveled the roads of war in a soldier's uniform, he saw and sensed the material in the same way as the director. The passionate, indignant words of the voiceover he wrote intensified the effect of the visual images[;] at times they brought a note of philosophical reflection, at times [they] strengthened its emotional resonance.
>
> Gorbatov's text was not at all like a normal voiceover commentary: it was a direct speech addressed to those whose faces were shown on the screen, a wrathful monologue, and sometimes the phrases were as rhythmical and expressive as poetry.[60]

Shifting Soviet attitudes toward the Holocaust, however, led the film's makers to significantly revise the commentary during the summer and early autumn of 1946. The earlier version contains much more material about the Jews, including extracts from a diary entry by one of the defendants, a former governor-general of Poland, Hans Frank, concerning the destruction of the Warsaw ghetto: "This neat album of photographs contains SS *Obergruppenfuhrer* General ——'s report on the annihilation of the Warsaw ghetto. In a few days —— thousand Jews—women, old children and children—were incinerated or shot. We turn the pages of the album. Terrifying photos: women and children shot point-blank. The faces of the murdered insane with terror. People throwing themselves from the upper floors of burning houses."[61]

The striking emphasis here on mass killings, specifically of Jews, is conveyed through powerful visual images that appear as the commentary mentions the Warsaw ghetto and its Jewish population. A subsequent draft of the screenplay removes this episode and all references to the destruction of the Warsaw ghetto but nevertheless quotes another excerpt from

Hans Frank's diary: "Jews are a race that must be annihilated. Wherever we catch them, every last one, they will be done away with. Here we started with three and a half million Jews, now all that's left of them is a few work teams. As for the rest—we will say at some point—they emigrated."[62] Incredibly, the final version of *The Judgment of the Nations* still refers to Frank's genocidal intention by quoting this passage from his diary, but it weakens the force of this sentiment by detaching the description from the images that were to have illustrated the other passage in the previous version.

Similarly, the earlier draft's text refers to scenes depicting Jewish shops smashed during Germany's Kristallnacht, 9–10 November 1938, describing the event as a "Jewish pogrom," and this sequence is followed by images of Julius Streicher (fig. 7.4), whom the commentary describes as "the organizer of anti-Semitic pogroms in Germany, the ideologue of the extermination of the Jewish people."[63] In the final film, however, the images of Kristallnacht come elsewhere and can be identified as showing a "Jewish pogrom" only if the spectator is able to pause the frame and read the word *Juden* on a Nazi placard exhorting passers-by to boycott Jewish businesses and extrapolate from that to the more extreme instances

FIGURE 7.4. Julius Streicher. From *Judgment of the Nations*.

FIGURE 7.5. Kristallnacht 1938, Nazis picket Jewish-owned shops. From *Judgment of the Nations*.

of Nazi anti-Jewish measures (fig. 7.5). In the predigital age of 1946, few viewers possessed the means to pause such films and thus could not grasp their oblique references.

This passing mention of Nazi anti-Semitism, detached from its visual depiction, makes this sequence in the final film far less powerful than its counterpart in the version planned earlier. Moreover, even though Roman Rudenko, the chief Soviet prosecutor at Nuremberg, referred to the Nazis' intentions to kill all Jews when he made his opening statement,[64] on 8 February, he offered the reference for the benefit of an international audience, not a domestic one.

Ultimately, even though the final version of Karmen's film mentions the Nazi persecution of Jews, it downplays any sense of the systematic attempt at genocide; even Karmen's earlier drafts for the screenplay made that case more strongly. Yet the film's most marked gesture with regard to representing Nazi atrocity in general and the Holocaust in particular lies in the director's decision not just to silence the witnesses who testified at the trial but to omit them entirely.

## Documents versus Witnesses

*The Judgment of the Nations* received many reviews from Soviet critics, a couple of whom pointed to the absence of witnesses. Thus M. Gus, writing in *Sovetskoe iskusstvo,* praises the film but laments the decision to omit all the witness testimonies against the Nazis, instead using film itself as a form of testimony.[65] Iu. Korol´kov makes the same point in a review appearing in *Literaturnaia gazeta:* "Unfortunately, the witnesses who spoke at the trial are not shown in the film either. This is unfortunate, as the subject is a worthwhile one: the testimony of the witnesses, representatives of the widest range of nationalities, provided exceptionally persuasive confirmation that Fascism brought slavery and death to all the peoples of the world."[66]

What explains the absence of witness testimony from Karmen's film? In contrast, recent documentaries of the trial concentrate on this testimony, such as that of Friedrich von Paulus, which Karmen later described as an "atom bomb" and had included not only in an earlier draft of the film but also in his two-reel special-release newsreel *At the Trial of the Major War Criminals in Nuremberg (Na protsesse glavnykh voennykh prestupnikov v Niuremberge* [1946]).[67] He might also have included the testimony of Marie-Claude Vaillant-Couturier, a former inmate of Auschwitz who provided a high-quality witness account of the camp and features prominently in Delage's film,[68] or the Russian-language testimony of Severina Smaglevskaia, who attested to the overwhelming numbers of Jews murdered at Auschwitz. In total, the court heard ninety-four witnesses, thirty-three for the prosecution and sixty-one for the defense.[69] This is not a large number given the trial's ten-month duration, and the relative paucity of witnesses reflects the preference of the chief prosecutor, among others. Justice Jackson insisted that documents play a more important role than witnesses, some of whom Jackson put on the stand only after pressure from journalists and the staff of the U.S. prosecutorial delegation.[70] The issue even led him to sack his first deputy, William J. Donovan, who disagreed with and criticized this strategy, arguing instead for the use of eyewitnesses to give the trial a more powerful human dimension.[71] Even when they got to the stand, the witnesses were not used effectively, as Annette Wieviorka stresses: "The witnesses had not been called upon to tell their stories, to move the judges or the public present at the trial, but essentially to confirm, comment on, and supplement the content of written documents. The Nuremberg trials marked the triumph of the written over the oral."[72]

To compensate, George Stevens structured the U.S. film *Nazi Concentration Camps* in a way intended to replace witnesses: "the filmic witness could offer pictures where speech failed; it could produce visual knowledge of atrocities that resisted summary in the words of eyewitness testimonials."[73] In his depiction of the trial, Karmen goes further and entirely dispenses with any witnessing other than photographic images showing the aftermath of Nazi atrocities. This decision stemmed partly from Karmen's desire to enliven the film by escaping the confines of the courtroom: "The principle behind the film's structure was based upon avoiding the boredom which might easily have resulted had we kept the spectator in the courtroom for all six reels, and so we constantly take the spectator beyond the courthouse and show what these criminals did, then we show the material our Soviet cameramen recorded following hot on the heels of the army."[74] The indictment for crimes against humanity, spoken by the Soviet prosecutor Rudenko and rendered in synchronous sound, is illustrated through close-ups of the defendants, images of their acts, and documents illustrating their guilt. The editing is fast and persuasive, but there is no place for witness testimony.

Yet for Karmen, the footage of Nazi atrocities *was* witness testimony—unlike other journalists, people who film for newsreels must be present at the scenes they report. In photographing these grisly scenes, Karmen and his colleagues saw themselves as collecting evidence that ultimately would help indict the Nazis. In certain cases, such as that of El´bert, who had taken the images of Volokolamsk, the cameramen had fallen in action and were unavailable to corroborate the footage they had taken. Karmen, however, was now determined to make the footage for which he could vouch the very center of his film: "When we filmed during the war, we said at all the triumphant meetings and in our articles we wrote that we shall at some point present this document at the court of nations. But that 'at some point' was very distant and vague, but now victory really has come, and the court of nations has come too."[75] One of Karmen's earlier drafts of the voiceover emphasized this process by which Nazi Germany was brought to account. The victories at Moscow and Stalingrad enabled revelations of the Nazis' crimes, and the film was to include the following commentary accompanying images of a cameraman standing on an advancing tank filming from a hatch with an Eyemo camera:

FIGURE 7.6. Soviet prosecutor Colonel Pokrovskii: "The dead never lie." From *The Judgment of the Nations.*

Together with the forward units of the Red Army, Soviet newsreel cameramen advanced too. They knew that Hitler's criminals would appear before a court of nations. They knew that every frame they took would enter history as a powerful document for the prosecution of the Fascist hangmen. Filming, we knew that the day would come when these terrifying film documents would be presented as evidence of the inexcusable crimes of Fascism. THIS DAY HAS COME.

SO LOOK, MURDERERS, AT YOUR WORK!

Pan of the bench of the accused. GÖRING. KEITEL. KALTEN-BRUNNER. FRANK. PAPEN. FRICH.

LOOK! YOUR VICTIMS HAVE COME TO IDENTIFY YOU.[76]

The final screenplay discarded this reflexive sense of the film's creation and of the rationale behind taking these images. Nevertheless, these frames—overwhelmingly of the dead—are used as a form of witness. Karmen's final version tellingly quotes the Soviet prosecutor Colonel Pokrovskii speaking after *Film Documents of Atrocities* was screened at the tribunal: "Gentlemen judges! Before you there have passed tens of thousands of witnesses. I cannot name them, you cannot swear them in, but it is impossible not to believe them, for the dead never lie" (fig. 7.6).

Then again, perhaps the dead do sometimes lie, as when the reasons for their deaths are not elucidated and they are made to articulate a misleading or biased representation. At the same time, like the Soviet films of the camps (see chapter 6), Karmen's film does effectively draw attention to the essential paradox of the witness in representations of the Holocaust: being dead, their corpses obliterated, the truest witnesses are unable to testify. Thus the attempt to make the dead serve as witnesses may be seen as a rather significant one, since they are the best qualified. Karmen's film, though, puts words in their mouths and makes them less witnesses than echoes of the Soviet prosecution: "The living and the dead have come to the court of the peoples. They are invisibly present in the courtroom. They are on the prosecutors' stand."

Some Russian legal historians have stressed the way in which Soviet courtroom practice consistently undermined the independent legal function of witnesses. Thus, particularly during the Great Terror, witnesses were treated like the accused and similarly intimidated, tortured, and told what to say.[77] Witness statements were usually supplied by OGPU/NKVD agents not identified as such, even to the courts. They were not even called to testify unless there was doubt about their statements, an exceptional situation since the defense was almost nonexistent.[78] On the rare occasions when they were called, any witness who forgot something was supplanted by previously written testimony that was then read into evidence.[79] Similarly, in Karmen's film, the dead do not contravene but only confirm the preestablished Soviet line, as they had been made to do throughout Soviet wartime film. Although Karmen thought about reflecting on the origins of the images, ultimately all questions concerning both provenance (who took the footage, in what circumstances, and to what purpose) and editorial considerations (what to use and what to omit) are pushed from the viewers' minds as the shocking contrasts, the pace of the editing, and the sharply polemical voiceover absorb their focus. Indeed, Karmen faced great difficulty in shaping a strong narrative from the lengthy and disparate elements of the Nuremberg Tribunal, where all the proceedings were simultaneously translated into four languages. In fact, the trial's organizers no doubt eschewed witnesses in part to cut down on such simultaneous translation, for documents could be translated in advance.[80] Similarly, from a technical point of view, synchronous sound footage was far harder to edit and manipulate than were silent images, to which the filmmaker could give almost any meaning.[81]

Karmen's distrust of synchronous sound was an extension of a wider distrust of witness testimony at the trial, especially among the Soviets.[82] Karmen treated synchronously recorded testimony much as Soviet authorities treated the witness Abraham Sutzkever, a Yiddish-language poet and partisan of the Vilnius ghetto whom they asked to testify at the Nuremberg Tribunal. Sutzkever insisted on testifying in Yiddish, seeing himself as a "living witness to the immortality of [his] people": "I will go to Nuremberg. . . . I feel the crushing responsibility that I bear on this journey. I pray that the vanished souls of the martyrs will manifest themselves through my words. I want to speak in Yiddish[;] any other language is out of the question. . . . I wish to speak in the language of the people whom the accused attempted to exterminate."[83] Sutzkever became increasingly uncertain as to whether he would be allowed to testify, noting in his diary: "I sense that there are some reservations about my appearance on the witness stand."[84] Finally he did speak, on 27 February 1946, but in Russian.[85] For the Soviets, to permit Sutzkever to testify at Nuremberg in Yiddish would be to allow the Jewish narrative of the Holocaust undue prominence, which was why he was forced to use Russian. Likewise, Soviet authorities prevented the publication of Ehrenburg and Grossman's *Black Book* principally because of the firsthand nature of the accounts, mostly from Jews, that it contains.[86]

Having excluded such firsthand accounts, the final version of Karmen's film adds a further chapter to the consistent picture of Soviet discomfort over witness testimony, especially of Nazi atrocities. Witnesses' exclusive relation to the traumatic event grants them an authority not conferred by the structures of the state or the party. Moreover, witness testimony expresses memory in its most individual, emotionally charged, and inchoate form; it is difficult if not impossible to control and does not necessarily adhere to the overarching historical narrative.[87]

*Judgment of the Nations* instead conveys a highly Sovietized narrative of the trial. Always intended at least in part for export, the film enjoyed the scoop factor of being "the first complete story" of the trial to be released in the United States.[88] *The Nuremberg Trials,* as its English-language version was named, ran for a month and was cleverly promoted, with over two thousand lawyers and law students in the metropolitan New York area invited to screenings.[89] Nevertheless, the film so relentlessly emphasizes both the Soviet role in the trial and the Nazis' crimes against the Soviet peoples that even some of the Soviet Union's supporters in the West, such as Paul Rotha, called the English version's commentary "naïve to the point of embarrassment."[90] Although positive reviews appeared in the *New York Times* and elsewhere,[91] the *New York Herald Tribune* condemned the film in no uncertain terms:

> If the Russians prefer to use the Nuremberg trials for their peculiar propaganda purposes, it is alright with this reviewer. The thing is that the Soviets ought to keep such a film as "The Nuernberg Trials" [*sic*] strictly for home consumption. The reiteration of the propaganda line that the Nazi menace was about to engulf the world until halted by the Red armies is not likely to win friends.
>
> There is nothing new in the current film, an elongated newsreel. Strange as it seems, the pictures of the Nazi atrocities have somehow lost their steam through constant repetition. This moviegoer has developed a defense mechanism where a flat picture having no depth or color is only a bad dream to be forgotten as quickly as possible.[92]

Karmen's film duly was forgotten, especially as momentum was growing in the campaign to root out communist influence in Hollywood. Nonetheless, while it has been called offensive,[93] as have the other films I have considered in the previous pages, its value as a representation of the Nazis' Final Solution, like that of *Film Documents of Atrocities,* depends on a historical and filmic recontextualization, a sense of the representational choices it makes, of what it does not say as much as what it does.

# Epilogue

***The Unvanquished*** may be seen as one of several early, faltering attempts by Soviet Jews to rethink their identity by depicting what we now term the Holocaust.[1] *The Black Book,* Ilya Ehrenburg and Vasilii Grossman's 1945 compilation of Nazi crimes against Soviet Jewry, was another such attempt, and when the two men assembled it, there was still hope that it would be published in the Soviet Union.[2] Such efforts, however, were increasingly denounced as Jewish nationalism and repressed, and this era saw an upsurge in anti-Semitism, including a pogrom in Kiev in 1945, not long before the release of Donskoi's film.[3] Mentioning the Nazis' persecution specifically of Jews soon became almost impossible in Soviet cinema, as it was in Soviet historiography and journalism. The subject would not again be addressed in the Soviet Union until the "Thaw" era.

*The Black Book* was banned in 1947; the victims of a subsequent wave of intensified anti-Semitic terror included Veniamin Zuskin, the actor who had portrayed Dr. Fishman in the *The Unvanquished*. After Mikhoels was murdered, in 1948, Zuskin took over the State Jewish Theater in Moscow but was arrested the same year and later murdered by the MGB, as were other members of the Jewish Antifascist Committee in August 1952.[4] The rise of postwar Soviet anti-Semitism is key to understanding why this and other similar films were forgotten. For a time, this wave of anti-Semitism prevented filmmakers from extending the group of films I have considered in this book.

## Soviet Postwar Anti-Semitism

As I have shown, the war initially served to interrupt the rising tide of Soviet-inflected Russian nationalism and permitted some appeals to Jews as Jews, especially in the darkest days of 1941 and 1942. Even Stalin himself publicly condemned the Nazis' killings of Jews in November 1941.[5] Nevertheless, as I discussed in chapters 2 and 3, references to and depictions of Jews and their fate under the Nazis were kept within strictly controlled limits, and the initial still-limited openness ultimately proved to have been a brief hiatus in the increasingly ethnic Russian underpinning to expressions of Soviet identity, which received an enormous boost from the war and was celebrated triumphantly in Stalin's victory-day toast to the Russian people.[6] When this renewed force confronted the resurgence of Jewish cultural self-definition and self-assertion in the wake of the Holocaust, interethnic tension increased.

The historian Amir Weiner has ably and sensitively analyzed the shift in Soviet identity that occurred during World War II and the attendant rise in anti-Semitism. He sees this as a gradual transition from defining opponents in class terms to defining them in ethnic terms, which he calls a "thorough ethnicization of the Soviet world before, during, and after the war." The war aided this shift.[7] Interestingly, however, Weiner rejects the notion that this new Sovietized Russian nationalism marked only a return to the old "Russian anti-Semitism" evident in the czarist period. Instead, Weiner argues the more important point to be not that the discourse was already present in the culture but that it became hegemonic. The question then becomes how and why it attained hegemonic status.[8]

One dimension of this development was a rising level of grassroots anti-Semitism, which in part resulted from Nazi propaganda, especially in the occupied territories.[9] Populations there resented Jews returning with the Red Army or from evacuation.[10] This led to pogroms such as the one in Kiev in 1945.[11] The contagion, however, spread more widely. It was related to another expression of this anti-Semitism, one that was more systematic and related just as much to areas that remained thousands of miles from the front throughout the war. This form of the poison came not from below but from above and initially involved things like the relocation of arts and science institutions back to Moscow from beyond the Urals, where they had been placed during the war. In the process, Jews were sometimes effectively left behind in the Far East, as occurs to the main character, Viktor Shtrum, in Vasilii Grossman's historical novel *Life and Fate* (*Zhizn' i sud'ba*, finished in 1959 but published only in 1980). Similarly, officials attempted to replace Jews with non-Jews in various other institutions, including Mosfil'm.[12]

These tendencies were already significant by 1944, years before the formation of the state of Israel, with memories of the war and the Holocaust playing a central role in the deterioration of relations between Jews and non-Jewish segments of Soviet society. Weiner stresses the importance of commemoration of the Holocaust:

> Conventional wisdom points to the establishment of the state of Israel and the unfolding cold war as the primary causes for the deterioration in the status of the Jewish community within the Soviet polity. Indeed, the creation of the Israeli state transformed Soviet Jewry overnight into a diaspora nation with a highly active external homeland. In the 1930s a similar situation cost Polish and German minorities in the Soviet Union dearly. Often glossed over, however, is the centrality of the living memory of the war and the Jewish genocide in shaping the course of Soviet-Jewish relations and providing them with a constant point of reference in the years following the war.[13]

As I have discussed, several works in both film and print attempted to depict the Holocaust in the immediate postwar period, but they all met persistent and increasing opposition. Nevertheless, as the Israeli historian Kiril Feferman has pointed out, references to the fate of the Jews under the Nazis continued to be published fitfully throughout this period; Ehrenburg's 1948 novel *The Storm* (*Buria*) even received a Stalin prize, despite its portrayal of Babyi Iar in a passage that clearly indicates the victims as Jewish.[14]

After the state of Israel had been established, however, the Soviet state came to see Jews as potential enemies, an attitude that helped lead to the 1949 campaign against "cosmopolitans," which in fact targeted Jews, and the arrest of the members of the Jewish Antifascist Committee. These circumstances made depicting the Jewish Holocaust virtually impossible and the potential dangers of doing so more severe than ever. The war became an important subject for late Stalin-era Soviet cinema, but the initial emphasis was on victory and Stalin's role in it rather than on the terrible price paid, especially by Soviet Jews. Instead, Jews were doubly marginalized by public memory of the war, which emphasized both "ethnic hierarchies of heroism and the simultaneous leveling of suffering."[15] Even when the post-Stalin era reintroduced the possibility of considering the price paid for victory, the Jewish tragedy was effectively subsumed into a universalized Soviet suffering.[16]

In her book about the Soviet, and especially Russian, culture of World War II commemoration, Nina Tumarkin attributes this elision of the Jewish fate to "the psychological economy of suffering: from the point of view of official Soviet historiography, the Germans had meted out to all the Soviet peoples a most horrible fate; to have granted to the Jewish people an equal or (in terms of this logic) higher status on the pecking order of martyred nationalities would have vitiated somewhat the Soviet claims on behalf of their own victimization, and was therefore impermissible."[17] The wartime depictions of particular Jewish suffering were now simply ignored, which was easy enough, because such representations were already both rare and marginal. During the Stalin era, for example, Veniamin Zuskin's murder by the MGB (successor to the NKVD), which occurred as part of the campaign against the Jewish Antifascist Committee, made it impossible to publicly screen *The Unvanquished*. Even after Stalin died, in 1953, the film was rarely discussed and never screened publicly. During the subsequent de-Stalinization of the 1960s, the central event to which the film alludes, the Babyi Iar massacre, served as the focus of a controversial poem by Evgenii Evtushenko and a heavily censored documentary novel by Anatolii Kuznetsov, with both works taking their titles from the site, and calls for the erection of a memorial to the victims were voiced repeatedly.[18] Nevertheless, though they occasionally discussed Dr. Fishman's Jewish ethnicity, the few specialist articles and books that bothered to analyze the film rigorously avoided mentioning Babyi Iar as the site where Donskoi shot the footage.[19] And only Miron Chernenko's recent history of the representation of Jews in Soviet cinema makes any attempt to relate the film to the broader context of Holocaust cinema.

Clearly, then, *The Unvanquished* was deliberately forgotten in the Soviet Union because officials and others there construed it as a film that unacceptably overemphasized the fate of Jews and thus failed to tell the "correct" story about the occupation. This covers only part of the story, however, for it does not explain why *The Unvanquished,* as well as the other Soviet films that depict the fate of Jews under Nazi rule, have been even more completely forgotten in the West, even though they were shown in many countries there, including France, Italy, and the United States.[20]

## How the West Forgot

The mirror image of this Sovietization, wherein themes of the larger Soviet society subsumed the particularity of the Jewish Holocaust, can be found in the Americanization of the Holocaust.[21] The former phenomenon is to some extent readily intelligible; after all, though the Nazis killed millions of Soviet citizens simply for being Jewish, they killed even more across the Soviet Union as a whole. But how did the Holocaust achieve such enormous importance in the United States? The question seems puzzling, for as Judith E. Doneson points out, despite playing a direct role in the lives of very few Americans, the Holocaust has become a powerful symbol in the American psyche.[22]

As a consequence, many Americans derive much of their vocabulary of catastrophe from the Holocaust, which has become "a model, a paradigm, or a framework for understanding history." The process of creating such a paradigm, however, has necessarily wrought a distorting influence on depictions of the actual events, for they consequently employ "American symbols and language to convey an American perception of the (European) Holocaust."[23] The results of this distortion appear, for example, in the vestibule of the United States Holocaust Memorial Museum, which contains the regimental standards of U.S. army units that liberated the concentration camps of Western Europe, even though these were peripheral sites of the Holocaust.

This Americanization of the Holocaust may place an overarching "emphasis on the saving power of individual moral conduct" and promote an optimism that shields the bleak realities.[24] Lawrence L. Langer has suggested that adaptations of the *Diary of Anne Frank* produced in America do just that, but so too does *Schindler's List*.[25] In addition, and significantly, the Holocaust has served as an important symbol for Jewish American identity, which sometimes conflicts with a broader desire, both in the United States and beyond, to see the Holocaust as a universal symbol.[26] Terri Ginsberg has even argued that interpretations emphasizing the "Jewish particularity" of the Holocaust use the symbol of Jews' sufferings to deflect criticism from contentious dimensions of modern Israel's political and military actions.[27]

Yet one of my purposes in writing this book has been to challenge this kind of systematic distortion, primarily in its Soviet guise but also, less explicitly, in its American or any other guise. To accomplish the latter task, it is important briefly to consider the acts of systematic forgetting that founded the memory of the Holocaust as such in the West.

The key decades here are those from the end of the war until the Eichmann trial in 1961; the development of the term *Holocaust* and the first histories of the events therein were also written at that time.[28] Many writers seem to see this initial postwar period as one when little was written about the Holocaust, but recent studies by Lawrence Baron and Hasia Diner have asserted that, at least in the United States, Jews living roughly in this period already "considered it their duty to recite the story of the six million."[29] Nevertheless, Baron concedes that that the Holocaust did not occupy the prominent place in the public consciousness that it now holds.[30]

While the onset of the cold war did not silence discussion of the Holocaust, as has previously been argued,[31] it certainly entailed reluctance to consider the fate that befell Soviet Jews, killed by the Nazis for their association with communism as well as Judaism. Anticommunist sentiment played a role in the United States as well. Members of the American Left were often among the first to publicize Nazi atrocities as they were occurring, and this was one reason for the broader American public's skepticism toward such claims. In addition, the years following World War II witnessed the systematic attempt to eradicate perceived communist influence in the media. Consequently, individuals involved in making films that displayed sympathy toward the Soviet Union came under intense suspicion; in particular, Albert Maltz, who had written the English-language commentary to *Moscow Strikes Back,* was one of the ten "unfriendly" witnesses who refused to testify to the House Un-American Activities Committee (HUAC). Understandably, few people wanted to recall how these films had influenced them, just as few filmmakers in this atmosphere wanted to recall their work on the U.S. releases of such movies. Those associated with them suffered; Edward G. Robinson, a major actor who voluntarily appeared before the committee to persuade them that he was not involved with communism, nevertheless remained on something of a gray list that precluded him from working in the top films.[32] His voiceover narration for *Moscow Strikes Back* certainly did not help dispel the suspicions.

Various parties have claimed that HUAC was anti-Semitic, an accusation that at the time was leveled by those whom the committee investigated or blackballed, many of whom were Jews.[33] Yet the committee's anticommunism initially played a greater role in blocking the emergence of memory of the Holocaust. The Soviet war films depicting the Holocaust that had reached American spectators were soon forgotten in the atmosphere of McCarthyism. Only once these initial attempts to portray the Nazi genocide in the East had been thoroughly consigned to oblivion could Holocaust film proper begin, and with it the Americanization of the Holocaust.

The cold war thus helped excise the memory of the films that form the subject matter of this book, in the Soviet Union, the United States, and in all other countries where they were shown. With the end of the cold war, these films have become available, along with enough of the material commenting on their evolution that we can now examine them and see them as the first, fragmented, flawed attempts to represent and interpret the Holocaust in film. To do so, it has been necessary to adopt and adapt a methodology from the emerging field of ethical enquiry in film studies, paying due attention to the silences and ellipses of these works. A process that muffled or silenced heterodox voices defined Soviet representations of Nazi atrocity and the Holocaust, and it has been the task of this book to enable these voices to be heard.

## Introduction

1. Judith E. Doneson, *The Holocaust in American Film,* 2nd ed. (Syracuse, N.Y.: Syracuse University Press, 2002), 4; Norman G. Finkelstein, *The Holocaust Industry: Reflections on the Exploitation of Jewish Suffering,* rev. ed. (New York: Verso, 2001), 11.

2. The term "spontaneous destalinization" comes from Mikhail Gefter, *Iz tekh i etikh let* (Moscow: Progress, 1991), 418.

3. Zvi Gitelman, "Politics and the Historiography of the Holocaust in the Soviet Union," in *Bitter Legacy: Confronting the Holocaust in the USSR*, ed. Zvi Gitelman (Bloomington: Indiana University Press, 1997), 20.

4. Giorgio Agamben, *Remnants of Auschwitz: The Witness and the Archive,* trans. Daniel Heller-Roazen (New York: Zone, 1999), 27–31.

5. Agamben, *Remnants of Auschwitz,* 31.

6. United Nations, "Resolution Adopted by the General Assembly on the Holocaust Remembrance (A/RES/60/7, 1 November 2005)," http://www. un.org/holocaustremembrance/docs/res607.shtml (accessed 23 Sept. 2010).

7. In starting at this point, I follow the great majority of contemporary historians of the Holocaust. Raul Hilberg begins his narrative in 1933, before the start of the systematic killings; see Hilberg, *The Destruction of the European Jews,* 3 vols. (New York: Holmes and Meier, 1985). A similar timeframe is adopted by other prominent histories of the Holocaust: see, e.g., Martin Gilbert, *The Holocaust: The Jewish Tragedy* (London: Fontana, 1987); as well as Lucy S. Dawidowicz, *The War against the Jews: 1933–1945,* 10th anniversary ed. (Harmondsworth, U.K.: Penguin, 1990). Daniel Goldhagen insists on the long

roots of Nazism; see Goldhagen, *Hitler's Willing Executioners: Ordinary Germans and the Holocaust* (London: Abacus, 2006).

8. Yuri Slezkine, *The Jewish Century* (Princeton, N.J.: Princeton University Press, 2004), 116.

9. Ibid., 110–17.

10. Zvi Gitelman, *A Century of Ambivalence: The Jews of Russia and the Soviet Union, 1881 to the Present* (London: Viking, 1988), 64.

11. Ibid., 64–65.

12. Slezkine, *Jewish Century*, 242–54.

13. Timothy Snyder, *Bloodlands: Europe between Hitler and Stalin* (New York: Basic, 2010), 89–109; Genadii Kostyrchenko, *Tainaia politika Stalina: Vlast'i antisemitizm* (Moscow: Mezhdunarodnye otnosheniia, 2003), 132.

14. Kostyrchenko, *Tainaia politika Stalina*, 200.

15. Ibid., 140–217.

16. These figures come from Dawidowicz, *War against the Jews,* 480. Recent English-language historical work on the Holocaust and Soviet Jews includes Karel C. Berkhoff, *Harvest of Despair: Life and Death in Ukraine under Nazi Rule* (Cambridge, Mass.: Belknap, 2004); Christopher R. Browning, with a contribution by Jürgen Matthäus, *The Origins of the Final Solution: The Evolution of Nazi Jewish Policy 1939–1942* (Lincoln/Jerusalem: University of Nebraska Press/Yad Vashem, 2005); Wendy Lower, *Nazi Empire-building and the Holocaust in Ukraine* (Chapel Hill: University of North Carolina Press, 2007); Yitzhak Arad, *The Holocaust in the Soviet Union* (Lincoln: University of Nebraska Press, 2009); Kiril Feferman, *Soviet Jewish Stepchild: The Holocaust in the Soviet Mindset, 1941–1964* (Saarbrücken, Germany: Verlag Dr Müller, 2009).

17. See, e.g., Lyn Smith, *Forgotten Voices of the Holocaust* (London: Ebury, 2005). Such testimony would have to be collected in Eastern Europe, for survivors of the camps were more likely to end up in Western Europe and the United States, where their testimony could be recorded. Those making it to the West disproportionately originated in Poland.

18. Il'ia Al'tman, *Zhertvy nenavistsi: Kholokost v SSSR 1941–1945 gg* (Moscow: Fond "Kovcheg"/ Kollektsiia "Sovershenno sekretno," 2002), 454. Also see Zvi Gitelman's use of the same figures in "The Soviet Politics of the Holocaust," in *The Art of Memory: Holocaust Memorials in History,* ed. James E. Young (New York/ Munich: Jewish Museum/Prestel, 1995), 139. For the more common figure of Soviet Jewish victims, see Dawidowicz, *War against the Jews,* 480.

19. See the exhibition's catalog by Jehudit Shendar, *Private Tolkatchev at the Gates of Hell: Majdanek and Auschwitz Liberated: Testimony of an Artist,* http://www1.yadvashem.org/exhibitions/tolkatchev/index.html (accessed 1 September 2010).

20. David Shneer, *Through Soviet Jewish Eyes: Photography, War, and the Holocaust* (New Brunswick, N.J.: Rutgers University Press, 2010).

21. Vasilii [as Vasily] Grossman, *Everything Flows,* trans. Robert and Elizabeth Chandler (London: Harvill Secker, 2010); Vasilii [as Vasily] Grossman, *A Writer at War: Vasily Grossman with the Red Army 1941–1945,* trans., ed., and with a commentary by Liuba Vinogradova and Antony Beevor (London: Pimlico, 2006); Joshua Rubenstein, *Tangled Loyalties: The Life and Times of Ilya Ehrenburg* (Tuscaloosa: University of Alabama Press, 1999).

22. See Jeremy Hicks, "Lost in Translation? Did Sound Stop Soviet Films Finding Foreign Audiences?" in *Screening Intercultural Dialogue: Russia and Its Other(s) on Film,* ed. Stephen Hutchings (London: Routledge-Curzon, 2008), 113–29; Jeremy Hicks, "The International Reception of Early Soviet Sound Cinema: *Chapaev* in Britain and America," *Historical Journal of Film, Radio and Television* 25, no. 2 (2005): 273–90.

23. See the accounts of the book's fate in Il´ia Erenburg [as Ilya Ehrenburg] and Vasilii [as Vasily] Grossman, *The Complete Black Book of Russian Jewry,* trans. and ed. David Patterson (New Brunswick, N.J.: Transaction, 2003), xiii–xix. Also see Arno Lustiger, *Stalin and the Jews: The Tragedy of the Jewish Anti–Fascist Committee and the Soviet Jews* (New York: Enigma, 2003), 157–69.

24. Tony Kushner, *The Holocaust and the Liberal Imagination: A Social and Cultural History* (Oxford: Blackwell, 1994).

25. Hannah Caven, "Horror in Our Time: Images of the Concentration Camps in the British Media, 1945," *Historical Journal of Film, Radio and Television* 21, no. 3 (2003): 227.

26. Joshua Hirsch similarly notes the extent to which American photographers' images from World War II lack explicit traces of violence; see Hirsch, *Afterimage: Film, Trauma, and the Holocaust* (Philadelphia: Temple University Press, 2004), 15. Barbie Zelizer discusses how the level of violence depicted in the images increased during the course of the war. Authorities in the United States decided to be more explicit in 1943, showing images of a U.S. Army amputee in August 1943 and, six months later, in September, of U.S. war dead. By D-Day such images had become a regular occurrence in the U.S. press, but the British remained much more reticent about showing images of their own dead; see Barbie Zelizer, *Remembering to Forget: Holocaust Memory through the Camera's Eye* (Chicago: University of Chicago Press, 1998), 34. Zelizer claims that the Soviets did not publicize the liberation of Auschwitz until after the liberation of the Western camps. This is not true, in that Polevoi's article was published in *Pravda* within a week of the camp's capture (see chapter 6). She also argues that the Soviets did not publicize the liberation of the death camps at Bełżec, Sobibór, and Treblinka, but this is not entirely true, and in any case, the

traces had been hidden by the time the Soviets arrived (Zelizer, *Remembering to Forget,* 50). Indeed, the English-language British press, such as the *London Illustrated News,* also printed, for example, the Soviet materials on the liberation of Majdanek, some of which was graphic; see Janina Struk, *Photographing the Holocaust: Interpretations of the Evidence* (London: I. B. Tauris, 2004), 142–46.

27. Robert H. Abzug, *Inside the Vicious Heart: Americans and the Liberation of Nazi Concentration Camps* (New York: Oxford University Press, 1985), xi; Caven, "Horror in Our Time," 231; Exhibition organized by Mémorial de la Shoah under the curatorship of Christian Delage, "Filming the Camps: John Ford, Samuel Fuller, George Stevens (from Hollywood to Nuremberg)," Paris, 10 March to 31 August 2010. This substantially ignores the Soviet images of death camps.

28. Abzug, *Inside the Vicious Heart,* xi.

29. Qtd. in Zelizer, *Remembering to Forget,* 88.

30. Qtd. in ibid., 71.

31. Ibid., 88–89.

32. See discussion of the Einsatzgruppen images in Hirsch, *Afterimage,* 1–3. For discussion of the photographs taken in the camps, see Struk, *Photographing the Holocaust,* 99–123; Libby Saxton, *Haunted Images: Film, Ethics, Testimony and the Holocaust* (London: Wallflower, 2008), 56–60.

33. In this regard LaCapra distinguishes between "primary" and "secondary" memory; see Dominick LaCapra, *History and Memory after Auschwitz* (Ithaca, N.Y.: Cornell University Press, 1998), 20–21. LaCapra nonetheless insists that "no memory is purely primary."

34. Michael Bernard-Donals, *Forgetful Memory: Representation and Remembrance in the Wake of the Holocaust* (Albany: State University of New York Press, 2009), 5. Also see Jay Cantor, "Death and the Image," in *Beyond the Document: Essays in Nonfiction Film,* ed. Chales Warren (Hanover, N.H.: Wesleyan University Press/University Press of New England, 1996), 23–50, esp. 26.

35. LaCapra, *History and Memory,* 9–11; Hirsch, *Afterimage,* 10–26.

36. Saxton, *Haunted Images,* 15. One starting point for the consideration of the ethical stance of the documentary filmmaker can be found in Bill Nichols, *Representing Reality: Issues and Concepts in Documentary* (Bloomington: Indiana University Press, 1992), 76–103. Nichols, however, is far less interested in the kinds of blind spots and gaps that Saxton's approach emphasizes.

37. Amir Weiner, *Making Sense of War: The Second World War and the Fate of the Bolshevik Revolution* (Princeton, N.J.: Princeton University Press, 2001), 208; Lustiger, *Stalin and the Jews,* 178–80.

38. Doneson, *Holocaust in American Film,* 4.

39. Norman Davies, *No Simple Victory: World War II in Europe, 1939–1945* (New York: Penguin, 2008), 367.

40. For an analysis showing how and why the emerging narrative focused on Soviet heroism rather than victimhood, see Weiner, *Making Sense of the War.* Few of the films I discuss in this book portray Jews as resisters, with Boris Barnet's *Priceless Head* (1942) and *Secretary of the Regional Party Committee* (1942) being partial exceptions. For a discussion of the symbolic importance of the war in post-Soviet Russia, see Floriana Fossato, "Vladimir Putin and the Russian Television 'Family,'" *Les Cahiers russes* 1 (2006): 13–15.

41. Donald Bloxham comments that a failure to do this was a central problem with the Nuremberg Tribunal; see Donald Bloxham, *Genocide on Trial: War Crimes Trials and the Formation of Holocaust History and Memory* (Oxford: Oxford University Press, 2003), 152. Interestingly, Lanzmann's *Shoah* retains and highlights the language barrier between the director and the subjects interviewed.

42. Alvin Rosenfeld, *The End of the Holocaust* (Bloomington: Indiana University Press, 2011), 51–94.

43. Susan Sontag, *Regarding the Pain of Others* (London: Penguin, 2004), 63.

44. Jeffrey Brooks comments that Soviet wartime propaganda repeatedly appealed to the instincts of hatred and revenge; see Brooks, "Pravda Goes to War," in *Culture and Entertainment in Wartime Russia,* ed. Richard Stites (Bloomington: Indiana University Press, 1995), 14. Peter Kenez also comments on the depiction of "devastation and pain" as a way of increasing hatred against the Nazis and argues that Soviet war films also show Nazi brutality to demonstrate that there was no alternative to armed resistance; see Kenez, "Black and White: The War on Film," in *Culture and Entertainment in Wartime Russia*, ed. Richard Stites (Bloomington: Indiana University Press, 1995), 163, 167.

45. Lustiger, *Stalin and the Jews,* 131–36; Weiner, *Making Sense of the War,* 114–21, 191–235; Kostyrchenko, *Tainaia politika Stalina,* 242–49.

46. A post on the Botinok blog on the subject "Byl li kholokost v Rostove?" (Did the Holocaust occur in Rostov?) quotes an archive document (RGASPI 625/1/25, sheets 401–18) containing an April 1943 report by Kazimir Mette, leader of the Mogilev underground; see http://botinok.co.il/node/34279 (accessed 1 Sept. 2010).

47. Peter Kenez, *The Birth of the Propaganda State: Soviet Methods of Mass Mobilization, 1917–1929* (Cambridge: Cambridge University Press, 1985), 36.

48. The French film historian Christian Delage discounts the Soviet footage of the liberation of the camps because of the reconstruction used in the Auschwitz film (see chapter 6). Yet this was the exception, and we cannot discard all this footage because of a single instance of reconstruction. As Helen Lennon recently put it when commenting on the affidavit that preceded *Film Documents of Nazi Atrocities,* the Soviet film shown at the Nuremberg Tribunal, as well as the film submitted by the United States, *Nazi Concentration Camps*: "While this

was effective in fortifying the visual evidence of atrocities such as the murder of women and children, soldiers bound and gagged and the existence of mass graves, doubts about who in fact perpetrated these crimes persisted, especially with regard to allegations that many of the massacres in the eastern territories were in fact committed by Stalin's Red Army" (Lennon, "A Witness to Atrocity: Film as Evidence in International War Crimes Tribunals," in *Holocaust and the Moving Image,* ed. Toby Haggith and Joanna Newman [London: Wallflower, 2005], 68).

49. Brian Winston, *Lies, Damned Lies and Documentaries* (London: BFI, 2000), 106.

50. Walter Benjamin, "A Short History of Photography," *Screen* 13, no. 1 (Spring 1972): 25.

51. Bernard-Donals, *Forgetful Memory,* 13.

52. Qtd. in Saxton, *Haunted Images,* 4–5.

53. Catherine Merridale, *Night of Stone: Death and Memory in Twentieth-Century Russia* (New York: Viking 2001), 311.

54. Saxton, *Haunted Images,* 54.

55. Cantor, "Death and the Image," 31.

56. Shoshana Felman and Dori Laub, *Testimony: Crises of Witnessing in Literature, Psychoanalysis, and History* (New York: Routledge, 1992), 3; Annette Wieviorka, *The Era of the Witness,* trans. Jared Stark (Ithaca, N.Y.: Cornell University Press, 2006 [1998]), 144, 149.

57. Shoshana Felman, *The Juridicial Unconscious: Trials and Traumas in the Twentieth Century* (Cambridge, Mass.: Harvard University Press, 2002), 133.

58. Marina Sorokina, "People and Procedures: Toward a History of the Investigation of Nazi Crimes in the USSR," *Kritika: Explorations in Russian and Eurasian History* 6, no. 4 (Fall 2005): 829.

## Chapter 1. "Right off the Top of the News": *Professor Mamlock* and Soviet Antifascist Film

1. David Platt, *Celluloid Power: Social Film Criticism from "The Birth of a Nation" to "Judgment at Nuremberg"* (Metuchen, N.J.: Scarecrow, 1992), 333. As Tony Kushner notes, anti-Semitic disturbances occurred in New York, Boston, and London cinemas, too, when British and American wartime films were shown depicting the persecution of Jews (Kushner, *Holocaust and the Liberal Imagination,* 143).

2. Otis Ferguson, "Whether to Laugh or Cry," *New Republic,* 14 December 1938, 174. One earlier film, *The Eternal Wanderer (Der vanderner Yid),* a Yiddish-language film made in the United States and directed by George Roland, shows newsreel footage of the Nazis' book burnings, which it describes as the burning of "Jewish books." This is a brief episode in the film that implies but does not

depict anti-Semitic violence against people. My thanks to Gil Toffell for bringing this film to my attention.

3. Nicholas Napoli, "Sovetskie fil'my v SshA," *Iskusstvo kino* 4 (1946): 29.

4. Ibid.

5. Patricia Erens, *The Jew in American Cinema* (Bloomington: Indiana University Press, 1984), 152 (Erens incorrectly states that *Professor Mamlock* was released in the United States in 1939; it was in fact released in October 1938); Annette Insdorf, *Indelible Shadows: Film and the Holocaust,* 3d ed. (Cambridge: Cambridge University Press, 2003), 153–56. More frequently histories completely ignore the film; Vincent Lowy, for example, claims films of this sort not to have existed at the time (see Lowry, *L'Histoire infilmable: Les camps d'extermination à l'écran* [Paris: L'Harmattan, 2001], 21).

6. Peter Galway, *New Statesman and Nation,* 30 April 1938, 728.

7. Raymond Fielding, "Mirror of Discontent: The *March of Time* and Its Politically Controversial Film Issues," *Western Political Quarterly* 12, no. 1, pt. 1 (1959): 148.

8. Thus Judith E. Doneson, in examining American film treatments of the Holocaust, does not address the fact that the first Hollywood treatments of the subject followed the success of *Professor Mamlock.* They were not direct responses to the Nazi threat but partially mediated ones. See Doneson, *Holocaust in American Film,* 30.

9. United Kingdom, *Parliamentary Debates,* Commons (debate on British Broadcasting Corporation [Propaganda], 8 Apr. 1943), 5th ser., vol. 388 (1943), cols. 835–925, http://hansard.millbanksystems.com/commons/1943/apr/08/british-broadcasting-corporation#S5CV0388P0_19430408_HOC_293 (accessed 27 Jan. 2010).

10. "Dr Hans Mamlok, Subject of Play," *New York Times,* 12 November 1940, 30. Also see Nina Dymshits, "Antifashistskoe kino v izgnanii: K teme," *Kinovedcheskie zapiski* 59 (2002): 134.

11. Fridrikh Vol'f (Friedrich Wolf), *P'esy,* ed. Aleksandr Dymshits, with notes by A. Levinton (Moscow: Iskusstvo, 1963), 643–44; "Milestones" (obituary for Alexander Granach), *Time,* 26 March 1945, 75.

12. The use of the term *ambivalent* to describe Russian and Soviet attitudes toward the Jewish minority comes from Gitelman's *Century of Ambivalence.*

13. Insdorf, *Indelible Shadows,* 155. One can take issue with using the notion of the Holocaust in reference to Nazi repression of the Jews in 1933, but the usage follows major trends in historiography, as illustrated in works by Raul Hilberg. (See the introduction to this book for more on this issue.)

14. Feuchtwanger's novel is better known in English as *The Oppermann Family.* Wulf Koepke writes that when the novel was completed, in September 1933, and submitted to its publisher in Amsterdam, it bore its original title,

*Die Geschwister Oppermann* (literally, "The Oppermann Siblings"). "However, a competitor of Feuchtwanger's brother Ludwig in the publishing industry and high-ranking Nazi named Oppermann protested against the misuse of his 'good' German name in the novel and threatened Ludwig with a concentration camp. As a result, the German edition in Amsterdam appeared first as *Die Geschwister Oppenheim*" (Koepke, "Lion Feuchtwanger," in *Holocaust Literature: An Encyclopedia of Writers and Their Work*, ed. S. Lillian Kremer, 2 vols. [New York: Routledge, 2003], 1:341). It is strange that the Soviet film does not restore the original title.

15. Miron Chernenko incorrectly claims the film was adapted from a work by Willi Bredel; see Chernenko, *Krasnaia zvezda, zheltaia zvezda: Kinematograficheskaia istoriia evreistva v Rossii, 1919–1999* (Moscow: Tekst, 2006), 94–95. Bredel, however, is the author of *Die Prüfung* (1934), which was probably the first literary account of German concentration camps. Langhoff's work was first published in 1935. Taylor and Short suggest that the work uses an original screenplay; see K. R. M. Short and Richard Taylor, "Soviet Cinema and the International Menace, 1928–1939," *Historical Journal of Film, Radio and Television* 6, no. 2 (1986): 145. In fact, though the two works differ substantially, the title and many episodes originate in Langhoff's memoir.

16. Chernenko (*Krasnaia zvezda,* 127) sees *Mamlock* as a superior work, in part because of the higher quality of its original source.

17. Short and Taylor, "Soviet Cinema," 131.

18. See Gitelman, "Politics and Historiography," 18.

19. I thank Olga Gershenson for her intellectual generosity in drawing my attention to this film.

20. Larry Ceplair, *Under the Shadow of War: Fascism, Anti-Fascism, and Marxists, 1918–1939* (New York: Columbia University Press, 1987), 207.

21. Jay Leyda, *Kino: A History of the Russian and Soviet Film* (London: Allen and Unwin, 1983), 346.

22. Short and Taylor, "Soviet Cinema," 131.

23. Ibid., 153. The original novel, *The Oppenheim Family,* had sold 257,000 copies in 1934 alone and was translated into fifteen languages (Koepke, "Lion Feuchtwanger," 341).

24. A. Minkin, "Bol′she antifashistskikh fil′mov," *Kino,* 29 July 1938, 2. In addition to *Ruddi's Career,* the Gustav von Wagenheim film *Fighters* (*Bortsy* [1936]), produced by Mezhrabpomfil′m, is set in an accurately depicted Germany and features Georgii Dmitrov's actual Reichstag speech. A. Masliukov's *Karl Brunner* (1936), produced by Ukrainfil′m, uses a similarly authentic German set. Neither mentions the circumstances then facing European Jews. For a discussion of these films, see Dymshits, "Antifashistskoe kino v izgnanii," 133.

25. N. Kovarskii, "Obvinitel´nyi akt protiv fashizma," *Iskusstvo kino* 9 (1938): 28.

26. Grigorii Roshal´, "Fil´my za 1938 goda 'Sem´ia Oppengeim,'" *Kino,* 5 July 1938, 2.

27. Il´ia Trauberg, "Utrachennye illiuzii: O novom fil´me 'Professor Mamloke,'" *Komsomol´skaia pravda,* 13 September 1938, 4. Also see Kovarskii, "Obvinitel´nyi akt protiv fashizma," 28.

28. Olaf Möller and Barbara Wurm, "Von forcierter Diskretion: Passage durch Filme von Gerbert Rappaport," in *Regie: Rappaport: Ein sowjetischer Filmemacher aus Wien,* ed. Michael Omasta and Barbara Wurm (Vienna: Synema, 2008), 11.

29. Semen Mezhinskii, "Kak sozdavalsia obraz Mamloka," *Kino,* 23 September 1938, 4.

30. Lotte H. Eisner, *The Haunted Screen: Expressionism in the German Cinema and the Influence of Max Reinhardt* (Berkeley: University of California Press, 1973), 119.

31. Eisner, *Haunted Screen,* 122.

32. Thomas Elsaesser, *Weimar Cinema and After: Germany's Historical Imaginary* (London: Routledge, 2000), 319.

33. Ibid., 313.

34. Aleksandr Dymshits, "Fridrikh Vol´f i ego p´esy," in Vol´f, *P´esy,* 9.

35. Minkin, "Bol´she antifashistskikh fil´mov," 2.

36. Trauberg, "Utrachennye illiuzii," 4.

37. S. Tsimbal, "'Professor Mamlok' Novaia rabota Lenfil´ma," *Kino,* 11 August 1938, 2.

38. By contrast, Oleg Zhakov had already played a number of prominent film roles, including ones in Efim Dzigan's *We from Kronstadt* (*My iz Kronshtata* [1936]) and *The Baltic Deputy.* Interestingly, he plays a role similar to that of Rolf Mamlock in *Swamp Soldiers.*

39. Kovarskii, "Obvinitel´nyi akt protiv fashizma," 31.

40. Ibid., 30.

41. Vol´f, *P´esy,* 168.

42. For an account of Soviet Yiddish culture in this period, see Ber Boris Kotlerman, *In Search of Milk and Honey: The Theater of "Soviet Jewish Statehood" (1934–49)* (Bloomington, Ind.: Slavica, 2009), esp., 3, 13, 21, 166–67.

43. Vol´f, *P´esy,* 200.

44. Paradoxically, Western narratives tend to express the opposite narrative, suggesting that Jews resisted only as Zionists. An example of this opposite emphasis can be found in Marvin J. Chomsky's popular television series *Holocaust* (1978). Representations of specifically Zionist resistance were, however, permissible on the Soviet stage.

45. Insdorf, *Indelible Shadows,* 156.

46. Chernenko, *Krasnaia zvezda,* 97–99.

47. Ibid., 113–14 and passim.

48. Ibid., 99.

49. For an investigation of the ways in which Soviet fears about foreigners affected the national cinema, see Jamie Miller, "The Purges of Soviet Cinema, 1929–39," *Studies in Russian and Soviet Cinema* 1, no. 1 (2007): 5–16.

50. L. V., "Uspekh fil´ma 'Professor Mamlok' na Moskovskikh ekranakh," *Vecherniaia Moskva,* 14 September 1938, 3.

51. *Vecherniaia Moskva,* 1 September 1938, 4.

52. L. V., "Uspekh fil´ma 'Professor Mamlok,'" 3.

53. "Uspekh fil´ma 'Professor Mamlok,'" *Kino,* 23 September, 1938, 4.

54. L. V., "Uspekh fil´ma 'Professor Mamlok,'" 3. Trauberg ("Utrachennye illiuzii," 4), for example, also stresses the importance of the film for Western spectators.

55. "Uspekh fil´ma 'Professor Mamlok,'" 4.

56. Leonid Rozenfeld, interview by Zhanna Litinskaya, Kiev, June 2003, http://www.centropa.org/index.php?nID=30&x=PXVuZGVmaW5lZDsgc2V hcmNoNoVHlwZTiCaW9EZXRhaWw7IHNlYXJjaFZhbHVlPTI3OTsgc2Vh cmNoU2tpcD0xMA== (accessed 5 July 2012).

57. Crispin Brooks, the curator of the Shoah Foundation Institute, has remarked on the frequency with which the film is mentioned in testimony (personal correspondence with author, January 2009). Anna Shternshis has also collected survivor testimonies about the important role the film played in alerting Soviet Jews to Nazi anti-Semitism; see Shternshis, "Evacuation and Escape of Jewish Civilians in the Soviet Union during World War II" (working paper presented at the University of Colorado at Boulder, 2 Nov. 2010), http://www .jewishmovers.org/uploads/File/Anna%20Shternshis,%20WWI,%20Jews,%20 and%20Evacuation.pdf (accessed 16 Aug. 2010).

58. N. Kruzhkov, "Professor Mamlock," *Pravda,* 28 July 1938, 6. Also see Tsimbal, "Professor Mamlok," 2.

59. Mezhinskii, "Kak sozdavalsia obraz Mamloka," 4.

60. Ibid.

61. Grigorii Roshal´, "Fil´my za 1938 goda 'Sem´ia Oppengeim,'" *Kino,* 5 July 1938, 2. However, Roshal´ stresses that all these changes were made with the agreement of Feuchtwanger himself. Indeed, in a later article Roshal´ argued that the addition of the line of communist resistance anticipated a shift in Feuchtwanger's own thinking (*Kino,* 23 November, 1938, 2).

62. Harvey Asher points to the wealth of coverage of this theme (twenty-nine reports, articles, and commentaries about attacks on Jews under German rule) that appeared in *Pravda* between 11 November 1938 and the end of June

1939; see Asher, "The Holocaust and the USSR," in *Lessons and Legacies,* vol. 7: *The Holocaust in International Perspective,* ed. Dagmar Herzog (Evanston, Ill.: Northwestern University Press, 2006), 256. Also see Mordechai Altshuller, "Escape and Evacuation of the Soviet Jews at the Time of the Nazi Invasion," in *The Holocaust in the Soviet Union: Studies and Sources on the Destruction of the Jews in Nazi-Occupied Territories of the USSR, 1941–1945,* ed. Lucjan Dobroczynski and Jeffrey S. Gurock (Armonk, N.Y.: Sharpe, 1993), 77–104.

63. Viktor Fink, "Sem´ia Oppengeim," *Literaturnaia gazeta,* 1 December 1938, 4.

64. Insdorf, *Indelible Shadows,* 155.

65. Kushner, *Holocaust and the Liberal Imagination,* 49.

66. "Screen," review of *Professor Mamlock, American Hebrew,* 18 November 1938, 17. The *Daily Worker* made the same point; see David Platt, "World's Strongest Anti-Fascist Film to Date," *Daily Worker,* 10 November 1938, 7.

67. Ferguson, "Whether to Laugh or Cry," 174.

68. Peter Kenney, "Professor Mamlock: 'If Anybody Is Going to Die, It Is Not We Comrades,'" *Daily Worker,* 19 November 1938, 7.

69. See, for example, "Cinema: The New Pictures," *Time,* 21 November 1938, which calls the film a "powerfully realistic investigation of the effects of Nazi government upon a Jewish surgeon" (53).

70. The substantial Jewish readership is evident from its advertisement of Yiddish-language plays. Anti-Semitic violence in the United States was also extensively documented by the *Daily Worker,* which reported, for example, an incident that occurred shortly before the New York premiere of the film in nearby Irvington, New Jersey, where a Jewish boy was beaten up and had a swastika branded on his arm by Nazis of Italian and German origin. The local newspaper had not covered the incident. See Louise Mitchell, "Jewish Mothers of Irvington Fear for Children after Brutality to Boy," *Daily Worker,* 15 October 1938, 1.

71. "Playing the Fascists in Films," *Daily Worker,* 14 November 1938, 7.

72. Lester Rodney, "Jewish and Communist Propaganda," *Daily Worker,* 22 November 1938, 7.

73. Frank S. Nugent, "'Professor Mamlock,' A Russian Appraisal of Nazi Culture, Has its Premiere at the Cameo," *New York Times,* 8 November 1938, 26.

74. Ibid., 26.

75. Frank S. Nugent, "Russia Grasps a Nettle," *New York Times,* 13 November 1938, 9:5.

76. David Platt, "Film Critics Stirred to Praise of Soviet 'Professor Mamlock,'" *Sunday Worker* (New York), 20 November 1938, 13.

77. Chernenko, *Krasnaia zvezda,* 97–99; Insdorf, *Indelible Shadows,* 156.

78. Kenney, "Professor Mamlock," 7.

79. Doneson, *Holocaust in American Film,* 7.

80. Prominent recent examples include the Steven Spielberg film *Schindler's List* (1993) and *Holocaust.* Edward Zwick's post–cold war film *Defiance* (2009) shows a specifically Jewish resistance to the Nazis that was oriented toward saving lives, contrasting it to the communists' brutal resistance.

81. Browning with Matthäus, *Origins of the Final Solution,* 110, 245, 294; Christian Streit, "The German Army and the Policies of Genocide," in *The Policies of Genocide: Jews and Soviet Prisoners of War in Nazi Germany,* ed. Gerhard Hirschfeld (London: German Historical Institute/Allen and Unwin, 1986), 1–14; Pavel Polian, "First Victims of the Holocaust: Soviet-Jewish Prisoners of War in German Captivity," *Kritika: Explorations in Russian and Eurasian History* 6, no. 4 (Fall 2005): 763–87.

82. Kushner, *Holocaust and the Liberal Imagination,* 36, 125. On the postwar period, see Finkelstein, *Holocaust Industry,* 15. Also see chapter 6 of this book.

83. Peter Kenney, "On and Off the Screen," *Sunday Worker* (New York), 20 November 1938, 13.

84. Ibid., 13.

85. Platt, "World's Strongest Anti-Fascist Film," 7.

86. Insdorf, *Indelible Shadows,* 155.

87. *Times Film Corp. v. Chicago,* 365 U.S. 43 (1961), http://caselaw.lp.findlaw.com/scripts/getcase.pl?navby=case&court=us&vol=365&invol=43 (26/09/10). For more on the ban, see Caroline Joan Picart, ed., *The Holocaust Film Sourcebook,* vol. 2: *Documentary and Propaganda* (Westport, Conn.: Praeger, 2004), 308.

88. Gerald A. DeLuca, "Avon Cinema, Providence, RI," http://cinematreasures.org/theater/465/ (accessed 24 Nov. 2006).

89. http://cinematreasures.org/members/profile.php?id=1878Ibid.

90. Napoli, "Sovetskie fil′my v SshA," 29.

91. "Right off the Reels," *Daily Worker,* 11 March 1939, 7.

92. *Time,* 11 September 1939, http://www.time.com/time/magazine/article/0,9171,711737–2,00.html (accessed 25 Nov. 2006). The film that replaced it is incorrectly described as *Lenin in 1917*; see "Soviet Withdraws Anti-Nazi Movie," *New York Times,* 30 August 1939, 12. Also see "Anti-German Films Banned," *New York Times,* 7 September 1939, 3:4.

93. Platt, *Celluloid Power,* 334.

94. Bosley Crowther, "Little Caesar Wants His Chance," *New York Times,* 22 January 1939, 9:5. Robinson is quoted: "'I would give my teeth,' he said, 'to do an American version of *Professor Mamlock.*'" Also see Allen Rostron, "'No War, No Hate, No Propaganda': Promoting Films about European War and Fascism during the Period of American Isolationism," *Journal of Popular Film and Television* 30, no. 2 (Summer 2002): 85–96.

95. Platt, "World's Strongest Anti-Fascist Film," 7. The Cliveden set was a group in the British establishment sympathetic to the Nazis and favoring appeasement.

96. A 1935 London performance was mysteriously stopped in rehearsals, days before its opening night, probably the result of Foreign Office unofficial pressure. The lack of a formal ban, however, meant that a January 1939 performance was reluctantly permitted in Nottingham when the lord chamberlain's office realized at the eleventh hour that it had already permitted the play to be performed in 1935. Nevertheless, the performance attracted little comment nationally. See Anthony Aldgate and James Crighton Robertson, *Censorship in Theatre and Cinema* (Edinburgh: Edinburgh University Press, 2005), 50–51. It was also performed in 1942, when it was perceived as an adaptation of the film; see "Austrian Theatre Club 'Professor Mamlock' (Reviews)," *Times* (London), 17 March 1942, 8.

97. This is effectively the penultimate film ever shown by the Film Society, the last being Sergei Eisenstein's *Aleksandr Nevskii* (1938).

98. A[rthur] V[esselo], review of *Professor Mamlock, Monthly Film Bulletin* 6, no. 64 (30 Apr. 1939): 79.

99. "A Film to Show," *News Chronicle,* 28 March 1939, 10.

100. Basil Wright, "The Cinema: 'Professor Mamlock' at the Film Society," *The Spectator,* 31 March 1939, 532. Curiously, Graham Greene reviewed the film for the same publication on its release at the Academy Cinema in September and did not mention the ban or even refer to the previous review. Greene objects to the film's preachiness. See Greene, review of *Professor Mamlock, The Spectator,* 1 September 1939, 325.

101. Arthur Vesselo, "The Grand Alliance," *Sight and Sound* 8, no. 29 (Spring 1939): 33. In the original, Vesselo had written "politically biased" but corrected this in the next issue of the magazine; see "Misprints and Limitations," *Sight and Sound* 8, no. 30 (Summer 1939): 77.

102. *Times* (London), 20 April 1939, qtd. in Aldgate and Robertson, *Censorship in Theatre and Cinema,* 52.

103. "British Censors Ban Anti-Nazi Film: Distributors Will Launch Protest," *Glasgow Herald,* 20 April 1939, 12.

104. "Film Society Performance; Correspondence and Other Material Related to the Films Shown, Season 14 (1938–39) *Professor Mamlock,*" BFI Special Collections, Film Society Collection.

105. For reference to the bonds required for refugees, see Andrew Sharf, *The British Press and Jews under Nazi Rule* (London: Oxford University Press, 1964), 156.

106. A. T. B[orthwick], "L.C.C. Passes Russian Anti-Nazi Film," *News Chronicle,* 27 July 1939, 3.

107. Ibid. Aldgate and Robertson (*Censorship in Theatre and Cinema,* 52) assert that the LCC required no cuts, but all other sources contradict this claim. In particular, the British trade publication *Kinematograph Weekly* states that the print shown at the Film Society ran to 9,669 feet and the print passed by the LCC in August, to only 9,360 feet. Evidently 309 feet (a little over three minutes) had been cut. Herbert Morrison, speaking in Parliament on 31 October 1939, also refers to the LCC's making cuts; see United Kingdom, *Parliamentary Debates,* Commons (debate on British Broadcasting Corporation [Propaganda], 8 Apr. 1943), 5th ser., vol. 388 (1943), cols. 835–925, http://hansard.millbank systems.com/commons/1939/oct/31/emergency-powers-defence-act-1939#S5 CV0352P0_19391031_HOC_457 (accessed 27 Jan. 2010).

108. "London to See Banned Films," *Daily Herald,* 27 July 1939, 5.

109. "Middlesex Bans Anti-Nazi Films," *Jewish Chronicle,* 25 August 1939, 34; P. L. Mannock, "Banned Film Shown," *Daily Herald,* 29 August 1939, 9; Walter Holmes, "A Worker's Notebook: Anti-Nazi Film Banned," *Daily Worker* (London), 28 August 1939, 2.

110. Holmes, "A Worker's Notebook," 2.

111. Jane Morgan, "Banned Picture You Can See at Last," *Daily Worker* (London), 28 August, 1939, 7.

112. See listings in the *London Film Guide* 55 (Sept. 1939): 3. In fact, it was licensed not only by the LCC but also by the local authority in Surrey, according to the *Daily Herald*; see Mannock, "Banned Film Shown," 9.

113. Anthony West, review of *Professor Mamlock, New Statesman and Nation,* 2 September 1939, 342.

114. C. A. Lejeune, "Films of the Week: There's a Happy Film Somewhere," *Observer,* 3 September 1939, 7.

115. "Professor Mamlock," review, *Kinematograph Weekly,* 31 August 1939, 14.

116. P. L. Mannock, "All Cinemas Will Be Open To-day," *Daily Herald,* 15 September 1939, 1. *Mamlock* is mentioned as one of the films to be resumed. The closing time for London cinemas, however, was initially set as 6 p.m. The print in question was 9,126 feet—in other words, it had lost a further two minutes from the LCC print.

117. Guy Morgan, "Stalin Makes a Film Hit," *Daily Express,* 26 October 1939, 6.

118. G. A. Rink, letter to the editor, *Times* (London), 14 October 1939, 6.

119. U.K., *Parliamentary Debates,* Commons, 31 Oct 1939. See also "War Time Film Censorship under Criticism: H. Morrison Demands a Reversal to Normal," *Kinematograph Weekly,* 9 November 1939, 9.

120. "Anti-Nazi Film a Big Success," *Kinematograph Weekly,* 16 November 1939, 6. A whole issue of *Cinegram Preview,* a national film fan magazine with

highbrow pretentions, was devoted entirely to *Mamlock*. See *Cinegram Preview* 5, no. 713 (Dec. 1939).

121. While, generally speaking, France was a more fruitful market for Soviet film than was Britain, on this occasion the film was banned; see "Un Film soviétique anti-nazi 'Professeur Mamlock' passe triomphalement en Angle-terre," *Cinématographie française,* [14] October 1939, 1. This ban occurred because France was following the same appeasement policy as Britain was, but more consistently and with a more intensely pro-German zeal, especially in cinema, where a special agreement was signed (see, e.g., *Le Cinéma français,* Jan.-Feb. 1939). Although, as in Britain, the film had been shown in at least one film club there, a print appears to have been available for showing after the outbreak of war made France, too, rue the doomed policy of appeasement. Adding insult to injury, the French also interned the author of the original play, Friedrich Wolf, at the start of the war, in Le Vernet concentration camp, and he was released only when the Soviet Union granted him citizenship (see A. Dymshits, "Frid-rikh Vol´f," 9). Luxembourg was another country that banned the film; see Paul Lesch, "Film and Politics in Luxembourg: Censorship and Controversy," *Film History* 16, no. 4 (2004): 439.

122. Trauberg, "Utrachennye illiuzii," 4.

123. Minkin, "Bol´she antifashistskikh fil´mov," 2.

124. The book is often dated to 1940, when Kerido published the first com-plete German-language edition in Amsterdam. *Pravda*, however, had published extracts earlier, in July 1938, and an incomplete Russian translation appeared in the journal *International´naia literatura* in 1939, which is why Russian discussions of the novel date it a year earlier.

125. "Zapiska V. M. Molotova v Politbiuro TsK VKP (b) ob ekranizatsii romana L. Feuchtwangera 'Izgnanie'" (memorandum), in *Kremlevskii kinoteatr, 1929–1953: Dokumenty,* ed. G. N. Bondareva (Moscow: Rosspen, 2005), 549.

126. Documents relating to *Professor Mamlock,* Gosfil´mofond Archive, sect. I/3/1/1985.

127. Leyda, *Kino,* 356.

128. Naum Kleiman, "Neosushchestvlennye zamysly Eizenshteina," *Iskusstvo kino* 6 (1992): 19–20.

## Chapter 2. "The Beasts Have Taken Aim at Us": Soviet Newsreels Screen the War and the Holocaust

1. See Gilbert, *The Holocaust,* 154–78; Hilberg, *Destruction of the European Jews,* 1:273; Yitzhak Arad, "The Destruction of the Jews in German-Occupied Territories of the Soviet Union," in *The Unknown Black Book: The Holocaust in the German-Occupied Soviet Territories,* ed. Joshua Rubenstein and Ilya Altman

(Bloomington: Indiana University Press, 2008), xiii; Streit, "The German Army," 2.

2. See Karel Berkhoff, "'Total Annihilation of the Jewish Population': The Holocaust in the Soviet Media, 1941–45," *Kritika: Explorations in Russian and Eurasian History* 10, no. 1 (Winter 2009): 66; Al´tman, *Zhertvy nenavistsi,* 386.

3. Martin Gilbert, *Auschwitz and the Allies: The Truth about One of This Century's Most Controversial Episodes* (London: Mandarin, 1991); Walter Laqueur, *The Terrible Secret: An Investigation into the Suppression of Information about Hitler's "Final Solution"* (London: Weidenfeld and Nicolson, 1980); Sharf, *British Press and Jews,* 193; Deborah Lipstadt, *Beyond Belief: The American Press and the Coming of the Holocaust 1933–1945* (New York: Free Press, 1986).

4. David Shneer succinctly summarizes the reasons for Western "lack of awareness or interest" in Soviet depictions of the Holocaust; see Shneer, "Picturing Grief: Soviet Holocaust Photography at the Intersection of History and Memory," *American Historical Review* 115, no. 1 (2010): 29.

5. These accounts are surveyed in Berkhoff, "Total Annihilation," 62–65. Kiril Feferman (*Soviet Jewish Stepchild,* 7–25) briefly refers to one or two of the film representations.

6. "Brat´ia evrei vsego mira," *Pravda,* 25 August 1941, 3. An English translation appears in Shimon Redlich, *War, Holocaust and Stalinism: A Documented History of the Jewish Anti-Fascist Committee in the USSR* (Luxembourg: Harwood, 1995), 178.

7. Redlich, *War, Holocaust and Stalinism,* 178.

8. Ibid., 182.

9. David Shneer discusses these images in *Through Soviet Jewish Eyes,* 99.

10. For an estimate that places Rostov's prewar Jewish population at 27,000, see Electronic Jewish Encyclopedia, s.v. "Rostov-na-Donu," http://www .eleven.co.il/?mode=article&id=13587&query=%D0%CE%D1%D2%CE%C2 (accessed 16 June 2010). The Russian-language Jewish magazine *Lechaim* provides the same figure for the city's prewar Jewish population, but by November 1941 refugees had raised the figure to around 50,000; see I. Karpenko, "Rostov evreiskii," http://www.lechaim.ru/ARHIV/163/VZR/017.htm (accessed 16 June 2010).

11. "Kinodokumenty Velikoi voiny," *Literatura i iskusstvo,* 14 February 1942, 1; A. Levitan, "Kinofal´shivki Gebbel´sa," *Literatura i iskusstvo,* 3 February 1942, 3.

12. Valerii Fomin, ed. and comp., *Kino na voine: Dokumenty i svidetel´stva* (Moscow: Materik, 2005), 138.

13. For a summary of these expectations, see Catherine Merridale, *Ivan's War: The Red Army 1939–45* (London: Faber and Faber, 2005), 21–26.

14. Fomin, *Kino na voine,* 141–42.

15. For an account of the evolution of still photographers' attempts to convey Nazi atrocities, see Shneer, *Through Soviet Jewish Eyes,* 96–111.

16. Fomin, *Kino na voine,* 142.

17. This combination was distinct to Soviet film. In Western documentaries, as Ron Barnouw has shown, films initially acted as a "bugler" encouraging the armies as an "adjunct to military action, [a] weapon of war," before turning to the role of "prosecutor of war crimes" toward the end of the war. For the Soviets, the roles were combined from the beginning; see Barnouw, *Documentary: A History of the Non-Fiction Film* (New York: Oxford University Press, 1974), 139–82.

18. Al´tman, *Zhertvy nenavisti,* 274. Here the figure is given as 1,000, but Al´tman has since clarified that this was a typographical error (personal communication with author, 8 Sept. 2010).

19. "Pis´mo zhitelei Rostova-na-Donu, komandiram i politrabotnikam 9-i i 56-i armii," *Pravda,* 1 December 1941, 3. Strangely, this source refers to the Germans as having killed "Red Army men, professors, women and children." The Russian Jewish Encyclopedia says that only thirty Jews were shot in Nakhichevan´; see s.v. "Nakhichevan´-na-Donu," http://www.rujen.ru/index .php (accessed 8 July 2012).

20. F. D. Sverdlov, ed., *Dokumenty obviniaiut: Kholokost—svidetel´stva Krasnoi Armii* (Moscow: Rosiiskaia biblioteka Kholokosta, 1996), 86, qtd. in Al´tman, *Zhertvy nenavisti,* 274. Much of Rostov's prewar Jewish population appears to have survived this brief period of occupation, only to be destroyed in a mass killing spree at Zmievskaia balka when the Nazis retook the city in July 1942 and slaughtered 15,000–27,000 people (Al´tman, *Zhertvy nenavisti,* 274–75).

21. A. Matskin, B. Sobolev, "Kak khozainichili nemtsy v Rostove," *Pravda,* 7 December 1941, 2.

22. In Sverdlov, *Dokumenty obviniaiut,* 81. The source is a protocol compiled on 30 November 1941 by five residents, witnessed by a Red Army officer, and sent to the Political Directorate of the Army.

23. See Katerina Migulina, "Golubinyi razvedchik," *Trud,* 10 May 2007, http://www.trud.ru/article/10–05–2007/115772_golubinyj_razvedchik.html (accessed 16 June 2010).

24. Evgenii Margolit, "Barnet i Eizenshtein v kontekste sovetskogo kino," *Kinovedcheskie zapiski* 17 (1993): 172.

25. Vladimir Mikhailov, "Fil´m o pervoi pobede," in *Iz istorii kino: Dokumenty i materialy,* vol. 10, ed. V. Mikhailov (Moscow: Iskusstvo, 1977), 85.

26. Matskin and Sobolev, "Kak khozainichili nemtsy v Rostove," 2. The newspaper puts his age at between twelve and thirteen and says he was killed for releasing his pigeons, as he did every day.

27. Sontag, *Regarding the Pain of Others,* 63.

28. Fomin, *Kino na voine,* 142.

29. The full official name of this body was the Extraordinary State Commission for the Establishment and Investigation of the Crimes of the Fascist German Invaders and Their Accomplices and of the Damage They Caused to Citizens, Collective Farms, Public Organizations, State Enterprises, and Institutions of the USSR.

30. Gefter, *Iz tekh i etikh let,* 418.

31. Lawrence Douglas, *Memory of Judgment: Making Law and History in the Trials of the Holocaust* (New Haven, Conn.: Yale University Press, 2001), 36.

32. Nina Markovna, *Nina's Journey: A Memoir of Stalin's Russia and the Second World War* (Washington D.C.: Regnery Gateway, 1989), 230–31. Thanks to Karel C. Berkhoff for pointing out this reference to me.

33. Matskin and Sobolev, "Kak khozainichili nemtsy v Rostove," 2.

34. Merridale, *Night of Stone,* 311.

35. Appeals to vengeance as a motivational force were not confined to the Soviets. The Warsaw Ghetto's Jewish Armed Resistance Organization (ZOB) issued a manifesto to Poles during the first days of the ghetto uprising, in April 1943, where similar calls to vengeance against the Germans for their crimes figure prominently. See Marek Edelman, *The Ghetto Fights: Warsaw 1941–43* (London: Bookmarks, 1994), 99–100. As soon as the conflict was over, such sentiments appeared inappropriate.

36. Gennadii L. Muravin, *Dvoe iz mnogikh tysiach* (Moscow: Sovetskii khudozhnik, 1967), 83.

37. Shneer, *Through Soviet Jewish Eyes.*

38. In his study of Soviet Jewish still photographers' depictions of the Holocaust, David Shneer emphasizes the images made of the liberation of Kerch and discounts the Rostov images: "These photographs had everything to do with the Nazis' violent occupation politics in the Soviet Union, but little to do with the Nazi war against the Jews. No Soviet photographer had witnessed the mass murders of Jews that were going on throughout the occupied Soviet Union in 1941" ("Picturing Grief," 33–34).

39. Khaldei's photographs can be viewed at "Kerch´: Bagerovskii Trench: Grigorii Berman beside the Bodies of His Wife and Children" (Jan. 1942), http://fotki.yandex.ru/users/khodak/view/202335?page=1 (accessed 15 Sept. 2010).

40. Il´ia Sel´vinskii, "Ia eto videl," *Ne zabudem, ne prostim!* (Moscow: Goskinizdat, 1942).

41. While the credits name Mazrukho and G. Popov, the Soviet film presented at the Nuremberg Tribunal, *Film Documents of Atrocities Committed by the German-Fascist Invaders,* states that it was Mazrukho who filmed these images.

42. Fomin, *Kino na voine,* 155.

43. Walter Benjamin uses the term *indeterminate* in "Short History of Photography," 25.

44. Al´tman, *Zhertvy nenavisti,* 286.

45. "Kaluga vziata," *Pravda,* 1 January 1942, 3.

46. Il´ia Al´tman, *Kholokost i evreiskoe soprotivlenie na okkupirovannoi territorii SSSR,* ed. A. G. Asmolov (Moscow: Fond "Kholokost"/ Kaleidoskop, 2002), 182; Al´tman, *Zhertvy nenavisti,* 266–67.

47. N. Mikhailov, "O vos´mi poveshennykh v Volokolamske," *Pravda,* 31 January 1942, 2.

48. V. Mikhailov, "Fil´m o pervoi pobede," 79.

49. Ibid., 85.

50. For an accessible English-language account of recording this speech, see Rodric Braithwaite, *Moscow 1941: A City and Its People at War* (London: Profile, 2006), 287–88. This is a further illustration of the organizational and technical difficulties with synchronously recording sound.

51. Fomin, *Kino na voine,* 191.

52. Felman and Laub, *Testimony,* 205–7. See also Saxton's excellent discussion of Felman and Laub in *Haunted Images,* 11–14.

53. Leonid Varlamov and Il´ia Kopalin, "Review, Articles, and Notes on the Film *Defeat of the Germans near Moscow,*" RGALI 1966/1/ 89. Note here the delayed, latent reaction described in the discourse of trauma theory.

54. Qtd. in Grigorii Tsitriniak, *Ne zabyto! rasskazy frontovykh kinooperatorov i kinorezhisserov* (Moscow: Soiuz kinematografistov SSSR Vsesoiuznogo biuro propagandy kinoiskusstva, 1986), 24. Although there was a codirector's credit, Il´ia Kopalin referred to himself as having edited the film; see Fomin, *Kino na voine,* 191.

55. Struk, *Photographing the Holocaust.*

56. The makers of *Razgrom* originally intended to make a two-reel special-release newsreel; see V. Mikhailov, "Fil´m o pervoi pobede," 77.

57. Or in the original formulation, on "the wide-scale robbery, the despoliation of the population, and the monstrous atrocities committed by the German authorities in the invaded Soviet territories."

58. Feferman, *Soviet Jewish Stepchild,* 15.

59. *Soviet Government Statements on Nazi Atrocities* (London: Hutchinson, 1946), 24.

60. Vsevolod Vishnevskii, *Leningrad: Dnevniki voennykh let: 2 noiabria 1941 goda-31 dekabria 1942,* vol. 1 (Moscow: Voenizdat, 2002), 121.

61. Qtd. in "Sovetskie fil´my za rubezhom: informatsionnyi biulleten´: po materialam inostrannoi pressy: Soiuzintorgkino 3, Jan 1943," RGALI 2918/2/19, sheet 39, obverse.

62. "'Moscow Strikes Back' Makes a Deep Impression in London," *Daily Worker,* 22 August, 1942, 7.

63. Manny Farber, "Zanuck at the Front," *New Republic,* 5 April 1943, 447.

64. Antonov to Bol'shakov, 30 April 1943, RGALI 2018/1/74.

65. Bolshakov to Shcherbakov, 15 March 1944, RGASPI, 17/125/291, sheet 27.

66. See, for example, Hirsch, *Afterimage,* 14–15; Caven, "Horror in Our Time." Caven claims that during World War II, the British public was sheltered from images of death and atrocity: "Images of horror and particularly images of death had been conspicuous by their absence from newspapers and newsreels" (227). As the representative of Soviet film in Britain commented, however, the British tried to remove images of *Defeat of the Germans near Moscow* (Fomin, *Kino na voine,* 648). Roger Manvell is one of few Western critics to mention these films, doing so in *Films and the Second World War* (London: Dent, 1974), 204.

67. Toby Haggith argues that when documenting Belsen, photographers with the Allies tended "to universalise the suffering and down-play the high number of Jews in the camp." Nevertheless, their dope sheets reveal the extent to which they were aware that most of the inmates of Belsen were Jews. See Toby Haggith, "Filming the Liberation of Bergen-Belsen," in *Holocaust and the Moving Image: Representations in Film and Television since 1983,* ed. Toby Haggith and Joanna Newman (London: Wallflower, 2005), 33–49 (quotation on 34).

68. Qtd. in Zelizer, *Remembering to Forget,* 39.

69. Lipstadt, *Beyond Belief,* 151.

70. Ibid., 139; Sharf, *British Press and Jews,* 91.

71. Lipstadt, *Beyond Belief,* 277. Sharf (*British Press and Jews,* 18–19) writes that the Catholic press in Britain reserved a particular venom and distrust for Bolshevik Russia, which it saw as being run by Jews.

72. Laqueur, *Terrible Secret,* 204.

73. Nicholas Pronay, "Defeated Germany in British Newsreels: 1944–45," in *Hitler's Fall: The Newsreel Witness,* ed. K. R. M. Short and Stephan Dolezel (London: Croom Helm, 1988), 41, 43.

74. Zelizer, *Remembering to Forget,* 42.

## Chapter 3. Imagining Occupation: Partisans and Spectral Jews

1. Fomin, *Kino na voine,* 89.

2. Vitalii Zhdan, *Velikaia otechestvennaia voina v khudozhestvennykh fil'makh* (Moscow: Goskinoizdat, 1947), 19–20.

3. T. K[alinovskaia], "Bestsennaia golova: stsenarii o bor'be pol'skikh patriotakh," *Vecherniaia Moskva,* 29 October 1941, 4.

4. This article and the latter review incorrectly call the hero "Dombrowski."

5. B. Petker, *Dissertatsiia Meri Archer* (Moscow: Vsesoiuznyi dom narodnogo

tvorchestva im. N. K. Krupskoi, 1950). This later play's concern with the fate of African Americans stands as analogous to the earlier work's interest in the fate of Jews. Certainly the emphasis on witty dialogue strongly suggests that the Jewish part of the screenplay belongs to Petker's pen. The play is effectively a typically Soviet antifascist work, with blacks in the role that Jews play in the earlier work. The black son-in-law of the would-be congressman says: "The children of Stalingrad kissed Paul Robeson, like one of their own, but you think your grandchildren are fit to be lynched" (Petker, *Dissertatsiia*, 8).

6. B. Petker, *Eto moi mir* (Moscow: Iskusstvo, 1968), 147. Petker and Mezhinskii, the actor who played Mamlock, were friends.

7. Untitled article, *Vecherniaia Moskva*, 8 January 1942, 4.

8. "V kinostudiiakh," *Literatura i iskusstvo*, 13 January 1942, 4.

9. I. Bol´shakov, "Rabotat´ voennymi tempami," *Literatura i iskusstva*, 14 March 1942, 1.

10. M. Il´ian, "Proizvodstvu fil´mov—voennye tempy," *Literatura i iskusstvo*, 4 April 1942, 4.

11. V. Smirnov, "Dve novelly," *Vecherniaia Moskva*, 2 June 1941, 3.

12. The doctor's name is Wladislawskii, and he is referred to as such by the Jew.

13. I. Vaisfel´d, "Kinonovella," *Literatura i iskusstvo*, 25 July 1942, 3.

14. Louise McReynolds and Joan Neuberger, eds., *Imitations of Life: Two Centuries of Melodrama in Russia* (Durham, N.C.: Duke University Press, 2002), 17.

15. Margolit, "Barnet i Eizenshtein," 167–68.

16. Marlen Khutsiev, Otar Ioseliani, and Genadii Poloka, "'On tak i ne nauchilsia snimat´ po zakazu': Vspominaia Barneta," *Kinovedcheskie zapiski* 61 (2002): 90, 92.

17. Evgenii Margolit, "Vremia i mesto Borisa Barneta," *Kinovedcheskie zapiski* 61 (2002): 100.

18. Ivan Bol´shakov, *Sovetskoe kinoiskusstvo v gody Velikoi Otechestvennoi voiny*, 2d ed. (Moscow: Goskinoizdat, 1950), 23.

19. Chernenko, *Krasnaia zvezda*, 115. The unnamed town nevertheless has a Częstochowska Street well known to the Jewish character. This might make it Białystok, which had been incorporated into the Soviet Union in 1939 and whose ghetto comprised a street of that name. Many other towns, however, have a street bearing that name.

20. Kotlerman, *In Search of Milk and Honey*.

21. Erens, *The Jew in American Cinema*, 14.

22. See M. Krutikova, ed., *Okkupirovannye strany pod fashistskim iarmom* (Moscow: Moskovskii rabochii, 1941). Published weeks after the Nazi invasion and drawn from reports that ran in the *Moskovskii Bol´shevik* newspaper, this

brochure accurately reported the creation of the Warsaw ghetto, stressing that the prisoners of the ghetto were suffering far more than other Poles (21). For Soviet press coverage of Nazi treatment of the Jews in Poland, see Al´tman, *Zhertvy nenavisti,* 408. Nevertheless, Chernenko (*Krasnaia zvezda,* 115) assumes that the scenarists and filmmakers could not have known about the conditions of the ghetto. In fact, they could have known, and given that they were writing and directing a film about it, it seems likely that they would have tried to read at least whatever appeared in the Soviet press, though nothing proves that they did.

23. Kalinovskaia, "Bestsennaia golova," 4.

24. *Fighting Film Collections* offers many examples of such eager self-sacrifice, one of the most extreme being Vsevolod Pudovkin and Mikhail Doller's *Feast in Zhirmunki* (*Pir v Zhirmunke* [1941]), where a hostess poisons her Nazi guests' food and, when they force her to eat some first, does so willingly to ensure that the Nazis are themselves killed.

25. Insdorf, *Indelible Shadows,* 153, 156.

26. This suggests that Avisar is incorrect to claim that centrality of children in early postwar Holocaust films arose through the influence of Italian neorealism, for Soviet films already do this; see Ilan Avisar, *Screening the Holocaust: Cinema's Images of the Unimaginable* (Bloomington: Indiana University Press, 1998), 40.

27. Margolit, "Barnet i Eizenshtein," 172.

28. Ibid., 167–68. Barnet's Russian biographer, Mark Kushnirov, mentions *A Priceless Head* as being better than the other wartime fictional shorts but does not say why; see Kushnirov, *Zhizn´ i fil´my Borisa Barneta* (Moscow: Iskusstvo, 1977), 167–68. For a contrasting view, see François Albera and Roland Cosandey, eds., *Boris Barnet: Ecrits, documents, études, filmographie* (Locarno, Switzerland: Editions du Festival International du Film de Locarno, 1985), which mentions the film but recounts the plot from Soviet written sources and omits the Jewish dimension. In addition, the timeline in this work misstates the film's release date. Evidently the film was not shown at the Locarno retrospective or the earlier La Rochelle festival held in 1982.

29. His first postwar film, *Exploits of a Spy* (*Podvig razvedchika* [1947]), does have a vehemently anti-Semitic Nazi character who gives his boss (an undercover Soviet spy) lists of Jews and Communists hiding in occupied Vinnitsa. The Soviet agent gets him arrested by the Gestapo by framing him as a Soviet spy.

30. Al´tman, *Zhertvy nenavisti,* 399–408.

31. David Bergel´son, "I Want to Live," literary film treatment, GARF R8114/1/1090, sheets 163–215.

32. Ibid., sheet 176.

33. A. Evseev, "Sekretar´ raikoma," *Literatura i iskusstvo,* 12 December 1942, 3.

34. M. P. Vlasov, ed., *Sovetskoe kino v gody Velikoi Otechestvennoi voiny (1941–1945)* (Moscow: VGIK, 1999), 26.

35. John A. Armstrong, ed., *Soviet Partisans in World War II* (Madison: University of Wisconsin Press, 1964), 279–80.

36. Iosif Leonidovich Prut, *P'esy* (Moscow: Sovetskii pisatel´, 1963), 199.

37. Ibid., 210–12.

38. Aleksei Kapler, *V tylu vraga* (Moscow: Pravda, 1942), 20.

39. Aleksei Kapler, *Partizany: P'esa v trekh deistviiakh, shesti kartinakh* (Moscow-Leningrad: Iskusstvo, 1943), 100.

40. This English translation has been transcribed from the original American release of the film, available from International Historic Films.

41. "Miting predstavitelei evreiskogo naroda," *Literaturnaia gazeta,* 27 August 1941, 3.

42. Svetlana Allilueva qtd. in Aleksei Kapler, *"Ia" i "My": Vzlety i padeniia rytsaria iskusstva* (Moscow: Kniga, 1980), 7.

43. Sergei Borodin, "Ona zashchishchaet rodinu," *Pravda,* 24 May 1943, 4.

44. Fomin, *Kino na voine,* 232.

45. Ibid., 276.

46. Ibid., 352.

47. Howard Barnes, "'No Greater Love'—Victoria," *New York Herald Tribune,* 25 February 1944, 10.

48. A. Sazonov, "Mark Donskoi Discusses 'The Rainbow,'" *Cinema/Film Chronicle* 1–2 (1944): 3.

49. Emilia Kosnichuk, "Vanda Vasilevskaia oboshla Fidelia Castro v rubke sakharnogo trostnika: K 100-letiiu so dnia rozhdeniia," *Ezhenedel'nik 2000,* 15 July 2005, http://2000.net.ua/2000/aspekty/kultura/19055 (accessed 26 Sept. 2010).

50. For the novel, see Wanda Wasilewska, *Raduga: Povest´,* trans. E. Usievich (Moscow: Ogiz, 1942). For her use of the journalistic source, see Wanda Wasilewska, *Tvori,* 8 vols. (Kiev: Dnipro, 1966), 1:55–56 . For the original article, see Oskar Kurganov, "Mat´," *Pravda,* 7 February 1942, 2; for an account of the murder of Jews in Uvarovka, see Sverdlov, *Dokumenty obviniaiut,* 77.

51. While it is sometimes claimed that Donskoi won an Oscar for *The Rainbow,* he in fact received an IFRG Unity award. The IFRG was the International Film and Radio Guild, a left-wing American media organization soon to be crushed in the McCarthy years.

52. Bosley Crowther, "Terror Reign by Nazis," *New York Times,* 23 October 1944, 14.

53. Howard Barnes, "On the Screen," review of *The Rainbow, New York Herald Tribune,* 23 October 1944, 10.

54. Manny Farber, "The Red and the Black," *New Republic,* 6 November 1944, 595.

55. James Agee, "The Rainbow," *The Nation,* 18 November 1944; repr. in James Agee, *Agee on Film: Reviews and Comments* (New York: McDowell-Obolensky, 1958), 125.

56. Jessica Smith, letter to the editor, *New Republic,* 4 December 1944, 749.

57. Mark Donskoi, "My Work on the Film 'Unvanquished,'" *Cinema Chronicle* 10 (Oct. 1945): 9–16.

58. Mark Donskoi, "Raduga," *Krasnoarmeets* 5 (Mar. 1944): 17.

## Chapter 4. Dovzhenko: Moving the Boundaries of the Acceptable

1. George O. Liber, *Alexander Dovzhenko: A Life in Soviet Film* (London: BFI, 2002), 188–89, 191.

2. Directors enjoyed greater scope when making feature-length documentaries, which were usually commissioned to represent specific battles. In these cases, the director often worked near the front, stationed with the army, and could assign camera operators specific tasks. Thus Aleksandr Medvedkin, in his plan for the film of the taking of Königsburg in February 1945, allocates roles to the members of his team; all of them were to film the fighting and images of the Red Army reaching the sea, but various pairs were instructed to record the town's defenses, artillery, the Gestapo HQ, and even "the sufferings of women and children" (Muzei kino, 56/1/9). Nevertheless, such plans suggest the habitual and predictable nature of these films, which could largely be planned in advance.

3. The phrase "Holocaust by bullets" comes from the title of a work by Father Patrick Desbois, *The Holocaust by Bullets: A Priest's Journey to Uncover the Truth behind the Murder of 1.5 Million Jews* (Houndmills, U.K.: Palgrave Macmillan, 2008).

4. These have yet to be published in full. The curently most complete edition appears, in its original Ukrainian, in Aleksandr (Oleksandr in the source) Dovzhenko, *Storinki shchodennika (1941–1956)* (Kiev: Vidavnitstvo gumanitarnoï literatury, 2004). Marco Carynnyk has produced an excellent translation of an earlier, less complete version: Alexander Dovzhenko, *The Poet as Filmmaker,* ed. and trans. Marco Carynnyk (Cambridge, Mass.: MIT Press, 1973).

5. The most famous formulation of this thesis is by Theodor Adorno. For a discussion of it, see Lawrence L. Langer, *The Holocaust and the Literary Imagination* (New Haven, Conn.: Yale University Press, 1975), 11–15; also see Ziva Amishai-Maisels, *Depiction and Interpretation: The Influence of the Holocaust on the Visual Arts* (Oxford: Pergamon, 1993), xxxi–ii.

6. Dovzhenko, *Poet as Filmmaker,* 35 (entry for Mar. 1942).

7. Dovzhenko, *Storinki shchodennika,* 130–31 (entry for 12 July 1942).

8. Dovzhenko, *Poet as Filmmaker,* 46 (entry for 2 Apr. 1942).

9. Ibid., 47 (entry for 2 Apr. 1942).

10. Aleksandr Dovzhenko, "War and the Cooperation of Allied Cinema" ("Voina i sotrudnichestvo kinematografii soiuznykh stran"), address to USSR Society for Cultural Relations with Foreign Countries (VOKS), RGALI, 2918/2/35. This speech was reprinted in full the following week in *Literatura i iskusstvo,* 29 August 1942, 2.

11. Vance Kepley Jr., *In Service of the State: The Cinema of Alexander Dovzhenko* (Madison: University of Wisconsin Press, 1986), 63.

12. Dovzhenko, *Poet as Filmmaker,* 34–35.

13. In writing the first English-language book-length study of Dovzhenko, Vance Kepley Jr. explained that he was not going to look at *The Battle for Our Soviet Ukraine* or its sequel, *Victory in Right Bank Ukraine,* for which, he said "Dovzhenko merely edited footage shot by others" (Kepley, *In Service of the State,* 9). Marco Carynnyk calls the wartime documentaries "the least known and studied of all Dovzhenko's work" but adds that they are "extremely important phases of his artistic development" (Carynnyk, "Introduction: The Mythopetic Vision of Alexander Dovzhenko," in Dovzhenko, *The Poet as Filmmaker,* ed. and trans. Marco Carynnyk [Cambridge, Mass.: MIT Press, 1973], xxxi). Similarly, Peter Kenez says that the film "deserves special attention . . . because it was . . . aesthetically the most satisfying film" among Soviet wartime documentaries, and he consequently devotes a whole paragraph of his generally rather conspectual book to it. He sees its merits as lying primarily in its images of nature, its editing, and its voiceover; see Kenez, *Cinema and Soviet Society from the Revolution to the Death of Stalin,* new rev. ed. (London: I. B. Tauris, 2001), 171.

14. See, e.g., Serhii Trimbach, *Oleksandr Dovzhenko: Zahibel' bogiv: Identifikatsiia avtora v natsional'nomu chaso-prostori* (Vinnitsa, Ukraine: Globus, 2007). The same can be said of other, less-accomplished scholarship, such as Ivan Koshelivets', *Oleksandr Dovzhenko vchora i s'ogodni: Zatemneni mistsia v biografii* (Lutsk, Ukraine: Teren/VMA, 2005).

15. Thus Dovzhenko himself complained in a diary entry for 3 January 1944 (*Storinki shchodennika,* 188) that despite the success of the film, Khrushchev dared not mention it to Stalin when "Ukraine in Flames" was being castigated.

16. Vladimir Mikhailov stresses that Dovzhenko uses enemy footage innovatively, not to depict the actual course of a battle, but rather to create "a generalized image of an enemy force." At the same time, Mikhailov insists that the documentary basis of the footage remains even though, in a classic example of the Kuleshov effect, Dovzhenko's use of montage suggests sadistic pleasure on the part of the German soldiers. He nevertheless more broadly treats the film as Dovzhenko's; see Vladimir Mikhailov, *Frontovoi kinoreportazh* (Moscow: Nauchno-issledovatel'skii institut teorii i istorii kino, 1977), 44, 153.

17. Dovzhenko and Solntseva had codirected the 1939 documentary *Bukovina Is Ukrainian Land* (*Bukovina—zemlia ukrain'ska*) and the 1940 documentary known as *Liberation*, the full title of which is *The Liberation of Polish and Belorussian Lands from the Polish "Pans" and the Unification of Brother Peoples into a Single Family* (*Osvobozhdenie ukrainskikh i belorusskikh zemel' ot pol'skikh panov i vossoedinenie narodov-brat'ev v edinuiu sem'iu*). The latter to some extent shares the orientation toward synchronously recorded sound evident in Dovzhenko's wartime documentaries, especially in footage of Ukrainian-language speakers, but possesses none of its art. The former, however, with its ethnographic orientation, has more of the look of a Dovzhenko film.

18. Valentin Orliankin, "V kadre—pravda voiny," in *Dovzhenko v vospominaniiakh sovremennikov,* ed. L. I Pazhitnova and Iu. I. Solntseva (Moscow: Iskusstvo, 1982), 159.

19. Fomin, *Kino na voine,* 197–98.

20. Vladislav Mikosha, "'Ia ostanavlivaiu vremia': Vospominaniia frontovogo operatora," *Iskusstvo kino* 5 (2005): 115.

21. Boris Polevoi recalls seeing him eager to be among the first into liberated Kharkov; see Polevoi, *From Belgorod to the Carpathians: From a Soviet War Correspondent's Notebook* (London: Hutchinson, 1945), 44–45.

22. Valérie Pozner, "Les Actualités soviétiques de la seconde guerre mondiale," in *Le Cinéma "stalinien": Questions d'histoire,* ed. Natacha Laurent (Toulouse: Presses Universitaires du Mirail/La Cinémathèque de Toulouse, 2003), 129.

23. Barthélemy Amengual, *Alexandre Dovjenko* (Paris: Seghers, 1970), 109, 113; Jay Leyda, *Films Beget Films* (London: George Allen and Unwin, 1964), 68. Abram Krichevskii describes Dovzhenko and Solntseva looking through material, with Dovzhenko selecting particularly expressive moments; see Krichevskii, "Spiashchii batal'on," in *Dovzhenko v vospominaniiakh sovremennikov,* ed. L. I Pazhitnova and Iu. I. Solntseva (Moscow: Iskusstvo, 1982), 153.

24. Pozner, "Les Actualités soviétiques," 129. Mark Volotskii also highlights the film's use of the participants' voices; see Volotskii, "Zamknuta moia pravda," *Rodina* 4 (2000), http://www.istrodina.com/rodina_articul.php3?id=166&n=13 (accessed 20 Sept. 2010).

25. Speaking in a television documentary, Evgenii Margolit has described the whole film as a lament uttered by a bereaved mother (Margolit, "Dokumental'nyi Dovzhenko: rekviem po mechte," an installment of the series *Dokumental'naia kamera,* by Andrei Shemiakin, Kul'tura channel, 18 July 2008); see also Dovzhenko, *Poet as Filmmaker,* 43.

26. [Tsentral'nyi dom kino], "Stenogramma zasedaniia sektsii po obsuzhdeniiu fil'ma *Bitva za nashu sovetskuiu Ukrainu*," 28 October 1943, RGALI 2923/1/95, sheet 4.

27. Ibid., sheet 14.

28. Ibid., sheet 7.

29. Ibid., sheet 3.

30. Norman Davies (*No Simple Victory,* 366–67) estimates civilian Ukrainian deaths in the war as 5–8 million, not counting the approximately 900,000 Ukrainian Jews who perished. This is more, in both absolute and relative term, than the number of dead Polish, Russian, or even Belorussian civilians. Other historians provide lower figures, but most agree that Ukraine suffered the highest losses, both absolute and propotional, of all modern states. In her study of the Holocaust in Ukraine, Wendy Lower repeats Magocsi's estimates of nearly 4.1 million Ukrainian dead subsequent to the confluence of "Nazi-style militarism, colonialism and genocidal population policies" (*Nazi Empire-Building,* 2). Pavel Polian reproduces the figures set in 1946 by the Extraordinary State Commission on War Crimes, which states that apart from the 1.3 million Ukrainian POWs who perished, 3.1 million Ukrainian civilians, making up 52.3 percent of the republic's population, were killed, with both figures being the highest of their kind for all the Soviet republics; see Pavel Polian, *Zhertvy dvukh diktatur: Zhizn´, trud, unizhenie i smert´ sovetskikh voennoplennykh i ostarbait-erov na chuzhbine i na rodine,* 2d ed., rev. (Moscow: Rosspen, 2002), 11.

31. Volotskii, "Zamknuta moia pravda."

32. Kate Brown, *A Biography of No Place: From Ethnic Borderland to Soviet Heartland* (Cambridge, Mass.: Harvard University Press, 2004), 230.

33. Wieviorka, *Era of the Witness,* 143–44.

34. See Liber, *Alexander Dovzhenko,* 192–93, 202–3.

35. Saxton, *Haunted Images,* 109.

36. Shimon Briman, "Khar´kov, evrei, Izrail´: Pervoistolitse Ukrainy, gorodu s bogateishei evreiskoi istorii—350 let," http://gazeta.rjews.net/Lib /briman/040729-briman.shtml (accessed 2 Nov. 2009). Iuri Liakhovitskii states that Doctor Efros was killed in the city before the Germans killed the rest of the city's Jewish population; see Iuri M. Liakhovitskii, *Poprannaia Mezuza: Kniga Drobitskogo iara: Svidetel´stva, fakty, dokumenty o natsistskom genotside evreisk-ogo naseleniia Khar´kova v period okkupatsii 1941–1942,* vol. 1 (Kharkov, Ukraine: Osnova, 1991), 188.

37. Leonid Cherevatenko, "Osvobozhdennyi Dovzhenko," *Kinovedcheskie zapiski* 77 (2006): 105. Cherevatenko stresses that this accusation is accompanied by demonstrably false claims and is therefore almost certainly groundless, an attempt to twist Dovzhenko's Petliurite past against him.

38. Liber, *Alexander Dovzhenko,* 171–77. Also see Al´tman, *Zhertvy nenavisti,* 411.

39. For his denunciation of Nazi anti-Semitism in Dovzhenko's wartime journalism, see the article "K oruzhiiu" in Aleksandr Dovzhenko, *Sobranie*

sochinenii, comp. Iuliia Solntseva and ed. Sergei Drobashenko, 4 vols. (Moscow: Iskusstvo, 1967), 2:404. The persecution of Jews is also mentioned in Dovzhenko's notebooks (*Poet as Filmmaker,* 39).

40. Liber, *Alexander Dovzhenko,* 171–77.

41. Al´tman, *Zhertvy nenavisti,* 219–31.

42. Ibid., 412–13; Martin Dean, *Collaboration in the Holocaust: Crimes of the Local Police in Belorussia and Ukraine, 1941–44* (Houndmills, U.K.: Macmillan, 2000), 156–57.

43. Kostyrchenko, *Tainaia politika Stalina,* 354–55. Also see Lower, *Nazi Empire-Building,* 207.

44. Dovzhenko, *Poet as Filmmaker,* 90–91.

45. Margolit, "Dokumental´nyi Dovzhenko." Initial ideas that were to be developed in "Ukraine in Flames" can be found in the Dovzhenko's notebooks dating back to March 1942.

46. Sergei Borodin, "Chas otmshcheniia," *Ogonek,* 30 October 1943, 15.

47. Dovzhenko, *Sobranie sochinenii,* 2:209.

48. I. V. Stalin, "Ob antileninskikh oshibkakh i natsionalisticheskikh izvrashcheniiakh v kinopovesti Dovzhenko 'Ukraine v ogne,'" ed. Anatolii Latyshev, *Iskusstvo kino* 4 (1990): 84–96.

49. Dovzhenko, *Poet as Filmmaker,* 95.

50. Dovzhenko, *Sobranie sochinenii,* 2:166.

51. Al´tman, *Zhertvy nenavisti,* 24–27; Browning, *Origins of the Final Solution,* 234–43.

52. Dovzhenko, *Sobranie sochinenii,* 2:171.

53. Ibid., 2:197.

54. Ibid., 2:196.

55. In fact, Dovzhenko's widow, Solntseva, made the film after her husband's death, in 1967, calling it *Unforgettable* (*Nezabyvaemoe*), the title of one of the short stories on which it was based. None of original screenplay's references to the fate of Jews made it into this finished film.

56. Dovzhenko, *Poet as Filmmaker,* 94.

57. "'Ukraina' Stsenarnyi plan, diktorskii tekst A. P. Dovzhenko i perepiska Iu. Solntsevoi s rukovodtstom kinostudii o khode raboty nad fil'mom (1944)," RGALI 2487/1/719, sheet 24.

58. Ibid. At this point the film was called *The Battle for Our Soviet Ukraine (Part 2)* ("Bitva za nashu sovetskuiu Ukrainu II-iaia seriia").

59. Letter from Solntseva, April 1944, RGALI 2487/1/719, sheets 5–6.

60. Ibid., sheet 4 .

61. Ibid., sheet 8.

62. Agapov, nachal´nik redaktsii fil´mov, to A. A. Lebedev, 11 May 1944, RGALI 2487/1/719, sheet 17B.

63. The published text has changed *nemetskikh* (German) to *fashistskikh* (fascist); see Dovzhenko, *Sobranie sochinenii*, 2:379.

64. Dovzhenko, *Poet as Filmmaker*, 93.

65. Dovzhenko, *Sobranie sochinenii*, 2:383–84. Again the published text differs slightly from the commentary in the actual film, here toning down the full horror of the words with an ellipsis after "hiding in the woods."

66. Dovzhenko, *Poet as Filmmaker*, 121. Liber (*Alexander Dovzhenko*, 215) comments that Dovzhenko habitually quoted this inaccurate figure, which is probably twice the actual Ukrainian war losses.

67. Feferman, *Soviet Jewish Stepchild*, 42.

68. Dovzhenko, *Storinki shchodennika*, 150 (entry for 28 Aug. 1943).

69. Fomin, *Kino na voine*, 638.

70. "'Battle for the Ukraine': Horrors of Invasion," *Times*, 14 March 1944, 8. A copy of the British release, entitled *Battle for the Ukraine*, can be found at the National Film and Television Archive in London.

71. M. K. to Bol'shakov, 12 December 1943, in Fomin, *Kino na voine*, 602–3.

72. "Ukraine in Flames," *Variety*, 26 April, 1944, n.p.

73. Dovzhenko, *Poet as Filmmaker*, 105.

74. Dovzhenko, *Sobranie sochinenii*, 2:304.

75. Iu. Morozov and T. Derevianko, *Evreiskie kinematografisty v Ukraine, 1917–1945* (Kiev: Dukh i litera, 2004), 210.

**Chapter 5. Mark Donskoi's Reconstruction of Babyi Iar: *The Unvanquished***

1. The unsigned article "Khudozhestvennye fil'my 1944 goda" (*Literatura i iskusstvo*, 8 Jan. 1944) refers to *The Unvanquished*, which it calls *Sem'ia Tarasa*, as one of the year's films "about the courage and fearlessness of Soviet people languishing in Fascist captivity" (2).

2. Mark Donskoi, "'Nepokorennye': Fil'm o velikom gordom narode," *Pravda Ukrainy*, 1 November 1944, 4.

3. Morozov and Derevianko, *Evreiskie kinematografisty v Ukraine*, 210-11; Hans Klering "Trebovatel'nost'," in *Mark Donskoi: Sbornik: Mastera sovetskogo kino*, ed. Liudmilla Padzhitnova (Moscow: Iskusstvo, 1973), 259–60.

4. "Pervyi den' s"emki," *Izvestiia*, 24 August 1944, 3. Filming began on the first day with the factory scenes.

5. Donskoi ("My Work," 16) mentions Manny Farber and James Agee by name in an interview intended to publicize the film abroad.

6. As Elena Baraban points out, despite the Ukrainian setting, the words *Ukraine* and *Ukrainian* are never used in the film; see Baraban, "Semeinyi krug: traktovka rodstva, evreev i voennoplennykh v stalinskom kino o voine," *Ab Imperio* 3 (2009): 12.

7. Elena Baraban (ibid., 7–8, 22) sees the film's treatment of prisoners of

war as highly orthodox and Stalinist and (incorrectly, in my view) the film's depiction of the fate of the Jews as exploitatively utilitarian and Soviet. The distinctive nature of the film's treatment of this theme should be evident from a comparison with the other such representations discussed in this book.

8. Boris Gorbatov, *Sobranie sochinenii,* 5 vols. (Moscow: Gos. Izd. khudozhestvennoi literatury, 1955), 2:414–15.

9. Mark Donskoi and Boris Gorbatov, *Nepokorennye: Literaturnyi i rezhisserskii stsenarii* (Moscow: n.p., 1944), 23; a copy can be found at the Gosfil´mofond archive, section I/3/1/1489, "Nepokorennye."

10. Arkadii Bernshtein, "Drevo zhizni," *Kinovedcheskie zapiski* 62 (2003): 200.

11. Donskoi and Gorbatov, *Nepokorennye,* 23.

12. LaCapra, *History and Memory,* 9; Janet Walker, *Trauma Cinema: Documenting Incest and the Holocaust* (Berkeley: University of California Press, 1999), 19; also see Bernard-Donals, *Forgetful Memory,* 3–15.

13. See, for example, Alvin H. Rosenfeld, "Popularization and Memory: The Case of Anne Frank," in *Lessons and Legacies,* vol. 1: *The Meaning of the Holocaust in a Changing World,* ed. Peter Hayes (Evanston, Ill.: Northwestern University Press, 1991), 243–78.

14. Milena Musina, "Ischislenie roda," *Kinovedcheskie zapiski* 51 (2001): 197.

15. In *Nazi Empire-Building,* Wendy Lower refers to an overlap between Ukrainian resistance and collaboration: "Many resistance fighters worked undercover in the administration. Moreover, Ukrainian police collaborators and administrators who were central agents of the Nazi terror and Holocaust in 1941–42 later deserted their posts and joined the partisans in 1943–44," thus "blurring the categorical distinctions of victim, perpetrator and bystander" (11–12).

16. Evgenii Margolit, "Obraz nemtsa-okkupanta v voennykh fil´makh Marka Donskogo," in *Ukraina-Nimechchina: Kinematografichni zv´iazky,* ed. Hans-Joachim Schlegel and Serhii Trimbach (Vinnitsa, Ukraine: Globus, 2009), 202.

17. For an account of the story's close relation to the original Voroshilovgrad sources, see N. Velengurin, "Maloizvestnaia stat´ia Borisa Gorbatova," *Ural´* 5 (1965): 148–53. Martyn Merzhanov, a fellow *Pravda* wartime correspondent, claims Gorbatov drew some of his material, including a prototype for Taras, from Vladikazkaz; see Merzhanov, "V soldatskoi shineli," in *Vospominaniia o Borise Gorbatove,* ed. S. A. Savel´ev (Moscow: Sovetskii pisatel´, 1964), 364–65.

18. Galina Kolesnikova, "Tvorchestvo pisatelia-patriota (kritiko-biograficheskii ocherk)," in Gorbatov, *Sobranie sochinenii,* 1:39.

19. Hiroaki Kuromiya, *Freedom and Terror in the Donbas: A Ukrainian-Russian Borderland, 1870s–1990s* (Cambridge: Cambridge University Press, 1998), 271.

20. Gorbatov, *Sobranie sochinenii,* 2:415.

21. Donskoi, "My Work," 13.

22. Thus Ivan Bol´shakov asserted that the film, like the original novel, was based in the Donbass, or Donets Basin; see Bol´shakov, *Sovetskoe kinoiskusstvo v gody velikoi otechestvennoi voiny* (Moscow: Goskinoizdat, 1948), 51.

23. Elie Wiesel, foreword to *Indelible Shadows: Film and the Holocaust,* by Anette Insdorf, 3d ed. (Cambridge: Cambridge University Press, 2003), xii.

24. "Stenogram of Artistic Council of Cinema Committee—Viewing and discussion of film 'The Unvanquished,'" 21 June 1945, RGALI 2456/1/1056, sheet 8. The French term *guignol* refers to any puppet show akin to British Punch and Judy shows and featuring the character Guignol; in its Russian usage, it refers to the gory naturalism associated with the Théâtre du Grand-Guignol, a Parisian theater known for its bloody content whose popularity peaked during the interwar years.

25. Ibid., sheet 21. The figure of 3.5 million Jews appears a number of times in this period. See also Karmen's first draft for the voiceover for *Judgment of the Nations* (discussed in chapter 7).

26. Erenburg (as Ehrenburg) and Grossman, *Complete Black Book,* 8.

27. Amishai-Maisels, *Depiction and Interpretation,* 131.

28. Richard McBee, "Yad Vashem's Art," 9 August 2005, http://richardmcbee.com/26yad_vashem_1.htm (accessed 24 Sept. 2009).

29. In describing the Babyi Iar massacre scene, the script for a film about Donskoi made shortly after his death calls this "the oldest prayer on Earth"; see Grigorii Chukhrai, Iu. Shvyrev, and M. Volotskii, *"Ia nauchu vas mechtat´"*: *Rezhisserskaia razrabotka monografii o Marke Donskogo,* codirectors, G. Chukhrai, Iu. Shvyrev (Moscow: Kinostudiia im. Gor´kogo, 1983), 26; a copy is available at the Muzei kino, Mark Donskoi archive.

30. Abraham Sutzkever, "I Feel Like Saying a Prayer," in *Beyond Lament: Poets of the World Bearing Witness to the Holocaust,* ed. Marguerite M. Striar (Evanston, Ill.: Northwestern University Press, 1998), 141.

31. Donskoi saw the two films as linked ("Nepokorennye," *Pravda Ukrainy,* 1 Nov. 1944, 4).

32. Merridale, *Night of Stone,* 311.

33. Donskoi and Gorbatov, *Nepokorennye,* 52.

34. Il´ia Erenburg, *Sobranie sochinenii,* 5 vols. (Moscow: Gos. izd. khudozhestvennoi literatury, 1952–54), 2:245.

35. Donskoi and Gorbatov, *Nepokorennye,* 52.

36. Insdorf observes that, for a number of East European films, "Judaism hinders resistance" (*Indelible Shadows,* 155–56). As I will discuss, *Pravda*'s review condemned the portrayal of the victims as "passive."

37. Musina, "Ischislenie roda," 197; author's conversation with Alexander Markovich Donskoi, Moscow, June 2008.

38. Erenburg (as Ehrenburg) and Grossman, *Complete Black Book,* 8.

39. Donskoi and Gorbatov, *Nepokorennye,* 52.

40. Amishai–Maisels (*Depiction and Interpretation,* xxxi) nicely summarizes these dilemmas for artists of the Holocaust.

41. "Stenogram of Artistic Council," sheet 22.

42. "Nepokorennye," *Pravda Ukrainy,* 1 November 1944, 4.

43. "Stenogram of Artistic Council," sheet 6.

44. Ibid., sheet 27.

45. I. A. Pyr′ev, *Izbrannye proizvedeniia,* 2 vols. (Moscow: Iskusstvo, 1978), 1:209.

46. "Stenogram of Artsistic Council," sheets 45–50.

47. Borzenko's stature is clear from the awestruck account of *Pravda'*s chief correspondent, Boris Polevoi. Borzenko was a journalist who had assumed command of a group of assault troops during the Kerch offensive after their officers had been killed in action. He was able to lead the soldiers effectively while still sending dispatches to *Pravda.* See Boris Polevoi, *Sobranie sochinenii,* 9 vols. (Moscow: Khudozhestvennaia literatura, 1981–86), 8:28–29.

48. S. Borzenko, "Nepokorennye," *Pravda,* 24 October 1945, 3.

49. Iurii Buriakovskii, "Sem′ia Tarasa," *Pravda Ukrainy,* 18 October 1945, 4; I. Sokolov "'Nepokorennye': Novyi khudozhestvennyi fil′m," *Komsomol′skaia Pravda,* 21 October 1945, 4.

50. "Nepokorennye," Gosfil′mofond archive, 1/3/1/1489.

51. Bosley Crowther, review of "The Taras Family," *New York Times,* 9 December 1946, 9:36.

52. Wit, "The Taras Family," *Variety,* 18 December 1946, n.p.

53. Ibid.

54. The film was shown at the Venice Film Festival "with success"; see "Un regista russo: Marco Donskoi," *La critica cinematografica* 1, no. 5 (10 Dec. 1946): 6.

55. Umberto Barbaro, "Ancora un bel film sovietico," *L'unità,* 14 September 1946, 2.

56. J. H., "Tarass l'indompté," *La Cinématographie française,* 14 May 1949, 28. This review indicates a running time of ninety minutes, the length of the Russian print generally available, whereas the review in *Variety* claims a length of eighty-two minutes. The film was likely shortened for audiences in the United States, as Soviet films often were.

57. Raymond Barkan, "'*Taras L'Indompté*': La sensibilité de Donskoi au service de l'humanisme soviétique," *L'Écran français,* 10 May 1949, 11.

58. Qtd. in ibid.

59. It was shown in what was to become the German Democratic Republic (DDR) in 1948 but appears not to have been shown in West Germany.

60. Avisar, *Screening the Holocaust,* 38.

61. Monastyrskii had himself briefly worked with Dziga Vertov on *Three Songs of Lenin* (*Tri pesni o Lenine* [1934]). Monastyrski's work would have been familiar to the Poles, for *The Rainbow,* adapted from a work by the Polish writer Wanda Wasilewska, was one of the first films that the Soviets allowed to be subtitled for and distributed in postwar Poland. See Stanislaw Ozimek, *Film polski w wojennej potrzebie* (Warsaw: Państowy Instytut Wydawiczy, 1974), 191.

62. Insdorf, *Indelible Shadows,* 256–57.

63. Avisar, *Screening the Holocaust,* 38.

64. Chernenko, *Krasnaia zvezda,* 108.

65. "Stenogram of Artistic Council," sheets 2–3.

66. Kiril Feferman (*Soviet Jewish Stepchild,* 38–42) has illustrated how Soviet war losses were systematically scaled down toward the end of the war and thereafter.

## Chapter 6. Liberation of the Camps

1. Alexander Werth, in Moscow at the time, corroborated the shock with which these revelations were greeted; see Werth, *Russia at War, 1941-1945* (London: Barrie and Rockliff, 1964), 890.

2. Simonov's subsequently published wartime diary indicates that he arrived at the camp a week after its liberation, even though in his wartime articles he claims to have been there from the outset; see Konstantin Simonov, *Sobranie sochinenii,* 10 vols. (Moscow: Khudozhestvennaia literatura, 1979–85), 9:360.

3. Roman Karmen, *No pasaran!* (Moscow: Sovetskaia Rossiia, 1972), 199.

4. Stanislaw Ozimek quotes Stanislaw Wohl as saying that the Polish group entered the camp minutes after the Nazis had left it; see Ozimek, "The Polish Newsreel in 1945: The Bitter Victory," in *Hitler's Fall: The Newsreel Witness,* ed. K. R. M. Short and Stephan Dolozel (London: Croom Helm, 1988), 72. Ozimek sees this testimony as resolving a dispute between Richard Raack and Sergei Drobashenko as to whether the Polish or Soviet filmmakers arrived at the camp first. According to a biography of him, Karmen arrived in Majdanek by accident soon after the liberation of Lublin, while the ash was still warm in the crematoria. He then informed the Sovinformbureau, which sent journalists and more cameramen, while Karmen advanced with his unit; see N. Kolesnikova, G. Senchakova, and T. Slepneva, *Roman Karmen* (Moscow: Iskusstvo, 1959), 91-92. The letter of introduction referred to later suggests that Karmen did not just chance across the camp but was sent there, which would indicate that he probably arrived after the Poles. In their accounts, many of these cameramen claim to have been the first to see the camp. Stuart Liebman's account of the time frame of the filming follows that of the Polish sources; see Liebman, "Documenting the Liberation of the Camps: The Case of Aleksander Ford's *Vernichtungslager Majdanek—Cmentarzysko Europy* (1944)," in *Lessons and Legacies,*

vol. 7: *The Holocaust in International Perspective,* ed. Dagmar Herzog (Evanston, Ill.: Northwestern University Press, 2006), 336.

5. Red Army Political Directorate to Karmen, Muzei kino, 32/1/26.

6. Władysław Jewsiewicki, *Polscy Filmowcy na frontach drugiej wojny światowej* (Warsaw: Wydawnictwa Artystyczne i Filmowe, 1972), 176. For a full list of credits and summary of the content in German, see Fritz Bauer Institut, Cinematographie des Holocaust, "Kurz-dokumentarfilm," http://www.cine-holocaust.de/cgi-bin/gdq?dfw00fbw002859.gd (accessed 30 Dec. 2008).

7. Adorno explored this notion a number of times in his work. See Rolf Tiedemann, "Introduction: 'Not the First Philosophy, but a Last One': Notes on Adorno's Thought," in *Can One Live after Auschwitz? A Philosophical Reader,* by Theodor W. Adorno, ed. Rolf Tiedemann (Stanford, Calif.: Stanford University Press, 2003), xi–xxvii.

8. Hilberg (*Destruction of European Jews,* 3:1219) estimates that the German concentration camps each accounted for Jewish deaths "in the low tens of thousands or fewer," with a combined death toll of 150,000. Thus more Jews were killed in the death camp with the less-familiar name of Chełmno than in all the concentration camps of Germany.

9. Liebman, "Documenting the Liberation," 334.

10. Soviet newsreels had recorded Nazi prisoner of war camps, such as that at Bol´shaia Rossoshka, near Stalingrad, footage of which was included in the 1943 documentary *Stalingrad,* directed by Leonid Varlamov. Soviet POW camps were comparable to concentration camps, for inmates in them were barely fed, and over two million Red Army prisoners died in the first two years of the war. See Karel C. Berkhoff, "The Mass Murder of Soviet Prisoners of War and the Holocaust: How Were They Related?" *Kritika: Explorations in Russian and Eurasian History* 6, no. 4 (Fall 2005): 789–96; Christian Streit ("The German Army," 9, 11) has estimated that Soviet POWs died at a rate of 1 percent a day, mostly though starvation, and related this process to the Nazi killing of Jews. The Austrian-born American director Fred Zinnemann's film *The Seventh Cross* (1944) also depicts a concentration camp.

11. For an account of this tension in Soviet photography, see Shneer, *Through Soviet Jewish Eyes,* 149–64.

12. For inaccuracies in the Soviet film shown at the Nuremberg Tribunal, see chapter 7.

13. Liebman ("Documenting the Liberation," 337) does concede that the Polish film draws on the example of Soviet war documentaries but expands very little upon this point.

14. O. Leonidov, "Kinoletopis´ voiny: Den´ v tsentral´noi studii kinokhron-iki," *Vecherniaia Moskva,* 22 June 1942, 3; V. Smirnov, "'Nagrada rodiny' Poslednii kinoreportazh," *Vecherniaia Moskva,* 7 May 1942, 3.

15. Hilberg argues that the death camps were unprecedented because "never before had people been killed on an assembly-line basis" (*Destruction of European Jews,* 3:863).

16. The historian Tomasz Kranz argues that the political executions and racial exterminations carried out at Majdanek made it an unusual and special case in the Nazi system of camps; see Kranz, "Between Planning and Implementation: The Lublin District and Majdanek Camp in Nazi Policy," in *Lessons and Legacies,* vol. 4: *Reflections on Religion, Justice, Sexuality, and Genocide,* ed. Larry V. Thompson (Evanston, Ill.: Northwestern University Press, 2003), 220-21. The Majdanek film illustrates these two functions, but—typically for Soviet films—it fails to point out the significant distinction between the two kinds of murder and the Jewish identities of most of those gassed.

17. Douglas, *Memory of Judgment,* 36 (I discuss this term in chapter 2).

18. See Saxton, *Haunted Images,* 21.

19. Primo Levi, *If This Is a Man,* trans. Stuart Woolf (Harmondsworth, U.K.: Penguin, 2006), 96; Primo Levi, *The Drowned and the Saved,* trans. Raymond Rosenthal (Harmondsworth, U.K.: Penguin, 1989), 63-64.

20. Saxton, *Haunted Images,* 76-82.

21. Ibid., 54.

22. Liebman, "Documenting the Liberation," 337.

23. Boris Gorbatov, "Lager´ na Majdaneke," *Pravda,* 11 August 1944, 2. David Shneer (*Through Soviet Jewish Eyes,* 151) argues that these images have antecedents in photographs of Malyi Trostinets, near Minsk, taken weeks earlier.

24. Konstantin Simonov, *The Death Factory near Lublin* (London: Daily Worker League, 1944), 18. The translation, which is unattributed, idiosyncratically renders Simonov's three repetitions of *strashnyi* ("terrifying") as *gruesome* (twice) and *grim.*

25. Zelizer, *Remembering to Forget,* 57.

26. Levi, *If This Is a Man,* 96; Levi, *The Drowned and the Saved,* 63-64.

27. The Polish historian Tomasz Kranz devotes a whole chapter of his *Extermination of Jews at the Majdanek Concentration Camp* (Lublin, Poland: Państwowe Muzeum na Majdanku, 2007) to an examination of the various estimates of the total number of Jews who died at Majdanek. Lucy Dawidowicz (*War against the Jews,* 149) repeats the same estimated death toll for Majdanek used by the Soviets, 1,380,000, though unlike the Soviet film, she treats all these victims as Jewish. Raul Hilberg (*Destruction of European Jews,* 3:1219) puts the lower figure of Jews killed at 50,000. Kranz (*Extermination of Jews,* 75) concludes that 60,000 perished in all. This figure also appears on the Majdanek museum Web site, as does the figure of 80,000 total victims of the camp, recently revised downward based on Kranz's scholarship (Kranz is the director of research at the Majdanek

museum); see "History of the Camp," http://www.majdanek.eu/articles.php ?acid=45 (accessed 17 Aug. 2011). The United States Holocaust Memorial Museum broadly follows these figures; see "Lublin/Majdanek Concentration Camp: Areas of Research," http://www.ushmm.org/wlc/en/article.php ?ModuleId=10007299 (accessed 17 Aug. 2011). Generally, the highest of more recent estimates maintain that as many as 250,000 people perished in the camp; see Kranz, "Between Planning and Implementation," 222, 224, 230. *Cemetery of Europe* estimates the death toll at nearly 2 million.

28. This material is available in RGAKFD, Krasnogorsk, near Moscow. Much of the footage can also be viewed in Irmgard von zur Mühlen, dir., *Holocaust: The Liberation of Majdanek,* DVD (Artsmagic, 2006; original German-language version, *Majdanek 1944: Opfer und Täter* [1986]). This film omits the Soviet voiceover, however, and translates selectively through dubbing, making the original Polish, Russian, and German speech of those interviewed hard to discern.

29. The spelling was established by Liebman in "Documenting the Liberation," 349.

30. Ibid., 340.

31. Similarly, Liebman refers to the "unsettling" nature of the Ford and Bossak's film's narrative. As he puts it: "Without outrightly falsifying any details, the filmmakers chose to focus on certain images and to highlight certain voices that distort the reality of the camp in highly significant ways" (ibid., 335). However, print sources, especially Konstantin Simonov, do mention the Jews as important victims of the camp without ever really showing them to have suffered in greater proportion than the others. Simonov's articles for the important Red Army daily, Krasnaia zvezda, were speedily translated into many languages; see Simonov, Death Factory near Lublin.

32. Ozimek, "Polish Newsreel in 1945," 73.

33. I draw my argument here from Liebman, "Documenting the Liberation," 340.

34. Sontag, *Regarding the Pain of Others,* 55-57.

35. Abzug, *Inside the Vicious Heart,* 40-41. Newman's report, entitled "Nordhausen: A Hell Factory Worked by the Living Dead," appeared on 23 April 1945. Toby Haggith contests this interpretation of the Bergen-Belsen footage; see Haggith, "Filming the Liberation of Bergen-Belsen," in *Holocaust and the Moving Image: Representations in Film and Television since 1933,* ed. Toby Haggith and Joanna Newman (London: Wallflower, 2005), 37-38.

36. Abzug, *Inside the Vicious Heart,* 41-44. Meyer Levin had a similar experience at Buchenwald (ibid., 58-59).

37. Jeffrey C. Alexander, "On the Social Construction of Universal Morals: The 'Holocaust' from War Crime to Trauma Drama," in *Cultural Trauma and*

*Collective Identity,* ed. Jeffrey C. Alexander, Ron Eyerman, Bernhard Giesen, Neil J. Smelser, and Piotr Sztompka (Berkeley: University of California Press, 2004), 199.

38. Avisar, *Screening the Holocaust,* 35; Omer Bartov, *The "Jew" in Cinema: From "The Golem" to "Don't Touch my Holocaust"* (Bloomington: Indiana University Press, 2005), 179.

39. For the way in which Erenburg was made a scapegoat for this, see Berkhoff, "Total Annihilation," 96.

40. Ibid., 93. The accusation as to Shcherbakov's anti-Semitism is made in Kostyrchenko, *Tainaia politika Stalina,* 227.

41. Berkhoff, "Total Annihilation," 94.

42. Gilbert, *The Holocaust,* 735. For a discussion of the newspaper and extraordinary commission reports on the camps, see Berkhoff, "Total Annihilation," 87.

43. Valerii Fomin, personal archive.

44. Werth, *Russia at War,* 889-90.

45. Konstantin Simonov's description of Majdanek appeared in the *Times,* 12 August 1944, 3.

46. Werth, *Russia at War,* 889-90.

47. Gilbert, *The Holocaust,* 711.

48. In his article about the discovery of Auschwitz, the Soviet journalist Boris Polevoi claims that the attempt to dismantle it was undertaken in reaction to the revelations about Majdanek (Polevoi, "Kombinat smerti v Oswentsime," *Pravda,* 2 Feb. 1945, 4). The process of destroying the evidence at Auschwitz began in November 1944, when Himmler ordered the crematoria to be dismantled; see Gilbert, *Auschwitz and the Allies,* 331-36.

49. Listings, *Vecherniaia Moskva,* 4 January 1945, 3. Thus, with regard to its domestic distribution, at least, Barbie Zelizer is right to argue that "the Russians were curiously uneven in their attempts to make public what they found when they liberated the camps" (*Remembering to Forget,* 50).

50. See Berkhoff, "Total Annihilation."

51. Berkhoff suggests that the decision to publicize the Nazi persecution of Jews in Poland was taken in response to Nazi revelations about the Katyn and Viniitsa killings ("Total Annihilation," 91).

52. See E. Pomeshchikov, "Tragediia v Katynskom lesu," *Literatura i iskusstva,* 4 March 1944, 4.

53. Sylvie Lindeperg, *Clio de 5 à 7: Les Actualités filmés de la Libération: Archives du futur* (Paris: CNRS, 2000), 164.

54. Ibid.

55. Georges Sadoul, "Maideneck: Le Camp de l'extermination," *Les Lettres françaises,* 21 April 1945, 5.

56. Liebman, "Documenting the Liberation," 343.

57. As the instructors' notes used to train army cameramen clearly show, British army photographers were aware that Soviets had been filming atrocities; see Haggith's discussion of these notes for instructors, from the IWM department of documents, in Haggith, "Filming the Liberation," 37-38.

58. Caven, "Horror in Our Time," 238-43.

59. Vasilii Petrenko, *Avant et après Auschwitz,* trans. François-Xavier Nérard (Paris: Flammarion, 2000), 123.

60. Kutub-Zade's account is quoted in Aidyn Shem´i-zade, "Kenian Kutub-zade—avtor fil´ma 'Lager´smerti Osventsima,'" *Krymskii mir,* 10 May 2010, http://www.kr-alemi.com/index.php?name=News&op=article&sid=899 (accessed 30 June 2010). While I have been unable to find print originals of these memoirs, they nevertheless correspond in many details with facts established by other sources and should consequently be treated seriously.

61. "Correspondence with film group of the 1st Ukrainian Front," 2 January-29 June 1945, RGALI 2487/1/1021.8/7, sheet 55.

62. Ibid., sheet 76.

63. Speaking on the exhibition "Filmer les Camps" in a segment of the radio program *Le RenDez-Vous* (Radio France Culture, 17 Mar. 2010), the French film historian Christian Delage stressed that the Soviet forces liberating Auschwitz did not have a camera crew and implied that all the footage was staged later, after the model of the Polish women who reconstructed life in the barracks. From this flawed analysis he concludes that the Soviet footage as a whole should be discounted.

64. "Correspondence with film group," sheet 78.

65. Ibid., sheets 82-90.

66. Ibid., sheet 116.

67. Ibid., sheet 140. According to the Irmgard von zur Mühlen film *Holocaust: The Liberation of Auschwitz* (Artsmagic, 2005; German-language original, *Die Befreihung von Auschwitz*), the filming ended on 28 February. These documents show that it continued after that date.

68. Shtatland (political directorate of the front) to Oshurkov (film group), 3 April 1945, "Correspondence with film group," sheet 223.

69. "Auschwitz: Protocols of Inspections," GARF R7021/108/17, sheet 156.

70. In the only published analysis of the film, Vincent Lowy (*L'Histoire infilmable,* 43-45) stresses the images' "rough actuality" and "lack of distance." In fact, as I hope to show, they were shaped through various conventions so as to suggest a distinct Sovietized vision of the camp.

71. For confirmation of the fact that the twins were Jewish and a description of the ordeals they faced, see Gilbert, *The Holocaust,* 687-89.

72. See the report from the Soviet Extraordinary State Commission on War Crimes (GChK) in Erenburg (Ehrenburg) and Grossman, *Complete Black Book,* 510. Quoting a 1960s Polish source, Martin Gilbert (*Auschwitz and the Allies,* 337) puts the figure at 7,600, with 1,200 in the main camp, 5,800 at Birkenau, and 650 at Monowitz. The arithmetic is Gilbert's.

73. "'Osventsim': Stsenarii i stenarnyi plan I. I Bachelis,' signed by Svilova, 20 May 1945," RGALI 2487/1/509, sheet 14.

74. Pavlov's dope sheet, in Valerii Fomin's personal archive copy; for the Sovinformbureau report, see "Ot sovetskogo informbiuro," *Pravda,* 1 February 1945, 1.

75. Muravin, *Dvoe iz mnogikh tysiach,* 104; Zinovii Tolkachev, *Osventsim* (Moscow: Izobrazitel´noe izkusstvo, 1969), 21.

76. "The Last and Only," Tolkachev, *Osventsim,* pl. 61.

77. Vasilii (as Vasily) Grossman, "The Hell of Treblinka," in *The Road: Short Fiction and Essays,* by Grossman, trans. Robert and Elisabeth Chandler (New York: New York Review of Books, 2010), 126–79.

78. In von zur Mühlen, *Holocaust: The Liberation of Auschwitz.*

79. Ibid.

80. "'Osventsim': Stsenarii," sheets 8-21 (quotation on 10).

81. Ibid., sheet 12.

82. The act of surrender was signed late at night, and because of the two-hour time difference between Berlin and Moscow, the news was received in the Soviet Union on 9 May, the date on which it is still celebrated there.

83. On this aspect of the Nuremberg Tribunal, see Felman, *Juridicial Unconscious,* 132. Also see chapter 7 of the present work.

84. "'Osventsim': Stsenarii," sheet 13.

85. Ibid., sheet 15.

86. A. Krol´, "Oswentsim: Novyi dokumental´nyi fil´m," *Pravda Ukrainy,* 7 June 1945, 3.

87. See Kostyrchenko, *Tainaia politika Stalina,* 362.

88. "Correspondence with film group," sheet 295.

89. Lindeperg, *Clio de 5 à 7,* 167-68.

90. "Les Films soviétiques de demain," *Paris-cinéma,* 10 October 1945, 5.

91. G. Fradkin, Soiuzintorgkino representative in Berlin, to P. Brigadnov, manager of Soiuzintorgkino, 4 October, "Otchet o finansovom sostoianii predstavitel´stva 'Soiuzintorgkino' v Germanii po sostoainiiu na 1 oktiabria 1945 goda," RGALI 2918/1/142, sheet 10. These German versions were edited to remove the wartime narrative of victory and other elements irrelevant to the postwar situation.

## Chapter 7. "The Dead Never Lie":
## Soviet Film, the Nuremberg Tribunal, and the Holocaust

1. Review, articles, and notes on the film *Defeat of the Germans near Moscow,* RGALI 1966/1/89.

2. Ilya Bourtman, "'Blood for Blood, Death for Death': The Soviet Military Tribunal in Krasnodar, 1943," *Holocaust and Genocide Studies* 22, no. 2 (2008): 249.

3. Aleksandr Chubar´ian stresses that the Soviet government was the first to assert the idea of an international tribunal to judge Nazi war criminals; see Chubar´ian, "Niurnbergskii protsess i ego znachenie v istorii XX veka," in *Niurnbergskii protsess: Uroki istorii: Materialy mezhdunarodnoi konferentsii, Moskva, 20–21 noiabria 2006,* ed. N. S. Lebedeva and V. V. Ishchenko (Moscow: Institut vseobshchei istorii RAN, 2007), 13. Also see Natal´ia Lebedeva, "SSSR i Niurembergskii protsess," in *Niurnbergskii protsess: Uroki istorii: Materialy mezhdunarodnoi konferentsii, Moskva, 20–21 noiabria 2006,* ed. N. S. Lebedeva and V. V. Ishchenko (Moscow: Institut vseobshchei istorii RAN, 2007), 13.

4. Some Russian scholarship, however, stresses the importance of Soviet jurisprudence for the elaboration of the forms of law applied at Nuremberg; see G. I. Bogush, "A. N. Trainin i znachenie ego idei dlia Niurnbergskogo protsessa," in *Niurnbergskii protsess: Uroki istorii: Materialy mezhdunarodnoi konferentsii, Moskva, 20–21 noiabria 2006,* ed. N. S. Lebedeva and V. V. Ishchenko (Moscow: Institut vseobshchei istorii RAN, 2007), 166–73.

5. See Douglas, *Memory of Judgment,* 3. Ruth Bettina Birn makes the same point in "War Crimes Prosecutions: An Exercise in Justice? A Lesson in History?" in *Lessons and Legacies,* vol. 4: *Reflections on Religion, Justice, Sexuality, and Genocide,* ed. Larry V. Thompson (Evanston, Ill.: Northwestern University Press, 2003), 101–27.

6. Michael R. Marrus, *The Nuremberg War Crimes Trial, 1945–46: A Documentary History* (Boston: Bedford, 1997), 193. The tribunal also collated documents that were to form the basis of subsequent groundbreaking histories of the Holocaust; see Dan Stone, "The Holocaust and Its Historiography," in *The Historiography of Genocide,* ed. Dan Stone (Houndmills, U.K.: Palgrave Macmillan, 2008), 373.

7. Thus, Lawrence Douglas, in an article about the trial's use of film, concentrates exclusively on *Nazi Concentration Camps* as the most important film because it was central to the prosecution's key charge of aggressive war. Douglas does note that "films documenting atrocities in the east," as well as some made by the Nazis themselves, were shown but downplays their importance: "These films, however, were not placed at the rhetorical center of the prosecution's case as was *Nazi Concentration Camps*" (Douglas, "Film as Witness: Screening *Nazi Concentration Camps* before the Nuremberg Tribunal," *Yale Law*

*Journal* 105 [1995–96]: 460, 466). Christian Delage is the one scholar to discuss the film, which he does in *La Vérité par l'image: De Nuremberg au procès Milosevic* (Paris: Denoël, 2006), 143–47. Moreover, both there and in Delage, dir., *Le Procès de Nuremberg: Les Nazis face à leurs crimes,* DVD (Arte, 2006), Delage perpetuates a slightly erroneous version of the film's title, which he claims to be "Les Atrocités commises par les envahisseurs germano-fascistes *en URSS.*" This version appears to date back to the trial, for Telford Taylor similarly refers to the film as *The Atrocities Committed by the German Fascist Invaders in the USSR*; see Taylor, *The Anatomy of the Nuremberg Trials: A Personal Memoir* (London: Bloomsbury, 1993), 316.

In fact, as outlined in the following pages, the film comprises footage of the death camps of Auschwitz and Majdanek, and approximately half of it concerns atrocities committed outside the Soviet Union's borders, be they those of 1939, 1940, or 1945. Delage's book shows this to be the case but does not point out the discrepancy between title and content. Even in Russian-language accounts of Nuremberg, mention of the Soviet film is rare and insight rarer still. While Russian scholarly accounts rarely mention the film, their silence is preferable to the ignorance of Valerii Shatin's TV documentary *Nurnberg: posledniaia skhvatka* (2005), broadcast on Rossiia-1 channel, 1 May 2008, which claims the Soviet prosecution showed the film *Nazi Concentration Camps.*

8. William A. Schabas, "Prosecuting Genocide," in *The Historiography of Genocide,* ed. Dan Stone (Houndmills, U.K.: Palgrave Macmillan, 2008), 257.

9. Bloxham, *Genocide on Trial,* 57.

10. See James Gow, *The Serbian Project and Its Adversaries: A Strategy of War Crimes* (London: Hurst, 2003), 21–22.

11. Peter Novick and Lawrence Baron, "Letters to the Editor," *Holocaust and Genocide Studies* 18, no. 2 (2004) 358–75.

12. Bradley F. Smith, *Reaching Judgement at Nuremberg* (London: Andre Deutsch, 1977), 304.

13. Bloxham, *Genocide on Trial,* 2, 186, 57.

14. Douglas, "Film as Witness," 478. In fact, as Douglas notes, the film was used at the Eichmann trial and elsewhere as irrefutable proof of the Holocaust, an event its makers did not intend it to document.

15. Delage, *La Vérité par l'image,* 130.

16. Bloxham, *Genocide on Trial,* 108–9.

17. This is the present general consensus according to David Cesarani and Sarah Kavanaugh, *Holocaust: Critical Concepts in Historical Studies* (London: Routledge, 2004), 357.

18. Bloxham (*Genocide on Trial,* 188–89) notes, however, that his testimony later facilitated the so-called Einsatzgruppen trial.

19. Ibid., 190.

20. Wieviorka, *Era of the Witness,* 68.

21. Bloxham, *Genocide on Trial,* 152.

22. Delage, *La Vérité par l'image,* 146.

23. Ibid., 126.

24. Vsevolod Vishnevskii, *Sobranie sochinenii,* 5 vols. (Moscow: Khudozhest-vennaia literatura, 1960), 5:304.

25. Von zur Mühlen, dir., *Holocaust: The Liberation of Majdanek;* von zur Mühlen, dir., *Holocaust: The Liberation of Auschwitz.*

26. Gitelman, "Politics and Historiography," 14; Al'tman, *Zhertvy nenavistsi,* 303. I discuss the total numbers of Holocaust-related deaths in the Soviet Union in the introduction.

27. Berkhoff, "'Russian' Prisoners of War," 1. The key text making this case is Christian Streit, *Keine Kamaraden: Die Wehrmacht und die sowjetischen Kriegsge-fangenen 1941–1945* (Stuttgart: Deutsche Verlags-Anstalt, 1978). The whole of this work has never been translated into English.

28. Polian, "First Victims," 771.

29. *Kholokost na territorii SSSR: Entsiklopediia,* 2d ed., rev., s.v. "Rostov-na-Donu" (Moscow: Rosspen, 2011).

30. Marrus, *Nuremberg War Crimes Trial,* 191–92.

31. Delage, *La Vérité par l'image,* 109.

32. Douglas, "Film as Witness," 465. As Delage (*La Vérité par l'image,* 74) points out, the Americans themselves needed to discover camps before any films of these atrocities could make an impact.

33. For a detailed comparison of the uses of atrocity footage in Soviet news-reels and documentaries of the war, see Pozner, "Les Actualités soviétiques," 123–41.

34. Paul Celan, "Deathfugue," in *Selected Poems and Prose,* trans. John Felstiner (New York: W. W. Norton, 2001), 31.

35. I am thinking here in particular of Claude Lanzmann's *Shoah.* Douglas ("Film as Witness," 467) sees the presence of oral testimony in *Nazi Concentration Camps* as having been influenced by the U.S. legal tradition, where normally, entering a film into evidence would require having a witness testify to the accuracy of the film and answer questions about it.

36. Bourtman, "Blood for Blood," 246–65, 256–57. Ruth Bettina Birn ("War Crimes Prosecutions," 105) stresses the internal goals of the propaganda. However, Bourtman's argument that the trial is externally directed is cor-roborated by Marina Sorokina's ("People and Procedures," 807) analysis of the Soviet Extraordinary State Commission on War Crimes, which Sorokina demonstrates was oriented primarily toward external consumption.

37. The film may well have been intended primarily for domestic consump-

tion; Bourtman ("Blood for Blood," 258) stresses that the trial's message was principally oriented internally, intended to unify the fragmented Soviet polity.

38. Ibid., 257.

39. Alexander Solzhenitsyn, *The Gulag Archipelago* (London: Collins and Harvill, 1974), 60.

40. Rolf-Dieter Müller and Gerd R. Ueberschär, *Hitler's War in the East, 1941–1945: A Critical Assessment,* trans. Bruce D. Little, 2d ed. rev. (New York: Berghahn, 2002), 251.

41. "The Kharkov Trial: A Grim Newsreel Record," *Times,* 7 July 1944, 6. The film was also discussed widely when shown in France during April 1945. Some form of the film was presumably shown in the United States, for the Library of Congress holds an edited three-reel version of it under the title *The Kharkov War Trial,* but this short film appears to have attracted little press attention. The Library of Congress also holds a Spanish-language copy entitled *Paso a la justicia,* which further indicates film's perceived significance.

42. Douglas, "Film as Witness," 453. I draw the phrase "pageant and process" from Douglas J. Sylvester, "The Lessons of Nuremberg and the Trial of Saddam Hussein," in *Evil, Law and the State: Perspectives on State Power and Violence,* ed. John T. Parry (Amsterdam: Rodopi, 2006), 128.

43. Delage, *La Vérité par l'image,* 116–17.

44. V. Smirnov, *Dokumental'nye fil'my o Velikoi Otechestvennoi voine* (Moscow: Goskinoizdat, 1947), 255.

45. Stalin responded in the Soviet press on 16 March 1946.

46. Roman Karmen to Anna. L. Vinogradova, of Ts.S.D.F., 22 June 1946, Muzei kino, 32/1/1.

47. Lebedeva, "SSSR i Niurembergskii protsess," 152.

48. Ibid., 159.

49. Ibid., 153.

50. Ibid., 158.

51. Boris Polevoi, "Neistovyi Karmen," in *Roman Karmen v vospominaniiakh sovremennikov,* ed. A. L. Vinogradova (Moscow: Iskusstvo, 1983), 154.

52. Strangely, despite the wide coverage of the film's release in the Soviet press at the end of 1946 (e.g., Tat'iana Tess, "Tsennyi fil'm," *Izvestiia,* 28 Nov. 1946, 2), Delage (*La Vérité par l'image,* 197) claims its May 1947 screening in New York took place before it was screened in Moscow.

53. More recent portrayals of the tribunal have similarly concentrated on the defendants. See, for example, Nigel Paterson, dir., *Nuremberg—The Nazis on Trial,* BBC/Discovery Channel coproduction, BBC Two, 26 Sept.–9 Oct., 2006.

54. Ravit Pe'er-Lamo Reichman, "Committed to Memory," *Law and Catastrophe,* ed. Austin Sarat, Lawrence Douglas, and Martha Merrill Umphrey (Stanford, Calif.: Stanford University Press, 2007), 190.

55. M. Iu. Raginskii, "Vospominaniia uchastnika Niurnbergskogo protsessa," in *Niurnbergskii protsess i sovremennost'*, ed. V. V. Pustogarov (Moscow: Institut gosudarstva i prava AN SSSR, 1986), 63.

56. Kolesnikova, Senchakova, and Slepneva, *Roman Karmen*, 102–3.

57. Douglas, "Film as Witness," 456.

58. Karmen, *No Pasaran!* 34.

59. Il'ia Ehrenburg, "Vasilisk," *Krasnaia zvezda*, 19 September 1941, 3.

60. Kolesnikova, Senchakova, and Slepneva, *Roman Karmen*, 106.

61. [TsSDF,] "Sud narodov," RGALI 2487/1/690, sheet 172.

62. Ibid., sheet 47.

63. Ibid., sheet 13. Broadly the same description of Streicher is used in Karmen's two-reel special-release newsreel *At the Trial of the Major Nazi War Criminals in Nuremberg.*

64. Taylor, *Anatomy of the Nuremberg Trials*, 307.

65. M. Gus, *Sovetskoe iskusstvo* 12 (1946), review of *Judgment of the Nations* in press cuttings relating to that film, RGALI 1966/1/147.

66. Iu. Korol'kov, "Vozmezdie i groznoe predosterezhenie," *Literaturnaia gazeta*, 30 November 1946, 4.

67. Karmen, *No pasaran!* 159. Von Paulus's testimony is also treated as a dramatic pinnacle of the trial in *Posledniaia skhvatka.*

68. Delage, *Le Procès de Nuremberg*. Bloxham (*Genocide on* Trial, 101) similarly highlights the quality of her testimony about Auschwitz.

69. Marrus, *Nuremberg War Crimes Trial*, v.

70. Bloxham, *Genocide on Trial*, 60–61.

71. Douglas, *Memory of Judgment*, 16.

72. Wieviorka, *Era of the Witness*, 67.

73. Douglas, "Film as Witness," 452.

74. "Stenogramma obsuzhdeniia dokumental'nogo fil'ma R. L. Karmena 'Sud narodov' v Leningradskom dome kino 29 November 1946," RGALI, 2091/2/663, sheet 5. In the same discussion, Trauberg goes out of his way to praise Svilova and links her name with Vertov, despite this being a period in which Vertov was being persecuted more than ever before.

75. Ibid.

76. [TsSDF,] "Sud narodov," sheet 41.

77. V. Kudriavtsev and A. Trusov, *Politicheskaia iustitsiia v SSSR* (Moscow: Nauka, 2000), 246–47.

78. The legal function of the defense has been even further devalued in Soviet legal tradition. Igor' Iartykh argues that Russian historiography of the Nuremberg tribunal has practically ignored the defense, whose statements have been published only in an eight-volume specialist publication in 1998; see Iartykh, "Pravo na zashchitu na Niurembergskom protsesse (istorikio-

filososkii aspekt)," in *Niurnbergskii protsess: Uroki istorii: Materialy mezhdunarodnoi konferentsii, Moskva, 20–21 noiabria 2006,* ed. N. S. Lebedeva and V. V. Ishchenko (Moscow: Institut vseobshchei istorii RAN, 2007), 210. Possibly indicative of a continuation of these attitudes in the post-Soviet period, Iartykh's article is accompanied by a disclaimer from the editors.

79. Kudriavtsev and Trusov, *Politicheskaia iustitsiia v SSSR,* 245.

80. Delage, *La Vérité par l'image,* 117.

81. The absence of witness testimony in the film is not due to technical reasons, since documents show that Karmen got the sound engineer Viktor Kotov to station himself with an Akilei sound camera near the prosecution witnesses and record their statements; see Viktor Kotov, "Vsei zvukovoi palitroi mira," in *Roman Karmen v vospominaniiakh sovremennikov,* ed. A. L. Vingradova (Moscow: Iskusstvo, 1983), 271.

82. Deborah E. Lipstadt has shown persuasively how the Eichmann trial made witness testimony central to understandings of the Holocaust; see Lipstadt, *The Eichmann Trial* (New York: Nextbook/Schocken, 2011), 200–203.

83. Sutzkever qtd. in Wieviorka, *Era of the Witness,* 31; see also Avrom [Avram] Sutzkever, "Mon témoinage au procès de Nuremberg," *Les Ecrivains et la guerre,* special issue of *Europe* (Aug.–Sept. 1995): 140–41.

84. qtd. in Wieviorka, *Era of the Witness,* 32.

85. Ibid. Wieviorka (*Era of the Witness,* 149) notes that the Eichmann trial revalorized Yiddish by permitting testimony in it, which was the language spoken by the majority of those murdered.

86. Gitelman, "Politics and Historiography," 19.

87. Felman and Laub, *Testimony,* xvi; Wieviorka, *Era of the Witness,* 144.

88. Advertisement, *New York Herald Tribune,* 23 May 1947, 18.

89. "'Nuremberg' Film Attracts Lawyers," *Daily Worker,* 6 June 1947, 11.

90. Paul Rotha, *The Film till Now: A Survey of World Cinema,* 2d ed., with an additional section by Richard Griffith (London: Vision, 1949), 580.

91. Bosley Crowther, "Goering with Swagger Lacking, in 'Nuremberg Trials,' at Stanley," *New York Times,* 26 May 1947, 24.

92. J. P., "'The Nuernberg Trials'—Stanley," *New York Herald Tribune,* 26 May 1947, 16.

93. Delage, *La Vérité par l'image,* 10.

## Epilogue

1. Maxim Shrayer has collected and translated a number of Russian-language literary treatments of the subject published at the time; see Shrayer, ed. and trans., *An Anthology of Jewish-Russian Literature: Two Centuries of Dual Identity in Prose and Poetry,* 2 vols. (Armonk: M. E. Sharpe, 2007), 1:513–606.

2. Genadii Kostyrchenko, *Out of the Red Shadows: Anti-Semitism in Stalin's Russia* (Amherst, N.Y.: Prometheus, 1995), 66.

3. Ibid., 44, 52.

4. Gorbatov, who wrote the material on which the film was based, also suffered under this wave of postwar Soviet anti-Semitism, and his wife was arrested. It is unclear whether this was related to the fate of the film or not. See ibid., 132, 168.

5. Kostyrchenko, *Tainaia politika Stalina,* 226.

6. For more on this victory-day toast, which took place on 24 May 1945, see Weiner, *Making Sense of War,* 208.

7. Ibid., 138–54, 365 (quotation). Slezkine charts the same process in *The Jewish Century,* 276–81.

8. Weiner, *Making Sense of War,* 209.

9. Al´tman, *Zhertvy,* 412. Robert Abzug has talked of "race-bigotry" as a virus spread by the Nazis that infected European culture; see Abzug, *American Views of the Holocaust, 1933–1945: A Brief Documentary History* (Boston/New York: Bedford/St. Martins, 1999), 117.

10. Al´tman, *Zhertvy,* 412.

11. Weiner, *Making Sense of War,* 193.

12. Al´tman, *Zhertvy,* 412; Kostyrchenko, *Tainaia politika Stalina,* 262–64. For other examples, such as the prewar replacement of Jews in the Ministry of Foreign Affairs and the Central Committee, as well as wartime and postwar purges of the arts and media, see Kostyrchenko, *Tainaia politika Stalina,* 196–99, 266–71.

13. Weiner, *Making Sense of War,* 208.

14. Feferman, *Soviet Jewish Stepchild,* 26.

15. Weiner, *Making Sense of War,* 208.

16. Feferman, *Soviet Jewish Stepchild,* 7.

17. Nina Tumarkin, *The Living and the Dead: The Rise and Fall of the Cult of World War II in Russia* (New York: Basic, 1994), 50.

18. Feferman, *Soviet Jewish Stepchild,* 46–53.

19. In the most substantial work on Donskoi's wartime films, O. Iakubovich identifies the victims as Jewish but does not mention the fact that the incident was reenacted at the site of Babyi Iar; see Iakubovich, "Voennye fil'my Marka Donskogo," in *Kino i vremia,* vol. 4, ed. O. Iakubovich (Moscow: Iskusstvo, 1965), 18–102.

20. See Jeremy Hicks, "Confronting the Holocaust: Mark Donskoi's *The Unvanquished,*" *Studies in Russian Soviet Cinema* 3, no. 1 (2009): 33–51.

21. Doneson, *Holocaust in American Film,* 4.

22. Ibid.

23. Ibid., 7.

24. Rosenfeld, *End of the Holocaust*, 60.

25. Langer, *Using and Abusing the Holocaust*, 19.

26. Flanzbaum, *Americanization of the Holocaust*, 13–14.

27. Summarized in Terri Ginsberg, *Holocaust Film: The Political Aesthetics of Ideology* (Newcastle, U.K.: Cambridge Scholars, 2007), 12. Ginsberg is targeting Doneson in particular here. Finkelstein (*The Holocaust Industry*, 36–38) argues something similar of wider treatments of the Holocaust produced in the United States. The Soviet Jewish experience is very different from the experience of Jews in the United States, where the emphasis is, if possible, placed on heroism as a category that confers greater status rather than victimhood. Thus, while the proposed *Black Book*, detailing Jewish wartime victimhood, was never published, it came quite close, but the proposed *Red Book*, detailing Jewish wartime heroism, was rejected out of hand; see Weiner, *Making Sense of War*, 208.

28. The first edition of Raul Hilberg's seminal history *The Destruction of the European Jews* came out in 1961 (London: W. H. Allen).

29. Hasia R. Diner, *We Remember with Reverence and Love: American Jews and the Myth of Silence after the Holocaust, 1945–1962* (New York: New York University Press, 2009), 11.

30. Novick and Baron, "Letters to the Editor," 370.

31. Peter Novick, *The Holocaust and Collective Memory: The American Experience* (London: Bloomsbury, 2000), 63–103; Finkelstein, *Holocaust Industry*, 14.

32. Michael Freedland with Barbara Paskin, *Hollywood on Trial: McCarthyism's War against the Movies* (London: Robson, 2007), 29.

33. Freedland with Paskin, *Hollywood on Trial*, 214–17. For an example of the claim of anti-Semitism leveled at the time, consider the following description of the committee taken from an account of its activities: "a committee serving as a sounding board for the anti-Negro and anti-Semitic utterances of Congressman John Rankin that has led to the present growth of lynchings and the increase of anti-Semitism everywhere" (Civil Rights Congress, *America's Thought Police: Record of the Un-American Activities Committee* [New York: Civil Rights Congress, 1947], 1–2).

## Archival Sources

British Film Institute, London
    BFI Special Collections, Film Society Collection

Museum of Cinema, Moscow
    Muzei kino, 32 (Frontline Cameramen)
    Muzei kino, 56 (Aleksandr Medvedkin)
    Muzei kino (Mark Donskoi, uncataloged)

Russian Federation State Archive (GARF), Moscow
    GARF R8114 (Jewish Antifascist Committee)
    GARF R7021 (Extraordinary State Commission)

Russian State Archive of Film and Photo Documents (RGAKFD), Krasnogorsk

Russian State Archive of Literature and Art (RGALI), Moscow
    RGALI 1966 (Sedykh)
    RGALI 2091 (Vertov)
    RGALI 2456 (USSR Ministry of Cinematography)
    RGALI 2487 (Central Studio of Documentary Films)
    RGALI 2918 (Sovexportfilm)
    RGALI 2923 (Central House of Cinema)

Russian State Archive of Social and Political History (RGASPI)
    17 (Central Committee of Communist Party)

State Film Collection of Russia (Gosfil'mofond Rossii), Moscow (Belye stolby)
    Section I/3 (collections under name of film)

## Books and Articles

Abzug, Robert H. *American Views of the Holocaust, 1933–1945: A Brief Documentary History.* Boston/New York: Bedford/St. Martins, 1999.

———. *Inside the Vicious Heart: Americans and the Liberation of Nazi Concentration Camps.* New York: Oxford University Press, 1985.

Agamben, Giorgio. *Remnants of Auschwitz: The Witness and the Archive.* Translated by Daniel Heller-Roazen. New York: Zone, 1999.

Agee, James. *Agee on Film: Reviews and Comments.* New York: McDowell-Obolensky, 1958.

Albera, François, and Roland Cosandey, eds. *Boris Barnet: Ecrits, documents, études, filmographie.* Locarno, Switzerland: Editions du Festival International du Film de Locarno, 1985.

Aldgate, Anthony, and James Crighton Robertson. *Censorship in Theatre and Cinema.* Edinburgh: Edinburgh University Press, 2005.

Alexander, Jeffrey C. "On the Social Construction of Universal Morals: The 'Holocaust' from War Crime to Trauma Drama." In *Cultural Trauma and Collective Identity,* edited by Jeffrey C. Alexander, Ron Eyerman, Bernhard Giesen, Neil J. Smelser, and Piotr Sztompka, 196–263. Berkeley: University of California Press, 2004.

Al'tman, Il'ia. *Kholokost i evreiskoe soprotivlenie na okkupirovannoi territorii SSSR.* Edited by A. G. Asmolov. Moscow: Fond "Kholokost"/Kaleidoskop, 2002.

———. *Zhertvy nenavistsi: Kholokost v SSSR 1941–1945 gg.* Moscow: Fond "Kovcheg"/Kollektsiia "Sovershenno sekretno," 2002.

Altshuller, Mordechai. "Escape and Evacuation of the Soviet Jews at the Time of the Nazi Invasion." In *The Holocaust in the Soviet Union: Studies and Sources on the Destruction of the Jews in the Nazi-Occupied Territories of the USSR, 1941–1945,* edited by Lucjan Dobroczynski and Jeffrey S. Gurock, 77–104. Armonk, N.Y.: Sharpe, 1993.

Amengual, Barthélemy. *Alexandre Dovjenko.* Paris: Seghers, 1970.

Amishai-Maisels, Ziva. *Depiction and Interpretation: The Influence of the Holocaust on the Visual Arts.* Oxford: Pergamon, 1993.

———. *Soviet Government Statements on Nazi Atrocities.* London: Hutchinson, 1946.

Arad, Yitzhak. "The Destruction of the Jews in German-Occupied Territories of the Soviet Union." In *The Unknown Black Book: The Holocaust in the German-Occupied Soviet Territories,* edited by Joshua Rubenstein and Ilya Altman, xiii–xxxix. Bloomington: Indiana University Press, 2008.

———. *The Holocaust in the Soviet Union: Comprehensive History of the Holocaust.* Lincoln: University of Nebraska Press, 2009.

Armstrong, John A., ed. *Soviet Partisans in World War II.* Foreword by Philip E. Mosely. Madison: University of Wisconsin Press, 1964.

Asher, Harvey. "The Holocaust and the USSR." In *Lessons and Legacies,* vol. 7: *The Holocaust in International Perspective,* edited and with an introduction by Dagmar Herzog, 253–68. Evanston, Ill.: Northwestern University Press, 2006.

Avisar, Ilan. *Screening the Holocaust: Cinema's Images of the Unimaginable.* Bloomington: Indiana University Press, 1998.

Baraban, Elena. "Semeinyi krug: traktovka rodstva, evreev i voennoplennykh v stalinskom kino o voine." *Ab Imperio* 3 (2009): 1–25.

Barnouw, Ron. *Documentary: A History of the Non-Fiction Film.* New York: Oxford University Press, 1974.

Bartov, Omer. *The "Jew" in Cinema: From "The Golem" to "Don't Touch My Holocaust."* Bloomington: Indiana University Press, 2005.

Benjamin, Walter. "A Short History of Photography." *Screen* 13, no. 1 (Spring 1972): 5–26.

Berkhoff, Karel. *Harvest of Despair: Life and Death in Ukraine under Nazi Rule.* Cambridge, Mass.: Belknap, 2004.

———. "The Mass Murder of Soviet Prisoners of War and the Holocaust: How Were They Related?" *Kritika: Explorations in Russian and Eurasian History* 6, no. 4 (Fall 2005): 789–96.

———. "The 'Russian' Prisoners of War in Nazi-Ruled Ukraine as Victims of Genocidal Massacre." *Holocaust and Genocide Studies* 15, no. 1 (2001): 1–32.

———. "'Total Annihilation of the Jewish Population': The Holocaust in the Soviet Media, 1941–45." *Kritika: Explorations in Russian and Eurasian History* 10, no. 1 (Winter 2009): 61–105.

Bernard-Donals, Michael. *Forgetful Memory: Representation and Remembrance in the Wake of the Holocaust.* Albany: State University of New York Press, 2009.

Bernshtein, Arkadii. "Drevo zhizni." *Kinovedcheskie zapiski* 62 (2003): 189–215.

Birn, Ruth Bettina. "War Crimes Prosecutions: An Exercise in Justice? A Lesson in History?" In *Lessons and Legacies,* vol. 4: *Reflections on Religion, Justice, Sexuality, and Genocide,* edited and with an introduction by Larry V. Thompson, 101–27. Evanston, Ill.: Northwestern University Press, 2003.

Bloxham, Donald. *Genocide on Trial: War Crimes Trials and the Formation of Holocaust History and Memory.* Oxford: Oxford University Press, 2003.

Bogush, G. I. "A. N. Trainin i znachenie ego idei dlia Niurnbergskogo protsessa." In *Niurnbergskii protsess: Uroki istorii: Materialy mezhdunarodnoi konferentsii, Moskva, 20–21 noiabria 2006,* edited by N. S. Lebedeva and V. V. Ishchenko, 166–73. Moscow: Institut vseobshchei istorii RAN, 2007.

Bol´shakov, Ivan. *Sovetskoe kinoiskusstvo v gody velikoi otechestvennoi voiny.* Moscow: Goskinoizdat, 1948.

———. *Sovetskoe kinoiskusstvo v gody Velikoi Otechestvennoj voiny.* 2d ed. Moscow: Goskinoizdat, 1950.

Bondareva, G. N., ed. *Kremlevskii kinoteatr, 1929–1953: Dokumenty.* Moscow: Rosspen, 2005.

Bourtman, Ilya. "'Blood for Blood, Death for Death': The Soviet Military Tribunal in Krasnodar, 1943." *Holocaust and Genocide Studies* 22, no. 2 (2008): 246–65.

Braithwaite, Rodric. *Moscow 1941: A City and Its People at War.* London: Profile, 2006.

Briman, Shimon. "Khar´kov, evrei, Izrail´: Pervoi stolitse Ukrainy, gorodu s bogateishei evreiskoi istorii—350 let." http://gazeta.rjews.net/Lib/briman/040729-briman.shtml.

Brooks, Jeffrey. "Pravda Goes to War." In *Culture and Entertainment in Wartime Russia,* edited by Richard Stites, 9–27. Bloomington: Indiana University Press, 1995.

Brown, Kate. *A Biography of No Place: From Ethnic Borderland to Soviet Heartland.* Cambridge, Mass.: Harvard University Press, 2004.

Browning, Christopher R., with a contribution by Jürgen Matthäus. *The Origins of the Final Solution: The Evolution of Nazi Jewish Policy 1939–1942.* Lincoln, Neb.: Arrow, 2005.

"Byl li kholokost v Rostove?" http://botinok.co.il/node/34279.

Cantor, Jay. "Death and the Image." In *Beyond the Document: Essays in Nonfiction Film,* edited by Charles Warren, 23–50. Hanover, N.H.: Wesleyan University Press/University Press of New England, 1996.

Carynnyk, Marco. "Introduction: The Mythopetic Vision of Alexander Dovzhenko." In *The Poet as Filmmaker,* by Aleksandr Dovzhenko, edited, translated, and with an introduction by Marco Carynnyk, ix–lv. Cambridge, Mass: MIT Press, 1973.

Caven, Hannah. "Horror in Our Time: Images of the Concentration Camps in the British Media, 1945." *Historical Journal of Film, Radio and Television* 21, no. 3 (2003): 205–53.

Celan, Paul. "Deathfugue." In *Selected Poems and Prose,* by Celan, trans. John Felstiner, 31–33 (New York: W. W. Norton, 2001).

Ceplair, Larry. *Under the Shadow of War: Fascism, Anti-Fascism, and Marxists, 1918–1939.* New York: Columbia University Press, 1987.

Cesarani, David, and Sarah Kavanaugh. *Holocaust: Critical Concepts in Historical Studies.* London: Routledge, 2004.

Cherevatenko, Leonid. "Osvobozhdennyi Dovzhenko." *Kinovedcheskie zapiski* 77 (2006): 105–7.

Chernenko, Miron. *Krasnaia zvezda, zheltaia zvezda: Kinematograficheskaia istoriia evreistva v Rossii, 1919–1999.* Moscow: Tekst, 2006.

Chubar´ian, Aleksandr. "Niurnbergskii protsess i ego znachenie v istorii XX veka." In *Niurnbergskii protsess: Uroki istorii: Materialy mezhdunarodnoi konferentsii, Moskva, 20–21 noiabria 2006,* edited by N. S. Lebedeva and V. V. Ishchenko, 9–21. Moscow: Institut vseobshchei istorii RAN, 2007.

"Cinema: The New Pictures." *Time,* 21 November, 1938, 53.

Civil Rights Congress. *America's Thought Police: Record of the Un-American Activities Committee.* Foreword by Henry A. Wallace. New York: Civil Rights Congress, 1947.

Davies, Norman. *No Simple Victory: World War II in Europe, 1939–1945.* New York: Penguin, 2008.

Dawidowicz, Lucy S. *The War against the Jews: 1933–45.* 10th anniversary ed. Harmondsworth, U.K.: Penguin, 1990.

Dean, Martin. *Collaboration in the Holocaust: Crimes of the Local Police in Belorussia and Ukraine, 1941–44.* Houndmills, U.K.: Macmillan, 2000.

Delage, Christian. *La Vérité par l'image: De Nuremberg au procès Milosevic.* Paris: Denoël, 2006.

DeLuca, Gerald A. "Avon Cinema, Providence, RI." http://cinematreasures.org/theater/465/.

Desbois, Patrick. *The Holocaust by Bullets: A Priest's Journey to Uncover the Truth behind the Murder of 1.5 Million Jews.* Foreword by Paul A. Schapiro. Houndmills, U.K.: Palgrave Macmillan, 2008.

Diner, Hasia R. *We Remember with Reverence and Love: American Jews and the Myth of Silence after the Holocaust, 1945–1962.* New York: New York University Press, 2009.

Doneson, Judith E. *The Holocaust in American Film.* 2d ed. Syracuse, N.Y.: Syracuse University Press, 2002.

Donskoi, Mark. "My Work on the Film 'Unvanquished.'" *Cinema Chronicle* (USSR Society for Cultural Relations with Foreign Countries) 10 (Oct. 1945): 9–16.

Douglas, Lawrence. "Film as Witness: Screening *Nazi Concentration Camps* before the Nuremberg Tribunal." *Yale Law Journal* 105 (1995–96): 449–81.

———. *The Memory of Judgment: Making Law and History in the Trials of the Holocaust.* New Haven, Conn.: Yale University Press, 2001.

Dovzhenko, Aleksandr. *The Poet as Filmmaker.* Edited, translated, and with an introduction by Marco Carynnyk. Cambridge, Mass.: MIT Press, 1973.

———. *Sobranie sochinenii.* Compiled by Iuliia Solntseva and edited by Sergei Drobashenko. 4 vols. Moscow: Iskusstvo, 1967.

——— [as Oleksandr]. *Storinki shchodennika (1941–1956).* Kiev: Vidavnitstvo gumanitarnoï literatury, 2004.

Dymshits, Aleksandr. "Fridrikh Vol´f i ego p´esy." In *P´esy,* by Fridrikh Vol´f, edited by Aleksandr Dymshits, 5–22. Moscow: Iskusstvo, 1963.

Dymshits, Nina. "Antifashistskoe kino v izgnanii: K teme." *Kinovedcheskie zapiski* 59 (2002): 131–35.

Edelman, Marek. *The Ghetto Fights: Warsaw 1941–43.* Introduction by John Rose. London: Bookmarks, 1994.

Eisner, Lotte H. *The Haunted Screen: Expressionism in the German Cinema and the Influence of Max Reinhardt.* Berkeley: University of California Press, 1973.

Elsaesser, Thomas. *Weimar Cinema and After: Germany's Historical Imaginary.* London: Routledge, 2000.

Erenburg, Il´ia. *Sobranie sochinenii.* 5 vols. Moscow: Gos. izd. khudozhestvennoi literatury, 1952–54.

Erenburg, Il´ia [as Ehrenburg, Ilya], and Vasilii [as Vasily] Grossman, eds. *The Complete Black Book of Russian Jewry.* Translated and edited by David Patterson. New Brunswick, N.J.: Transaction, 2003.

Erens, Patricia. *The Jew in American Cinema.* Bloomington: Indiana University Press, 1984.

Farber, Manny. "The Red and the Black." *New Republic,* 6 November 1944, 595.

———. "Zanuck at the Front." *New Republic,* 5 April 1943, 447.

Feferman, Kiril. *Soviet Jewish Stepchild: The Holocaust in the Soviet Mindset, 1941–1964.* Saarbrücken, Germany: VDM Verlag, 2009.

Felman, Shoshana. *The Juridicial Unconscious: Trials and Traumas in the Twentieth Century.* Cambridge, Mass.: Harvard University Press, 2002.

Felman, Shoshana, and Dori Laub. *Testimony: Crises of Witnessing in Literature, Psychoanalysis, and History.* New York: Routledge, 1992.

Ferguson, Otis. "Whether to Laugh or Cry." *New Republic,* 14 December 1938, 174.

Fielding, Raymond. "Mirror of Discontent: The *March of Time* and Its Politically Controversial Film Issues." *Western Political Quarterly* 12, no. 1, pt. 1 (1959): 145–52.

Finkelstein, Norman G. *The Holocaust Industry: Reflections on the Exploitation of Jewish Suffering.* rev. ed. London: Verso, 2001.

Flanzbaum, Hilene, ed. *The Americanization of the Holocaust.* Baltimore, Md.: Johns Hopkins University Press, 1999.

Fomin, Valerii, ed. and comp. *Kino na voine: Dokumenty i svidetel´stva.* Moscow: Materik, 2005.

Fossato, Floriana. "Vladimir Putin and the Russian Television 'Family.'" *Les Cahiers russes* 1 (2006): 13–15.

Freedland, Michael, with Barbara Paskin. *Hollywood on Trial: McCarthyism's War against the Movies.* London: Robson, 2007.

Gefter, Mikhail. *Iz tekh i etikh let.* Moscow: Progress, 1991.

Gilbert, Martin. *Auschwitz and the Allies: The Truth about One of This Century's Most Controversial Episodes.* London: Mandarin, 1991.

———. *The Holocaust: The Jewish Tragedy.* London: Fontana, 1987.

Ginsberg, Terri. *Holocaust Film: The Political Aesthetics of Ideology.* Cambridge: Cambridge Scholars, 2007.

Gitelman, Zvi, ed. *Bitter Legacy: Confronting the Holocaust in the USSR.* Bloomington: Indiana University Press, 1997.

———. *A Century of Ambivalence: The Jews of Russia and the Soviet Union, 1881 to the Present.* London: Viking, 1988.

———. "Politics and the Historiography of the Holocaust in the Soviet Union." In *Bitter Legacy: Confronting the Holocaust in the USSR,* edited by Zvi Gitelman, 15–42. Bloomington: Indiana University Press, 1997.

———. "The Soviet Politics of the Holocaust." In *The Art of Memory: Holocaust Memorials in History*, edited by James E. Young, 138–47. New York/Munich: Jewish Museum/Prestel, 1995.

Goldhagen, Daniel Jonah. *Hitler's Willing Executioners: Ordinary Germans and the Holocaust.* London: Abacus, 2006.

Gorbatov, Boris. *Sobranie sochinenii.* 5 vols. Moscow: Gos. Izd. khudozhestvennoi literatury, 1955.

Gow, James. *The Serbian Project and Its Adversaries: A Strategy of War Crimes.* London: Hurst, 2003.

Grossman, Vasilii [as Vasily]. *Everything Flows.* Translated by Robert and Elizabeth Chandler. London: Harvill Secker, 2010.

——— [as Vasily]. "The Hell of Treblinka." In *The Road: Short Fiction and Essays,* by Grossman, translated by Robert and Elisabeth Chandler, 126–79. New York: New York Review of Books, 2010.

——— [as Vasily]. *A Writer at War: Vasily Grossman with the Red Army 1941–1945.* Translated, edited, and with a commentary by Liuba Vinogradova and Antony Beevor. London: Pimlico, 2006.

Haggith, Toby. "Filming the Liberation of Bergen-Belsen." In *Holocaust and the Moving Image: Representations in Film and Television since 1983,* edited by Toby Haggith and Joanna Newman, 33–49. London: Wallflower, 2005.

Hicks, Jeremy. "Confronting the Holocaust: Mark Donskoi's *The Unvanquished.*" *Studies in Russian Soviet Cinema* 3, no. 1 (2009): 33–51.

———. "The International Reception of Early Soviet Sound Cinema: *Chapaev* in Britain and America." *Historical Journal of Film, Radio and Television* 25, no. 2 (2005): 273–90.

———. "Lost in Translation? Did Sound Stop Soviet Films Finding Foreign Audiences?" In *Screening Intercultural Dialogue: Russia and Its Other(s) on Film,* edited by Stephen Hutchings, 113–29. London: Routledge-Curzon, 2008.

Hilberg, Raul. *The Destruction of the European Jews.* 3 vols. New York: Holmes and Meier, 1985.

Hirsch, Joshua. *Afterimage: Film, Trauma, and the Holocaust.* Philadelphia: Temple University Press, 2004.

"History of the Camp" (Majdanek). http://www.majdanek.pl/articles.php?acid=45.

Iakubovich, O. "Voennye fil'my Marka Donskogo." In *Kino i vremia,* vol. 4, edited by O. Iakubovich, 18–102. Moscow: Iskusstvo, 1965.

Iartykh, Igor´ S. "Pavo na zashchitu na Niurembergskom protsesse (istorikio-filososkii aspekt)." In *Niurnbergskii protsess: Uroki istorii: Materialy mezhdunarodnoi konferentsii, Moskva, 20–21 noiabria 2006,* edited by N. S. Lebedeva and V. V. Ishchenko, 208–18. Moscow: Institut vseobshchei istorii RAN, 2007.

Insdorf, Annette. *Indelible Shadows: Film and the Holocaust.* 3d ed. Cambridge: Cambridge University Press, 2003.

Jewsiewicki, Władysław. *Polscy Filmowcy na frontach drugiej wojny światowej.* Warsaw: Wydawnictwa Artystyczne i Filmowe, 1972.

Kapler, Aleksei. *"Ia" i "My": Vzlety i padeniia rytsaria iskusstva.* Moscow: Kniga, 1980.

———. *Partizany, P'esa v trekh deistviiakh, shesti kartinakh.* Moscow-Leningrad: Iskusstvo, 1943.

———. *V tylu vraga.* Moscow: Pravda, 1942.

Karmen, Roman. *No pasaran!* Moscow: Sovetskaia Rossiia, 1972.

Kenez, Peter. *The Birth of the Propaganda State: Soviet Methods of Mass Mobilization, 1917–1929.* Cambridge: Cambridge University Press, 1985.

———. "Black and White: The War on Film." In *Culture and Entertainment in Wartime Russia,* edited by Richard Stites, 157–75. Bloomington: Indiana University Press, 1995.

———. *Cinema and Soviet Society from the Revolution to the Death of Stalin.* New rev. ed. London: I. B. Tauris, 2001.

Kepley, Vance, Jr. *In Service of the State: The Cinema of Alexander Dovzhenko.* Madison: University of Wisconsin Press, 1986.

Khutsiev, Marlen, Otar Ioseliani, and Genadii Poloka. "'On tak i ne nauchilsia snimat´ po zakazu': Vspominaia Barneta." *Kinovedcheskie zapiski* 61 (2002): 87–99.

Kleiman, Naum. "Neosushchestvlennye zamysly Eizenshteina." *Iskusstvo kino* 6 (1992): 9–21.

Klering, Hans. "Trebovatel´nost´," in *Mark Donskoi: Sbornik: Mastera sovetskogo kino,* edited by Liudmilla Padzhitnova, 259–60. Moscow: Iskusstvo, 1973.

Koepke, Wulf. "Lion Feuchtwanger." In *Holocaust Literature: An Encyclopedia of Writers and Their Work*, edited by S. Lillian Kremer, 2 vols., 1:340–43. New York: Routledge, 2003.

Kolesnikova, Galina. "Tvorchestvo pisatelia-patriota (kritiko-biograficheskii ocherk)." In *Sobranie sochinenii,* by Boris Gorbatov, 5 vols., 1:17–50. Moscow: Gos. Izd. khudozhestvennoi literatury, 1955.

Kolesnikova, N., G. Senchakova, and T. Slepneva. *Roman Karmen*. Moscow: Iskusstvo, 1959.

Korneichuk, Aleksandr. "Partizany v stepiakh Ukrainy," *Novyi mir* 1–2 (1942): 43–63.

———. *Zibrannia tvoriv.* 5 vols. Kiev: Naukova duma, 1986–88.

Koshelivets′, Ivan. *Oleksandr Dovzhenko vchora i s′ogodni: Zatemneni mistsia v biografii.* Lutsk, Ukraine: Teren/VMA, 2005.

Kostyrchenko, Genadii. *Out of the Red Shadows: Anti-Semitism in Stalin's Russia.* Amherst, N.Y.: Prometheus, 1995.

———. *Tainaia politika Stalina: Vlast′ i antisemitizm.* Moscow: Mezhdunarodnye otnosheniia, 2003.

Kotlerman, Ber Boris. *In Search of Milk and Honey: The Theater of "Soviet Jewish Statehood" (1934–49).* Bloomington, Ind.: Slavica, 2009.

Kotov, Viktor. "Vsei zvukovoi palitroi mira." In *Roman Karmen v vospominaniiakh sovremennikov,* edited by A. L. Vinogradova, 270–74. Moscow: Iskusstvo, 1983.

Kovarskii, N. "Obvinitel′nyi akt protiv fashizma." *Iskusstvo kino* 9 (1938): 28–32.

Kranz, Tomasz. K. "Between Planning and Implementation: The Lublin District and Majdanek Camp in Nazi Policy." In *Lessons and Legacies,* vol. 4: *Reflections on Religion, Justice, Sexuality, and Genocide,* edited and with an introduction by Larry V. Thompson, 215–35. Evanston, Ill.: Northwestern University Press, 2003.

———. *Extermination of Jews at the Majdanek Concentration Camp.* Lublin, Poland: Państwowe Muzeum na Majdanku, 2007.

Kremer, S. Lillian, ed. *Holocaust Literature: An Encyclopedia of Writers and Their Work.* 2 Vols. New York: Routledge, 2003.

Krichevskii, Abram. "Spiashchii batal′on." in *Dovzhenko v vospominaniiakh sovremennikov,* edited by L. I Pazhitnova and Iu. I. Solnsteva, 149–55. Moscow: Iskusstvo, 1982.

Krutikova, M., ed. *Okkupirovannye strany pod fashistskim iarmom.* Moscow: Moskovskii rabochii, 1941.

Kudriavtsev, V., and A. Trusov, *Politicheskaia iustitsiia v SSSR.* Moscow: Nauka, 2000.

Kuromiya, Hiroaki. *Freedom and Terror in the Donbas: A Ukrainian-Russian Borderland, 1870s–1990s.* Cambridge: Cambridge University Press, 1998.

Kushner, Tony. *The Holocaust and the Liberal Imagination: A Social and Cultural History.* Oxford: Blackwell, 1994.

Kushnirov, Mark. *Zhizn′ i fil′my Borisa Barneta.* Moscow: Iskusstvo, 1977.

LaCapra, Dominick. *History and Memory after Auschwitz.* Ithaca, N.Y.: Cornell University Press, 1998.

————. *Writing History, Writing Trauma*. Baltimore, Md.: John Hopkins University Press, 2001.

Langer, Lawrence L. *The Holocaust and the Literary Imagination*. New Haven, Conn.: Yale University Press, 1975.

————. *Using and Abusing the Holocaust*. Bloomington: Indiana University Press, 2006.

Laqueur, Walter. *The Terrible Secret: An Investigation into the Suppression of Information about Hitler's "Final Solution."* London: Weidenfeld and Nicolson, 1980.

Lebedeva, Natal´ia. "SSSR i Niurembergskii protsess." In *Niurnbergskii protsess: Uroki istorii: Materialy mezhdunarodnoi konferentsii, Moskva, 20–21 noiabria 2006,* edited by N. S. Lebedeva and V. V. Ishchenko, 139–65. Moscow: Institut vseobshchei istorii RAN, 2007.

Lennon, Helen. "A Witness to Atrocity: Film as Evidence in International War Crimes Tribunals." In *Holocaust and the Moving Image: Representations in Film and Television since 1983,* edited by Toby Haggith and Joanna Newman, 65–73. London: Wallflower, 2005.

Lesch, Paul. "Film and Politics in Luxembourg: Censorship and Controversy." *Film History* 16, no. 4 (2004): 437–46.

Levi, Primo. *The Drowned and the Saved*. Translated by Raymond Rosenthal and with an introduction by Paul Bailey. Harmondsworth, U.K.: Penguin, 1989.

————. *If This Is a Man*. Translated by Stuart Woolf and with an introduction by Paul Bailey and an afterword by the author. Harmondsworth, U.K.: Penguin, 2006.

Leyda, Jay. *Films Beget Films*. London: Allen and Unwin, 1964.

————. *Kino: A History of the Russian and Soviet Film*. London: Allen and Unwin, 1983.

Liakhovitskii, Iuri M. *Poprannaia Mezuza: Kniga Drobitskogo iara: Svidetel´stva, fakty, dokumenty o natsistskom genotside evreiskogo naseleniia Khar´kova v period okkupatsii 1941–1942.* Vol. 1. Khar´kov: Osnova, 1991.

Liber, George O. *Alexander Dovzhenko: A Life in Soviet Film*. London: BFI, 2002.

Liebman, Stuart. "Documenting the Liberation of the Camps: The Case of Aleksander Ford's *Vernichtungslager Majdanek—Cmentarzysko Europy* (1944)." In *Lessons and Legacies,* vol. 7: *The Holocaust in International Perspective,* edited and with an introduction by Dagmar Herzog, 333–51. Evanston, Ill.: Northwestern University Press, 2006.

Lindeperg, Sylvie. *Clio de 5 à 7: Les actualités filmés de la Libération: Archives du futur.* Paris: CNRS, 2000.

Lipstadt, Deborah E. *Beyond Belief: The American Press and the Coming of the Holocaust*. New York: Free Press, 1986.

————. *The Eichmann Trial*. New York: Nextbook/Schocken, 2011.

Lower, Wendy. *Nazi Empire-Building and the Holocaust in Ukraine.* Chapel Hill: University of North Carolina Press, 2005.

Lowy, Vincent. *L'Histoire infilmable: Les camps d'extermination à l'écran.* Paris: L'Harmattan, 2001.

Lustiger, Arno. *Stalin and the Jews: The Tragedy of the Jewish Anti-Fascist Committee and the Soviet Jews.* With an introduction by Roman Brackman and a foreword by Yefim Etkind. New York: Enigma, 2003.

Manvell, Roger. *Films and the Second World War.* London: Dent, 1974.

Margolit, Evgenii. "Barnet i Eizenshtein v kontekste sovetskogo kino." *Kinovedcheskie zapiski* 17 (1993): 165–80.

———. "Obraz nemtsa-okkupanta v voennykh fil′makh Marka Donskogo." In *Ukraina-Nimechchina: Kinematografichni zv′iazki,* edited by Hans-Joachim Schlegel and Serhii Trimbach, 195–208. Vinnitsa, Ukraine: Globus, 2009.

———. "Vremia i mesto Borisa Barneta." *Kinovedcheskie zapiski* 61 (2002): 99–101.

Markovna, Nina. *Nina's Journey: A Memoir of Stalin's Russia and the Second World War.* Washington, D.C.: Regnery Gateway, 1989.

Marrus, Michael R. *The Nuremberg War Crimes Trial, 1945–46: A Documentary History.* Boston, Mass.: Bedford, 1997.

McBee, Richard. "Yad Vashem's Art." 9 August 2005. http://richardmcbee. com/26yad_vashem_1.htm.

McReynolds, Louise, and Joan Neuberger. "Introduction." In *Imitations of Life: Two Centuries of Melodrama in Russia,* edited by Louise McReynolds and Joan Neuberger, 1–24. Durham, N.C.: Duke University Press, 2002.

Merridale, Catherine. *Ivan's War: The Red Army 1939–45.* London: Faber and Faber, 2005.

———. *Night of Stone: Death and Memory in Twentieth-Century Russia.* New York: Viking, 2001.

Merzhanov, Martyn. "V soldatskoi shineli." In *Vospominaniia o Borise Gorbatove,* edited by S. A. Savel′ev, 356–83. Moscow: Sovetskii pisatel′, 1964.

Mikhailov, Vladimir. "Fil′m o pervoi pobede." In *Iz istorii kino: Dokumenty i materialy,* vol. 10, edited by Vladimir Mikhailov, 76–92. Moscow: Iskusstvo, 1977.

———. *Frontovoi kinoreportazh.* Moscow: Nauchno-issledovatel′skii institut teorii i istorii kino, 1977.

Mikosha, Vladislav. "'Ia ostanavlivaiu vremia': Vospominaniia frontovogo operatora." *Iskusstvo kino* 5 (2005): 91–115.

Miller, Jamie. "The Purges of Soviet Cinema, 1929–39." *Studies in Russian and Soviet Cinema* 1, no. 1 (2007): 5–16.

Möller, Olaf, and Barbara Wurm. *Regie: Rappaport: Ein sowjetischer Filmemacher aus Wien.* Vienna: Synema, 2008.

Morozov, Iu., and T. Derevianko. *Evreiskie kinematografisty v Ukraine, 1917–1945.* Kiev: Dukh i litera, 2004.

Müller, Rolf-Dieter, and Gerd R. Ueberschär. *Hitler's War in the East, 1941–1945: A Critical Assessment.* 2d rev. ed. Translated by Bruce D. Little and with a foreword by Gerhard L. Weinberg. New York: Berghahn, 2002.

Muravin, Gennadii L. *Dvoe iz mnogikh tysiach.* Moscow: Sovetskii khudozhnik, 1967.

Musina, Milena. "Ischislenie roda." *Kinovedcheskie zapiski* 51 (2001): 189–203.

Napoli, Nicholas. "Sovetskie fil´my v SshA." *Iskusstvo kino* 4 (1946): 28–31.

Nichols, Bill. *Representing Reality: Issues and Concepts in Documentary.* Bloomington: Indiana University Press, 1992.

Novick, Peter. *The Holocaust and Collective Memory: The American Experience.* London: Bloomsbury, 2000.

Novick, Peter, and Lawrence Baron. "Letters to the Editor." *Holocaust and Genocide Studies* 18, no. 2 (2004): 358–75.

Orliankin, Valentin. "V kadre-pravda voiny." In *Dovzhenko v vospominaniiakh sovremennikov,* edited by L. I Pazhitnova and Iu. I. Solnsteva, 158–60. Moscow: Iskusstvo, 1982.

Ozimek, Stanislaw. *Film polski w wojennej potrzebie.* Warsaw: Państowy Instytut Wydawiczy, 1974.

———. "The Polish Newsreel in 1945: The Bitter Victory." In *Hitler's Fall: The Newsreel Witness,* edited by K. R. M. Short and Stephan Dolezel, 70–79. London: Croom Helm, 1988.

Pazhitnova, Liudmilla, ed. *Mark Donskoi: Sbornik: Mastera sovetskogo kino.* Moscow: Iskusstvo, 1973.

Pazhitnova, Liudmilla, and Iu. I. Solnsteva, eds. *Dovzhenko v vospominaniiakh sovremennikov.* Moscow: Iskusstvo, 1982.

Petker, Boris. *Dissertatsiia Meri Archer.* Moscow: Vsesoiuznyi dom narodnogo tvorchestva im. N. K. Krupskoi, 1950.

———. *Eto moi mir.* Moscow: Iskusstvo, 1968.

Petrenko, Vasilii. *Avant et après Auschwitz.* Translated by François-Xavier Nérard. Paris: Flammarion, 2000.

Picart, Caroline Joan, ed. *The Holocaust Film Sourcebook,* vol. 2: *Documentary and Propaganda.* Westport, Conn.: Praeger, 2004.

Platt, David. *Celluloid Power: Social Film Criticism from "The Birth of a Nation" to "Judgment at Nuremberg."* Metuchen, N.J.: Scarecrow, 1992.

Polevoi, Boris. *From Belgorod to the Carpathians: From a Soviet War Correspondent's Notebook.* London: Hutchinson, 1945.

———. "Neistovyi Karmen." In *Roman Karmen v vospominaniiakh sovremennikov,* edited by A. L. Vinogradova, 151–54. Moscow: Iskusstvo, 1983.

————. *Sobranie sochinenii.* 9 vols. Moscow: Khudozhestvennaia literatura, 1981–86.

Polian, Pavel. "First Victims of the Holocaust: Soviet-Jewish Prisoners of War in German Captivity." *Kritika: Explorations in Russian and Eurasian History* 6, no. 4 (Fall 2005): 763–87.

————. *Zhertvy dvukh diktatur: Zhizn', trud, unizhenie i smert' sovetskikh voennoplennykh i ostarbaiterov na chuzhbine i na rodine.* 2d ed., rev. Moscow: Rosspen, 2002.

Pozner, Valérie. "Les Actualités soviétiques de la seconde guerre mondiale." In *Le Cinéma "stalinien": Questions d'histoire,* edited by Natacha Laurent, 123–41. Toulouse: Presses Universitaires du Mirail/La Cinémathèque de Toulouse, 2003.

Pronay, Nicholas. "Defeated Germany in British Newsreels: 1944–45." In *Hitler's Fall: The Newsreel Witness,* edited by K. R. M. Short and Stephan Dolezel, 28–49. London: Croom Helm, 1988.

Prut, Iosif Leonidovich. *P'esy.* Moscow: Sovetskii pisatel', 1963.

Pyr'ev, Ivan. *Izbrannye proizvedeniia.* 2 vols. Moscow: Iskusstvo, 1978.

Raginskii, M. Iu. "Vospominaniia uchastnika Niurnbergskogo protsessa." In *Niurnbergskii protsess i sovremennost',* edited by V. V. Pustogarov, 58–73. Moscow: Institut gosudarstva i prava AN SSSR, 1986.

Redlich, Shimon. *War, Holocaust and Stalinism: A Documented History of the Jewish Anti-Fascist Committee in the USSR.* Luxembourg: Harwood, 1995.

"Un regista russo: Marco Donskoi." *La critica cinematografica* 1, no. 5 (10 Dec. 1946): 6.

Reichman, Ravit Pe'er-Lamo. "Committed to Memory." In *Law and Catastrophe,* edited by Austin Sarat, Lawrence Douglas, and Martha Merrill Umphrey, 91–130. Stanford, Calif.: Stanford University Press, 2007.

Rosenfeld, Alvin H. *The End of the Holocaust.* Bloomington: Indiana University Press, 2011.

————. "Popularization and Memory: The Case of Anne Frank." In *Lessons and Legacies,* vol. 1: *The Meaning of the Holocaust in a Changing World,* edited by Peter Hayes, 243–78. Evanston, Ill.: Northwestern University Press, 1991.

Rostron, Allen. "'No War, No Hate, No Propaganda': Promoting Films about European War and Fascism during the Period of American Isolationism." *Journal of Popular Film and Television* 30, no. 2 (2002): 85–96.

Rotha, Paul. *The Film till Now: A Survey of World Cinema.* 2d ed. With an additional section by Richard Griffith. London: Vision, 1949.

Rozenfeld, Leonid. Interview with Zhanna Litinskaia, Kiev, June 2003. http://www.centropa.org/index.php?nID=30&x=PXVuZGVmaW5lZDsgc2VhcmNoVHlwZTiCaW9EZXR haWw7IHNlYXjjaFZhbHVlPTI3OTsgc2VhcmNoU2tpcDoxMA==.

Rubenstein, Joshua. *Tangled Loyalties: The Life and Times of Ilya Ehrenburg.*
Tuscaloosa: University of Alabama Press, 1999.

Saxton, Libby. *Haunted Images: Film, Ethics, Testimony and the Holocaust.* London:
Wallflower, 2008.

Saxton, Libby, and Lisa Downing. *Film and Ethics: Foreclosed Encounters.* London:
Routledge, 2010.

Sazonov, A. "Mark Donskoi Discusses 'The Rainbow.'" *Film Chronicle* 1–2
(1944): 1–3.

Schabas, William A. "Prosecuting Genocide." In *The Historiography of Genocide,*
edited by Dan Stone, 253–70. Houndmills, Basingstoke, U.K.: Palgrave
Macmillan, 2008.

Sel´vinskii, Il´ia. "Ia eto videl." In *Ne zabudem, ne prostim!* by Sel´vinskii, n.p.
Moscow: Goskinizdat, 1942.

Sharf, Andrew. *The British Press and Jews under Nazi Rule.* London: Oxford
University Press, 1964.

Shendar, Yehudit. *Private Tolkatchev at the Gates of Hell: Majdanek and Auschwitz
Liberated: Testimony of an Artist.* Exhibition catalog. http://www1.yadvashem.
org/exhibitions/tolkatchev/index.html.

Shneer, David. "Picturing Grief: Soviet Holocaust Photography at the Intersection of History and Memory." *American Historical Review* 115, no. 1 (2010):
28–52.

———. *Through Soviet Jewish Eyes: Photography, War, and the Holocaust.* New
Brunswick, N.J.: Rutgers University Press, 2010.

Short, K. R. M., and Richard Taylor. "Soviet Cinema and the International
Menace, 1928–1939." *Historical Journal of Film, Radio and Television* 6, no. 2
(1986): 131–59.

Shrayer, Maxim D., ed. and trans. *An Anthology of Jewish-Russian Literature:
Two Centuries of Dual Identity in Prose and Poetry.* 2 vols. Armonk, N.Y.: M. E.
Sharpe, 2007.

Shternshis, Anna. "Evacuation and Escape of Jewish Civilians in the Soviet
Union during World War II." Paper delivered at University of Colorado,
Boulder, 2 November 2010. http://www.jewishmovers.org/uploads/File/
Anna%20Shternshis,%20WWI,%20Jews,%20and%20Evacuation.pdf.

Simonov, Konstantin. *The Death Factory near Lublin.* London: Daily Worker
League, 1944.

———. *Sobranie sochinenii.* 10 vols. Moscow: Khudozhestvennaia literatura,
1979–85.

Slezkine, Yuri. *The Jewish Century.* Princeton, N.J.: Princeton University Press,
2004.

Smirnov, V. *Dokumental´nye fil´my o Velikoi Otechestvennoi voine.* Moscow:
Goskinoizdat, 1947.

Smith, Bradley F. *Reaching Judgement at Nuremberg.* London: Andre Deutsch, 1977.

Smith, Lyn. *Forgotten Voices of the Holocaust.* London: Ebury, 2005.

Snyder, Timothy. *Bloodlands: Europe between Hitler and Stalin.* New York: Basic, 2010.

Sontag, Susan. *Regarding the Pain of Others.* London: Penguin, 2004.

Sorokina, Marina. "People and Procedures: Toward a History of the Investigation of Nazi Crimes in the USSR." *Kritika: Explorations in Russian and Eurasian History* 6, no. 4 (Fall 2005): 797–831.

Stalin, Iosif. "Ob antileninskikh oshibkakh i natsionalisticheskikh izvrashcheniiakh v kinopovesti Dovzhenko 'Ukraine v ogne.'" Edited by Anatolii Latyshev. *Iskusstvo kino* 4 (1990): 84–96.

Stone, Dan. "The Holocaust and Its Historiography." In *The Historiography of Genocide,* edited by Dan Stone, 373–99. Houndmills, Basingstoke, U.K.: Palgrave Macmillan, 2008.

Streit, Christian. "The German Army and the Policies of Genocide." In *The Policies of Genocide: Jews and Soviet Prisoners of War in Nazi Germany,* edited by Gerhard Hirschfeld and with an introduction by Wolfgang J. Mommsen, 1–14. London: German Historical Institute/Allen and Unwin, 1986.

———. *Keine Kamaraden: Die Wehrmacht und die sowjetischen Kriegsgefangenen 1941–1945.* Stuttgart: Deutsche Verlags-Anstalt, 1978.

Struk, Janina. *Photographing the Holocaust: Interpretations of the Evidence.* London: I. B. Tauris, 2004.

Sutzkever, Avram [as Abraham]. "I Feel Like Saying a Prayer." In *Beyond Lament: Poets of the World Bearing Witness to the Holocaust,* edited by Marguerite M. Striar, 141. Evanston, Ill.: Northwestern University Press, 1998.

——— [as Avrom]. "Mon témoignage au procès de Nuremberg." *1945–1995: Les Ecrivains et la guerre,* special issue of *Europe* (Aug.–Sept. 1995): 140–53.

Sverdlov, F. D., ed. *Dokumenty obviniiaut: Kholokost: Svidetel'stva Krasnoi Armii.* Moscow: Rosiiskaia biblioteka Kholokosta, 1996.

Sylvester, Douglas J. "The Lessons of Nuremberg and the Trial of Saddam Hussein." In *Evil, Law and the State: Perspectives on State Power and Violence,* edited by John T. Parry, 127–41. Amsterdam: Rodopi, 2006.

Taylor, Telford. *The Anatomy of the Nuremberg Trials: A Personal Memoir.* London: Bloomsbury, 1993.

Tiedemann, Rolf. "Introduction: 'Not the First Philosophy, but a Last One': Notes on Adorno's Thought." In *Can One Live after Auschwitz: A Philosophical Reader,* by Theodor W. Adorno, edited by Rolf Tiedemann, xi–xxvii. Stanford, Calif.: Stanford University Press, 2003.

*Times Film Corp. v. Chicago,* 365 U.S. 43 (1961). http://caselaw.lp.findlaw.com/scripts/getcase.pl?navby=case&court=us&vol=365&invol=43.

Tolkachev, Zinovii. *Osventsim*. Repr. Foreword by Aleksandr Borshchagovskii. Moscow: Izobrazitel´noe izkusstvo, 1969.

Trimbach, Sergii. *Oleksandr Dovzhenko: Zahibel´ Bogiv: Identifikatsiia avtora v natsional´nomu chaso-prostori*. Vinnitsa, Ukraine: Globus, 2007.

Tsitriniak, Grigorii, ed. *Ne zabyto! Rasskazy frontovykh kinooperatorov i kinorezhis-serov*. Moscow: Soiuz kinematografistov SSSR Vsesoiuznogo biuro propagandy kinoiskusstva, 1986.

Tumarkin, Nina. *The Living and the Dead: The Rise and Fall of the Cult of World War II in Russia*. New York: Basic, 1994.

United Kingdom. *Parliamentary Debates*. Commons (debate on Emergency Powers [Defence] Act, 31 Oct. 1939), 5th ser., vol. 352 (1939), cols. 1829–1902. http://hansard.millbanksystems.com/commons/1939/oct/31/emergency-powers-defence-act-1939#S5CV0352P0_19391031_HOC_457.

———. *Parliamentary Debates*. Commons (debate on British Broadcasting Corporation [Propaganda], 8 Apr. 1943), 5th ser., vol. 388 (1943), cols. 835–925. http://hansard.millbanksystems.com/commons/1943/apr/08/british-broadcasting-corporation#S5CV0388P0_19430408_HOC_293.

United Nations. "Resolution Adopted by the General Assembly on the Holocaust Remembrance (A/RES/60/7, 1 November 2005)." http://www.un.org/holocaustremembrance/docs/res607.shtml.

Velengurin, N. "Maloizvestnaia stat´ia Borisa Gorbatova." *Ural´* 5 (1965): 148–53.

V[esselo], A[rthur]. "The Grand Alliance." *Sight and Sound* 8, no. 29 (Spring 1939): 33–35.

———. "Misprints and Limitations." *Sight and Sound* 8, no. 30 (Summer 1939): 77–79.

———. Review of *Professor Mamlock*. *Monthly Film Bulletin* 6, no. 64 (30 April 1939): 79.

Vishnevskii, Vsevolod. *Leningrad: Dnevniki voennykh let: 2 noiabria 1941 goda–31 dekabria 1942*. Vol. 1. Moscow: Voenizdat, 2002.

———. *Sobranie sochinenii*. 5 vols. Moscow: Khudozhestvennaia literatura, 1960.

Vlasov, M. P., ed. *Sovetskoe kino v gody Velikoi Otechestvennoi voiny (1941–1945)*. Moscow: VGIK, 1999.

Vol´f, Fridrikh [Wolf, Friedrich]. *P´esy*. Edited by Aleksandr Dymshits and annotated by A. Levinton. Moscow: Iskusstvo, 1963.

Volotskii, Mark. "Zamknuta moia pravda." *Rodina* 4 (2000). http://www.istrodina.com/rodina_articul.php3?id=166&n=13.

Walker, Janet. *Trauma Cinema: Documenting Incest and the Holocaust*. Berkeley: University of California Press, 1999.

Wasilewska, Wanda. *Raduga: Povest'*. Translated by E. Usievich. Moscow: Ogiz, 1942.

———. *Tvori*. 8 vols. Kiev: Dnipro, 1966.

Weiner, Amir. *Making Sense of War: The Second World War and the Fate of the Bolshevik Revolution*. Princeton, N.J.: Princeton University Press, 2001.

Werth, Alexander. *Russia at War, 1941–1945*. London: Barrie and Rockliff, 1964.

Wiesel, Elie. Foreword. In *Indelible Shadows,* by Annette Insdorf, 3d ed., xi–xii. Cambridge: Cambridge University Press, 2003.

Wieviorka, Annette. *The Era of the Witness*. Translated by Jared Stark. Ithaca, N.Y.: Cornell University Press, 2006.

Winston, Brian. *Lies, Damned Lies and Documentaries*. London: BFI, 2000.

Zelizer, Barbie. *Remembering to Forget: Holocaust Memory through the Camera's Eye*. Chicago: University of Chicago Press, 1998.

Zhdan, Vitalii. *Velikaia otechestvennaia voina v khudozhestvennykh fil'makh*. Moscow: Goskinoizdat, 1947.

## Soviet Films and the Holocaust, 1938–1946

This filmography does not pretend to be exhaustive. The Russian, Ukrainian, and Belorussian archives likely contain other wartime films that depict or deliberately obscure the fate of Jews under the Nazis, but either I was unable to find them, or I failed to identify them as relevant. In some cases, footage that I treat as part of feature-length films may have initially appeared in newsreels, or further contextualization may enable the identification of other films as relating to the Nazis' killing of Jews.

I have not included films I mention in the text that relate to the Holocaust but neither mention Jews nor record sites of killing, for in my view, such works ought not be considered films *of* the Holocaust. Similarly, I have not included non-Soviet films mentioned in the text, with the exception of Ford's *Majdanek Death Camp—The Cemetery of Europe,* since this is in part a Soviet film.

The films are listed in chronological order according to release or, in the case of unreleased footage, the release of the related film.

### Newsreels and Documentaries

*Soiuzkinozhurnal* no. 84, *Radio Meeting of Representatives of the Jewish People* (*Radiomiting predstavitelei evreiskogo naroda*). 30 August 1941. Director: Irina Setkina; camera: Ivan Beliakov, Mark Troianovskii, Arkadii Levitan, Konstantin Pisanko, and G. Fomin.

*Soiuzkinozhurnal* no. 114, *In Rostov* (*V Rostove*). 23 December 1941. Director: Roman Gikov; camera: Arkadii Levitan, Georgii Popov, and Andrei Sologubov.

*Soiuzkinozhurnal* no. 9. 30 January 1942 (Livny). Director: Roman Gikov; camera: Boris Vakar, M. Gol´dbrikh, Izrail´ Gol´dshtein, Evgenii Mukhin, and Grigorii Ostrovskii.

*Soiuzkinozhurnal* no. 10. 6 February 1942 (Kerch). Director: Nikolai Karmazinskii; camera: Mikhail Oshurkov.

*Defeat of the Germans near Moscow (Razgrom nemetskikh voisk pod Moskvoi).* 1942. Directors: Il´ia Kopalin and Leonid Varlamov; camera: Ivan Beliakov, G. Bobrov, Teodor Bunimovich, Pavel Kasatkin, Roman Karmen, Anatolii Krylov, Aleksei Lebedev, Boris Makaseev, Boris Nebylitskii, Vasilii Solov´ev, Moisei Shneiderov, Viktor Shtatland, S. Sher, Aleksandr Shchekut´ev, Aleksandr El´bert, and Mariia Sukhova. The same footage was used in a version substantially reedited by Slavko Vorkapovich with an entirely different commentary by Albert Maltz for release in the United States under the title *Moscow Strikes Back*.

*Soiuzkinozhurnal* no. 27. 30 March 1942 (Barvenkovo). Director: Irina Setkina; camera: Leon Mazrukho.

*We Shall Be Avenged! Film Documents of the Monstrously Evil Deeds, Atrocities and Violence of the German-Fascist Invaders (Otomstim! Kino-dokumenty o chudovishchnykh zlodeianiiakh i nasiliiakh nemetsko-fashistskikh zakhvatchikov).* 1942. Director: Nikolai Karmazinskii; camera: unknown (film compiled from more than one source).

*The Battle for Our Soviet Ukraine (Bitva za nashu sovetskuiu Ukrainu).* 1943. Directors: Iuliia Solntseva and Iakov Avdeenko; artistic director: Aleksandr Dovzhenko; camera: V. Afanas´ev, Konstantin Bogdan, Nikolai Bykov, Vladimir Frolenko, Mikhail Glider, M. Gol´brikh, Izrail´ Gol´dshtein, M. Kapkin, Pavel Kasatkin, Isaak Katsman, Vladimir Komarov, Yuli Kun, Grigorii Mogilevskii, Valentin Orliankin, Boris Rogachevskii, S. Semenov, Viktor Smorodin, Avenir Sof'in, Semen Sheinin, Viktor Shtatland, Sergei Urusevskii, Boris Vakar, I. Zaporozhskii, and others.

*Darnitsa Prisoner of War Camp (Lager' voennoplennykh v Darnitse).* 1943 (unreleased). Director: unknown; camera: Valentin Orliankin.

*The People's Verdict: Special-Release Release Newsreel about the Trial in the Case of the German-Fascist Invaders and Their Accomplices on the Territory of the Town of Krasnodar and the Krasnodar Region during Their Temporary Occupation (Prigovor naroda: Spetsial'nyi vypusk o sudebnom protsesse po delu nemetsko-fashistskikh zakhvatchikov i ikh posobnikov na territorii goroda Krasnodara i Krasnodarskogo kraia v period ikh vremennoi okkupatsii).* 1943. Director: Irina Setkina; camera: Mark Troianovskii.

*Justice Is Coming (Sud idet).* 1943 (Kharkov trial). Director: Il´ia Kopalin; camera: V. Frolenko, Aleksei Lebedev, A. Shapovalov, and Andrei Laptii.

*Majdanek Death Camp—The Cemetery of Europe* (*Vernichtungslager Majdanek— Cmentarzysko Europy*). 1944. Director: Aleksander Ford; camera: Wladyslaw Forbert, Olgierd Samucewicz, Stanislaw Wohl, Avenir Sof´in, Roman Karmen, and Viktor Shtatland.

*Majdanek: Film Documents of the Monstrously Evil Deeds of the Germans in the Extermination Camp of Majdanek, in the Town of Lublin* (*Majdanek: Kino-dokumenty o chudovishchnykh zlodeianiiakh nemtsev v lagere unichtozheniia na Majdaneke v gorode Lublin*). 1944. Director: Irina Setkina; camera: Avenir Sof´in, Roman Karmen, and Viktor Shtatland.

*Salaspils Concentration Camp* (Kontsentratsionnyi lager´ Salaspils). 1944 (unreleased). Director: unknown; camera: unknown.

*The Liberation of Soviet Belorussia* (*Osvobozhdenie sovetskoi Belorussii*). 1944. Directors: V. Korsh-Sablin and Mikola Sadkovich; camera: Teodor Bunimovich, Roman Karmen, O. Reizman, S. Shkol´nikov, V. Tsesliuk, Avenir Sof´in, Viktor Shatland Mariia Sukhova, and others.

*Klooga Death Camp* (*Klooga—lager´ smerti*). 1944. Director: S. Iakushev; camera: O. Ivanov and Efim Uchitel´.

*The Battle for the Baltic* (*Bitva za Pribaltiku*). 1944. Director: unknown; camera: V. Mass, K. Shirnin, M. Segal´, M. Prudnikov, O. Ivanov, Efim Uchitel´, S. Shkol´nikov, A. Akekseev, E. Alekseev, I. Gelein, I. S. Gutman, and A. Gaft.

*News of the Day* (*Novosti dnia*) no. 18, *The Judgment of Majdanek's Hangmen* (*Sud nad palachami Majdaneka*). 1944. Director: unknown; camera: David Ibragimov and Avenir Sof´in.

*Victory in Right Bank Ukraine and the Expulsion of the German Invaders from the Boundaries of Soviet Ukrainian Lands* (*Pobeda na Pravoberezhnoi Ukraine i izgnanie nemetskikh zakhvatchikov za predely ukrainskikh sovetskikh zemel´*). 1945. Directors: Aleksandr Dovzhenko and Iuliia Solntseva; camera: Konstantin Bogdan, Boris Vakar, Nikolai Vikhirev, Vladimir Voitenko, Izrail´ Gol´dshtein, Viktor Dobronitskii, David Ibragimov, Pavel Kasatkin, Isaak Katsman, Aleksander Kovalchuk, Abram Krichevskii, Iulii Kun, Kenian Kutub-Zade, Andrei Laptii, Grigorii Mogilevskii, Valentin Orliankin, M. Otsep, Pavel Rusanov, Aleksei Semin, Avenir Sof´in, Nikolai Topchii, and David Sholomovich.

*Auschwitz: Film Documents of the Monstrous Crimes of the German Government in Auschwitz* (*Kinodokumenty o chudovishchnykh prestupleniiakh germanskogo pravitel´stva v Osventsime*). 1945. Director: Elizaveta Svilova; camera: Mikhail Oshurkov, Nikolai Bykov, Kenian Kutub-Zade, A. Pavlov, and Aleksandr Vorontsov.

*The Smolensk Trial* (*Sudebnii protsess v Smolenske*). 1945. Director: Esfir´ Shub; camera: A. Brantman and Arkadii Levitan.

*The Kiev Trial* (*Kievskii protsess*). 1946. Director: unknown; camera: Gol´brakh, Shapovalov, V. Voitenko, and Mestechko.

*At the Trial of the Major Nazi War Criminals in Nuremberg* (*Na protsesse glavnykh voennykh prestupnikov v Niuremberge*). 1946. Director: Roman Karmen; camera: Boris Makaseev, S. Semenov, and Viktor Shtatland.

*Film Documents of Atrocities Committed by the German-Fascist Invaders* (Kino- dokumenty o zverstvakh nemetsko-fashistskikh zakhvatchikov). 1946. Director: uncredited; camera: Aleksandr Vorontsov, Rafail Gikov, Viktor Dobronitskii, Vladimir Eshurin, Arkadii Zeniakin, Roman Karmen, Kenian Kutub-Zade, Arkadii Levitan, Vladislav Mikosha, Evgenii Mukhin, Ivan Panov, Mikhail Posel´skii, Mikhail Segal´, Vasilii Solov´ev, Andrei Sologubov, and Mark Troianovskii.

*The Judgment of the Nations* (*Sud narodov*). 1946. Directors: Roman Karmen and Elizaveta Svilova; camera: Roman Karmen, Boris Makaseev, S. Semenov, and Viktor Shtatland.

*The Bobruisk Trial* (*Sudebnyi protsess v Bobruiske*). 1947. Director: Iu. Stal´makov; camera: M. Berov and V. Kitas.

## Fiction Films (Features and Shorts)

*Ruddi's Career* (*Kar´era Ruddi*). 1934. Director: V. Nemoliaev; screenplay: A. Golovnia and V. Nemoliaev.

*Professor Mamlock* (*Professor Mamlok*). 1938. Directors: Adol´f Minkin and Herbert Rappoport; screenplay: Friedrich Wolf, Adol´f Minkin, and Herbert Rappoport.

*Peat-Bog Soldiers* (*Bolotnye soldaty*). 1938. Director: Aleksandr Macheret; screen- play: Iurii Olesha.

*The Oppenheim Family* (*Sem´ia Oppengeim*). 1938. Director: Grigorii Roshal´; screenplay: S. Roshal´.

*A Priceless Head* (*Bestsennaia golova*). 1942. Director: Boris Barnet; screenplay: Boris Petker and G. Rublev.

*Secretary of the Regional Party Committee* (*Sekretar´ raikoma*). 1942. Director: Ivan Pyr´ev; screenplay: Iosif Prut.

*Partisans of the Ukrainian Steppe,* aka *Ukraine, 1941* (*Partizany v stepiakh Ukrainy*; *Ukraina 1941*). 1943. Director: Igor´ Savchenko; screenplay: Igor´ Savchenko (from the play by Aleksandr Korneichuk).

*She Defends the Motherland* (*Ona zashchishchaet rodinu*). 1943. Director: Fridrikh Ermler; screenplay: Ivan Bondin and Mikhail Bleiman (Aleksei Kapler uncredited).

*The Unvanquished* (*Nepokorennye*). 1945. Director: Mark Donskoi; screenplay: Boris Gorbatov and Mark Donskoi.

Note: Page numbers in italic type indicate illustrations.

crematoria, 162, 172, 182, 189
crimes against humanity, 188–89, 194,
206. *See also* war crimes
Crowther, Bosley, 102, 153
culture, destruction of, 41–42, 67, 192

Dachau, 158
*Daily Express* (newspaper), 40
*Daily Telegraph* (newspaper), 75
*Daily Worker* (London) (newspaper), 39
*Daily Worker* (New York) (newspaper),
32–37, 75, 229n70
Darlow, Michael, 1
Dawidowicz, Lucy, 254n27
the dead: artifacts of, 9; children among,
52–53; evidence of, 162–64, *163*, 176,
194; identities of, 120–21, 125–26,
165–66, 169, 171, 176–77, 189, 190–91,
193–94; photographs of, 8–9, 13,
53–54, 62, 165, 179, 221n26; relation of
spectators/liberators to, 13, 55, 166–68,
179–83, 189, 191; relatives of, 55, *56*,
65; representation of, 131, 176–77,
180, 194–95; rhetorical use of, 15; as
witnesses, 207–8
death: in Donskoi's work, 147; in
Dovzhenko's work, 111–12, 117, 119–23;
religious response to, 169
death camps. *See* camps
*Defeat of the Germans near Moscow* (film),
64–69, *65, 66, 68,* 73–78, 98, 116, 192,
238n66
Delage, Christian, 191, 205, 223n48,
257n63, 259n7
Desbois, Patrick, 242n3
*The Destruction of Works of Art and Artifacts
of National Culture, Wrought by the Nazis
on the Territory of the USSR* (film), 192
*The Diary of Anne Frank,* 215
Dinamo Moscow, 152
Diner, Hasia, 216
Dmitrov, Georgi, 26, 227n24
documentary film, 14, 79–80. *See also* film
documents
Doller, Mikhail, *Feast in Zhirmunki* (with
Vsevolod Pudovkin), 240n24
Doneson, Judith E., 12, 215, 225n8

Donovan, William J., 205
Donskoi, Alexander, 148, *149*
Donskoi, Mark, 101, 102, 104–5, 133–56,
*135,* 265n19; *Hello, Children,* 145; *The
Rainbow,* 100–105, *102,* 134, 135, 147,
242n50; *The Unvanquished,* 16, 133–56,
166, 211, 214
dope sheets, 14, 171, 238n67
Douglas, Lawrence, 189, 259n7, 260n14,
261n35
Dovzhenko, Aleksandr, 16, 106–33,
166; *Arsenal,* 110, 122; *The Battle for
Our Soviet Ukraine,* 108, 112–23, *115,
116, 119–21,* 131, 159, 243n13, 244n15;
*Bukovina Is Ukrainian Land* (with Iuliia
Solntseva), 42, 122, 244n17; "Chronicle
of Flaming Years," 131–32; *Earth,* 111,
117; *Ivan,* 111; *Liberation* (with Iuliia
Solntseva), 122, 244n17; reported anti-
Semitism of, 122, 246n37; on represen-
tation of atrocity, 109–12; *Shchors,* 122;
and synchronous sound, 114, 117–18;
"Ukraine in Flames," 105–6, 108, 109,
124–27, 131, 247n55; *Victory in Right
Bank Ukraine* (with Iuliia Solntseva),
108, 127–31, *130,* 243n13
Dreiman, Aleksandra, 101, 104
Drobitskii Iar, 108, 118–20, *119, 120,* 194
Durbin, Deanna, 152

Efimov, Boris, 199
Efros, Aleksandr Mikhailovich, 121
Ehrenburg, Ilya, 46, 201; *Black Book of
Russian Jewry* (with Vasilii Grossman),
6, 7, 209, 211, 265n27; *The Storm,* 147,
213
Eichmann, Adolf, 199
Eichmann trial, 199, 264n82, 264n85
Einsatzgruppen, 142, 148, 189, 190, 193
Eisenhower, Dwight, 55
Eisenstein, Sergei, 6, 42; *Battleship
Potemkin,* 18, 48, 149
Eisner, Lotte, 24
El´bert, Aleksandr, 72, 206
ellipses and silences in Holocaust films, 9,
10–11, 15, 73, 97–98, 217
Epstein, Berthold, 176

73, 174; British, 2, 8–9, 13, 73, 174; contents of, 54; emotions portrayed in, 55–57; on liberation of camps, 174–85; public familiarity with, 1; purpose of, 48, 172–73; Rostov-on-Don, 47–58, *50–53, 56*; of short-lived liberations, 58–64; used in Soviet films, 23; of war crimes trials, 195–96, 197. *See also* documentary film; Soviet wartime and Holocaust films

Nikolaev, Lev, 114

NKVD (People's Commissariat for Internal Affairs), 4, 45, 122, 173, 198

*No Greater Love* (film), 99. See *She Defends the Motherland*

nonaggression pact. *See* Molotov-Ribbentrop nonaggression pact

Novick, Peter, 188–89

Nugent, Frank S., 34–35

Nuremberg trials, 186–210; distortions arising out of, 189–91; documentary of, 195, 196–210; films shown at, 74, 159, 185, 187–95, 224n48, 259n7; and genocide, 188, 190; Holocaust and, 187–89; newsreels made in anticipation of, 182; as pageant, 197; significance of, 187, 188, 197

*The Nuremberg Trials* (film), 209–10. See *The Judgment of the Nations*

*Observer* (newspaper), 39

*Ogonek* (magazine), 124

Ohlendorf, Otto, 190

Orliankin, Valentin, 112

Orlova, Vera, 84, 85

Oshurkov, Mikhail, 60, 174–75, 180, 184

Ostrovskii, Grigorii, 58

Oxford University Refugee Committee, 38

Pabst, Georg Wilhelm, 23

Palestine, 38

*Paris-cinéma* (magazine), 185

Parloff, Morris, 168

partisan movement, 91, 93, 96

Paulus, Friedrich von, 205

Pavlov, A., 179

peepholes, 161, *162*

Petker, Boris, *Mary Archer's Dissertation*, 83–84, 239n5

Petliura, Symon, 122

Pioneer movement, 51–52

Platt, David, 34

pogroms, 3–4, 30, 123, 203, 211, 212

Pokrovskii (Soviet prosecutor), *207*

Poland, 5, 88, 155, 240n22

Polevoi, Boris, 174, 256n48

Polish-Soviet Extraordinary Commission for Investigating the Crimes Committed by the Germans in the Majdanek Extermination Camp in Lublin, 160–61, 169

Political Directorate of the Red Army, 64

Popov, Georgii, 49

Poslavskii, Boris, 93

Pozner, Valérie, 114

*Pravda* (newspaper), 29, 50, 53, 56, 58, 96, 98, 135, 152, 163, 169, 172, 174

*Pravda Ukrainy* (newspaper), 153, 184

*Priceless Head* (film), 16, 81–91, *82, 83, 89*, 223n40; Jewish theme of, 83, 86–88, 90–91; production of, 84; reception of, 84–86; story of, 81–82

prisoners of war, 128, 193, 253n10

*Professor Mamlock* (film), 18–43, *25*, *31*; American reception of, 31–37; anti-Semitism in, 27, 29–35; British reception of, 19, 37–41; censorship of, 18, 19, 36–40, 233n121; communism in, 33; influence of, 91; international audience for, 28–29; play as basis of, 20; reception of, 18–20, 28–41; setting of, 22–23; Soviet message adapted to, 20, 24–28; Soviet reception of, 28–31; Soviet withdrawal of, 42; symbolism in, 23–24

Pronay, Nicholas, 77–78

propaganda: calls for justice as, 187, 195; dismissal of information as, 77; *Professor Mamlock* as, 34; Soviet cinema as, 13–15; in Soviet wartime films, 49

Protazanov, Iakov, 85

Prut, Iosif, 92–93

Pudovkin, Vsevolod, 84, 117, 125, 166;

Feast in Zhirmunki (with Mikhail Doller), 240n24; *The Murderers Leave for the Road* (with Iuryi Tarych), 101
Pyr´ev, Ivan, 151–52; *Conveyor of Death*, 21; *Secretary of the Regional Party Committee*, 79, 92–95, *94*, *95*, 223n40

Radok, Alfred, *Distant Journey*, 155
Raginskii, M., 199
Rappoport, Herbert, *Professor Mamlock*, 18–43
Rappoport, Nahum, 60, *61*
Red Army, 57, 67, 76, 128, 157, 174–75, 191, 194, 253n10
refugee organizations, 38
Reingold, Iakov, 62, *62*
representation, issues in: atrocities, 9, 16, 75, 109–12, 143–44, 177–78; the dead, 9, 131, 164–65, 169, 176–77, 180, 194–95; evidentiary function, 15; the Holocaust, 9–12, 15, 16, 140, 143–44, 148, 177–78, 180, 182, 208; survivors, 178; testimony, 15; violence, 52; war crimes trials, 197
resistance: Jews and, 27, 45, 90; Soviet, 11, 12, 26
Resnais, Alain, *Night and Fog*, 1, 10, 174
Riumkin, Iakov, 162, 172
Robinson, Edward G., 76, 216
Rodger, George, 9
Rodianskii, Zinovii, 135
Roland, George, *The Eternal Wanderer* (film), 225n2
Romm, Mikhail, 144, 151
Roosevelt, Franklin, 183
Roshal´, Grigorii, 229n61; *The Oppenheim Family*, 21, 23, 27, 31, 42; *Salamander*, 25
Rostov-on-Don, 47–58, 64, 193
Rotha, Paul, 210
Rudenko, Roman, 204, 206
ruins, 49
Russia, 3–4. *See also* Soviet Union
Russian Revolution, 4

sadism, 161
Sadoul, Georges, 173
Samucewicz, Olgierd, 159

Savchenko, Igor´, *Partisans of the Ukrainian Steppes*, 95
Saxton, Libby, 10, 119, 161
Second Ukrainian Front, Red Army, 175
Segal, Daniil, 136
Sel´vinskii, Il´ia, 60
Setkina, Irina, 60, 158–69, 172; *The People's Verdict*, 195–96; *Tragedy in the Katyn Wood*, 14, 173
Shatin, Valerii, *Nurnberg*, 260n7
Shcherbakov, Aleksandr, 169
*She Defends the Motherland* (film), 91, 95–100, *97*, 126
Shevchenko, Taras, 127
Shingeladze (doctor), 114
Shishkin, Vladimir, 84
Shneer, David, 58, 236n38
Shoah, 3
Shoah Foundation, 29
shoes, 162–64, *163*, *164*, 180
show trials, 6, 187, 195–96
Shtatland, Viktor, 159
Shumiatskii, Boris, 24
*Sight and Sound* (magazine), 38
silences in Holocaust films. *See* ellipses and silences in Holocaust films
Simonov, Konstantin, 155, 157, 162–64, 171–72, 252n2, 255n31
Slezkine, Yuri, 4
Smaglevskaia, Severina, 205
Smith, Bradley F., 189
Smith, Jessica, 103–4
Sobibór, 158, 189
Sof´in, Avenir, 159
*Soiuzkinozhurnal*, 45–64, 160
Solntseva, Iuliia, 112–13; *Bukovina Is Ukrainian Land* (with Aleksandr Dovzhenko), 42, 122, 244n17; *Liberation* (with Aleksandr Dovzhenko), 122, 244n17; *Unforgettable*, 247n55; *Victory in Right Bank Ukraine* (with Aleksandr Dovzhenko), 108, 127–28, *130*, 243n13
Sologubov, Andrei, 49
Solzhenitsyn, Alexander, 196
Sontag, Susan, 53, 167
Sorokina, Marina, 261n36
sound. *See* synchronous sound

*Sovetskoe iskusstvo* (newspaper), 205

Soviet cinema, 6–9, 13–15, 27–28, 32, 211, 213, 214. *See also* feature films; newsreels; Soviet wartime and Holocaust films

Soviet Extraordinary State Commission on War Crimes (ChGK), 17, 55, 64, 175, 191, 236n29, 245n30, 261n36

Soviet Union: anti-Semitism in, 4–5, 13, 42, 122–23, 211–14; atrocities committed by, 173, 186–87, 195; attitudes toward Nazi Germany in, 25–26; culture of, Nazi destruction of, 41–42, 67, 192; and German nonaggression pact, 6, 7, 39, 41, 42; and the Holocaust, 7, 12–14, 22, 202, 211, 213; and international tribunal, 186–87; Jews killed in, 5–6, 7, 44–45, 50–51, 67, 69, 118, 120–21, 125, 134–51, 193, 235n20; nationalism in, 212; and Nuremberg trials, 209–10, 263n78; *Professor Mamlock*'s reception in, 28–31; repression by, 197–98; war death toll in, 12, 131, 253n10; Western distrust of, 187

Soviet wartime and Holocaust films: conventions of, 8, 16, 79, 159; cross-referencing of, with other documentation, 14, 16; *Defeat of the Germans near Moscow*, 64–69; ellipses and silences in, 9, 10–11, 15, 73, 97–98, 217; as evidence, 15, 54, 72, 161–65, 168, 172–73, 182–83, 185, 186, 188, 206–7; feature films and, 91; genesis of, 1–2; Germans as portrayed in, 54, 56, 58, 100–101; ignorance/neglect of, 1–2, 8, 19, 77, 173, 187–88, 214–17, 223n48; influence of, 173, 256n57; on liberation of camps, 157–85; propaganda in, 49; reconstructions in, 14–15, 78–80, *150*, 180–81, *181*, 191–92, 257n63; rhetorical construction and function of, 14–15, 47–78, 166–67, 176–85, 191, 208 (*see also* Holocaust, Sovietization of); symbolism in, 49, 51–53; twofold purpose of, 54–55, 73–77, 105, 187; violence as represented in, 52; Western reception of, 74–78. *See also* newsreels

Sovinformbureau, 179, 252n4

*Spectator* (newspaper), 37, 39

Spielberg, Steven, 29; *Schindler's List*, 1, 140, 161, 215, 230n80

SS (Schutzstaffel), 168, 174

Stalin, Joseph, 5, 44–45, 69, 98, 108, 124–25, 153, 183, 198, 212, 213, 214, 244n15

Stalin, Svetlana, 98

Stamp, Reginald, 38–39

Star of David, 62, 81, 87, 137, 171, 176, 194

Stevens, George, 187, 206

Straukh, Maxim, 84

Streicher, Julius, *203*

Struk, Janina, 73

suffering: depictions of, 13, 48, 55; giving meaning to, 35, 47–48, 57, 68; Jewish, 34–35, 69, 189, 193, 215; nationalization/universalization of, 67, 71, 72, 112, 167, 179, 192–94, 214, 238n67; responses to, 13, 57

Supreme Soviet, 186

Sutzkever, Abraham, 147, 209

Sverdlov, Iakov, 4

Svilova, Elizaveta, 201

symbolism: children, 90, 178, 192, 240n26; in *Professor Mamlock*, 23–24; of Soviet martyr's funeral, 15, 57, 147; in Soviet wartime films, 49, 51–53; steps, 88; in *The Unvanquished*, 145–46

synchronous sound: *The Battle for Our Soviet Ukraine* and, 114, 117–18; *Defeat of the Germans near Moscow* and, 69–71; difficulties with, 70–71; *Film Documents of Atrocities* and, 195; *The Judgment of the Nations* and, 206; newsreels and, 160, 166, 168, 175; testimony presented with, 17, 69–71; *Victory in Right Bank Ukraine* and, 127–28; war crimes trials films and, 196, 208

Taganrog, 194

tallits, 145–46, 176, *177*

*The Taras Family* (film), 153–54

Tarych, Iuryi, *The Murderers Leave for the Road* (with Vsevolod Pudovkin), 101

tattoos, 176, 177, *179*

Taylor, Telford, 259n7

Tchaikovsky, Pyotr, *Sixth Symphony*, 57

testimony: absent, 182; American attitude toward, 261n35; in *The Battle for Our Soviet Ukraine*, 114–16, 120; characteristics of, 209; from the dead, 207–8; and the Holocaust, 264n82; in Holocaust films, 15, 17; at Nuremberg trials, 204–9, 263n81; in *The People's Verdict*, 196; silent footage as, 71–73, 206–7; Soviet attitude toward, 17, 208–9; synchronous sound for conveyance of, 70; visual vs. verbal, 195

Tetlow, Edwin, 9

Thames TV, *World at War*, 1, 174

*Times* (London) [newspaper], 40, 196

Tolkachev, Zinovii, 6, 57–58, 145–46, 180; *Occupiers*, 58; *Taleskoten*, 145

Trauberg, Il´ia, 23, 41; *Maxim* (with Grigorii Kozintsev), 26

Treblinka, 158, 180, 189

*Tribune* (newspaper), 75

*trombity*, 127

Trotskii, Lev, 4

Tseitlin, Boris, 48

TsOKS studio, 81

Tumarkin, Nina, 214

twins, 177–78, *179*

Uchitel´, Efim, 171

Ukraine: anti-Semitism in, 123, 126, 128; in Dovzhenko's work, 108, 117–18, 120–22, 124–33; Holocaust in, 151; Jews in, 101–2; liberation of, 106; nationalism in, 108, 122–23, 127–28; occupation of, 100–102, 124, 131; Soviet Union's relations with, 124; war death toll in, 118, 245n30

*Ukraine in Flames* (film), 132

Ukrainian Commission Investigating German War Crimes, 107

Ukrainian Communist Party, 125

*L'Unità* (newspaper), 154

United Nations, 3, 188

United States: anti-Semitism in, 77; *The Battle for Our Soviet Ukraine* in, 131–32; censorship in, 36–37, 132; and communism, 77, 210, 216–17; and the Holocaust, 12, 35, 141, 215–17; and international tribunal, 187; *Majdanek* in, 174; *Moscow Strikes Back* in, 75–76; newsreels made by, 2, 8–9, 13, 73, 174; and Nuremberg trials, 187, 190; Nuremberg Tribunal films made by, 187–94, 206; *Professor Mamlock* in, 31–37; *The Rainbow* in, 135; Soviet feature films shown in, 99–100, 102–3; Soviet newsreels shown in, 8; *The Taras Family in*, 153–54

universalization/nationalization of suffering, 67, 71, 72, 112, 167, 179, 192–94, 214, 238n67

*The Unvanquished* (film), 133–56, *138*, *139*, *141*, *143*, *145*, *146*, *149*, *150*, 211; Eastern Europe's reception of, 155–56; influence of, 155; Jews represented in, 134–56; massacre scene in, 141–51; reception of, 151–56; Soviet Union's reception of, 151–53, 214; story of, 136; symbolism in, 145–46; Ukrainian occupation depicted in, 136–40; Western reception of, 153–55

Vaillant-Couturier, Marie-Claude, 205

Vakar, Boris, 58

Vanin, Vasilii, 92

Vannik, Abram Moisevich, 171

*Variety* (magazine), 153–54

Varlamov, Leonid, 69; *Stalingrad*, 253n10

Vasiliev, Georgii and Sergei, *Chapaev*, 144

*Vecherniaia Moskva* (newspaper), 83, 84–85

vengeance, 13, 55, 57, 65, 67, 74, 98–99, 103, 116, 119, 120, 147, 178, 236n35. See also justice

Vertov, Dziga, 6, 93, 201, 251n61

Vesselo, Arthur, 37–38

victory, as theme in Soviet wartime culture, 15, 57, 131, 147, 213

Vinnitsa, Ukraine, 44, 256n51

Vishnevskii, Vsevolod, 74

voiceover commentary: in *Auschwitz*, 181–82; in *The Battle for Our Soviet Ukraine*, 112, 114–18, 121; evidentiary function of, 172; in *Film Documents of*